TWENTIETH-CENTURY
AME

*Politics and Power in the United
States, 1900–2000*

M. J. HEALE
*Emeritus Professor of American History,
Lancaster University, UK*

ARNOLD

A member of the Hodder Headline Group
LONDON

Distributed in the United States of America by Oxford University
Press Inc., New York

First published in Great Britain in 2004 by
Arnold, a member of the Hodder Headline Group,
338 Euston Road, London NW1 3BH

http://www.arnoldpublishers.com

Distributed in the United States of America by
Oxford University Press Inc.
198 Madison Avenue, New York, NY 10016

The advice and information in this book are believed to be true and
accurate at the date of going to press, but neither the authors nor the publisher
can accept any legal responsibility or liability for any errors or omissions.

British Library Cataloguing in Publication Data
A catalogue record for this book is available from the British Library

Library of Congress Cataloging-in-Publication Data
A catalog record for this book is available from the Library of Congress

ISBN 0 340 61408 0 (hb)
ISBN 0 340 61407 2 (pb)

1 2 3 4 5 6 7 8 9 10

Typeset in Sabon 10pt by Charon Tec Pvt. Ltd, India
Printed and bound in Malta

What do you think about this book? Or any other Arnold title?
Please send your comments to feedback.arnold@hodder.co.uk

For Lesley, as always

Contents

Preface

History is about both continuity and change. In the middle of the twentieth century one influential group of American historians tended to emphasize the continuities in the American experience. According to these 'consensus' scholars, what characterized most Americans at most points in time was an agreement on values and fundamentals: a commitment to the United States Constitution, a belief in private property and a capitalist culture, a faith in individualism and opportunity, the tolerance of a competitive electoral system in which the major parties seemed more in agreement than in serious dispute. This was an American history which stretched almost seamlessly into the past, a history in which class conflict was muted and in which ideological polarization was all but absent. But consensus history was a precarious construction and subsequent generations of historians have rediscovered the conflict and variety in American life. Tensions associated with race, class and gender came to be regarded as key to an understanding of American history, which was punctuated by periods of turmoil and change. But, of course, there were continuities too: Americans remained attached to their Constitution, the individualist ethic and a capitalist economy.

This political history of the United States divides the twentieth century into three parts, or what are here called political orders, that is to say, broad patterns of political activity. These orders happen to coincide roughly with the first, middle and final thirds of this hundred-year period. Each is defined by its continuities, but none could resist change, which ensured that the first two orders eventually disappeared and the third may expect the same fate. Yet the American republic is still recognizably the one of which Theodore Roosevelt took command in September 1901. The Constitution has been amended in important ways, but its federal principles and determined separation of powers continue to structure the political system. The powers of government have grown and the 'free enterprise' economy is not as unregulated as once it was, but the American love affair with private enterprise shows no sign of abating. The Democratic and Republican parties, as in Theodore Roosevelt's day, continue to confront one another in state and national elections.

While several chapters in this book largely focus on the national admin-istrations, American politics cannot be understood by a narrow focus on Washington, DC alone. The Washington political class has always largely consisted of well-to-do white men, but they are hardly typical of the society over which they have tried to preside. Even the politically powerless can affect the shape of a political system by their very presence. As the homoge-neous vision of consensus historians lost its appeal, scholars came to accord larger roles to African-Americans, women, working people and minorities of many kinds in the making and evolution of American political society.

These categorizations, of course, are not mutually exclusive. An American citizen could at once be black, female and a wage-earner, and some damage is done to historical complexity when the interlocking themes of race, class and gender are pulled apart. Historians have come to recognize too that these themes may reflect perceptions and ideology more than any objective 'reality'. Many modern scientists, for example, doubt the validity of dividing humankind into distinct races, while the official US classification of racial groups – recently White, Black, Hispanic, Native American and Asian – seems particularly arbitrary in a society in which 'mixed' marriages are not uncom-mon. Hispanics were counted as white until the 1970s, and once upon a time even a person confident of an overwhelmingly Anglo-Saxon lineage would be classified as black if just a drop of black blood had somehow entered the genetic chain. Notions of social class too have been socially constructed, and social scientists have used a surfeit of definitions in analyses of the American social order. Americans have sometimes been resistant to what might be seen as the application of Marxist-inspired theory to their society – what President Eisenhower once described as 'the invention of a lonely refugee scribbling in a dark recess of the British Museum' – and in social surveys high propor-tions have liked to describe themselves as middle class. But even if defini-tions of social class can be agreed, history does not stand still. While a substantial blue-collar workforce was clearly present in the industrial econ-omy of the mid-twentieth century, the boundaries between the conventional classifications became blurred with the subsequent rapid expansion of white-collar work. Even gender distinctions appear to be less clear-cut than was once assumed to be the case, and recent demands for a recognition of identity by sexuality have further undermined traditional understandings.

Nonetheless, despite the slipperiness of such concepts as race, class and gender, they remain indispensable categories in any examination of American political history, and this book attempts to trace in particular the changing roles of organized (and disorganized) labour, immigrants, women and African-Americans in the American political system. Some scholars have also stressed the essential interdependence of such concepts as race and class. One argument of a recent series of 'whiteness studies' is that important in the formation of working-class identity in the United States was the tendency of immigrants to emphasize their common whiteness with American-born white workers. They were thus implicated in the intricate process by which African-Americans

were so long excluded from the political nation. If these categories sometimes reinforce one another (generally African-Americans have been disad-
vantaged by both race and social class), there can also be tensions between
them. It is suggested in this book that the women's movement tended to
flourish in the absence of a strong labour movement and vice versa.

This book's division of twentieth-century America into three political
orders is also a matter of interpretation and definition. Some historians would
resist the labels applied here, others might use similar terms but choose different dates, and yet others might agree on the periods but assign them different names. Such terms as the 'New Deal Order', while familiar enough in the
writings of American political scientists, will not be found in all histories of
the United States; Americans living through the years of the New Deal Order
would not have used the phrase, any more than contemporary Americans,
apart from a few academics, would speak of the Divided Political Order. But
these conceptualizations may assist in an understanding of both the changes
and the continuities in twentieth-century American political history.

Part I of this book examines the Progressive Order, which took shape as
the nineteenth century turned into the twentieth, and which lasted until the
Great Crash of 1929 and the subsequent Depression brought it tumbling
down. Historians have commonly recognized a Progressive Era, characterized by the movements for political and social reform between about 1900
and 1917, but while the reform spirit weakened after the First World War,
many of the era's characteristics continued through the 1920s. This was a
polity largely governed by Anglo-Saxon élites, for the most part imbued by
a strong Protestant morality, responding to the disruptive processes of rapid
industrialization and urbanization and massive immigration. In their struggles to preserve social order they retreated from the *laissez-faire* prescriptions of the nineteenth century and sought – not altogether successfully – to
redefine the relationship between state and citizen. This Anglo-American
establishment, confident of the virtues of their civilization, also sought to
define a role for the United States in the world, which Woodrow Wilson
believed could be an elevating one. As it happened, Wilson was a Democrat,
but a major feature of the Progressive Order was the ascendancy of the
Republican Party, with its ties to the flourishing urban-industrial sector and
its identification with progress. It was also a world in which African-
Americans (and other non-whites) were strictly segregated, women were
mostly held to occupy a separate sphere (though one that tended to reinforce the Progressive Order) and immigrants and American-born wage-
earners also found their political roles severely circumscribed. After the Great
Crash destroyed the credibility of the Republican administrations, immigrants, industrial workers and African-Americans assisted in the process of
fashioning an alternative to the Progressive Order.

The inauguration of Franklin Roosevelt as president in 1933 marks the
advent of the New Deal Order, the subject of Part II, which essentially survived until the late 1960s. The Democratic Party became the majority party,

rooted in a disparate electoral coalition that included both Southern whites and Northern urban workers (many of recent European immigrant stock). Organized labour won significant influence in an increasingly pluralistic and secular political society, and other groups too established a political presence, among them African-Americans. The prescriptions of the Progressive Order had been found wanting, and the federal government for the first time assumed a substantial role as guardian of the country's economic and social well-being. More than in the Progressive Era, and in contrast to traditional *laissez-faire* ideas, American liberals became identified with a willingness to employ the institutions of government to solve social problems. Liberal ambitions were often frustrated by a resilient conservative resistance, but it was liberals, from Franklin Roosevelt to Lyndon Johnson, that tended to set the public agenda. The centrality of Washington, and particularly the White House, in the American system of government, was also furthered by foreign crises, most notably the Second World War and the Cold War, which to the New Deal state added the growth of the national security state. But the New Deal coalition depended on the subordination of race and gender to class priorities, and when African-Americans and women demanded liberation its fragility was exposed. The tendency of the governments of the New Deal Order to attempt to impose their will abroad eventually led to a humiliating exposure of the limits of American might and contributed to the end of Democratic ascendancy.

Part III of this book examines the Divided Order of the last third of the century. No political party established hegemony in this period, when usually Republican presidents faced Democratic Congresses, and the White House and Congress competed with one another for authority. As the economy encountered troubled times, faith in the 'big government' philosophy of the New Deal Order waned, and the Republican Party was better placed to set the political agenda, although even during the presidency of the popular Ronald Reagan its conservative precepts were often frustrated. In the middle decades of the century, Democrats and Republicans had tended to contest one another on economic and welfare policies, but during the subsequent era cultural and lifestyle issues – abortion, school prayer, pornography, gun control – cut across the traditional alignments. The centrifugal tendencies in American politics were abetted by the course of events abroad, as the bipolar configuration of East and West gave way to more complex patterns and the Cold War itself eventually came to a stupefying end. With elected politicians often unable to provide sustained leadership, it sometimes seemed that policy decisions were in effect being taken by bureaucrats or even the courts. Organized labour lost much of its clout, but the fading of traditional class issues allowed women to exert a new influence in this political culture, even if this revitalized feminism was fiercely opposed by a moralistic New Right. The momentum of the African-American movement slowed, but other ethnic groups were inspired to assert their identities, and the return of large-scale immigration furthered the recognition that the

United States was a multicultural – if fragmented and quarrelsome – society. The fractious temper of American politics perhaps served to deepen the disenchantment of many voters. Only about half of the potential electorate bothered to go to the polls in presidential elections in the final decades of the twentieth century; in this confused system of government the political nation was matched by the apolitical nation.

This book owes something to my students and colleagues, reflecting as it does the history courses I have taught, particularly with my former colleague, Bob Bliss. I am also very grateful to the friends who have read parts of it and improved my understanding of American history, notably Jay Kleinberg, Iwan Morgan, Robert Harrison, John Thompson, Gareth Davies and Patrick Hagopian.

THE PROGRESSIVE POLITICAL ORDER, 1900–33

|1|

The Progressive Order
1900–33

In the last three decades of the nineteenth century an industrial colossus was erected in the United States, a complex process that not only transformed economic and social relationships but also triggered far-reaching changes in the political realm. New patterns of American politics emerged and government itself gradually, if erratically, took on a different shape. The early decades of the twentieth century are usually known as the Progressive Era, because of the presence of bands of 'progressives' who spurred on the cause of reform, but with or without them American governing structures were not going to stay the same. What might be called the Progressive Political Order came into being, and it broadly remained in place throughout the first third of the twentieth century.

The polity of which Herbert Hoover took command in 1929 was no longer the flimsy edifice admired by nineteenth-century Americans. The historian Robert H. Wiebe has spoken of the 'island communities' of the nineteenth century, characterizing a largely agrarian America as a confederation of loose-knit townships that mostly governed their own affairs and had little sense of a managerial hierarchy above them. The political scientist Stephen Skowronek has defined the nineteenth-century polity as one of 'courts and parties'. The island communities were not immune to party politics. Indeed for much of the century national political parties straddled the land and generated an extraordinary degree of partisan excitement; it was not uncommon for 80 per cent of the electorate to flock to the polls in presidential elections, a proportion unknown to the twentieth century. But these parties were more interested in winning elections, allocating resources (like land) and distributing patronage than in the kind of managerial functions or positive governmental programmes offered by their modern descendants. State legislatures were arenas for party competition rather than sustained policy-making, and they were keener to promote than to regulate economic enterprise. It was often the courts rather than the legislatures which regulated public affairs, such as by determining the boundaries of trade union activity. Constrained in any case by traditional *laissez-faire* doctrines, neither federal nor state governments expected to assume many responsibilities.

The 'island communities' had lost much of their autonomy and the polity of 'courts and parties' had been obliged to experiment with forms of regulation before the end of the nineteenth century. The great and intertwining forces of industrialization, urbanization and immigration were not only disrupting American society but also promoting new values and organizational forms. The rapid growth of urban and national markets created pressures for economic rationalization, but these sat uneasily with a political system governed by an eighteenth-century Constitution, with its emphasis on checks and balances and the broad dispersal of power. Yet ways had to be found to resolve conflict and bring order to an ever fluid world. In the years after about 1900 the outlines of a new political system came into clearer focus.

The emergence of the urban-industrial order was accompanied by the political ascendancy of the Republicans. The Republican Party was the majority party during the first third of the twentieth century, even though a split within it allowed Woodrow Wilson to capture the White House for the Democrats in 1912. For the most part (and with some influential exceptions) Republicans were not greatly enamoured of political and social reform, but they were attuned to the values of the urban and business worlds. American public life in these years was also in effect presided over by an essentially Anglo-Saxon and Protestant establishment, that is to say by men who would later be characterized as Wasps (white Anglo-Saxon Protestants), or as we might call them, Anglo-Americans. Close to this establishment was a significant number of upper- and middle-class citizens who were eager to uplift the huddled urban masses and adapt American institutions to the needs of a modern society. Partly as a result of their efforts, though more because the political system in a host of ways was responding to the pressures created by industrialization, the nature of American government changed vitally. In the individualistic nineteenth century, it might be argued, citizens had relied for guidance on the consciences implanted deep within them by their parents and teachers, but in the interdependent and impersonal industrial society of the twentieth century, in which organized groups jostled for influence, such internal imperatives needed to be supplemented by external rules. The formulation of regulations implied a more active role for government, though in the fitful creation of regulatory structures the United States took a distinctive route of its own. These characteristics – Republican Party ascendancy, Anglo-American hegemony and the cautious governmental retreat from *laissez-faire* traditions – together constituted the Progressive Order. It was essentially a white world. A kind of counterpoint to this political order was the separate sphere occupied by black Americans. Also excluded from the political nation were Chinese and Japanese immigrants on the West Coast and Native Americans in reservations.

Sustaining the emerging order was a mostly buoyant economy. After the severe depression of 1893–6 had been shaken off, the United States entered a long period of economic expansion. At the turn of the century Gross National Product was estimated to be $37.1 billion (in 1929 prices); by 1929 it had reached a phenomenal $104.4 billion, an almost threefold increase over three decades. This formidable economic growth was not uninterrupted, and there was a financial panic in 1907 and a jarring post-war depression in 1920–1, but the setbacks were short-lived and many Americans enjoyed steadily improving standards of living through these decades. Increased productivity owed something to technological innovation, most graphically illustrated by the mass arrival of the automobile. That industry barely existed in 1900, when just 4192 motor cars were produced; in 1929 some 4.9 million rolled off the assembly lines. Lifestyles were changing too. The average life expectancy in 1900 was 47.3 years; in 1930 it was a healthier 59.7. Just 6.4 per cent of seventeen-year-olds graduated from high school in 1900, but the proportion had more than quadrupled by 1930 to 29 per cent. If such figures suggest an enrichment of the quality of life, by the end of the period the emblems of material affluence were to be found almost every-where – over 23 million cars (almost one per household), 10 million radios, 6.8 million vacuum cleaners, 5 million washing machines. Not everyone shared in the prosperity, but it underpinned the pervasive optimism which characterized American life through much of the period. The Great Crash of 1929 not only devastated the economy but was also to spell the end for the Progressive Order.

The twentieth century may have opened with an economic boom, but by that date many Americans had become acutely aware that industrialization was exacting costs as well as bestowing rewards. As the island communities had been sucked into a national economy, so their inhabitants had become increasingly vulnerable to the pressures of impersonal market forces. One way of achieving a measure of security in this uncertain world was to band together. In the closing decades of the nineteenth century the organizational impulse had appeared in virtually every sector, as people struggled to secure a degree of control over their environment, whether in business corporations, trade unions, farmers' alliances, professional bodies or ethnic societies. There was safety in numbers, as politicians had long since realized when they had created mass political parties to secure leverage in the national political system. Now the parties, themselves weakened by new curbs being placed on political machines, were being joined in the public arena by a host of other organizations.

Most conspicuous were the business corporations. The large corpor-ation, representing millions of dollars of capital and employing thousands of workers, was a new phenomenon (railroad companies apart). Even in 1900 most firms were small or family firms, employing no more than a handful of people, but an extraordinary merger movement was taking place which transformed the economy. Between 1895 and 1905 nearly 300 businesses a year were taken over by bigger businesses. The consolidation movement was dramatically symbolized in 1901 by the combination of 138 steel firms into the mammoth United States Steel Corporation, with capital of $1.4 billion. As such giants came to tower over whole industries, they acquired complex hierarchical structures which distanced them even more from the small family firms of old. Less subject to the whims of individual proprietors, the corporations were bureaucracies in their own right, increasingly controlled by boards of managers interested in long-term planning. They had the resources to lobby governments and cultivate friends in the press. In short, they became significant players in the political arena. When President Theodore Roosevelt came to deliver his first Annual Message to Congress in December 1901, he took the precaution of showing the first draft of it to George Perkins, a partner in the great banking firm, J. P. Morgan and Company.

The arrival of corporations was an unnerving phenomenon for many. Big businesses, of course, featured in other industrial economies, but nowhere did their appearance meet with such suspicion as in the United States. This was partly a product of the country's particular ideological traditions. The American economy was meant to be open to all. The emergence of the large corporation, capable of exercising monopolistic power, contradicted this essentially American concept of equality of opportunity. Also, over a third of economically active Americans were still farmers or farm workers, many of them deeply suspicious of the price-fixing activities of industrial and railroad monopolies. In addition, the power of big business was not confined to the economic sphere. By the end of the nineteenth century scandal after scandal had revealed the extent to which the corporations were able to influence city councils, state legislatures and even Congress.

The emergence of the corporation as a political player, seemingly usurping the rights of the electorate, became one of the major issues of the day, generating prolonged debate over the role of big business in the American system of government. But corporations were not alone in seeking to influence public policy. The organizational impulse produced interest groups of all sorts. Trade unions could not command nearly the same influence as the major corporations, but organized labour was mostly growing in the late nineteenth and early twentieth centuries. Total union membership expanded from about 500,000 at the end of the nineteenth century to over 2 million in 1910. The greater part of these unionists were members of unions affiliated to the American Federation of Labor (AFL). While the AFL did not carry much political clout, it did seek to influence public policy on labour issues, such as by bringing pressure to bear on candidates in congressional and state elections. At city level local labour federations made their presence felt. And other organizations also sought a voice in the political arena. Farm groups were active and the National Farmers' Union occasionally won a hearing on legislation affecting its members. Very formidable was the Anti-Saloon League, single-mindedly pursuing the cause of the prohibition of alcohol. Exerting some influence with local and state governments were such groups as the

American Medical Association and the National Education Association. There were veterans' groups like the Grand Army of the Republic, social work organizations like the National Conference of Charities and Corrections, and immigrant mutual aid associations like the Order of Sons of Italy. The agreement in 1907 between the Ancient Order of Hibernians and the German–American Alliance to oppose all forms of immigration restriction helped for a time to deter Congress from imposing a literacy test on immigrants.

The advent of a society of organized and contending interests put new pressures on government. Politicians, of course, could become the paid lackeys of wealthy lobbies, as some did, but they were also increasingly called upon to lay down the rules of the game. The courts might decide in principle what constituted legitimate conduct in an industrial society, as they had long done, but they were not well suited to resolving complex economic and technical issues, and in any case their conservatism meant that they did not command general confidence. Many citizens and groups looked to the legislative and executive branches to formulate rules of behaviour. Greater public regulation was inescapable, with government often being obliged to broker an agreement between competing interests. Sometimes consensus could not be reached and, on occasion, government simply imposed its own solution. In a variety of ways, government at all levels – city, state and national – was prodded into taking a more active role in resolving the conflicts inherent in an urban-industrial society.

Economic growth had accentuated class divisions, generating great fortunes for a few, good livings for a growing and increasingly professional middle class, a modest affluence for well-paid skilled workers and economic precariousness for millions of labourers and domestic workers. The gaping class divisions and the urban blight worried many well-to-do Americans, and before the turn of the century, fostered by the return of prosperity, there emerged a popular mood broadly sympathetic to proposals for economic, social and political reform. What is usually called the 'progressive movement' will be examined more fully in later chapters, but reforms were pressed by a variety of groups and individuals. Partly because of their actions, as well as the evolutionary trajectory of their urban-industrial society, a new and distinctive political system was being created – the Progressive Order.

Some scholars prefer the term the Republican Political System to characterize the pattern of politics that obtained between the late 1890s and the early 1930s. There are advantages in this terminology, since it does not exaggerate the reform aspects and underlines the dominance of the Republican Party. In the period 1875–97 the major political parties had been relatively evenly matched in terms of voting support, and there were only four years when one party simultaneously commanded the White House and enjoyed majorities in both houses of Congress. But in the mid-1890s an electoral realignment took place that made the Republican Party the normal 'majority party'. Through the North and Midwest, voters from many social groups switched from Democrat to Republican and maintained the allegiance well into the new century. The realignment also emphasized the Republicans' identification with urban-industrial America, many city workers now joining the middle and commercial classes in the party of order. In some parts of the country, most notably the South, the Democratic Party maintained its dominance, but only in unusual circumstances could it hope to win national elections. Of the seventeen Congresses elected between 1896 and 1928, the Republicans commanded majorities in the Senate in fourteen and in the House of Representatives in thirteen of them. A Republican occupied the White House for twenty-eight of the thirty-six years between 1897 and 1933. The Great Crash was to destroy this Republican ascendancy, and in the 1930s the Democratic Party assumed the role of majority party, which was to last for a generation and more.

Not all Republicans were of the ilk of the inimitable Theodore Roosevelt – who momentarily broke with party regulars to run for president as a Progressive Party candidate in 1912 – and Republican rule did not guarantee much sympathy for reform. But several prominent Republicans, from Theodore Roosevelt to Herbert Hoover, did at times avow themselves 'progressives', and Republicans of this generation showed some interest in the deployment of federal governmental powers. Support for reform was more consistently displayed by the Democrats, however. The realignment of the 1890s had identified the Democratic Party even more than previously with rural America, with its suspicion of moneyed interests and business-oriented governments, though it increasingly won support from labour groups also interested in progressive causes.

Republican dominance served to weaken the party system (as did Democratic dominance in the South): as elections in much of the country became less competitive, voters had less reason to cast their ballots. Party organization was also hampered by the attempts of progressive politicians to reduce the influence of political machines. Nonetheless the ascendancy of the Republican Party from the mid-1890s may have eased the adaptation of American government to the needs of an urban-industrial society.

The political realignment of the 1890s and the curbs on machine politics also reinforced the tendency of Anglo-Saxon Protestants to preside over the affairs of state and society. Republican ascendancy promoted the salience of Protestant values, reducing the access of urban ethnics (such as recent European immigrants) to high political councils, while the weakened party system allowed greater influence to new institutions like business corporations, professional associations and missionary societies. These institutions, concerned to articulate the public good, tended also to be managed by Anglo-Saxon Protestants. Not a few members of this Waspish hegemony, liberals among them, accepted the prevalent racial theories of the period, which imputed superiority not merely to whites but to those of Northern or Western European descent, and many were imbued too with a powerful missionary imperative. Evangelical Protestantism was expanding around the turn of the century.

A Christian moralism animated the highest in the land. Theodore Roosevelt saw the world in terms of good and evil, and while he acknowledged that there were faults in the body politic that needed to be exposed, these were defined in terms of individual morality. It was necessary to make war on 'grave evils', to expose 'every evil man' and 'every evil practice', to respect the 'honest man' and where possible to despatch the 'unscrupulous scoundrel' to the penitentiary. Roosevelt's theme song at the Progressive Party convention of 1912 was 'Onward, Christian Soldiers'. Even more imbued with a Christian morality was that son of the manse Woodrow Wilson, who read the Bible daily and believed that he had been sent to the White House by God. It was said of Herbert Hoover's aspirations for his administration that, 'It was as if a new paradise had burgeoned on earth for the exclusive benefit of the Americans and that God had blessed them with the perpetual improvement of this providential condition'. Christian moralists could be stand-pat conservatives or crusading radicals, but a Protestant spirit permeated the political culture of the period.

The Anglo-American establishment also tended to assume that American civilization, whatever its imperfections, was God's gift to humankind. Josiah Strong, a prominent Protestant cleric, believed that 'God ... is here training the Anglo-Saxon race for an hour sure to come in the World's future', and asked rhetorically whether this divinely favoured race was 'destined to dispossess many weaker ones, assimilate others, and mould the remainder, until in a very true and important sense, it has Anglo-Saxonized mankind?' Unlike democracy in Europe, Woodrow Wilson once observed, American democracy 'has had ... a truly organic growth. There was nothing revolutionary in its movements'. America's own history showed the way, and few doubted that other peoples would want to follow the American model.

The powerful religious faith of many in public life was allied to a lively respect for science, expertise and professionalism. In an increasingly urban-industrial society, governments were coming to recognize that they needed specialist advice on a range of issues. Experts in many areas were emerging. The late nineteenth and early twentieth centuries witnessed increasing professionalism in such fields as law, medicine, education and social work. Training improved and professional associations were founded or strengthened. In the universities the newer disciplines like sociology, psychology and public administration established themselves more securely, as did professional graduate schools. Specialists of various sorts offered advice on public policy. As Walter Lippmann observed in 1913 of the prospective governmental mechanisms, 'We shall use all science as a tool and a weapon'.

Many of these experts were convinced that it was possible for humankind to control its environment and they lent their support to the emerging progressive movements. Their prescriptions often implied a more active role for government, such as in regulating public health, but they were recommending them to a public that had little confidence in governments apparently captured by special interests. Before effective economic and social reform could take place, the political system had to be cleansed. The varieties of progressivism will be examined later, but the attempts to democratize American politics need to be discussed here. As earlier pointed out, the political order was changing in response to the pressures triggered by industrialization, but the political progressives also left their mark.

It seemed to many that the tensions that threatened the peace of American society stemmed in no small degree from the malfunctioning of the political system. Government no longer reflected the will of the whole community; special interests, particularly 'the trusts', had insinuated themselves at strategic junctures, often grasping monopoly privileges, manipulating systems of taxation and generally warping public policies. Party political machines too had intruded between the citizenry and the government, illicitly perpetuating their own power and promoting the interests of their particular clients (often local businesses, but they could also be beholden to labour groups or immigrant communities). A series of scandals, graphically publicized by the popular press, helped to turn public opinion against both the boss system and the involvement of business in government. (This also helps to explain the progressives' readiness to nominate for office men untainted with conventional politics, such as the academic Woodrow Wilson and the lawyer Charles Evans Hughes.) The idea of purifying politics by restoring power to 'the people', that is, promoting forms of 'direct democracy', proved to have wide support. In the Western states it drew on the old agrarian suspicion of the trusts. In the industrial states some labour groups hoped that the democratization of the political system would enhance the power of the working class. Many members of the Wasp establishment could enthusiastically embrace the cause of democratization both because it comported with their ideals and because it offered a means of curbing rival sources of authority.

To the progressive Republican Robert M. La Follette of Wisconsin, the 'will of the people' was to be the 'law of the land'. One way of implementing this vision was to trim the powers of party machines. Thus between 1903 and 1908 some thirty-one states passed laws requiring political parties to hold primary elections to choose their candidates for major offices. Increasingly, states also found ways of electing US senators by popular choice rather than by the state legislature, as prescribed by the Constitution, and direct election was ratified by the 17th Amendment in 1913. Many states sought to vest a measure of legislative authority directly in the electorate, with the introduction of such devices as the initiative (allowing voters to petition to vote directly on a measure) and the referendum. Women's suffrage was another reform demanded by many progressives. Women had traditionally represented spirituality and wholesomeness, and some suffrage supporters argued that enfranchising women (who were thought to be naturally non-partisan) would end bossism and corruption. Women's suffrage was achieved on the national level with the 19th Amendment to the Constitution in 1920.

But the thrust towards direct democracy was not as simple as it seemed. It was powered in part by a determination to end the business corruption of politics, and to that extent was an attack on party machines suspected of taking graft. Between 1903 and 1908 some twenty-two states outlawed campaign contributions by corporations. The introduction of the direct primary was meant to enable voters to circumvent the bosses. But direct democracy was not the only way to attack machine politics, and other attempts to curb corruption tended to put limits on popular participation. One was the enactment of tighter voter registration and residency laws, limiting access to the electoral rolls. Literacy tests, introduced in sixteen states, both North and South, between 1889 and 1913, had the same effect, excluding many immigrants and blacks. Another favourite measure was the so-called Australian ballot, that is, a secret ballot using forms printed by the government. This ended the practice whereby parties printed their own tickets and helped voters fill them in, but the new forms in effect discouraged illiterate voters who were unable to read them. In other ways too popular participation in politics was curbed. In many cities government was put in the hands of city commissions or city managers, supposedly expert administrators who might run their cities as businesses; while they were elected, elections had to be formally non-partisan and took place on a city-wide basis, making it more difficult for working-class districts to make their mark.

These various measures, designed to curb party abuses, had the broad effect of making politics a less popular pastime. In the twentieth century, turnout at elections began to drop dramatically. There were a number of reasons for this, among them the voter realignment of the mid-1890s that had left one party or the other dominant in many states. With election outcomes often a foregone conclusion, not only was voter interest diminished but divisions within each party tended to deepen as each faction sought the party nomination for its own candidate, and such unseemly quarrels may have done something to disenchant the public. The increasing centralization and bureaucratization of American political life also militated against popular involvement; decisions were being taken by remote officials and impersonal agencies. The carnival atmosphere of campaigns declined, as did turnout at the polls. Voter turnout dipped below 70 per cent in the presidential election of 1904 for the first time since the two-party system had taken shape in the late 1830s; in 1912, turnout was down to below 60 per cent, and in 1920 and 1924 it fell to below 50 per cent. Low turnouts were to remain characteristic of the new system of politics. Among other things, they meant that Southern blacks, poor whites and recent immigrants in the Northern cities were pushed to the margins of the political nation.

While the purification of American politics could arguably restore a sense of community, some Americans began to see the potential of rules and regulations in bringing order to a fluid urban-industrial world. The individual conscience beloved of nineteenth-century moralists no longer seemed a sufficient guide. The competing and interwoven interests of modern society might best be able to function together within some kind of administrative framework, that is, the goal of social harmony might be achieved by bureaucratic means. The elaboration of systemic rules implied a more active role for government, and in the Progressive Era, city, state and national governments did find themselves formulating regulations of many kinds.

The regulatory impulse was an essential component of progressivism, but it did not necessarily imply active governmental control. Most reformers, not to mention the armies of conservatives determined to maintain the status quo, were fervent believers in individual values and had no wish to create an overpowerful state. Allied to traditional anti-state attitudes was a growing distrust of politicians; the flagrant instances of bossism and corruption made many Americans wary of enlarging the power of government. An ingenious solution emerged to the problem of reconciling the tradition of limited government with the imperatives of industrial society: have the rules drawn up by bodies established by government but independent of it. A distinctive feature of American government was the reliance on semi-autonomous commissions or bureaus to formulate guides to conduct and to supervise behaviour. This was also related to another progressive characteristic, the faith in the expert. Such bodies, it was trusted, would be composed of disinterested professionals, specialists with expertise in the area in question. Order would be introduced into modern society by the application of knowledge and science.

The vision of the cooperative commonwealth, helped to function smoothly through flexible rules and the guidance of experts, was a meritocratic one, and it is hardly surprising that it was embraced by many members of the middle and upper classes anxious to defuse social conflict. In some respects the changes to the governing system in these years served to strengthen the hegemony of the Anglo-American élite. The creation of administrative hierarchies in the economic realm provided members of the educated classes with new governing tools. This is not to suggest that the process did not arouse misgivings. 'What I fear is a government of experts', said Woodrow Wilson in commenting on the tendencies he discerned in 1912, and being 'scientifically taken care of by a small number of gentlemen who are the only men who understand the job.'

Centralization and regulation, however, proceeded by fitful stages. At the opening of the twentieth century the notion that the federal government was strictly limited in its power was deeply engrained in constitutional thought. The power to regulate, in so far as it existed at all, was held to reside with the state governments, not with Washington (other than for interstate commerce). This was made clear in a Supreme Court decision of 1895, which held that: 'The power of a State to protect the lives, health, and property of its citizens, and to preserve good order ... is a power originally and always belonging to the States, not surrendered by them to the general government.' The establishment of semi-autonomous regulatory agencies helped to overcome the ideological scruples. The Interstate Commerce Commission (ICC) had been founded as early as 1887, somewhat ineffectually, but its powers were increased in 1906 and 1910. When the Hepburn Act of 1906 gave the ICC authority to supervise the railroads and fix their prices, it set a major precedent for the way in which the public welfare in the United States would be served through the use of disinterested administrative machinery. 'Its actual impact on the development of the railroad system was much less than its significance for the development of the American system of government', Robert Harrison has written. In 1914 the Federal Trade Commission was established. At state level, too, public service commissions made their appearance to regulate public utilities like gas or electricity, which were normally in private hands.

While the powers of these various commissions naturally varied, broadly they were expected to see that the relevant businesses operated in a proper manner. They might investigate suspected abuses, rule against unfair business practices, and publish reports and make recommendations for changing laws or regulations. They had little say over the internal management of individual companies, and usually they could not control prices. Sometimes businessmen themselves saw an advantage in cooperating with these regulatory initiatives, but in many cases compliance was reluctant. A railroad president complained in 1907 that President Roosevelt and his progressive allies were 'consciously or unconsciously ... trying to concentrate all power in Washington ... and to govern the people by commissions and bureaus'.

The comment was hardly fair, for state regulation of the market was for the most part 'indirect'. In theory it would have been possible to contemplate extensive state control or public ownership, of public utilities at least, but this was not to be the American way. Government was moving away from the *laissez-faire* tradition of the nineteenth century, but not in a manner that threatened private property. It was also moving away from the courts – a decision on what was a legitimate practice was to rest with an agency possessed of relevant expertise, not by an appeal to jurists unversed in economics. Commission members would normally be appointed by the executive, but would otherwise operate within the terms of the law establishing the agency rather than under the direction of government. In principle, they were to be public-spirited specialists in the area in question rather than party hacks. Responsibility for defining relations between government and business was thus being removed from parties, legislatures and courts and vested in formally non-partisan panels. Often, however, those appointed to regulate business were businessmen themselves.

Some of the agencies that emerged in these years were more administrative than regulatory. Facts and figures had to be compiled to assist in the making of policy and decisions had to be implemented. The Bureau of Labor Statistics had been established as early as 1884, the Bureau of Corporations in 1903 (before it was supplanted by other measures), and specialist bureaus appeared in existing government departments, like the Bureau of Chemistry within Agriculture and the Children's Bureau within the Department of Labor. (Kriste Lindenmeyer has identified the Children's Bureau as 'the first governmental agency in the world created solely to consider the problems of the child.') Policing another area of American public life was the Bureau of

Investigation, established in 1908, reconstituted under J. Edgar Hoover in 1924, and finally acquiring the word Federal in its title in 1935.

Within the civil service, too, expertise and efficiency, if not always in evidence, at least were becoming more highly valued. A beginning had been made in the 1880s with the replacement of patronage appointments to federal offices by a system of open competitive examinations, but the proportion of classified positions of this sort swelled from 22 per cent in 1891 to 44 per cent in 1901 and to 76 per cent in 1920. The states had begun to introduce the merit system too, and they sometimes replaced elective offices with appointive ones, further restricting the role of the voter but arguably locating public responsibility in expert hands. Specialists of various sorts – lawyers, scientists, economists – were recruited to federal or state government service. While the civil service in the United States was not as strong as it was in some European countries and party appointments were slow to disappear, it became more professional in nature.

The degree to which American government was bureaucratized should not be exaggerated. By European standards, the federal governmental framework in particular remained a very modest construction, and when the United States was pitched into the First World War the inadequacy of the administrative and regulatory machinery was exposed. Some progressives tried to seize the opportunity to add to governmental authority, though for the most part the emergency powers assumed by Washington were abandoned again after the war.

The Progressive Order was also based on the principle of exclusion. While the authentic democratic creed of progressives like La Follette cannot be doubted, in some ways, as already remarked, the democratic reforms of these years served to limit popular participation. For many members of the Anglo-Saxon élite, the curbs on political machines, the tightening of voter registration procedures and the transfer of decision-making to non-elective experts marked steps in the direction of good government. But governance of this kind also excluded many members of society from significant participation.

The major business corporations usually enjoyed access to government, but the role accorded to organized labour was very limited. The AFL enjoyed a modicum of influence in federal councils during the First World War, when the Wilson administration was anxious to recruit it to the war effort, but in the 1920s the labour movement was crumbling and its political voice was minimal. The political role of women also was a subordinate one, as will be argued in the next chapter, despite their extraordinary activity in the social sphere. Immigrants too enjoyed very limited access to high political councils, and legislation of the 1920s largely restricted future immigration to the countries of Northern and Western Europe. African-Americans were kept almost completely outside the political pale.

The essentially exclusive nature of the Progressive Order is nowhere more apparent than in its treatment of black Americans. It was in these years that

African-Americans were most rigorously excluded from the political nation. Discrimination had long existed, but blacks were now systematically disfranchised and 'Jim Crow' laws bolted segregation firmly into place in the South, the location of 89 per cent of African-Americans in 1910. Neither the Supreme Court nor the federal government offered them much protection. Most progressives displayed little sympathy for blacks (though it was sometimes argued in private that it was better to get good men into government before addressing the race question). Theodore Roosevelt may have raised Southern hackles by inviting the prominent black educator Booker T. Washington to lunch at the White House, but there was no mention of the plight of African-Americans in the Progressive Party platform of 1912. If anything, the federal authorities tended to reinforce discrimination. President Taft saw no case for supporting voting rights for blacks, who were but 'political children, not having the mental status of manhood', and in 1913 the sometime university professor Woodrow Wilson introduced segregation into federal employment.

The era of Republican ascendancy in effect left African-Americans politically impotent. The Republican Party had conceded the South to the Democrats, where most blacks could not vote. Outside the South, in much of the North and West, the Republicans normally enjoyed safe majorities in most states, so that the tiny black vote (which was Republican anyway) could not exert even marginal influence. The one-sided contests throughout the country allowed racial minorities no electoral leverage. Few congressmen through the first third of the twentieth century needed to heed black constituents, and Congress's influential Southern bloc ensured failure for any measure that might disturb the white South. When the House of Representatives passed an anti-lynching bill in 1921, Southern senators killed it with a filibuster.

The segregation laws and local ordinances introduced in the South between about 1890 and the First World War ensured that blacks were educated (up to a modest point) in separate schools, and that public places and private services were similarly segregated – hospitals, trains, parks, toilets, barber shops and even cemeteries. The Supreme Court, in *Plessy v Ferguson* in 1896, legitimized segregation on the premise that the equal rights of blacks were not infringed by separate treatment. The doctrine of 'separate but equal' underpinned Jim Crow, though the separate treatment of blacks was rarely if ever equal. In this separate world, African-Americans could fashion, to a degree, a culture of their own and draw strength from their churches, but they were hardly in a position to confront the white power structure and its laws. As if law was not enough, lynching also kept blacks in their place. Lynching reached a peak in the 1890s, when over a hundred incidents were usually recorded annually; but there were still several dozen a year in the 1900s and 1910s. Not until the end of the era – in 1929 – did recorded lynchings dip into single figures.

What made segregation virtually impregnable was the exclusion of most Southern blacks from the suffrage. The purpose of Virginia's constitutional convention in 1900, according to one frank delegate, was 'to discriminate to the very extremity of permissible action under the limitations of the federal Constitution, with a view to the elimination of every Negro voter who can be gotten rid of legally, without materially impairing the numerical strength of the white electorate'. Progressive reformers sometimes joined the disfranchisement cause, believing that blacks – like immigrants in Northern cities – were manipulated by corrupt white politicians. As it happened, the poll taxes and other devices used to disfranchise blacks also had the effect of keeping many poor whites off the electoral registers, so that Southern élites were well protected from a plebeian insurgency.

Yet beneath the surface, the foundations of this racist system of politics were being chipped away gradually. Blacks were leaving the land for the city and the North. What became known as the Great Migration was an epochal episode in African-American history. A few blacks had trickled North through the middle decades of the nineteenth century, and towards its end the migration swelled. By 1910 there were 440,000 Southern-born blacks living in the North out of a total Northern black population of just over 1 million. Then the 1910s, when war erupted in Europe, saw a massive exodus from the South, an estimated net out-migration of 432,000. The accelerating demands of war industries, combined with the dwindling of foreign immigration, greatly increased black opportunities for jobs, especially in the Middle Atlantic states and the industrial Midwest. Once unleashed, the flood of migrants mounted even more in the 1920s, to around 750,000. By 1930 there were nearly 2.5 million Northern blacks. Then the Depression checked this massive relocation of people, although it did not stop it.

Almost overnight, Northern cities found themselves with considerable black populations. For many blacks, 'freedom land' meant Chicago, with its relatively easy rail and road access from the Mississippi Delta and the Deep South. In 1910 there had been 44,000 blacks in Chicago; by 1930 there were 233,000. But other Northern and Midwestern cities experienced similar explosions in their black populations. These newcomers were not always made welcome. In particular, the conditions associated with the First World War, when American-born workers, immigrants and blacks scuffled unhappily for housing and jobs in the congested cities, exacerbated racial tensions. There were vicious race riots in East St Louis in 1917, and in Washington, DC, Chicago and elsewhere in the 'Red Summer' of 1919.

Black ghettos expanded in these cities, with implications for black consciousness, black culture and black politics. The growth of black communities outside the South and an educated black middle class made possible a modicum of organization. Some black activists joined with white liberals and intellectuals in 1910 to form the National Association for the Advancement of Colored People (NAACP), which dedicated itself to securing equal rights for black Americans. Through the years prior to the Great Depression, the NAACP remained primarily a Northern organization. The vulnerable black sharecroppers and tenant farmers of the South could not be organized easily. Another biracial body appeared in 1911 in New York in the form of the National Urban League, which worked to improve conditions for black Americans in Northern cities, in particular helping Southern migrants to adapt to urban life. African-Americans were learning the value of organization, even if it meant working with sympathetic whites. The socialist A. Philip Randolph saw another opportunity for blacks in the labour movement now that they were finding jobs in the industrial economy, and in 1925 he organized the all-black Brotherhood of Sleeping Car Porters. The existing unions offered little succour to black workers.

Another sign of the growing political consciousness of urban blacks emerged with Marcus Garvey. A Jamaican immigrant, Garvey won prominence in the 1920s with his Universal Negro Improvement Association (UNIA). He caught the imagination of the black masses with his programme of black nationalism, 'back to Africa', black economic independence and his liking for flamboyant pageantry. He spoke of a black-owned merchant fleet sailing to Africa and black-owned factories and stores. UNIA claimed 500,000 members by 1925, far exceeding the number enrolled by the NAACP. Garvey thus became the first man to lead a black mass movement in the United States. The popularity of his nationalist appeal owed something to the widespread perception among blacks that there was little prospect of significant concessions from the existing political system. Garvey's financing of his black enterprises, however, ran into trouble, and in 1925 he went to prison for fraud; on release he was deported to England. In the early 1920s, however, his message of black pride and his emphasis on African ancestry caught the imagination of the black masses, excluded as they were from the conventional polity.

The growth of black ghettos and a heightened African-American consciousness held out the possibility of a new political strategy for blacks. Southern blacks may have been kept off the electoral rolls, but the growing numbers in the Northern cities did have the right to vote. Their concentration in particular districts occasionally gave them some political leverage. In 1928 a Chicago district elected the first Northern black man to Congress, and occasional blacks were also elected to the city councils of New York and Chicago in the 1920s and 1930s. These first black politicians were often Republicans, faithful to the party of Abraham Lincoln and Emancipation, but there were signs that the accord between the Republican Party and black Americans was weakening. 'Racial amalgamation there cannot be', said President Warren Harding, resisting any suggestion of social equality. During the presidential election of 1928, some blacks were attracted to the Democratic Party by the reformist urban politics of Al Smith, presaging the great switch of black allegiances to the New Deal in the 1930s. During the Hoover administration the Illinois black leader Roscoe Conkling Simmons was once moved to stand beneath a window of the White House and forlornly implore: 'Speak, Mr President, speak. Tell us that Lincoln still lives.'

But the Emancipator was long dead. The NAACP may have won occasional court battles, a few blacks may have joined trade unions, and black politicians may have been elected to local offices occasionally, but there were only the faintest of cracks in the monstrous edifice of white supremacy. As Robert Cook has written: 'By 1930 ... protest activity had failed to undermine significantly the nationwide system of segregation and discrimination which confined most blacks to the bottom of the pile.' The Progressive Order was not responsible for this racial subjugation, which had long existed, but the dominant political currents of these years reinforced it. The progressive doctrine of good government was used to justify the disfranchisement of black Americans. White Americans of all political persuasions generally subscribed to the racial theories of the time, which assumed a hierarchy of ethnic and racial types in which Caucasians (and especially those held to be of Anglo-Saxon stock) ranked highest. The progressives' esteem for experts contributed to this understanding. The intelligence tests developed by Lewis Terman and other psychologists during the 1910s seemed to prove the intellectual inferiority of those of African descent. The barriers erected against the participation of African-Americans in the polity were no anomaly, for in the Progressive Order, women, white ethnics and the labouring classes were also consigned to separate spheres for the most part.

When Herbert Hoover entered the White House in 1929 the political order seemed more secure than ever. Republican presidents were being elected by huge popular majorities and the Republicans usually enjoyed handsome majorities in both houses of Congress. The Republican ascendancy reinforced the influence of Anglo-Saxon Protestants, as did those reforms to the electoral system which were ostensibly democratic but tended to limit popular participation. The restriction of immigration to the peoples of Northern and Western Europe sought to ensure the continued supremacy of Anglo-Americans. Government had been fortified by an array of semi-autonomous commissions and specialized bureaus and by an increasingly professional civil service, and in theory, at least, was better equipped to mediate the conflicts that arose in a society of contending interest groups. But the foundations of this system of politics, with its exclusion or subordination of so many restless people, were more vulnerable than was generally recognized. In the event, a major crash on the stock market would not only fell the economy but also bring down the Progressive Order.

|2|

Immigrants, Workers and Women
1900–33

The Progressive Order was not an inclusive one. As we have seen, as the new century opened, black Americans were already being bound in their place and few whites questioned their exclusion from political society. Other groups, too, were expected to assume a subordinate position in a political society mostly governed by well-bred Anglo-Americans. Industrial workers began to establish their own organizations, but their more radical fraternities were treated as un-American, while even moderate labour unions found that their legal status was weaker than that of business corporations. There was considerable public debate over whether immigrants from Southern and Eastern Europe were entitled to the same rights as those old-stock Americans whose ancestors had built the United States; eventually they were refused entry to the country. There was disagreement also over the status of women. Well-educated middle-class women sometimes wondered why they were excluded from the suffrage while illiterate (male) European peasants were not, and some of them mobilized to claim a political voice. Only partly because of the strategies employed by the élites, the major labour and women's groups were to evolve more as allies than as critics of the Progressive Order.

The greatest threat to social order in the early years of the twentieth century seemed to come from below, that is, from the multitude of impoverished foreigners pouring into American cities and from the growing industrial working class. In part, the attempts to reconstruct the political system in these years were designed to avert subversion by these elements. As with black Americans, coercive and restrictive instruments were employed to contain the danger, but a major part of the strategy of the governing authorities was amelioration. To a significant degree progressive reform was designed to heal the class and ethnic sores of the body politic. American women sensed an opening for themselves in this, for they were to play a major role in fashioning institutions that reached into the immigrant and working-class communities.

In the late nineteenth century the Anglo-Saxon and Northern European peoples who had long populated North America confronted the 'new immigration' from Southern and Eastern Europe, as well as Chinese and Japanese newcomers on the West Coast. By 1900 over 70 per cent of immigrants came from such countries as Italy, Russia, Poland, Greece and the Austro-Hungarian empire, bringing with them customs, religions and tongues which seemed to set them disturbingly apart from old-stock Americans. Then the numbers increased, over 8 million pouring through American ports in the first decade. This spectacular figure would have been exceeded in the 1910s had it not been for the disruptive outbreak of the First World War; after it, large-scale immigration resumed. Although Congress began to enact legislation to restrict entry, not until the Great Crash added its deterrent effect was immigration significantly reduced. The first three decades of the century saw nearly 19 million people enter the United States, and the composition of urban America changed rapidly. The proportion of Protestant immigrants plummeted; many of the newcomers were Roman Catholic, some were from the Orthodox Churches, and substantial numbers were Jewish. By 1910 immigrants (including American-born children of foreign parents) accounted for three-quarters of the population of many cities.

This alien torrent troubled many of those even of progressive disposition. Woodrow Wilson expressed concern about admitting to American society 'multitudes of men of the lowest class' and feared that 'a miscellaneous immigration' was creating 'social chaos'. The progressive academic Edward A. Ross worried that 'American blood' would be overwhelmed by these newcomers, who would reduce social standards to 'their brawls and their animal pleasures'. Many public figures, both liberal and conservative, accepted supposedly scientific evidence that the peoples of Southern and Eastern Europe were genetically inferior to those of Anglo-Saxon or Nordic stock. In principle there were two ways in which the subversive potential of this great invasion could be countered – immigrants could be socialized into American ways or excluded from the country. The Progressive Order was to be protected by the adoption of both strategies.

Middle-class social workers in the cities tried to integrate immigrants into American society for years. Patriotic societies, like the Daughters of the American Revolution, sponsored lectures and classes to teach newcomers the principles of American citizenship. 'We must Americanize them in every way, in speech, in political ideas and principles, and in their way of looking at the relations between Church and State', said Theodore Roosevelt. Social workers, patriotic groups and employers' associations each had their reasons for wishing to educate and socialize the growing numbers of strangers. Party machines often offered their mediating services to immigrants, some of whom voted, though the electoral revisions of the period, as we have seen, tended to limit their political voice. (Many immigrants, in fact, were slow to naturalize and become citizens.) In New York in the Progressive Era, Frances Kellor led campaigns to secure better education and protective welfare legislation for immigrants. In 1914 she and others formed the Committee for Immigrants in America, and the outbreak of the First World War gave considerable impetus to the Americanization movement.

The war frayed the nerve endings of an ethnically diverse society, and after it public sentiment turned sharply against European influences. Americanization became identified with the strident patriotism of 'One Hundred Percent Americanism'. The American Legion established a National Americanism Commission, whose goal was to realize in the United States 'the basic ideal of ... one hundred percent Americanism through the planning, establishment, and conduct of a continuous, constructive, educational establishment'. To this end it urged English and civics courses for immigrants, encouraged patriotic rituals in schools and distributed patriotic literature. Other groups followed suit. An emphasis on cultural homogeneity displaced the humane Americanization ideas of Frances Kellor, designed as much to protect as to educate immigrants. This was a goal of a revitalized Ku Klux Klan, which between 1920 and 1926 enrolled over 3 million members and became a political force in several Midwestern and Southern states. While traditional anti-black racism was present, in the 1920s the dominant Klan prejudice was anti-Catholicism, an expression of its fear of the alien hordes. As the Grand Wizard expressed it: 'We are demanding ... a return of power into the hands of the everyday, not highly cultured ... but unspoiled and not de-Americanized, average citizen of the old stock.' Some Klansmen worked responsibly to restore traditional moral values to local communities, but others succumbed to vigilante action against labour radicals, Jews and Catholics. Eventually incidents of scandal and violence so tarnished the Klan's reputation that respectable citizens deserted it, but not before it had testified to a popular belief that the route to political and social security lay in the restoration of a uniform cultural order.

Cultural homogeneity could also be achieved by excluding unwanted categories from the country. In the aftermath of the First World War, the nativist crusade was reaching its peak, heightened by racist fears that the dilution of Anglo-Saxon blood could undermine the achievements of American civilization and by the anxieties of old-stock Americans over their status and jobs. These pressures proved irresistible. Chinese immigration had been largely stopped in 1882 and Japanese in 1907, but after the First World War a Supreme Court decision decreed East and South Asians ineligible for citizenship. The immigration acts of 1921 and 1924 for the first time put a ceiling – a low one – on the number of foreigners from outside the western hemisphere annually settling in the United States. Virtually all Asian immigration was prohibited, and the eventual permanent formula assigned a quota to each European nationality, reflecting its overall contribution to the white population in 1920. Thus only those countries that had been sending immigrants for generations, like Britain and Germany, could expect significant quotas. The National Origins Quota System was designed to perpetuate the existing ethnic composition of American society. It excluded the supposedly inferior and dangerous races of Southern and Eastern Europe, thereby preserving the primacy of American Wasps.

By the end of the first third of the twentieth century the 'immigrant question' had been largely resolved. Immigrants themselves tended to form their own communities, often in ghettos, and found reassurance in their own churches, synagogues and ethnic clubs. Often culturally and politically conservative, very few wished to challenge the structures of American society. The schools taught their children something of American values, and many of the adults obligingly cast ballots for the regular parties in accordance with the wishes of their employers or local party chieftains. Simultaneously, the progressive curbs on machine politics increasingly limited the political influence of new immigrants, while the barriers erected in the 1920s ensured that their communities would not be supplemented by fresh arrivals. In 1933 the number of immigrants sank to a hundred-year low.

By this date too the ruling classes had answered the related 'labour question'. The industrialized world had been highly conscious of the bloody potential of class conflict, at least since the Paris Commune of 1871. American authorities had been alarmed by the social disturbances that had marked the severe depression of 1893–6, while the emergence of radical socialist groups in the first decade of the twentieth century was no more reassuring. In principle, labour could aspire to a number of roles. In some industrial countries, such as Britain, a labour party emerged to represent the interests of the working class within the prevailing constitutional structure. In Russia the Bolsheviks sought to impose the dictatorship of the proletariat and replace capitalism with collective ownership. There were advocates of both these approaches in the United States, but the bulk of American workers avoided the political route and adopted an economic strategy, forming trade unions to protect their interests within the capitalist system. This strategy, of course, had a political dimension, for the unions could function as pressure groups.

The two related questions – why there was no strong labour or socialist party and why organized labour did not achieve the potency it did elsewhere – have been exhaustively discussed by scholars. The problem was famously posed in 1906, when the German sociologist Werner Sombart asked, not quite accurately: why is there no socialism in the United States? One major set of explanations has focused on the distinctive nature of the American working class itself, composed of elements that did not lend themselves to organization and radicalism. A second set has emphasized the particular economic, constitutional and political environments in which American workers found themselves, environments capable of absorbing, dissipating or repressing labour aspirations. Together these two approaches provide much of the answer. But labour weakness did not mean quiescence. American workers indeed were exceptionally militant – in the early twentieth century the incidence of strikes in the United States was very high, and appalling violence marked industrial relations.

Organizing American workers was never going to be easy. There was the problem of numbers. The world's leading industrial power did not possess a particularly large working class. Even in their numerical heyday, industrial wage-earners were a minority class in the United States. In Britain in 1910 the proportion of the workforce employed in the secondary or industrial sector was about 51 per cent; in the United States it was only 31 per cent. American workers usually had a rural and middle-class majority arrayed against them, at least potentially. This was probably one reason why employers and governments were able quite often to crush industrial action brutally. Disruptive workers did not often command public sympathy.

The divisions within the working class represented another problem. Skilled workers were separated from unskilled labourers by both income and ethnicity. Skilled workmen tended to be native-born Americans or old-stock immigrants, and they enjoyed relatively high wages compared to their counterparts in Britain. They could believe that America was indeed the land of opportunity, and for the most part they were firm enough supporters of the status quo. Many were Roman Catholic, encouraged by their Church to be wary of socialist remedies. Courted by local bosses, they put their trust in the existing parties. But unskilled workers experienced very different conditions, not to mention some hostility from American-born labour. Their wages were often pitifully low and employment uncertain. Many had been European agricultural workers and craftsmen and had brought with them their own customs and values; their traditional folk cultures often rendered them less than receptive to class appeals. The transiency of many immigrants – high proportions returned to their homelands – also militated against class solidarity. In any case, most immigrants found security in ethnic cultures rather than in class activity. Such workers, as historian John Bodnar has shown, gave their primary loyalties to family and ethnic community. Cut off from one another by income, ethnicity, race and occupation, the condition of American wage-earners was less conducive than in Europe to either trade unionism or a class-conscious political movement.

The larger political environment did not lend itself to exploitation by labour movements. American workers had never been wholly excluded from the conventional political system. In the early decades of the nineteenth century the suffrage became all but universal – for white men. By the 1840s two mass political parties had been organized, achieving turnouts of up to 80 per cent in presidential elections. The parties, pragmatic guardians of a capitalist economy and an ostensibly democratic polity, had succeeded in mobilizing most ordinary citizens, adroitly making concessions to their working-class constituents when the occasion demanded. And whatever their ethnic differences, these workers, it has been argued, at least shared an awareness of their common 'whiteness', which may have cemented their loyalty to the dominant political institutions (as well as reinforcing the exclusion of African-Americans from the polity). Further, the American constitutional structure did not facilitate the successful creation of third parties, at least on a national scale. Labour parties might be formed in certain industrial cities, but they were unlikely to capture even the state legislatures – in which rural areas were over-represented – let alone mobilize successfully across the immensity of the United States.

Most American workers never even organized into unions. At the height of the early union effort, in 1920, the unionized proportion of the non-agricultural workforce was still under 20 per cent. The unions had enjoyed some success in what were by now relatively traditional sectors of the economy, such as construction, mining and the railroads, but large areas were barely touched, most notably the fast-growing mass-production industries such as steel, textiles and automobiles. This is not to suggest an absence of class conflict. On the contrary, workers were often highly aware of social distinctions and recognized the need for concerted action. But their actions often did not take an expressly socialist form. In local communities workers found collective purpose in immigrant societies, neighbourhood groups, cooperative stores and, indeed, in meetings and strikes, many of the latter conducted by non-unionized workers. In the opening years of the twentieth century, proportionately speaking, there were more strikes and strikers in the United States than in any European country other than Italy. Employer hostility helps to explain the protracted and violent nature of many strikes.

In these conditions radical movements tended to encounter both the indifference of most workers and the hostility of the authorities. One group to challenge the established order were the Industrial Workers of the World, or Wobblies. Formed in 1905, the IWW constituted evidence of the authentic class conflict that flickered in the mines, lumber camps and fields of the West and South-West. Denying that workers and employers shared common interests, the Wobblies argued that between these two classes 'a struggle must go on until the workers of the world organize as a class, take possession of the earth and the machinery of production, and abolish the wage system'. Their defiant poses seemed tantamount to insurrection to many businessmen and government officials, and a number of Western states in effect declared war on them, particularly as the First World War added to fears of subversion. Extensive vigilante and legal offensives, and disavowal by the major trade unions, largely destroyed the Wobblies even before the post-war Red Scare mopped up the relics.

Barely more successful were those who sought to further the cause of labour through political action. Formed in 1901, the Socialist Party of America spread with remarkable rapidity, supporting many of the causes of progressive reform while hoping eventually to bring much of the economy under collective ownership. By 1912 it claimed nearly 118,000 members. Most immigrants resisted the lure of socialism, but the party found some support among Jewish and other Eastern European immigrants and some skilled German workers. Conspicuously absent were the Irish Catholics, who made up a large part of the older urban working class. From 1904 the party regularly contested presidential elections, reaching a high point in 1912, when Eugene V. Debs won

6 per cent of the popular vote. Since the British Labour Party, with a much more cautious approach to socialism, had polled only 7 per cent in December 1910, Debs's showing was not unimpressive. The Socialists tended to fare best in small communities – in 1911 they elected seventy-three mayors or other major municipal officers – but they could not break out of their scattered urban redoubts. When the party defiantly opposed both preparedness and intervention during the First World War, prominent supporters defected, some members fell foul of state sedition laws, Debs himself was arrested and prosecuted and Socialist newspapers were banned from the mail. As the party reeled under these blows, the Russian Revolution added its disruptive impact, inspiring some on the left to sheer away into more radical alternatives. Two new parties were formed in September 1919, the Communist Party, identified strongly with Eastern European immigrants, and the Communist Labor Party, led by the American-born John Reed. Within a year they too were being eviscerated by the Red Scare and internal division. The Socialist Party lingered but was never to play a significant role in American politics. It failed to mobilize the working class at the polls or win control of organized labour. The communists, united after a fashion into the Communist Party by 1923, similarly remained on the margins, distrusted by mainstream organizations as subject to the imperatives of Moscow.

These various radical eruptions had some political effect. The subversive threat they supposedly represented provided an excuse to extend governmental authority. States enhanced their police powers as they adopted a panoply of anti-anarchy and sedition laws between 1917 and 1921. The federal government also expanded its capacity. The Immigration Act of 1918 made it easier for the federal authorities to deport dissident aliens, while within the Bureau of Investigation the General Intelligence Division was created under J. Edgar Hoover to subject left-wing activity to surveillance. It was the fate of the various radical groups to be large enough to be noticed and small enough to be crushed.

The very enmity of corporations and the state (including the courts) helped to persuade some labour leaders that radicalism was not the way forward in the American environment. Better, they concluded, to support the political order while building resilient organizations of their own. Determining an economic strategy, these leaders wanted to keep the state out of labour relations and focus on negotiating with employers on such issues as hours and wages. Some employers themselves recognized the value of encouraging a form of labour organization compatible with the capitalist system. In 1900 the National Civic Federation (NCF) was created, composed of representatives of business, labour and the public, with the object of promoting industrial peace through an acceptance of trade unionism and the use of conciliation and arbitration. Some of the country's biggest businessmen identified themselves with this body, which saw trade unionism as 'consonant with American institutions' and an 'antidote for the socialistic propaganda', even if they did not always recognize unions within their own companies.

But even a unionism antipathetic to socialism encountered obstacles. Many employers rejected the very assumption that unions were a legitimate part of American political economy and courts viewed them with the deepest suspicion. Trade unions as such were never declared unlawful, but their methods frequently inspired judicial disapproval. A union might call a strike, but if it engaged in 'intimidatory' action it risked being placed outside the law. Secondary boycotts and sympathy strikes were generally deemed illegal. In the 1890s the Supreme Court legitimized attempts to turn the Sherman Anti-Trust Act against union activity. When threatened by industrial action, employers frequently turned to the courts, asking for an injunction prohibiting strikes on pain of costly contempt proceedings. This court hostility, perpetuating unions in a semi-outlaw status, helps to explain the distinctive course taken by organized labour in the United States.

Self-help was the answer. Unions would have to be strong enough to confront employers but they would not expect anything from the state – except recognition. Like Churches, they would be voluntary organizations in the American polity. But there was a cost to this self-help philosophy. Union dues had to be high, since benefits and permanent officials had to be paid for, a circumstance which largely excluded unskilled workers. It was skilled workers, a relatively small segment of the working class, who came to be mobilized in the emerging craft unions. These workers tended also to be distanced from other wage-earners by ethnicity and race. They were often wary of 'new' immigrants and reinforced segregation in their reluctance to admit African-Americans to their unions.

A group of craft unions had formed the American Federation of Labor (AFL) in 1886, and this was to become the major labour organization through the first third of the twentieth century. Repudiating socialist doctrines, the AFL worked to secure acceptance by employers as the sole acceptable adversary. By the turn of the century the AFL and other unions enjoyed considerable success. Total union membership passed 2 million in 1904 and by 1920 there were 5 million union members, 4 million of them in the AFL. As defined by Samuel Gompers, its president for nearly forty years, the AFL was a firm believer in 'voluntarism'. He aspired to strength in the workplace and took an adversarial attitude towards management, while wary of remedies that might make labour dependent on a political party or government. He had no interest in his members becoming the employees of an untrustworthy state and saw little need for public ownership or even minimum wage laws. He told a congressional committee in 1916 that unemployment insurance was 'socialist' and that it was better for workers to suffer than to 'give up one jot of the freedom ... to strive and struggle for their own emancipation through their own efforts'. Whether any other strategy would have served the interests of the mainstream labour movement better is debatable, but to Gompers voluntarism recognized the realities of American legal, political and economic life. (The failure of government and the Democratic Party to protect labour in the last third of the twentieth century, a resurrected

Gompers might have argued, vindicated his stance.) Nonetheless, the strategy did depend on trade unions being recognized as bargaining agents, the objective of much of the strike activity of these years.

Increased employer attacks on labour after 1903 pushed the AFL reluctantly toward political action. Above all it wanted the removal of injunctions as a weapon of management and the exemption of unions from prosecution under the Sherman Act. In 1906 the AFL actively involved itself in congressional elections for the first time, targeting a number of anti-labour congressmen for defeat. Two years later the Democrats inserted an anti-injunction plank in the national party platform and the AFL endorsed the Democratic ticket. During the 1910s organized labour glimpsed the prospect of expanding its political role. At state level it sometimes helped to secure progressive reforms, like workmen's compensation for injury. In the 1912 presidential campaign the AFL backed a winner in Woodrow Wilson, and his administration paid some heed to its labour constituents, creating a Department of Labor with a former trade union official as its head. The Clayton Act of 1914 sought to exempt unions from the anti-trust laws and related injunctions, although the courts soon decided otherwise. The Adamson Act of 1916 gave railroad workers an eight-hour day, and in the election of that year Gompers campaigned for Wilson and encouraged his members to vote for pro-labour Democrats.

With the outbreak of the First World War the AFL saw an opportunity to become a kind of junior partner of government and to discredit its socialist rivals. Gompers wrote to Wilson in August 1917 that unless government and employers dealt with the AFL they would have 'the alternative of being forced to take the consequences of the so-called IWW with all that implies'. The administration, anxious to maximize war production at a time of exceptional industrial militancy, was responsive. With government blessing, the AFL secured substantially better wages and widely achieved an eight-hour day; in return it discouraged strikes. The National War Labor Board brought considerable pressure on employers to recognize trade unions and union membership boomed. But the romance between the AFL and the Wilson government proved ephemeral. Once the war ended, Washington had less reason to mediate between labour and capital. The labour movement, eager to protect wartime gains and win compensation for galloping inflation, itself adopted a more belligerent posture, which employers were not slow to impute to Bolshevist influence. Industrial relations rapidly soured, presaging a ferocious Red Scare (as discussed in Chapter 5) and the year 1919 established a new strike record. With public opinion turning against strikers the Democrats were less inclined to protect them and the disappointed AFL distanced itself from the party.

The Red Scare and its aftermath took their toll, union membership falling by 25 per cent between 1920 and 1923. The early 1920s witnessed powerful open-shop drives, as some employers sought to cripple unions by equating the closed shop with Bolshevism. As the decade progressed, other employers, equally concerned to disarm radicalism, experimented with welfare capitalism, such as company-sponsored pension and insurance plans. The anti-union offensives, the flowering of welfare capitalism and company unions, the general prosperity of the period and the relatively high wages all helped to weaken the labour movement. Many of the new industrial workers had had little or no previous industrial experience. Employers like Henry Ford paid high wages in return for hard work and no unionism, and many workers accepted this bargain. By the late 1920s the material and psychological rewards of a consumer-oriented capitalism had begun, as yet very modestly, to compensate for the demands of work; jobs were becoming instruments, not ends in themselves. Workers arguably became machine-like in the work-place, but a few enjoyed greater comforts at home.

Employer and court intransigence also put the AFL on the defensive. They used the injunction more widely than ever during the 1920s, its effectiveness greatly enhanced by the related use of the yellow dog contract, which bound employees not to join a union. If they did so an injunction might be secured and weak unions had no effective response to the combined application of the yellow dog/injunction strategy. The shaken AFL became yet more con-servative after William Green succeeded Gompers as president in 1924. It had always been cast as an adversary of management, but by the late 1920s it was promoting the doctrine of labour–management cooperation, to the pleasure of conservative progressives like Herbert Hoover. In 1930 William Green was awarded a medal by the Roosevelt Memorial Association for his services in overcoming industrial strife. The AFL, it seemed, had been fully co-opted to the Progressive Order. Nonetheless the acute social distress fol-lowing the Stock Market Crash did produce some public sympathy for orga-nized labour and growing support for its anti-injunction campaign. Congress finally responded in 1932, the Norris-La Guardia Act prohibiting the yellow dog contract, strictly limiting the use of injunctions and upholding labour's right to organize without interference.

If the political leaders of the Progressive Era had wished to encourage a 'responsible' labour movement, they had in large measure succeeded. The radical alternatives represented by the Wobblies and the Socialist Party had been seen off, partly because they held little appeal for the bulk of American workers and partly because of the corporate and governmental campaigns waged against them. Radicalism did not come easily to American working men, although militancy did. At the ballot box they broadly accepted the prevailing system of major non-ideological parties; in the workplace they often resorted to industrial action. Yet the success of the combative volun-tarism of Sam Gompers and the AFL was limited. There were gains, such as the establishment of the Department of Labor and the broader acceptance of the eight-hour day, and while union membership fell in the 1920s it remained significantly larger than it had been before the First World War. But organized labour had a distinctly minor role in the American polity, and the legal status of unions, unlike that of the corporations, remained ambiguous until at least 1932. Further, the AFL represented only a fraction of American wage-earners. In 1930 no more than 12 per cent of non-agricultural workers belonged to unions. The AFL had not reached the mass of unskilled and semi-skilled workers of the industrial economy.

If the political activity of labour was weaker in the United States than in some other industrial societies in the early twentieth century, the position of women was stronger and helped to shape the Progressive Era state. The two were not unrelated. In a sense, the limited public role of labour allowed women more space. Further, many well-to-do women saw themselves as the answer to 'the labour question' – they might work to socialize immigrants and build bridges between the classes. (Other women, of course, were both workers and immigrants.) In this sense the function of women was socially conservative, strengthening American economic and political systems by humanizing them.

Industrialization accentuated gender differences, as men offered their muscles and skills in the labour market and many women performed unpaid tasks at home. This division of labour provided a basis for the doctrine of separate spheres, the idea that men and women had different roles in life, and in attenuated form this became the Cult of True Womanhood, which held married women responsible for introducing spirituality to the family home (though the man remained head of the household). In fact, the real world never conformed to such urban, white middle-class notions. Many women entered the labour market, mainly single working-class whites and black, Hispanic and Asian women, both married and single. The increasing visibility of women in American public life in the early twentieth century was in part a consequence of continuing socio-economic change. The spread of business and government bureaucracy meant more typists and clerks, and a shopping boom provided employment for presentable white women as sales clerks. Office and sales work had once been dominated by men, but the flourishing bureaucratic and consumer cultures enabled women to sup-plant them. In 1890 the proportion of women in paid employment reached 19 per cent; by 1930 it was not quite 25 per cent (though about half of single women had jobs). The visible presence of women in the workplace, especially in white-collar jobs demanding competent minds rather than muscles, did something to weaken the doctrine of separate spheres.

One reason for the surge of women into employment was their sophistica-tion. In no other country were women so well educated. Over half of high school graduates at the beginning of the twentieth century were female (boys tended to drop out earlier to find jobs). Impressive numbers went on to higher education. By 1900 some 36 per cent of those attending college were women, and by 1920 the proportion had soared to nearly 50 per cent. These are extraordinary figures for a period when most European countries denied women significant entry to higher education. One calculation put the number of women in women's colleges in Britain in 1897 at a paltry 784, while in 1900 some 85,000 women were enrolled in higher education in the United States.

The young women graduating from these colleges itched to find socially useful roles for themselves. A remarkably high proportion, perhaps half, remained single. Many went into teaching, but other occupations were opening up, including social work, at the core of which in the United States was the settlement house movement. One of the first was Hull House in Chicago, founded in 1889 by Jane Addams. Established in poor urban areas, settlement houses became centres for social action, publicizing the plight of the desperately poor and offering them such services as playgrounds, public baths, classes for immigrants and guidance on dealing with officialdom. The idea had started in Britain, where settlement houses were largely run by young male graduates, but in the United States women predominated and they founded many more of them. There were under fifty social settlements in Britain in 1911 but hundreds in the United States, testimony to the determination of women to heal the wounds occasioned by industrialization. (At least the wounds inflicted on immigrants; black residents of Northern cities tended to be ignored.)

Other white middle-class women were drawn out of their homes and into their communities, legitimized by what some historians have called the Cult of True Womanhood, for as guardians of religion and morality they could engage in acts of benevolence. The notion of such an ideology has probably been exaggerated, but forms of domestic feminism did empower many women, including women of colour. Women's charities developed a kind of quasi-governmental function, as women's nurturing and domestic capabilities were turned to social amelioration. Many women joined local civic clubs. The General Federation of Women's Clubs (GFWC) was formed in 1890 and grew at a faster rate than any other middle-class movement of the period – from 20,000 individual members in 1892 to over a million by 1911. Clubwomen carried their maternal responsibilities over into the society around them, often becoming engaged in community reforms, such as free libraries, better schools or the establishment of juvenile courts. The amelioration of urban conditions was a major concern. One leading clubwoman argued in 1895 that by raising the condition of the working classes 'we shall have taken a most important step in the progress of civilization, and the consequent settlement of the labor question'. The club movement was distinctively American, with no close parallels in other countries.

Women seemed readier than men to build cross-class (if not cross-race) alliances. This ambition helped to inspire the Consumers' League. Josephine Shaw Lowell, an upper-class woman who came to believe that working women needed better wages and working conditions, organized a Consumers' League in New York, in which wealthy women used their influence to try to secure improvements in the pay and working conditions of sales clerks. Their success led to similar organizations in other cities, and in 1899 these groups formed the National Consumers' League (NCL). By 1905 the NCL encompassed sixty-four local leagues in some twenty states. These branches were often led by well-connected upper- and middle-class women, in a position to bring pressure to bear on local businesses and city and state governments. The NCL worked for protective legislation for working women and legislation regulating child labour. Such women's groups were less wary of extending the role of the state than was the AFL.

While other countries were experimenting with social insurance, pension systems and public housing, at the beginning of the twentieth century the United States remained largely bereft of such provision. But a distinctive welfare system was fitfully emerging. Excluded from the suffrage, their awareness heightened by operating in their own realm, women took to cooperating with one another and lobbying to secure benefits for mothers and children. This activity was consistent with the traditional wifely duty towards home and family, and also effective in a political world in which interest groups were beginning to compete with parties as instruments for bringing outside opinion to bear on government. In Britain, where labour organization was stronger, women's groups sometimes associated themselves with working-class political movements, but in the United States they remained independent, building cross-class alliances of women to confront the cross-class alliances of men in the political parties. Women functioned not by violating traditional values but by pushing outwards the boundaries of the female sphere. In so doing, they helped to create the beginnings of a 'maternalist' welfare state, one which conferred benefits on women, particularly mothers, rather than men.

The family, woman's traditional sphere, was the focus of the female reform groups' concern. After all, many impoverished families owed their plight to the absence of a male wage-earner. Virtually all the women's groups supported efforts to press the state legislatures to provide material aid at least to 'deserving' mothers, which usually meant widows. The movement proved a remarkably successful one, at least in terms of the number of state governments – forty by 1920 – that were willing to recognize the principle of mothers' aid (soon labelled mothers' pensions), if not in the generosity of the provision. The pensions were often hedged about with moralistic and other conditions, and many states allowed county governments to opt out. But at least they offered a little support to some needy mothers, and they survived to be absorbed in New Deal legislation. (Men were not entirely neglected by the state; war veterans could expect federal pensions.)

Mothers' pensions were part of the wider child-saving movement which preoccupied so many social reformers of both sexes in the early twentieth century. Male adults might be expected to fend for themselves, but it could hardly be argued that children should be entirely self-reliant. Much energy was put into improving schools and creating more wholesome environments, such as by providing playgrounds. One significant progressive reform was the juvenile court, which kept delinquent children out of the adult criminal justice system. The major child-saving cause was the ending or protection of child labour. Some 2 million children under the age of fourteen were employed in 1900, many in canning and textile and other factories, many in the fields and some down mines. Their plight was highlighted by the dramatic campaign in 1903 of labour activist Mary Harris Jones (better known as Mother Jones), who marched children from Philadelphia to President Roosevelt's summer home on Long Island. In the same year stronger child labour laws were adopted by Pennsylvania, New York and Illinois. In 1904 the National Child Labor Committee (NCLC) was formed and by 1916 most Northern states had enacted laws prohibiting the employment of young children in factories and street trades. Urban working-class families themselves did not always welcome this invasion of middle-class sensibilities, needing their children's wages to augment the meagre incomes of unskilled adult workers. The reluctance of Southern states to act encouraged reformers to turn to Congress, and in 1916 the Keating-Owen Act legislated against the factory employment of children under fourteen, although the Supreme Court soon struck it down. Nonetheless child labour was already in decline because of the spread of compulsory education and the increasing skills needed for many occupations.

A landmark in the establishment of the maternalist welfare state was the *Muller v Oregon* case of 1908. The American courts, imbued with *laissez-faire* business conservatism, had traditionally been hostile to legislation regulating the terms of employment. In 1905 the US Supreme Court had struck down a New York ten-hour law for (male) bakers on the grounds that it violated the constitutional rights of employers and employees to agree on their own contracts. Trade unions could bargain with employers over terms of employment and the courts were reluctant to interfere with such private arrangements. It was not clear that they would tolerate the new maximum-hours laws for women, but in the *Muller* case the Supreme Court decided that women were different, because a woman was a mother or potential mother: 'Differentiated by these matters from the other sex, she is properly placed in a class by herself, and legislation designed for her protection may be sustained, even when like legislation is not necessary for men.' This doctrine also eased the acceptance of other benefits for women. By 1921 some forty-one states had laws regulating the hours of women workers, and by 1923 fifteen had enacted minimum wage laws for women, though these were to fall foul of the Supreme Court.

The female reform network also had an impact on the shape of the federal government. Infant mortality rates were relatively high in the United States. The NCLC argued that the federal authorities should take at least as much interest in nurturing human lives as the Department of Agriculture did in encouraging the production of healthy farm crops. Such pressure secured the establishment in 1912 of the Children's Bureau in the Department of Labor. Its first head, Julia Lathrop, developed the Bureau as a major force in the welfare field, collecting data, advising government and distributing advice. In 1921 Congress, sensitive to the new women voters, passed the Sheppard-Towner Act authorizing the use of federal funds on a matching basis for state health-care services for mothers and infant children. The innovative programme used matching grants as a means by which the federal government could spur state governments to action, a feature which was later to become central to the American welfare state. Another bridgehead within the federal government was secured with the creation of the Women's Bureau (also in the Department of Labor) in 1918. The increasing employment of women had drawn attention to the conditions in which they worked, and the Women's Bureau exerted what influence it could against the unfair treatment of women in the workplace. Both the Children's and the Women's Bureau came under attack in the 1920s, but both survived, marks of the growing bureaucratization of the federal government.

Participation in the settlement house, child-saving and consumer movements often raised the political consciousness of these women. Many became feminists, interested in the suffrage as well as other female rights. Women could vote only in four Western states in the 1890s. There had been groups calling for the vote since the mid-nineteenth century, but the demand had long been seen as dangerously radical. It seemed to strike at the sanctity of the family, which in the United States – in the absence of the hierarchical institutions and deferential habits of the Old World – seemed almost the only bulwark against social chaos. But now the maternalist values radiating from the women's reform network allowed the suffrage cause to seem less threatening to family life.

In 1890 the two main suffrage organizations merged into the National American Woman Suffrage Association (NAWSA), but its appeal remained narrow. Membership was only about 17,000 in 1905, but by 1915 had spurted to about 100,000, still less than half the number in the Women's Christian Temperance Union, but the cause was making headway. In 1910 the state of Washington had granted the vote, soon followed by four other Western states. In 1912 Jane Addams seconded Theodore Roosevelt's nomination at the Progressive Party convention and the party itself made history by endorsing women's suffrage. NAWSA itself, restive with the slow state-by-state strategy, turned to seeking an amendment to the federal constitution, encouraged by Alice Paul, a young Quaker who had been inspired by the militancy of the British suffragettes. Paul assumed leadership of the Congressional Union (CU), a NAWSA affiliate, and adopted confrontational tactics to demand the vote. The CU's bellicosity proved too provocative for NAWSA and in 1916 the two groups split, the CU turning itself into the National Woman's Party. NAWSA divided its energies between the state and the federal campaigns and won other state victories, but the prize was the large state of New York. A women's suffrage referendum was finally successful there in 1917, with immigrant and Socialist votes contributing to victory.

American intervention in the First World War provided the campaigners for a constitutional amendment with another opportunity. By this time women voted in many states and much of the old resistance was crumbling. Further, NAWSA membership soared. Like the AFL, its leaders seized on the war situation. While the NWP agitated against the war as well as for the vote, NAWSA leaders swallowed their pacifist instincts, disavowed the NWP tactic of aggressive picketing, and sought quietly to reason with the White House and members of Congress. Some women took over men's jobs in factories and on the land and others sold war bonds, strengthening their claims to suffrage. This was no time to alienate them, or so it could be intimated,

NAWSA arguing that women's enfranchisement was needed 'as a war measure'. From the perspective of the political leadership, NAWSA provided a respectable alternative to the NWP and the war afforded an excuse to yield. Early in 1918 President Wilson called on Congress to support the federal amendment, later adding that it was 'vital to the winning of the war'. The 19th Amendment cleared Congress in 1919, and by August 1920 the states ratified it. Not entirely coincidentally, women's other favourite reform, Prohibition, was also adopted as a constitutional amendment at about the same time.

By 1919 NAWSA's membership had reached a stunning 2 million. In a remarkably short space of time the suffrage movement had been transformed from a minority to a mass movement. The war did something to bring it to its peak, but more importantly the suffrage had come to be perceived as compatible with family values. Suffrage campaigners, rather than demanding the vote as an individual right, tended now to agree with their opponents that women were different to men, that they possessed distinctive moral and mothering qualities, but they argued that these qualities were needed in modern politics. Jane Addams remarked that the modern city was beset with such problems as child labour and insanitary housing, precisely those problems that women were best equipped to handle: 'May we not say that city housekeeping has failed partly because women, the traditional housekeepers, have not been consulted as to its multiform activities?' In short, suffragists were now conceding that there was a woman's sphere but arguing that its boundaries spilled over into the political sector. Vital social reforms would follow the enfranchisement of women.

For the moment, as women gained the vote, the major parties treated them with wary respect. In 1922 the Cable Act accorded married women equal citizenship rights (previously women who married foreigners lost their US citizenship). Polling stations were moved out of saloons and barber shops and into schools, and women began to join men in jury service. But by the mid-1920s it became clear that there was not much of a woman's vote after all, women tending to vote in the same way as their husbands or fathers, and the major parties became less attentive to them. Like the labour movement after the war, too, women's groups endured serious red-baiting. But although weakened, they survived. Once the suffrage was achieved, Carrie Catt founded the League of Women Voters (LWV) to educate women in citizenship and it became a woman's non-partisan pressure group in the political arena. Alice Paul's NWP competed with it, emphasizing rights as individuals (rather than as women). In 1923 the NWP called for an Equal Rights Amendment (ERA) to the Constitution, to guarantee women the same rights as men, and introduced it into Congress. Almost every other women's group in the country, including the LWV, opposed the ERA. They believed that in stressing that women were identical to men the ERA threatened the protective legislation that had been achieved. The split in the women's movement was hardly a source of strength, but both organizations sought to give a political voice to women. In the 1920s their influence often seemed frustratingly limited, but their very existence was remarkable. Only in the United States did women continue to work for separate political expression after the suffrage had been won.

Nonetheless, like organized labour, by the end of the first third of the twentieth century women had only limited cause for celebration. The suffrage had been won but had not enabled women to change the course of American politics. It was not followed by legislation furthering a female agenda, as some feminists had promised, few women were elected to major offices and male politicians soon paid less attention to the women's vote than they had as it was being secured. Ultimately the maternalist project largely failed too. The Supreme Court struck down the Keating-Owen Child Labor Act, it moved against minimum wage laws for women in 1923 and Congress ended the Sheppard-Towner programme in 1929. Even mothers' pensions, modest as they were, reached less than 10 per cent of female-headed families in 1921, largely because local communities could usually opt out of state schemes. Women had carved a niche for themselves in the federal bureaucracy, but in the 1930s were to find that they were not strong enough to fashion the welfare state that emerged with the New Deal.

By the 1920s the Anglo-American élites probably felt secure enough with the order over which they presided. Political authority for the most part, if not exclusively, resided in people like themselves. Black Americans had been fenced off from political society, especially in the South, and the suspect Slav and Mediterranean races had been barred entry. Defences had been erected against political radicalism, which had not appealed greatly to the bulk of a variegated workforce anyway. Workers might be tiresomely strike-prone, but they generally gave their allegiance to pragmatic political parties managed by middle-class leaders, while the decline in voter turnout and the curbs on machine politics in any case limited the influence of the lower orders. The principal labour organization loyally supported the economic and political systems, despite its limited influence with government. Women also continued to occupy a subordinate role in the polity, although their heroic efforts in combating class tensions and creating a more caring form of capitalism had helped to win them the vote. But there were risks to the strategy of exclusion practised by the Progressive Order. Even if American women stood by their men, there was no guarantee that the ethnic communities, the great unorganized armies of semi-skilled and unskilled workers and the increasingly urbanized African-Americans, would continue to acquiesce in their fates.

|3|

Progressive Hopes:
from Roosevelt to Wilson
1900–17

The imperative need to adapt to the arrival of an industrial economy meant that American political and social practices could not avoid transformation in the early twentieth century. Something not entirely unlike what we have called the Progressive Order would have emerged even had there not been self-appointed 'progressives' ardently demanding reform. There would have been some enhancement of government authority and a growth of bureaucratic structures. Experts would have been called on to apply their professional skills and a Protestant morality would have suffused American public life. But the circumstances of the time did call forth energetic bands of reformers who accepted the designation 'progressive' and who offered their own remedies to the ills of American life. The progressive mood was particularly strong between about 1900 and 1917, when reformers won an unusual influence in city, state and national governments. These progressives did help to shape the new political order, even if they failed to achieve some of their most cherished objectives.

Progressivism was more a mood than a movement. The term – coined late in the period – signified a wish to see improvement in American public life and an assumption that improvement had to be helped along a bit. There were professional politicians in both the major parties who identified with the progressive persuasion, as did countless journalists, social workers, academics, feminists, trade unionists and businessmen. Progressive activists – like their conservative opponents – tended to be men and women of Anglo-Saxon descent and of the Protestant faith. Working-class constituencies sometimes gave crucial support to reform measures, but middle-class or upper middle-class citizens were usually at the core of the various campaigns. The prosperity of the new century fostered confidence and a popular mood broadly receptive to schemes to bridge the class divide. Fears of insurrection had subsided, while memories of the depression of the early 1890s prompted an interest in averting social discontent. And the processes of change had multiplied the number of professionals eager to apply their skills and placed them at critical junctures in the social structure.

Ameliorating class conflict had been a major objective of the influential religious and humanitarian movements that had emerged in the late nineteenth century. Some Protestant clerics resuscitated the old idea that churches might mediate between economy and society. 'A minister mingling with both classes can act as an interpreter to both', wrote Walter Raushenbusch. 'He can soften the increasing class hatred of the working class.' Raushenbusch was a leading proponent of the Social Gospel, which believed in the perfectibility of human nature and believed too that humankind could gain control of its environment and deliver a better world. Closely associated with the Social Gospel was a growing interest in social work, as exemplified by the Charity Organization Society movement, which came to have an appreciation of poverty's economic and social causes and developed an interest in environmental solutions, such as improved housing. In these years middle-class women and men moved into the slums to found settlement houses, where they could work with the poor.

If the swelling of humanitarian activity owed something to a resurgent evangelical Protestantism, something was also owed to a modernist faith in science. Some of the practitioners of the Social Gospel applied themselves to the study of such subjects as economics and sociology, in order the better to understand the forces shaping society; and social scientists, in turn, were often willing to put their disciplines to a spiritual purpose. The economist Richard T. Ely personified this convergence in *Social Aspects of Christianity* (1889), explaining that members of 'the ethical school of economists' wanted 'to ascertain the laws of progress, and to show men how to make use of them'. The social sciences, in short, offered Christians the means of furthering God's work and improving the human condition. The faith in progress – in applying scientific principles – put a premium on knowledge, expertise and competence. Efficiency became the watchword of a growing number of progressives. The best-known efficiency expert was Frederick W. Taylor, who promoted with a crusading zeal *The Principles of Scientific Management*, as the title of his 1911 book put it. He popularized a number of production techniques, such as time-and-motion studies.

Evangelical and scientific impulses did not always sit easily together, but they were among the qualities that distinguished this generation of reformers. Most shared other characteristics too. They were optimistic, believing as they did in the possibility of social betterment. More distinctively, and in contrast to the *laissez-faire* assumptions of many nineteenth-century theorists, progressives believed in purposive social action. Governments, groups and individuals, it was held, possessed the capacity to bring about change, and to bring about change for the better. Yet progressives also held fast to a consensual ideal. It was important to them to unite society: the tensions threatening the industrial order were to be resolved through better integration. Progressives sometimes spoke of the 'cooperative commonwealth', invoking a vision of a society in which citizens were aware of their fraternal obligations and in which selfish interests were subordinated to the public good. As always in American culture, this belief in the integrity of the community coexisted with a strong commitment to individualism. It was the attachment to both the harmonious ideal and individualism that made many progressives uneasy about the labour movement, which arguably put class before nation. Similar considerations were later to turn some surviving progressives against the New Deal.

The progressives' commitment to action combined with their respect for democracy gave rise to another characteristic, their belief in educating the public. They – or at least many of them – did not altogether trust in the intelligence of the lower orders. Good government, thought Woodrow Wilson, had to come from 'an educated élite' (though he also valued democracy because of its capacity to be refreshed from below). Their conception of political life resembled that of the Founding Fathers, who had conceived of republicanism as a form of government in which the people voluntarily chose the better sort to lead them. But as practical politicians, progressives realized that they could not prevail against special interests without popular support, and in any case their faith in democracy, however much it might need their guidance, meant that they had to put their case to the people. The progressive journalist Ray Stannard Baker later explained that 'I had a kind of faith, perhaps naïve faith, that if I could make people see the situation as clearly as I did they would immediately put an end to abuses'.

The journalism of the time added to the pressure on politicians to communicate their views as vividly as possible. The so-called 'yellow press' had emerged at the end of the nineteenth century, displacing staid party newspapers and seeking a mass audience through a sensational style. Newspapers like Joseph Pulitzer's *New York Evening World* and William Randolph Hearst's *New York Morning Journal* aligned themselves with the lower classes and boosted circulation by launching crusades against unpopular corporations and exposing political scandals. A number of relatively cheap, mass-circulation magazines appeared, such as *McClure's* and *Cosmopolitan*, and also turned to investigative journalism. Lincoln Steffens exposed the widespread corruption in municipal government in a series of articles known as 'The Shame of the Cities' in 1902–3, and Ida Tarbell similarly revealed the shady practices of the Standard Oil Company. It was in response to a series entitled 'Treason of the Senate' by David Graham Phillips that Theodore Roosevelt branded such writers as 'muckrakers', plucking the term from Bunyan's *Pilgrim's Progress*. Richard L. McCormick has shown that muckraking and other exposés reached their peak in the middle of the first decade of the twentieth century, triggering a popular awareness of public corruption and demands for reform at state level.

The very variety of interests that could be mobilized to support any given objective means that the phrase 'the progressive movement' is problematic. It has been argued that the phenomenon was neither progressive nor a movement, that it hid conservative impulses and in any case was too disparate in its constituents to possess any coherence. But whether or not there was *a* progressive movement, there was wide agreement on a number of issues among those trying to arouse public support for action. One was class tension and urban blight, that is, the misery, crime and poor housing associated with the overcrowded cities and the lower orders. Another was 'the trusts' (as discussed in Chapter 1), the conspicuous concentration of economic power in the big corporations, whose presence seemed to make a mockery of the traditional American ideal of free competition and opportunity for all. Uniting most progressives was a shared distrust of 'the bosses', the corrupt machines of the cities and the cosy relationship between many businessmen and politicians. 'Corruption' was a favourite bogey of progressives, an affront to both morality and efficiency. Addressing any of these issues tended to imply some kind of action from government.

In the opening years of the century, government for the most part did not mean Washington. The total spending of state and local government was roughly twice that of the federal government, and the ratio remained much the same until Franklin Roosevelt's New Deal. If businessmen wanted to pressure government, or if working men, consumers or high-minded reformers wanted government to intervene to correct a perceived injustice, they naturally looked first to their immediate representatives. Progressivism, it is often said, emerged in the cities, moved to the state legislatures and then finally arrived in national politics. As the 'island communities' were gradually absorbed into a national market, so competing interest groups naturally enough moved the focus of their attention to the larger arena.

Reform movements emerged in the cities in the 1890s, for the most part led by members of the white and Protestant middle class. Rapid urban growth had endangered public health, taxed police resources and created demands for a range of services such as education, transportation and lighting. Private corporations provided such services as gas, electricity and street railways, and they frequently secured franchises by bribing local councillors or contributing generously to party funds. In Chicago, for example, Charles T. Yerkes developed his utility businesses through financial favours to a compliant city council, but in 1896–7 a reform group of professional, clerical and business leaders won control of the council and helped to elect Carter Harrison Jr. as mayor. In Toledo, Ohio, a successful local businessman, Samuel M. ('Golden Rule') Jones, became mayor in 1897 and was outraged when he found he was expected to grant a street-railway franchise to his financial backers. He broke with the Republican machine and ran successfully for re-election as an independent, and as a reform mayor established public parks and free kindergartens, improved the pay of municipal employees and campaigned (unsuccessfully) for public ownership of local utilities. Another businessman-turned-reformer was Tom L. Johnson, elected mayor of Cleveland in 1901, who appointed talented officials, introduced fairer taxation and subjected the street railways to municipal regulation.

In other cities scattered across the country reform groups won control and tried, with varying degrees of success, to create more effective urban government. A major issue was tax policy. Utility companies had often been given generous tax breaks to get established, but major inequities developed as the companies flourished while ordinary citizens bore the tax burden. When Johnson took office in Cleveland, many business properties paid no tax while the utilities paid only 10 or 20 per cent of that paid by individual homeowners. In addition to fairer taxes, many reformers sought to police the utilities. While Americans tended to shy away from 'socialistic' remedies like municipal ownership, utilities were often brought under a degree of regulation. As reformers established the standard of the public good and aroused civic pride, they sometimes turned their energies to improving schools and the city environment.

Improvements of any kind, however, often meant protracted struggles with corrupt politicians and party machines, and reformers early concluded that the machinery of local government itself needed a fundamental overhaul. As noted in Chapter 1, they championed democratic reforms like direct primaries and the secret ballot as a means of bypassing the traditional machines, and several communities experimented with wholly new forms of city government. In Galveston, Texas, after a severe storm had inflicted extensive damage in 1900, the old mayoral and aldermanic offices were scrapped in favour of a five-man commission chosen by popular election. By 1914, some 400 cities had adopted this system of government by non-partisan commissioners. An alternative was the appointment of professional city managers, used by over 300 municipalities by the early 1920s. Commissioners and managers illustrated the progressive suspicion of bossism and the progressive impulses for expertise and the harnessing of government to the public good. Nonetheless these devices were confined to small and medium-sized cities, all the major cities retaining their traditional mode of government throughout the period, although they sometimes enhanced the powers of the mayors.

American cities were legally the creations of the states, and the struggle for municipal reform often moved to the state legislature. This could take the form of home rule – allowing cities greater control over their own affairs – and about a dozen states had moved in this direction by 1914. But many of the issues pressed by the municipal reformers could not be resolved easily. Large corporations prepared to buy up city councils were also adept at distributing their largesse in state capitals, which in any case were often dominated by rural interests suspicious of urban demands. In state after state in the early twentieth century, the old party bosses were challenged by insurgents who wanted to purify politics and put an end to the influence of shadowy special interests. In the East these progressive movements were often extensions of municipal reform; in the South, Midwest and Plains states urban reformers sometimes joined forces with older agrarian or populist elements long resentful of the political clout of the corporations. In Oregon William S. U'Ren pioneered several devices for democratizing the political system, such as the initiative (allowing a proportion of the electorate to initiate a legislative proposal), the referendum and the direct primary. By 1918 almost all states had adopted the direct primary (though only a few used it for presidential contests); twenty had adopted the initiative and referendum. In New York Charles Evans Hughes served as an anti-machine governor between 1907 and 1910, his election owed in part to public outrage over the exposure of the political influence of the insurance industry. In California Governor Hiram Johnson took on the notorious Southern Pacific Railroad.

Much the most celebrated state progressive was Robert M. La Follette, elected Governor of Wisconsin in 1900. La Follette had earlier entered politics as a congressman, but had rebelled when he found that he was expected to do the bidding of the machine boss. Building his own organization and presenting himself as the champion of the people rather than the corporations, La Follette triumphed over the machine and as governor pioneered the 'Wisconsin Idea', central to which was a close association with the University of Wisconsin, which provided experts to offer advice on a range of issues and serve on state agencies. The direct primary was introduced to constrain the power of the party machines; corporations were made to pay more in tax; railroads and state banks were subjected to greater public regulation; workmen got compensation for industrial accidents; forests and water power were conserved. So energetic was the La Follette administration that Theodore Roosevelt called Wisconsin 'the laboratory of democracy'.

Municipal and state progressivism were important because it was at these levels that most government took place. But once the progressive ethos had taken hold in the states it inevitably impinged on national politics. Some state progressives themselves moved to Washington, not least Robert M. La Follette, who was elected senator in 1906; and joining him there were other state reformers, such as Albert Cummins of Iowa in 1908 and Hiram Johnson of California in 1916. Some issues in any case forced their way onto the national agenda. By 1912 some twenty-nine states had adopted primaries for senatorial elections, preparing the way for the constitutional amendment formally transferring the choice from the state legislatures to the people. More significantly, it had long been clear that major corporations engaged in interstate commerce could not be regulated adequately by the states. An attempt to bring the railroad corporations to order had been made with the Interstate Commerce Act of 1887, but it had been a modest measure and the powers of the Interstate Commerce Commission had been further limited by Supreme Court decisions in the 1890s. Not until the Progressive Era were there sustained attempts to regulate big business at a national level.

When the assassination of President McKinley precipitated Theodore Roosevelt into the presidency in 1901 he possessed no specific reform agenda beyond making the government, as he later put it, 'the most efficient possible instrument' for improving the lot of the people. Yet he possessed a bolder conception of the presidential office than most of his immediate predecessors. 'I believe in a strong executive', he once observed, 'I believe in power.' In his first message to Congress, just three months after he had taken office, he warned that artificial bodies, 'such as corporations and joint stock or other associations … should be subject to proper governmental supervision'.

He quickly followed word with action, early in 1902 mobilizing the Sherman Anti-Trust Act against the Northern Securities Company, a railroad holding company formed in the recent wave of mergers. Anti-trust prosecutions had rarely been pressed vigorously, but Roosevelt was determined to apply the act to the new giant combinations. In 1904 the Supreme Court narrowly sided with the administration, ordering the break-up of Northern Securities. Even the richest men in the land were not above the law. Roosevelt also moved against another unpopular combination, the meat-packers' Beef Trust, and more prosecutions followed, especially in Roosevelt's second term. Before his accession only eighteen prosecutions had been brought under the Sherman Act; during his administration there were forty-three. In fact, Roosevelt had no objection to big businesses in principle and indeed regarded them as inevitable. Trusts, he believed, should be regulated rather than destroyed, and one reason for his actions was the reluctance of a conservative Congress to enact effective regulatory legislation. In 1903 a new cabinet department of Commerce and Labor was established, and it included a Bureau of Corporations empowered to investigate corporate practices. The Elkins Act of the same year curbed the rebates the railroad companies allowed to favoured shippers, another – albeit modest – attempt to promote fair competition.

In other ways too Roosevelt advanced his commitment to an active executive and his progressive belief that government should not be beholden to vested interests. Through the late nineteenth century, industrialists could usually count on state governments, whether manned by Republicans or Democrats, to assist in the breaking of strikes, and on occasion the federal government had used troops for the same purpose. In 1902 coalminers in the Pennsylvania anthracite fields went on strike, demanding higher wages, an eight-hour day and union recognition. The strike dragged on and a national coal shortage threatened, prompting Roosevelt in October to invite both sides to talks. Yet the intransigent owners were in no mood to deal with 'outlaws', insisting rather that Roosevelt intervene against the strikers. An angry president did threaten to send in troops – to take over the mines for the government, not to break the strike – and the employers gracelessly bowed to arbitration. The miners called off their action and in 1903 the arbitration commission allowed them a 10 per cent wage increase and a reduction in hours. Roosevelt subsequently observed that he had wanted to give both capital and labour a 'square deal'. Roosevelt was not a habitual friend of labour and there were occasions when he despatched troops during industrial disputes, but his highly publicized actions during the anthracite conflict helped to define his progressive principles. First, the federal government had a right to intervene in an industrial dispute and impose its own solution; and its intervention should be in the name of social justice – not in the interests of capital.

Roosevelt's high-profile incumbency, his jousting with big business and his winning of American rights to the Panama Canal Zone (discussed in Chapter 4) proved generally popular with the public, and he had no effective rival for the Republican nomination in 1904. The Democrats nominated a conservative jurist as their candidate, but Roosevelt's personal popularity sped him to a mighty victory, and the Republicans won large majorities in both houses of Congress too. 'Tomorrow I shall come into office in my own right', Roosevelt told a friend on the eve of his inauguration. 'Then watch out for me.' But conservatives remained strongly entrenched in Congress, and many of its members did not care for Roosevelt's attempts to make the executive the leading branch of government. 'Unless some restraint can be placed on the White House the Republican Party will be divided into hostile camps before 1906', grumbled one Republican senator.

But Roosevelt was now determined to use his authority to promote progressive reform. The time had come, he said, 'to assert the sovereignty of the National Government by affirmative action'. Reformers had long sought to limit the rates charged by railroads, which could be (though were not invariably) exploitative, and Roosevelt embarked on a push for railroad regulation. Many Western Republicans, responding to pressures from farmers and shippers in their own section, favoured regulation, as did Southern Democrats. For conservatives wedded to the enterprise system, however, the suggestion that prices should be set by some agency other than the businesses themselves was alarming, as were hints from Roosevelt that company books be inspected. But public opinion was with the president, as were a number of businessmen associated with the National Civic Federation, and the Hepburn Act eventually became law in 1906. It endowed the Interstate Commerce Commission with authority to fix reasonable rates and forbade certain unfair practices. The ICC was finally being given some teeth. The Hepburn Act was not as strong as some progressives wished, but it set a powerful precedent and represented a major milestone in the American (and progressive) way of ordering an industrial society through administrative commissions. Roosevelt himself had been at the heart of the struggle for the act, and it was an illustration too of what could be achieved by determined presidential leadership.

It was during Roosevelt's second term, following muckraking exposés, that the popular conviction that business was corrupting government was at its height, and state legislatures were busy introducing direct primaries, prohibiting corporations from making campaign contributions and establishing their own commissions to supervise utilities, railroads and insurance companies. At the same time the progressive wing of the Republican Party was growing. The president was thus afforded a fair wind to further his own attempts to influence business conduct.

The public's health, in Roosevelt's opinion, provided one legitimate reason to regulate business. In 1906 Samuel Hopkins Adams, in a series of magazine articles, focused on the harm done by patent medicines, and in the same year Upton Sinclair's pungent novel *The Jungle* publicized the unsavoury methods of the meat-packing industry. Sinclair's charges were endorsed by an inquiry ordered by Roosevelt. Bodies like the General Federation of Women's Clubs and the National Consumers' League joined the campaign for food and drug regulation. Chemists and medical specialists added their voices, reflecting the growing authority of the expert in American public life. The beleaguered meat-packers themselves adroitly decided to support an inspection law. In the summer of 1906 the Pure Food and Drugs Act and the Meat Inspection Act added to the regulatory power of the federal government. These two measures together with the Hepburn Act, observed Roosevelt, were a 'noteworthy advance in the policy of securing Federal supervision and control over corporations'. Before his term was over Roosevelt was also alarming corporations by supporting other proposals involving government interference in the business world, such as a federal income tax, an employers' liability law and restrictions on injunctions in labour disputes.

Such advocacy deepened the division between the progressive and the stand-pat factions in the Republican Party. In his last two years in office Roosevelt experienced greater difficulty with Congress, in which conservatives like Joseph G. Cannon, the powerful Speaker of the House of Representatives, fretted both at his radicalism and his attempts to enhance presidential authority. 'That fellow at the other end of the Avenue wants everything', Cannon complained on one occasion, 'from the birth of Christ to the death of the devil.'

Roosevelt defended his activism in terms of his duty to protect the public interest, a solicitude that was nowhere better reflected than in his zeal for preserving the continent's natural heritage. Conservationism was a cause in which various progressive impulses meshed together: respect for the common weal, a concern for efficiency, a suspicion of the cosy relationship between business and politics. The federal government had been slow to accept responsibility for the environment, but there was growing concern both about the profligate use of natural resources by businessmen and about such features as the dust bowls that had appeared on the Plains. Finally, in 1902 the Newlands Reclamation Act established the Bureau of Reclamation and empowered the federal government to undertake irrigation in Western states. Roosevelt enthusiastically pressed ahead with dam-building and reclamation projects, increased the federal forest reserve and closed off parts of Alaska and the North-West from business development. During his administration the acreage of government reserves roughly quadrupled. Sharing and partly inspiring Roosevelt's conservationist enthusiasm was the Department of Agriculture's Chief Forester, Gifford Pinchot. In 1908 Roosevelt raised public awareness of the environment by calling the National Conservation Commission, attended by most state governors.

Roosevelt may have been insisting that he had a responsibility to ensure that business practices did not harm the public interest, but he was far from hostile to the capitalist system. When banks and businesses began collapsing during a financial panic in 1907, Roosevelt conferred with the banker J. P. Morgan and arranged for public funds to be placed in New York banks, thus protecting them. Eventually calm was restored to the money markets, although businessmen and conservative Republicans blamed Roosevelt's interference in the economy for precipitating the panic. Roosevelt himself pointed the finger at 'certain malefactors of great wealth'. The souring of his relationship with powerful interests in his party if anything added to his progressive zeal. In the winter of 1907–8 he sent two messages to Congress demanding action on a long list of proposed reforms, including further regulations on business, and he returned to the attack in December 1908. By that date Roosevelt was about to leave the White House, though he had attempted to protect his progressive agenda by ensuring that the Republican nomination went to his fat friend and Secretary of War William Howard Taft.

Helped by Roosevelt's endorsement, Taft won the election and he did sustain some of Roosevelt's initiatives. Large corporations continued to be targeted under the Sherman Act, indeed more often than under Roosevelt. Where Roosevelt liked to pick and choose between good and bad trusts, Taft's legal-mindedness prompted him to enforce the law whenever it appeared to have been breached. The 1910 Mann-Elkins Act, supported by Taft, though strengthened by progressives in Congress, further enhanced the powers of the ICC to set railroad rates and brought telephone and telegraph systems into its remit. More land was taken into government reserves and an eight-hour day for federal employees was introduced.

Yet Taft proved a disappointment to Roosevelt and other progressives. A temporizer rather than a leader, his instinct was to work with the existing Republican leadership in Congress, despite its domination by the Old Guard. And he was less adroit than his predecessor in dealing with the divisive matter of the tariff. Taft failed effectively to come to the aid of the progressives when they sought substantial tariff reductions, and he compounded his offence by praising the protectionist tariff that emerged. The fight left the Republicans more disunited than ever and alienated the progressive insurgents from the White House. In part the stand-patters' capacity to obstruct reform measures lay in the dictatorial power of House Speaker Cannon, who could largely control the flow of business. In 1910 progressive Republicans and Democrats did succeed in curbing the speaker's powers, but Taft had sided with Cannon and thus further estranged his critics. But it was Taft's perceived betrayal of conservation that particularly upset his predecessor.

Taft's secretary of the interior, Richard A. Ballinger, withdrew some water sites from the national reserves, much to the fury of Chief Forester Gifford Pinchot. The affair escalated as Pinchot accused Ballinger of favouritism to businessmen, but he found it difficult to supply corroborating evidence and was eventually fired for insubordination. The issue became a major public controversy, with progressives taking up Pinchot's case and conservatives rallying to Ballinger. A congressional investigation found no criminal activity on Ballinger's part, but it was evident that he had little enthusiasm for conservation and the affair deepened the rift in the Republican Party. Progressive

Republicans began to look for an alternative candidate for the party's presidential nomination in 1912.

Robert M. La Follette hoped to fill that role, but he was widely regarded as too erratic and enjoyed little support outside the Midwest. The attention of the insurgents inevitably turned to Roosevelt, who after quitting the White House had travelled extensively in Africa and Europe, returning to a hero's welcome in New York in 1910. Still in his early 50s, the restless Roosevelt found it impossible to stand silently aside from the political fray, and he soon advocated strong progressive reforms. 'The New Nationalism', he said in a speech of that title, 'regards the executive power as the steward of the public service.' With leading progressives conspicuously visiting him at home, Roosevelt became an alternative power centre in the Republican Party, much to the frustration of President Taft. Early in 1912 Roosevelt agreed to be a candidate for the Republican nomination. Had the presidential primary, which was just being introduced, been used in more states, Roosevelt would probably have secured the nomination, but the party machinery was still controlled by the Old Guard and Taft was duly renominated. The angry Roosevelt forces charged that they had been cheated and defiantly organized another convention and a new Progressive Party. For the moment the progressive spirit had crystallized in distinct party form. Roosevelt, of course, was nominated for president and Hiram W. Johnson, the California governor, for vice-president.

The Progressive Party platform was a remarkable document, all the more so in that its authors nursed serious hopes of winning with what, in the context of the time, was a radical programme. The new party defiantly justified its own existence by bluntly stating that the existing parties had become 'the tools of corrupt interests'. Behind the ostensible government was an 'invisible government', and the first task of statesmanship was 'to dissolve the unholy alliance between corrupt business and corrupt politics'. The platform went on to offer a comprehensive list of progressive reforms: preferential primaries; women's suffrage; curbs on state courts and the banning of injunctions in labour disputes; health and safety legislation, the prohibition of child labour, minimum wages for women, the eight-hour day and social insurance for sickness and old age; the 'strong' regulation of big business; reform of the money and banking system; a vigorous policy of conservation; and selective downward revisions of the tariff. To Jane Addams, the Progressive Party was 'the American exponent of a world-wide movement toward juster social conditions'. Sweeping though it was, the platform did not quite embrace every progressive issue. There was no specific anti-trust plank; rather the emphasis was on the supervision and 'constructive regulation' of corporations engaged in interstate commerce – they were to be made to behave responsibly rather than broken up. And while the plight of working men, women and children was addressed and immigrants were promised fairer treatment, there was no mention of African-Americans.

The regular Republican platform had gone a modest way towards incorporating some progressive concerns, but its strong reaffirmation of the integrity of the judiciary signalled its conservative orientation. The Democratic platform called for tariff reduction, stronger anti-trust measures, presidential preference primaries, banking reform and curbs on injunctions in industrial disputes. But it could not match the Progressive platform for reform comprehensiveness. For president the Democrats nominated the Governor of New Jersey, Woodrow Wilson, a university professor and administrator recently turned politician.

The campaign of 1912 shaped up as a contest between Wilson and Roosevelt. In the country at large the progressive temper was peaking and the voters were drawn primarily to the two reform candidates, whose rival programmes became known respectively as the New Freedom and the New Nationalism, though the difference between them was more one of emphasis than of substance. Wilson's New Freedom reflected traditional anti-monopoly sentiments; government would use its powers to destroy the trusts and restore an economy based on competition between smallish businessmen – 'regulated competition'. Wilson was also keen to move towards free trade and, while he was not a doctrinaire believer in *laissez-faire*, his individualistic philosophy disposed him against the welfare proposals in the Progressive Party platform. Roosevelt, in contrast, argued that large corporations could be a source of economic strength and that the proper response was to regulate them – 'regulated monopoly'. His New Nationalism thus envisaged an activist federal government. But Roosevelt's candidacy also meant that the Republican Party was fatally split, thus delivering the election to Wilson. In the popular vote Taft trailed in a humiliating third and the Socialist Eugene Debs won a notable 6 per cent. If Wilson, Roosevelt and Debs are regarded as reform candidates, between them they accounted for 75 per cent of the popular vote, a suggestive sign of public opinion in 1912 (though voters were not responding to platforms alone).

The Democrats had also won control of both houses of Congress, and for the most part Wilson attempted to work through the Democratic majorities rather than construct a new progressive coalition. In the American system of government, he believed, the president should exercise leadership, not defer to Congress after the manner of several late nineteenth-century presidents. He dramatized this conception by appearing personally before Congress to address it. He took a close interest in the details of legislation and used his influence to promote his favoured issues and to obstruct others. This presidential commitment enabled a number of progressive measures to reach the statute books. In his first term in particular, as John A. Thompson has noted, he 'succeeded in enacting a more successful program of domestic legislation than any of his predecessors; among his successors only Franklin D. Roosevelt and Lyndon Johnson could boast of a comparably impressive record'. This accomplishment is testimony to a political pragmatism with which Wilson is not always credited; not so progressive was his decision that government departments should be racially segregated.

'It is in the tariff schedules that half the monopolies of the country have found cover and protection and opportunity', Wilson had said while seeking the Democratic nomination. An early victory for the president was the Underwood-Simmons Tariff Act of 1913, which did not end protection but did substantially reduce duties on a wide range of items. The lost revenue was instead to be raised by an income tax, possible now that the 16th Amendment had been ratified. A very low rate of taxation was introduced, but since the great majority of adult Americans did not fall into the tax bracket the new system was arguably fairer than the essentially regressive principle of the tariff.

The Democrats had also promised banking reform, the inadequacies of the monetary system having long been acknowledged. American banks were privately owned and largely independent of one another. There was no central bank, so coordinated action to resolve financial problems (such as bailing out a bank in distress) was difficult and the supply of money and credit was inflexible – the South and West in particular complained of lack of credit. Bankers and politicians had been arguing about reform since the 1890s, but no particular remedy commanded general support. A congressional commission had recommended a central bank controlled by private bankers, unacceptable to most Democrats, who feared the further enhancement of Wall Street power; others favoured a decentralized system of private banks; yet others pressed for greater federal governmental control. Wilson eventually agreed that there should be some public control and steered the Federal Reserve Act through Congress in 1913. Supervising the banking system would be a Federal Reserve Board, which included the secretary of the Treasury and a number of members appointed by the president, and the demand for decentralization was met by the establishment of twelve Federal Reserve banks in different parts of the country able to issue their own notes. The act was a classic progressive measure. The banks remained in private hands but became subject to a degree of public supervision. The new system was more efficient and seemed better suited to the needs of an industrialized society. And where the bankers had not been able to agree, the politicians, on expert advice, had imposed their own solution. Private interests had not dictated the structure of the system, even if they had limited the options available.

Woodrow Wilson was also determined that the public interest should prevail in the ongoing governmental contest with the trusts, although in office he retreated from the New Freedom solution of simply outlawing monopoly. Several corporate leaders themselves had come to favour some form of regulation, federal guidelines providing more certainty than the hazards of court action. In 1914 Wilson secured an act to establish a Federal Trade Commission, which was empowered to investigate the actions of large corporations and to disallow unfair practices. In fact the act fell short of the strong regulation advocated by Roosevelt, and the FTC failed to develop much authority. Another measure of 1914, the Clayton Act, sought to strengthen the Sherman Act by prohibiting certain practices that restricted competition, such as interlocking directorates in large industrial corporations. It also tried to protect trade unions from anti-trust prosecution. These two acts were hardly the assault on business that some radical Democrats hankered after, but Wilson had moved a little closer to the notion of regulating trusts. The regulation was hardly exacting, however, and did more to defuse the anti-trust movement than to handicap corporate America. The trust question largely disappeared from American life as a political issue.

If Wilson began to see some virtue in New Nationalism's approach to corporate America, he was slower to follow it on a range of social issues. He declined to support Prohibition and women's suffrage, and he regarded bills in favour of rural credit and against child labour as unconstitutional. He reluctantly signed the Seaman's Act of 1915 improving wage rates and safety standards on merchant vessels. But towards the end of his first term, when war was raging in Europe, his progressive zeal returned. Like most successful politicians, Wilson knew how to temper idealism with pragmatism, and the approach of the election of 1916 impressed on him the need to rally progressive-minded voters to his banner. A Federal Farm Loan Act established a string of rural land banks to provide long-term credit; the Keating-Owen Act legislated against child labour, and the Adamson Act gave an eight-hour day to railroad employees. Another measure of 1916 provided workmen's compensation for federal employees. Some of these measures were enacted after the Democratic national convention in June embraced them in its platform.

The platform also stressed preparedness and 'Americanism', and with a mighty war raging in Europe foreign issues dominated the campaign. The Republicans had more or less reunited and nominated the moderate progressive Charles Evans Hughes of New York for president, but Hughes proved an inept campaigner while the Democrats were able to rally behind Wilson with the cry 'He kept us out of war'. The European conflict had also boosted the American economy, so Wilson could offer the electorate the beguiling combination of peace and prosperity. Wilson was also keen to stress his reform record. 'We have in four years come very near to carrying out the platform of the Progressive Party as well as our own', he said in September, 'for we are also progressives.' The pro-labour and pro-farm stances that Wilson had taken in the last year perhaps helped to win over critical groups of voters, but probably more important was his success in keeping the United States out of war, and he was narrowly re-elected.

The First World War, of course, was soon virtually to monopolize the attention of the Wilson administration. By April 1917 the United States was a belligerent itself (though not formally an 'Ally' in Wilson's mind) and, Prohibition and women's suffrage apart, there was no further significant reform legislation during the Wilson administration. Wilson himself had a better grasp than most of what war could do to progressivism. 'Every reform we have won will be lost if we go into this war', he said in March 1917. As he was agonizing over asking Congress to declare war the president told a newsman: 'Once lead this people into war and they'll forget there was ever such a thing as tolerance.' In fact the war did not immediately kill progressive impulses. The need to mobilize for the war worked to the advantage of certain reform causes and some public figures seized the opportunity to further others. But the heyday of progressive reform was over and it was a crippled version that haunted the post-war years.

Further, some progressives were already beginning to lose faith in their cause. For many, progressive reform was the answer to the class conflict that accompanied rapid industrialization, but by the time of the First World War class conflict seemed to be increasing rather than diminishing. Labour historian David Montgomery has dubbed the 1910s the 'strike decade'; the number of strikes reached a new record during the year that the United States went to war. There were food riots in New York and Philadelphia in 1917, and five city-wide general strikes between September 1917 and April 1918. The prominence of Socialist and Wobbly leaders in some strikes enhanced the image of radicalism. Racial tensions were on the rise too, as evidenced by the fearful riots in East St Louis, Illinois in July 1917, when forty blacks and eight whites died. Some Americans concluded that the ameliorative strategies of progressivism were failing.

The accomplishments of the progressives were not insignificant. In the 1910s, as previously explained, women's groups and male social reformers at state level had peppered the statute books with laws regulating female and child labour, and providing mothers' pensions and workmen's compensation. The overhaul of municipal government had continued, and across the country city and state reformers were still working to democratize and purify political systems. A host of state and city commissions had been established to regulate public utilities and other businesses. At federal level both major parties were publicly committed to conservation, and constitutional amendments had been adopted to require the popular election of US senators and to authorize the introduction of an income tax. The tariff had been reduced, as Wilson had promised, the banking system overhauled, child labour and federal farm loan legislation enacted and anti-trust regulation extended. The Federal Trade Commission had been established to supervise big business. The authority of the federal government had been broadened and that of the presidency enhanced. Woodrow Wilson was exaggerating in 1916 when he claimed that his government had almost carried out the platform of the Progressive Party, but there was some truth in the claim. Nonetheless the progressive objective of social harmony remained frustratingly beyond reach, and Wilson was right in his perception that the coming of war would do more to endanger than to strengthen the cause of progressive reform.

|4|

The Progressives and the World
1900–33

The Progressive Era coincided with the emergence of the United States as a world power. 'A new consciousness seems to have come upon us – the consciousness of strength – and with it a new appetite, the yearning to show our strength', mused the *Washington Post* in 1898. The progressive temperament was by no means undivided in its understanding of the proper international role of the United States, and some political leaders were much keener than others to flex American muscles. But in the first third of the twentieth century the United States not only came to extend a proprietorial influence over a large part of Latin America, but also participated in international conferences, offered to mediate foreign quarrels and engaged as a major participant in a world war. American leaders through these years regularly commended to other peoples their own institutions as models for political development, and Woodrow Wilson embarked on an ambitious plan to fashion a new world order. Two Nobel Peace Prizes were won by American presidents and another by a secretary of state. But the world was to prove an obdurate place, and the attempts of the United States to guide the course of international events met with more failure than success.

No one better personified the American itch to reorder the world along American lines than Woodrow Wilson. 'The idea of America is to serve humanity', he said in 1914. His belief that the United States had a duty to the world was expressed again in January 1917, when he proposed that the European war should be settled on the principles of 'peace without victory' and 'government by the consent of the governed'. He concluded that these 'are American principles, American policies … They are the principles of mankind and must prevail'. Theodore Roosevelt was less messianic if more belligerent, but he too felt that the United States had something to teach the world. At any rate he was determined that 'Our place must be great among the nations'. Many Americans initially welcomed the Russian Revolution, assuming that the Russian people would follow the same liberating trail blazed by the

United States. 'It was the American flag that has brought about the peaceable revolution in Russia', said the Des Moines *Register* in March 1917. 'And it is the American flag that will bring about the revolution in Germany, peaceable or violent, for that revolution is bound to come. It is American ideals that dominate the world.'

Of course American foreign policy was not exclusively propelled by providential and humanitarian ideals. Americans were no less susceptible to the temptations of power politics and economic gain than other peoples. But such ideals coloured American actions. Other characteristics of Progressive America were also reflected in the nation's international stance. One was the instinct for action. After decades during which the United States had shown little interest outside the western hemisphere, many of the nation's political leaders seemed impatient for a role on the wider stage. The assumption of Great Power status came fairly naturally to a political class consisting largely of Anglo-Saxon Protestants. When the United States acquired colonial dependencies, its imperial politics paralleled domestic politics, as an Anglo-American ruling class wielded authority over a congeries of ethnic and racial groups. For some the expansion of American influence was an evangelical imperative. At this time American missionaries were spreading out across the world. One woman argued that foreign missionary work 'should appeal to every broad-minded Christian woman who is interested in education, civics, sanitation, social settlements, hospitals, good literature, the emancipation of children, the right of women to health, home and protection; and the coming of the Kingdom of our Lord'. In such hands, Protestant evangelicalism was almost indistinguishable from Americanization.

The United States' emergence on the world stage followed its emergence as the leading industrial power in the world. American cotton, wheat and beef had long been dependent on overseas consumers, but with the new century such products as steel and oil were commanding global markets. The *Journal of Commerce* in 1895 observed that no one could any longer 'imagine that we can maintain ourselves in isolation from the rest of the commercial world'. By this date the United States had become the world's second largest international trader. Hard-headed businessmen, uncertain about the domestic market, particularly through the depression of the 1890s, increasingly turned their attention to the prospect of foreign markets. 'We have the Anglo-Saxon thirst for wide markets growing upon us', observed the president of the National Association of Manufacturers in 1898. 'We have long been the granary of the world, we now aspire to be its workshop, then we want to be its clearing house.' By 1900 the value of American exports was about $1.6 billion; in 1920, bloated by wartime expansion, it was $10,264 billion. Exports were rising much faster than imports, and from 1896 the United States reversed the situation that had obtained during most of the nineteenth century and began to enjoy a positive balance of payments on goods and services, a feature it retained until the Nixon presidency.

The exercise of power abroad had implications for the American armed forces, which had traditionally been miniscule. Captain Alfred T. Mahan, whose book, *The Influence of Sea Power upon History*, had been published in 1890, argued that the historical record showed that national greatness was closely related to command of the seas. Major powers needed to expand to sustain their potency, expansion required foreign commerce, and such commerce in turn required a navy. The lessons for the United States were that overseas markets were necessary for its growing industrial production; a large navy would be needed to protect these markets; and servicing the navy in turn would require overseas bases or colonies. Mahan's ideas were eagerly embraced by rising politicians like Massachusetts senator Henry Cabot Lodge and the young Theodore Roosevelt. In the 1880s Congress had begun to replace the navy's handful of aging ships with more modern designs, and in the 1890s created a powerful fleet. A major attraction at the Chicago World's Fair of 1893 was an exhibition of the 'Great White Fleet' that was being built, including full-scale models of the new battleships. The number of American sailors increased more than fivefold between 1890 and 1910.

In 1898, having emerged from the depression of the 1890s, the United States went to war with a European power for the first time since the war of 1812. The Spanish–American War had complex roots, among them a popular empathy with the plight of Cubans fighting to cast off Spanish control and business and political worries about instability in the Caribbean, as well as sensationalist reporting by rival American newspapers. The United States speedily won what the secretary of state called a 'splendid little war', but in the course of it occupied the Philippines, Guam and Puerto Rico. Cuba's independence was recognized by the Paris Peace Treaty of 1898, but the Philippines were not so easily disposed of. McKinley had also taken the opportunity of the jingoistic wartime sentiment to annex Hawaii, which had effectively been under American control for some years.

Suddenly the United States had acquired an empire of sorts and there was outspoken opposition by those who insisted that America's own traditions required it to renounce imperialism. The acquisition of the extensive Philippine islands gave the president particular anguish. William McKinley felt that he could hardly give them back to Spain or hand them over to another imperial power; nor could they be left to themselves because 'they were unfit for self-government'. According to his own account he 'walked the floor of the White House night after night' and eventually fell to his knees to pray. 'And one night it came to me this way ... that there was nothing left for us to do but to take them all, and to educate the Filipinos, and uplift and civilize and Christianize them, and by God's grace to do the best we could by them ... ' Whatever epiphany President McKinley may have experienced, others held similar views, although their uplifting resolve was tested when Filipino insurgents revolted against American control. Woodrow Wilson did not doubt that Americans were the 'apostles of liberty and of self-government' in the Philippines, but that the Filipinos 'must first love order ... We are old in this learning and must be their tutors'. Thus might the United States 'seek to serve, not to subdue, the world'. In educating their Filipino charges American forces slew 15,000 of them, and many more died from deprivation. Similarly President Theodore Roosevelt's aim was 'progressively to increase the share' of the Filipinos in their government until they had learned to 'combine the enjoyment of liberty with the enforcement of order'. The American territorial empire would be paternalistic – but temporary. (One sceptical senator pointed out that it had taken Anglo-Saxons a thousand years to learn self-government.)

One consequence of the war was the permanent enhancement of the American military establishment. The ancient suspicion of a standing army, combined with geographical aloofness, had meant that American forces were tiny by the standards of the major European powers. For most of the period since the 1870s the total personnel of the army, navy and marines had fluctuated around 40,000. The Spanish–American War brought a massive increase to 236,000 in 1898, but even after the return of peace the establishment never again fell below 100,000. Further, in keeping with the imperatives of the Progressive Era, the armed forces were being centralized and professionalized. Both army and navy established their own war colleges. Also in 1903 the state militias were reorganized as the National Guard and became subject to federal authority. The American nation state was finally acquiring a military capability.

The stirring events of 1898 had given the United States a presence at strategic locations in the Caribbean and the Pacific. One of the reasons for the acquisition of the Philippines was the desire for a base for access to China, with which the United States had long enjoyed trade. But at the end of the nineteenth century a number of European powers and Japan threatened to carve up that vast country between themselves, cutting off markets to American business and a 'heathen' population to American missionaries. (In the 1890s the number of American missionaries in China doubled to over a thousand.) The United States insisted that the 'open door' to China must be preserved, so that any country could trade with any part of its vast territory, and the European powers and Japan complied. It was hardly American power that overawed them, for these nations had their own reasons for acquiescing in the open-door policy, but the United States had won a major diplomatic *coup*. Further, it had again displayed its opposition to European-style colonization and its commitment to American business and religious enterprise. The United States would conquer the world in its own way.

Access to the Pacific and China would also be facilitated by a canal across the Central American isthmus, a project long under discussion. It was during Theodore Roosevelt's presidency that the canal was built, although the United States had to encourage the Panamanians to revolt against their Colombian rulers before American rights to the Canal Zone were secured in 1903. Roosevelt happily claimed credit for the Panama Canal, although the matter was hardly conducted in accordance with international law. When asked whether he could provide any legal cover,

Roosevelt's Attorney-General replied that 'if I were you I would not have any taint of legality about it'. (When Panama was pressing its claims to the Canal Zone in the 1970s, one US senator defended retention on the grounds that 'we stole it fair and square'.) In 1904 the primacy of the United States in the Americas was reasserted by the Roosevelt Corollary to the Monroe Doctrine. European powers had been tempted to take action against Latin American governments to enforce the collection of debts, but now Roosevelt insisted that it was the prerogative of the United States alone to exercise police power in the hemisphere. He acted on his word in 1905 when he sent US forces to take over the customs houses of the Dominican Republic. Thereafter, during the first third of the twentieth century, the United States periodically despatched troops to such countries as Nicaragua and Haiti. Among the more active interventionists was President William Howard Taft, whose policy of 'dollar diplomacy' encouraged American investment in the region and protected it with American troops when it seemed jeopardized. During the Wilson administration William Jennings Bryan, as secretary of state, saw no contradiction between American hegemony and his anti-imperialist beliefs: 'Those Latin republics are our political children, so to speak. It is written that much is required of them to whom much is given, and this country will fall far short of its duty if it does not do more than any other country in the work of fellowship and brotherhood'. Several Caribbean countries in effect became American protectorates. The United States formally withdrew its claims on Haiti only in 1933 and on Cuba in 1934.

The Pacific could hardly be policed in the same way but the United States had interests there too. The open-door policy was threatened by the expansionism of Russia, but Japan was also an expansionist power and war broke out between the two in 1904. Japan quickly established its dominance. Theodore Roosevelt offered to mediate and the resulting Treaty of Portsmouth (New Hampshire) ended hostilities and secured Roosevelt the Nobel Peace Prize. The United States had won recognition as a major player in world politics. Roosevelt added to his diplomatic laurels in 1906, when he sent an American delegation to Algeçiras to help mediate a dispute between France and Germany over Morocco. A few years later he reflected that 'we ourselves are becoming, owing to our strength and geographic situation, more and more the balance of power of the whole globe'. After war broke out in Europe in 1914, President Wilson again offered to act as a mediator.

The United States might aspire to serve as a kind of global umpire, but – its dependencies apart – it could only bring its direct influence to bear on Latin America. Woodrow Wilson disavowed Taft's policy of 'dollar diplomacy', but he accepted that the United States had a legitimate interest in the region, which he wanted to encourage to develop democratic – which is to say, American-style – institutions. He hoped that business and democracy would go hand in hand, together edifying the less fortunate members of humankind. He told a group of businessmen to 'go out and sell goods that will make the world more comfortable and more happy, and convert them to the principles of America'. The difficulty was that democratic development would not only take time but was also contingent upon political stability, and Wilson proved himself even readier than his predecessors to despatch American forces to the countries of Central America and the Caribbean. Wilson's policy was one of 'missionary diplomacy', according to biographer Arthur Link. During his first year in office Wilson assured the Latin American countries that the United States would be a friend and benefactor: 'We dare not turn from the principle that morality and not expediency is the thing that must guide us and that we will never condone iniquity because it is most convenient to do so.'

The greatest challenge to Wilson's edifying foreign policy came in Mexico. There were extensive American investments and over 40,000 American citizens in this large neighbour, whose stability was a matter of concern. When revolution broke out in 1911 and the Mexican dictator was overthrown, it looked as if a form of democracy would emerge, but in 1913 General Victoriano Huerta seized power and executed the reform leadership. It had long been American practice to accord *de facto* recognition to an established government, but Wilson refused to abide by this convention in the case of Huerta. He would not, he said privately, recognize a 'government of butchers', and he told a British diplomat that he was going 'to teach the South American governments to elect good men'. The president provided diplomatic and economic support for the Constitutionalists under Venustiano Carranza, and even sent the navy to seize the port of Vera Cruz in April 1914 after some American sailors had been arrested. Huerta eventually fled the country and in 1915 Wilson recognized the Carranza government, but the civil war in Mexico damagingly continued. When a rebel force under Pancho Villa provocatively attacked a New Mexican town in March 1916, killing a number of American citizens, Wilson sent General John J. Pershing with a punitive expedition into Mexico, an embroilment which brought the United States into conflict with the legitimate Mexican authorities. The two countries came perilously close to war. In the event Carranza managed to subdue Villa, after which Pershing's force was recalled in January 1917 and the United States recognized a reconstituted Carranza regime. Wilson's intervention in Mexico had been at the cost of a few American and more Mexican lives, but he could claim that he had never sought Mexican territory and that, however frustratingly, he was trying to encourage the Mexicans to develop their politics along democratic lines.

But by this date Wilson was nourishing an even larger ambition, introducing a new order to the whole world. The Great War being bloodily waged in Europe represented at once a threat to American security and an opportunity for the United States to advance its own prescriptions for international understanding. Where Theodore Roosevelt had found an international role for himself as an arbiter, Woodrow Wilson dreamed of extending American values through the world.

As a major commercial power, the United States was inevitably affected deeply by the European conflict. Great Britain, France and Russia – the Allies – had been arrayed against the Central Powers of Germany and

Austria-Hungary since the summer of 1914. Since the time of George Washington it had been the policy of the United States to avoid direct implication in European quarrels and Wilson was quick to reassert this tradition, issuing a neutrality proclamation in August 1914 and calling on American citizens to be 'impartial in thought as well as in action'. At this stage a major consideration was domestic stability. 'We definitely have to be neutral', Wilson is reported to have said, 'since otherwise our mixed populations would wage war on each other.'

It was one thing, however, to proclaim strict neutrality in principle and another to implement it in practice. The rules of war entitled the British to use their large navy to blockade the continent, with the result that American trade with the Allies soared while that with the Central Powers dwindled. In 1914 the value of US exports to Britain and France totalled an estimated $754 million; by 1916 it was an astonishing $2.7 billion. The value of exports to Germany correspondingly collapsed. With European production disrupted, Allied demand for American foodstuffs, textiles and industrial goods, including munitions, seemed all but insatiable, but these exports also quickly mopped up their cash reserves. Britain and France needed loans to sustain their purchases, and these Woodrow Wilson was at first reluctant to permit. But in 1915, persuading himself that both the Allies and Germany would be free to negotiate loans from American bankers, and recognizing that the American economic boom was fuelled by burgeoning foreign commerce, Wilson allowed the loans to be made. Unsurprisingly given the pattern of trade, the vast bulk of these loans went to the Allies.

While there was a rationale to Wilson's claim that the principle of strict neutrality was being observed – all belligerents in principle had access to the private finance houses – it hardly seemed that the United States was remaining impartial in spirit. In any case, German actions were making it increasingly difficult for the American administration to steer an even course between the belligerents. From February 1915 Germany embarked on a campaign of submarine warfare as the only means of breaking the British blockade, and Allied shipping was subjected to attack. Submarines were a new weapon and could only operate effectively if they struck without warning, a breach of international law if they did so against merchant and passenger ships. Thus even citizens of neutral nations might be at risk when at sea. Wilson responded by insisting that the United States would hold Germany to 'strict accountability' for the loss of any American lives or ships. Germany tried to avoid provoking the United States, but in May 1915 a German submarine sank the British liner, the *Lusitania*, with the loss of nearly 1,200 lives, 128 of them American. This 'murder on the high seas' was traumatic for an age that had not witnessed the mass carnage that the twentieth century would visit on humankind. Germany rightly suspected the *Lusitania* of carrying munitions to Great Britain as well as passengers, but there was enormous public outrage in the United States. President Wilson sent a strong note of protest and demanded that Germany agree never again to strike at a passenger liner. Again he vehemently upheld neutrality rights, although in the particular conditions of warfare that obtained this interpretation served Allied rather than German interests. Wilson's secretary of state, William Jennings Bryan, resigned in June 1915, complaining that the president was more tolerant of British than of German violations of American rights. Germany bowed to Wilson's demands to the extent of avoiding attacks on liners, but merchant ships remained at risk. In March 1916 an unarmed French passenger steamer, the *Sussex*, was torpedoed, and a number of Americans aboard were hurt. Wilson despatched an ultimatum demanding that submarines refrain from attacking both merchant and passenger ships and threatening to sever diplomatic relations with Germany. Not wanting the United States in the war, Berlin issued the *Sussex* Pledge, agreeing to American demands.

The president was well aware of the precariousness of the situation: 'Any little German lieutenant can put us into war at any time by some calculated outrage.' Wilson had already begun a 'preparedness campaign', and in the summer of 1916 Congress agreed to a much larger navy. He had no wish to enter the war directly, but he hoped to mediate an end to the European conflict. The offer to mediate came to little, and in January 1917 Germany decided to try to force a quick victory by embarking on unrestricted submarine warfare. This meant that American vessels were subject to attack without warning; Wilson broke off diplomatic relations with Germany and ordered the arming of American merchant ships. American–German relations deteriorated further with the interception of the Zimmermann Telegram, a message from the German foreign minister inviting Mexico to attack the United States if it entered the war, holding out the prospect of the return of former Mexican territory.

The European war then took a dramatic turn in March when the Tsarist regime was overthrown in Russia, to be replaced by a seemingly liberal government promising to continue in the Allied cause. The war now more plausibly took the form of a contest between democratic and autocratic systems. 'The war which started as a clash of empires in the Balkans will dissolve into democratic revolution the world over', rejoiced the American journal the *New Republic*. As the momentous events were unfolding in Russia, in the Atlantic German submarines sank three American merchant ships on a single day. Early in April, at the request of the president, Congress finally declared war on Germany. 'The world must be made safe for democracy', said Wilson. By this date, in the face of German attacks on American shipping, Wilson had few options left, and one reason for his decision to intervene was to speed the war's end and give him a place at the peace conference. If the United States was not a belligerent, he told Jane Addams, his only role in the peacemaking would be to 'call' at members 'through a crack in the door'.

The intervention of the United States in the First World War, late though it was, made a vital difference. The German submarine campaign was proving effective in destroying merchant shipping bound for Britain, which was threatened with starvation, but American destroyers were quickly despatched to assist the Royal Navy in protecting merchant vessels and hunting down submarines. By the end of 1917, after the introduction of convoys, the war at sea had turned to the Allies' advantage. The land war was more problematic. The American army needed to be greatly enlarged before it could go into action, while the position of the Allied troops on the western front deteriorated after the Bolshevik Revolution in November and the withdrawal of Russia from the war. The Germans, with more troops at their disposal by early 1918 with the collapse of the Russian front, hoped to storm through the British and French lines before the Americans arrived in force. The Allied armies retreated under the German assault but they did not collapse, and during the summer, with the aid of a million American troops, the Allies were finally able launch a counter-attack. The German armies could not withstand this massive force and hostilities ended in November 1918.

Now Woodrow Wilson had an opportunity to try to shape a new world order in conformity with his ideals. As a German officer observed, the United States appeared to be 'the power to which, as far as anyone can tell, the future on this earth belongs'. In May 1916 Wilson had publicly called on the belligerents to end the war and support a 'universal association of nations' to keep the peace. At this point he was primarily trying to find a way of bringing the war to an end, assuming that participation in such an association would not mean abandoning his country's historic commitment to neutrality. The United States would be able to act as a world power, holding out its own values to the peoples of the world, while preserving a degree of detachment from foreign conflicts. In a speech to the Senate in January 1917, Wilson envisioned a world in which 'every people should be left free to determine its own polity'. He was gradually developing a vision of a new world order, one in which collectivism and independence could be held in harmonious equipoise, and which would be possible if peoples everywhere followed the American example.

Now a belligerent, Wilson amplified his views in January 1918 with his Fourteen Points, beginning with 'open covenants, openly arrived at' and concluding with the establishment of a league of nations. In September 1918, with the war drawing to a close, he spoke of a league of nations as the 'indispensable instrumentality' of permanent peace and called for its creation at the peace conference. Such a body could revolutionize international relations; for progressives like Wilson, the world as well as society could be changed and uplifted. The Allies unenthusiastically accepted the Fourteen Points as the basis for peace – France's Clemenceau complained, 'why, God Almighty has only ten!' – but the Paris Peace Conference proved to be fractious. Wilson was obliged to yield on a number of his Points. 'If I didn't feel that I was the personal instrument of God I couldn't carry on', muttered the president. Nonetheless, in attending the peace conference in person Wilson was underlining the global role now being assumed by the United States, and he did secure his overriding goal of the League of Nations.

In the spring of 1919 the Treaty of Versailles, with its incorporation of the Covenant of the League of Nations, seemed to be endorsed by popular opinion in the United States. But there was hostility from certain powerful groups. If the League represented one form of progressive thought, to other progressives it represented a betrayal of American ideals. Republican progressives like Hiram Johnson and William Borah feared that the League would be an entangling alliance, in particular ensnaring the United States in defending the imperial interests of Britain and France. To be 'the leading intellectual and moral power in the world', insisted Borah, the United States had to keep its distance. These 'irreconcilables' were determined to defeat the treaty. Conservative Republicans had their own problems with it, those around the powerful chair of the Senate Foreign Relations Committee, Henry Cabot Lodge, in principle accepting that the United States might enter a League but holding reservations about the document put before them. There were differences among the 'reservationists', but broadly they wanted the treaty amended before endorsing it.

The reservationists particularly objected to Article 10, which Wilson had called the 'heart of the Covenant', pledging members of the League to 'preserve as against external aggression' the territorial integrity and political independence of all members. Reservationists read this as an open-ended commitment, one that could draw the United States into armed support of questionable European governments. Lodge proposed a series of amendments, but Wilson felt that the treaty could hardly be renegotiated and launched on a speaking tour of the country in September 1919 to try to rally public opinion behind his handiwork. At the end of the month he was crippled by a stroke, but even from his sickbed Wilson continued to resist compromise. At this time the Red Scare was also sweeping the United States, serving to harden opinion against entanglements with a suspect Europe. In the event no version of the treaty put to the Senate was able to secure the necessary two-thirds majority. Another form of rejection came in the presidential campaign of 1920, which the president vainly trusted would be a 'solemn referendum' on the covenant. It could hardly be that, but in the event the Republicans won a handsome victory, killing any lingering hope that the United States might somehow take its place in the new world order as a leading member of the League of Nations. Wilson's dream of a League of Nations to keep the peace was fulfilled after a fashion, but without the United States. In 1920 Wilson was awarded the Nobel Peace Prize.

But even in 1920 the United States was not quite free of Old World entanglements. At the opening of that year there were American troops in Russia. They had been despatched in the summer of 1918, initially in an attempt to keep some kind of eastern front, but other considerations came to bear on their role. The revolution in Russia in March 1917 had been generally welcomed by Americans as heralding democracy, but the Bolshevik Revolution in November had introduced the disturbing spectre of anarchy to the propertied classes everywhere. As V. I. Lenin's regime took shape, assaulting private property and the Church and establishing workers' control in the factories, its direction became unmistakable, and was all the more alarming to Western leaders when it called for world revolution and the dissolution of capitalism everywhere. During his fateful speaking tour of September 1919, Woodrow Wilson identified Bolshevism as 'the poison of disorder', and emphatically denied that the principles of the American Revolution had anything to do with the violent regime in Russia, which represented 'the negation of everything that is American'. He was not alone in such opinions. When White Russians launched their own attack on the Bolshevik regime, influential figures among the Allies argued that it was in the West's interest to support their cause.

But intervention in Russia was not something that could be readily undertaken, especially by the United States and its high-minded president. In the event the Japanese, supported by Britain and France, did send forces into Siberia in April 1918, and when Wilson eventually sent battalions they were ostensibly to protect Allied military supplies placed there when Russia was an ally, and also to help a Czech force in the region with its own nationalist aspirations. In March 1919 Lenin established the Third International expressly to further world revolution, and before the end of 1920 his forces had seen off the White armies. American troops were withdrawn and Woodrow Wilson announced that the United States would not recognize the Soviet Union. As in the earlier non-recognition of the Huerta regime, Wilson was bucking tradition in not according *de facto* recognition to an established government. Rather as Theodore Roosevelt sought to distinguish between good trusts and bad trusts, Wilson distinguished between good and bad governments. Moral judgments were at the heart of progressive politics.

Progressive politics could have other side effects. One consequence of American intervention in the World War was a permanent enhancement of the American military establishment. As with the Spanish–American conflict, war had a major ratchet effect. Total membership of the armed forces had been 153,000 in June 1912; the war took it to 2,897,000 in June 1918. Over 4 million men served in uniform. With the return of peace the size of the armed forces dropped again, but not to the pre-war level, and for most of the 1920s and first half of the 1930s membership was around 250,000. This was roughly double the number of men the United States had usually kept under arms in the first decade of the twentieth century. The armed forces also secured a hefty and lasting budget increase. In 1913 the federal government had spent $245 million on the military; in 1922 (before war-related expenses had entirely disappeared) the figure was $864 million and in 1932 it was $702 million.

The United States had also achieved too large a role in the world to retreat completely into isolation, despite the popular repudiation of Old World values following the First World War. In certain respects the war had irrevocably increased American entanglements with the outside world, and the impulse to serve as an arbiter remained irresistible to policy-makers through the 1920s. Several of them shared Wilson's desire to reduce arms and outlaw war. One strand of thought was represented by Herbert Hoover as secretary of commerce between 1921 and 1929. Hoover advocated 'individualism in international economic life', or what biographer Joan Hoff Wilson has called 'independent internationalism', that is, asserting the American role in the world but keeping the United States free from collective obligations. Expanding American commerce did not mean a destructive trade war with other countries, in his progressive vision, but a mutually fruitful participation in a growing world economy: 'By contributing to peace and economic stability, by the loan of our surplus savings abroad for productive purposes, by the spread of inventions over the world, we can contribute to the elevation of standards of living in foreign countries and the demand for all goods.' The high tariff barriers constructed by the Republican administrations, however, militated against the fulfilment of this benevolent objective.

As Hoover recognized, the source of American authority in the outside world was ultimately economic, owing in part to its particular wartime experience. During the war years the United States had become a major net creditor. In mid-1914 foreign investments in the country had been about twice the value of American investments abroad; in 1919 the reverse obtained. Massive American loans had sustained the Allied war effort, and the United States was owed over $3.5 billion by the Allies by 1918. To a substantial degree the country was displacing Britain as the world's leading banker.

Thus the United States could hardly avoid being involved in the reconstruction of Europe. American loans made possible the stabilization of the currencies of Britain, Germany and Italy, and American monies helped rebuild factories and railroads in Europe. In order to circumvent tariff barriers, American companies bought or built plants abroad, one example being the acquisition of Britain's Vauxhall Motors by General Motors. In Washington government officials hoped that the expansion of commerce would promote international peace, but this economic activity, including the loans, was in private hands. Government advised and encouraged, but kept punctiliously clear of the arrangements themselves. The closeness between politicians and bankers sometimes led to jibes that American foreign policy was directed by Wall Street. Prominent theologian Reinhold Niebuhr observed in 1930 that the United States had become an empire but that 'our legions are dollars'.

The reluctance of the government to engage officially in negotiations about loans was also related to its insistence that the European nations repay the loans that the government had made from public funds during the war. The Allied countries wanted these debts to be linked to German reparations – if Germany made reparation payments to France and Belgium, for example, they would be better able to repay their debts to the United States. Washington refused to accept a linkage between reparations and debt repayments, and saw to it that private bankers rather than public officials attended conferences at which such matters might be raised. It was the Chicago banker Charles G. Dawes who headed the American delegation to the 1924 conference, and the resulting Dawes Plan carried his name, providing for a reduction in German reparation payments and for private bank loans to help the German economy. In 1929 it was another private citizen, the head of General Electric, Owen D. Young, who negotiated another agreement reducing German reparations. The American government monitored the actions of the bankers, encouraging some loans and discouraging others, but it was American bankers and American investors who helped to reconstruct the European economies.

If the government encouraged trade as one way of promoting peace, another way was through disarmament. Arms races were held to have been in significant part responsible for the outbreak of the First World War, and the popular reaction against war did something to strengthen the peace movement in the United States. Wilsonian dreams of fashioning a permanent peace were not entirely dead, and disarmament now became the means. As the war ended the United States was still constructing new battleships, as were Japan and Britain, and partly to avert an expensive naval race, though also because of unease over growing Japanese influence in the Pacific, the Americans called a conference of the naval powers to discuss arms limitations. This was something that surviving progressives could support, most notably Republican Senator William Borah of Idaho. The Washington Conference of 1921–2 agreed to limits for the navies of participating countries; the ratios of 5-5-3 were set for the United States, Britain and Japan respectively, with smaller ratios for Italy and France. Thus the US Navy would finally achieve parity with the Royal Navy; Britain, unable to afford an arms race with the United States, had to consent. Further disarmament discussions followed, the London Conference of 1930 extending the ratio principle to smaller ships. Herbert Hoover still floated disarmament proposals in 1932, suggesting a ban on all offensive weapons, but his refusal to enter into anything that looked like a commitment to collective security contributed to their failure. American governments in the 1920s – as they had done before the First World War – also continued to explore the use of arbitration treaties to resolve international disputes. The peace movement secured its greatest success in 1928 when Secretary of State Frank B. Kellogg helped to negotiate the Kellogg–Briand Pact, in which the major powers agreed to renounce war and settle disputes by peaceful means. Highly popular with the public, the Pact won Kellogg the Nobel Peace Prize, although seasoned veterans of the world of diplomacy doubted the efficacy of this 'international kiss'.

The veterans were right to be cynical. Ultimately the diplomacy of the conservative progressives of the 1920s was to prove no more successful than Woodrow Wilson's more idealistic version. In fact the State Department was not the servant of the banks and in time it was to be disappointed with the power of the dollar. Economic influence proved a poor substitute for political power. Major issues not readily amenable to financial pressures or inducements, such as the expansion of Japanese power and the role of the Soviet Union among the great powers, were never adequately addressed. In the aftermath of the Great Crash of 1929, American loans to Europe were widely repudiated and the work of the bankers was in ruins. The government's stubborn retention – and further raising – of protective tariffs deepened the subsequent international depression. Also destined to be disappointed was the Wilsonian notion of finding a mechanism to preserve international peace. The dream flickered on in the various arms and arbitration negotiations of the Republican administrations, but their futility was exposed in 1931 when Japan launched an invasion of Manchuria. War was returning to the world. The progressive vision was no closer to fulfilment abroad than it was at home.

5

Red Scare and Republican Ascendancy: from Wilson to Hoover 1917–33

By the 1920s the committed activists of progressive reform had for the most part been pushed to the margins of the political realm. Strands of the progressive persuasion survived, even in the federal government, but they were not the healthy sentiments that had invaded the administrations of Theodore Roosevelt and Woodrow Wilson. The First World War and its unhappy Red Scare aftermath were largely responsible for crippling the progressive persuasion, even though certain aspects of progressivism were strengthened by the war. Repression was replacing reform as the means of containing social discontent. The insular currents of the 1920s, when the United States sought to shake free of European influences, deepened the growing conservatism. A period of prosperity can release reform currents, but that of the 1920s seemed to reinforce the rule of tradition-minded members of the Wasp élite.

The very mobilization of government during the war emergency gave heart to some progressives. For the moment government was able to extend its authority, as many progressives had hoped, and war gave a fillip to particular causes. One such was women's suffrage. As discussed in Chapter 2, several states had already enfranchised women, but the war triggered the support of the Wilson administration and the final boost needed for the ratification of the 19th Amendment. The war similarly enabled the Prohibition movement to ram through its own amendment to the Constitution.

The crusade for Prohibition had emerged from the evangelical impulse within progressivism, as it also reflected the progressive willingness to turn to the state for regulation – though enforcement would mean more federal interference in the lives of ordinary citizens than in any other progressive cause. Rooted in the Victorian notion that respectability was a product of hard work and self-restraint, Prohibition won its key supporters among a farming middle class and white-collar workers and small businessmen in the cities – and their families. Its objective, in no small part, was to impose bourgeois values on the supposedly dissolute lower orders of the cities, many of whom were immigrants. The movement was most effectively led by the Anti-Saloon League, which developed as a potent pressure group, and by the Women's Christian Temperance Union, which enjoyed much influence among middle-class women.

In the absence of opinion-poll data it is difficult to know just how much sympathy Prohibition commanded in the country at large, but David Kyvig, in analysing an array of state referenda and legislative votes, has conjectured that it was supported by a slim majority of the electorate. Even before 1917 nineteen states had introduced their own bans on alcohol, but war provided additional arguments, notably that the grains used for alcohol should be conserved and that the war effort depended on sober workers and warriors. The Anti-Saloon League's influence grew and it pressed for an amendment to the federal Constitution. As it happened, brewing was largely in the hands of German–American firms and patriotic sentiments were readily turned against them. Congress in December 1917 adopted the 18th Amendment prohibiting the sale, manufacture or transportation of 'intoxicating liquors' (which the Volstead Act defined very narrowly) and by January 1919 it had been ratified by the necessary three-quarters of the states, a process facilitated by the over-representation of rural areas in most state legislatures. The progressive objective of purifying American life, however, was soon being mocked by the Prohibition experiment, which may have modestly curtailed alcoholic consumption but also spawned crime and new opportunities for business to corrupt politics.

Women's suffrage and Prohibition were not the only progressive causes furthered by the war, which created opportunities to reshape the administrative structure of the United States. During the emergency businessmen and others were hastily recruited to Washington, and some tried to fashion a more efficient economy, less dominated by the vagaries of a competitive market place. Government, corporations and labour unions also cooperated in the War Labor Board, set up to resolve industrial disputes, in the progressive tradition of the earlier National Civic Federation. But in the confusion of war government was inevitably pulled in different directions. While reformers sometimes secured the kind of rationalization they wanted, the businessmen in Washington tended to promote commercial values.

By the end of 1917 the federal government was assuming wide powers over the economy. The Food Administration enjoyed extensive influence over the pricing and even the consumption of foods, and the Fuel Administration held similar authority over coal. The government took control of the railroads, pumped millions of dollars into them and greatly improved the nationwide rail system. The Shipping Board developed shipyards and commandeered and constructed ships. A War Industries Board achieved some success in prioritizing the allocation of resources. Progressives could cite war mobilization as an example of the rational management of the economy, though of course most of the wartime agencies disappeared with the return of peace. Nonetheless there was a modest residue. A few agencies, such as the Shipping

Board, did survive. While the Railroad Administration surrendered its duties in 1920, a Railway Labor Board was created to mediate disputes.

Similarly in line with progressive values was the enhancement of the financial authority of the federal government. In the decade 1906–15 federal government receipts had usually been in the range of $600 or $700 million a year. During the war they rose rapidly, peaking at $6694 million in 1920, and while they eased thereafter they rarely fell below $4000 million a year in the 1920s. The enlargement of federal financial power was dramatic and permanent. One reason why the federal government had to maintain a high level of revenue after the war was to service the national debt, which had increased by about twenty times between 1915 and 1920.

The imperative need for increased revenue during the war gave congressional reformers hope that they could graft a clearly progressive tax system on the country. In this they were largely disappointed, since in the event about two-thirds of the war costs were covered by loans to the government, generated by Liberty Bond drives. Nonetheless some taxes had to be raised. In 1915 federal income tax had reached just 7 per cent on the top bracket; it rose to 77 per cent during the war. Tax cuts in the 1920s eventually reduced the top rate to 25 per cent, but even that was far above the pre-war level. The war also extended income tax to middle-class earners for the first time. And there were some far-reaching changes. Before the war nearly 75 per cent of the revenue of the federal government came from customs and excise taxes, essentially taxes on consumption that reached most Americans. After the war nearly 75 per cent of federal revenue came from taxes on incomes, profits and estates. Because of this and the upward adjustment of income tax, the rich did come to contribute a higher tax share.

But if world war served to advance certain progressive goals, its impact on the wider progressive persuasion was shattering. Some progressives, like Wilson and Roosevelt, believed the war a necessary and just one. Others came out against it. William Jennings Bryan resigned as secretary of state in protest as early as 1915, believing that Wilson's foreign policy was insufficiently neutral. Robert M. La Follette denounced American intervention, earning the lasting enmity of pro-war progressives. The quarrels over the peace terms, particularly the League of Nations, were further to split progressives.

The actions of the federal government itself served to undermine the progressive faith. Since 1914 public opinion had been generally against US entry into the European quarrel, and the homelands of millions of Americans lay within the territory of the Central Powers. Many progressives feared that the war would undo the cause of reform, and further left were groups like the Socialist party and the IWW who were outspoken critics of intervention. Such opposition could hamper the war effort and worse. Yet the slight federal government lacked even a police force to guard against possible sabotage. These circumstances had fateful consequences for progressivism. The administration had to rely on the uncertain techniques of persuasion to create a new consensus, embarking on a mammoth campaign to harness public opinion to the war. Patriotism, however, proved an ill-controlled emotion.

The principal responsibility for mobilizing public opinion was vested in the Committee on Public Information (CPI). Chaired by George Creel, who brought to his task a progressive faith in democracy, the CPI disseminated torrents of information that became increasingly indistinguishable from patriotic propaganda. The CPI's objective, Creel later explained, was to create 'a passionate belief in the justice of America's cause that should weld the people … into one white-hot mass of instinct'. For Creel and not a few progressives the war became a holy mission. 'Woe be to the man', said Wilson, 'that seeks to stand in our way.' The administration also quietly sponsored the American Protective League (APL), a private body using local volunteers to look for spies and undertake loyalty investigations. By 1918 there were some 250,000 leaguers, and while many behaved responsibly others disrupted Socialist meetings and beat up draft evaders. The APL was flanked by other patriotic associations, such as the American Defense Society, a champion of 'One Hundred Percent Americanism'. Legitimized by the government's propaganda campaign, patriot citizens joined these groups to serve their country in time of war, but when peace returned many were reluctant to abandon these gratifying vigilante activities.

Disquiet over the extent of anti-war feeling in the United States also fuelled demands for protective legislation. The states' rights tradition had left the federal authorities with few legal controls over American citizens, but the war emergency made possible some fitful extension of their powers. The 1917 Espionage Act made it a crime to obstruct enlistment or interfere with industrial production. The Sedition Act of May 1918 went further, prohibiting language disloyal to the American form of government or intended to promote the cause of the enemies of the United States. A disloyal statement could be punished by twenty years in jail – opponents criticized government policy at their peril. Among the critics of American intervention was the Socialist Party and the IWW, and the leaders of both were prosecuted under wartime legislation. The Espionage and Sedition Acts would expire with the war, but some officials wanted a more permanent weapon to turn against radicalism. A high proportion of the members of left-wing groups were immigrants, many still not naturalized. Make aliens readily deportable, it was calculated, and radicalism would be crippled. The Immigration Act of 1918 barred entry to those subscribing to theories advocating the violent overthrow of government and provided for the deportation of aliens subsequently found to hold such ideas. This law was to be the basis for the celebrated Palmer Raids of 1919–20.

Thus during the war an active citizenry had been awakened to guard the republic, while bureaucratic tools had been forged in the defence of national security. Events in the outside and post-war world interacted with this wartime heritage to unleash a fierce right-wing reaction. The Russian Revolution had at first been welcomed by the American public as a democratic uprising, but its later Bolshevik turn alarmed the propertied classes. Yet it exhilarated American radicals, and communist risings in Western and Central Europe in 1918 and 1919 immeasurably strengthened both radical hopes and conservative fears that the appeal of revolutionary communism knew no national boundaries. When in 1919 bombs exploded in several American cities and major steel and coal strikes wrenched at the very core of America's industrial capitalism, many were ready to believe that Bolsheviks were abroad in the land.

This intensification of class conflict itself was largely a consequence of the war. Major industrial corporations had emerged more prosperous than ever, while organized labour had also grown in size, and both businessmen and workers took the Armistice as a signal to turn on one another. Souring the atmosphere further was a sharp inflation that also cast doubts on the government's regulatory experiments. Public opinion, and for the most part the federal government, responded with hostility to the strikes of 1919–21; the strike wave did not abate until 1922. As industrial conflict increased, many progressive and middle-class citizens grew disenchanted with labour and reform. Paralleling the class conflict was an exacerbation of racial tension, as lynching increased in the South and race riots disfigured Washington and Chicago. The fading of progressive sentiment and the deepening fissures of class, ethnicity and race promoted a polarization of American politics, as public opinion at large moved to the right but tiny minorities embraced a revolutionary radicalism.

The celebrated Red Scare lasted little over a year in its most intensive phase. The city of Seattle was paralysed in February 1919 by a general strike, which Mayor Ole Hanson described as the work of men who 'want to take possession of our American Government and try to duplicate the anarchy of Russia'. The strike collapsed after four days and made Hanson a hero, and he toured the country giving lectures on the need to fight the red menace. The scare intensified in the spring, when several bombs addressed to distinguished figures were found in the mails, and in the autumn major coal and steel strikes gave some credence to conservative warnings, as did an unnerving strike by the police in Boston. It had been a Wobbly boast that 'every strike is a small revolution and a dress rehearsal for the big one', and the extraordinary eruption of industrial conflict, violence and political radicalism in 1919 suggested to many that the revolution was at hand.

Across the land, in countless official and vigilante actions, strikers were beaten and sometimes killed and socialist meetings and newspapers were suppressed. The high point came when Attorney-General A. Mitchell Palmer authorized raids in November and early January on radical organizations and over 6000 people were arrested. It was assumed that many would be aliens who could be deported under the 1918 Immigration Act. The enormous publicity the Palmer Raids generated briefly buoyed up the anti-radical elements, but the raids failed to uncover evidence of revolutionary conspiracy and their indiscriminate nature soon attracted criticism. The Supreme Court and the Department of Labor issued rulings protecting the rights of those arrested. The Red Scare waned as the abuses suffered by detainees became public and it became clear that there were no real grounds for fearing revolution.

Public sympathy for progressive reform had been disappearing even before the Red Scare. Wartime taxes, labour unrest and the embroilment in foreign quarrels had undermined confidence in activist government. 'Price fixing by the Government has worked nothing but mischief', complained Theodore Roosevelt during 1918. By this date progressive impulses had largely fled the Republican Party. One trajectory was illustrated by Roosevelt himself, who a few years earlier had enthusiastically embraced a sweeping progressivism, but who during the war avowed a superpatriotism that made little allowance for dissent. He supported loyalty oaths for teachers, excoriated conscientious objectors as 'slackers' and saw Bolshevik agitators behind labour unrest. While he did not altogether abandon his progressive convictions, they were overshadowed by a jingoistic patriotism that did nothing to hold back Red Scare sentiments.

Democrats and Republicans alike were moving to the right, and the progressives among them were losing their faith. Ole Hanson and A. Mitchell Palmer were but two examples of men who had once supported liberal causes but now regarded every strike as a prelude to revolution. Progressives of greater intellectual weight abandoned the cause of reform. Leading senator Albert J. Beveridge had denounced the 1916 Adamson Act, setting an eight-hour day for railroad employees, as a surrender by government to the 'threat of force by special interest'; he also came out against the income tax and in 1919 complained that constitutional government was being usurped by 'predatory groups'. Progressives were dismayed when class was put before commonwealth, a reaction which contributed to the retreat of the Democratic Party from the reform cause that it had supported so strongly in 1916.

For many progressives, particularly writers and intellectuals, the war and the peace were profoundly dispiriting. Some lost faith in the capacity of human beings to change society for the better, at least by democratic means. Lincoln Steffens found something to admire in the authoritarian regimes emerging in Europe. Walter Lippmann expressed his distrust of public opinion and yearned for greater authority to be accorded to experts. Walter Weyl referred to the 'tired radicals' that his generation of progressives had turned into. Many intellectuals retreated in dismay from public life, displaying little further interest in efforts to reform society.

While the Red Scare faded in the early 1920s, the forces on which it had fed remained formidable. The rejection of the European world and all it stood for let loose an ideological crusade that demanded adherence to the values of One Hundred Percent Americanism. In this divided and troubled society, conservative economic and ethno-cultural interests, particularly those feeling threatened by the cosmopolitan culture emerging in the cities, cleaved fiercely to traditional values. One manifestation of this parochial nativism was the

Ku Klux Klan, which (as discussed in Chapter 2) became an influential force for cultural and political conservatism. Another was the erection of barriers against immigration from outside the western hemisphere.

Statist solutions also fell under suspicion. Across the nation social reformers of various kinds found that there were limits to public sympathy for government-sponsored solutions. A social work editor saw little hope for a constitutional amendment to prohibit child labour, even though Congress endorsed it in 1924, since the separate state legislatures would have to ratify it: 'The familiar bogeys ... of states' rights, the prohibition analogy, the grasping bureaucrats of Washington, the sacred right of the seventeen-year old farm boy to pick blueberries on the hill, and all the rest – will no doubt troop from state capital to state capital to do their worst.' These were among the reasons for the conservative sentiments of the 1920s: memories of tiresome wartime constraints, fear of an overbearing Washington, disappointment at the sorry mess of the Prohibition experiment, suspicion of anything that undermined the autonomy of family life.

The Democratic occupancy of the White House could not survive the ending of the war and the widespread disillusionment with the European adventure, not to mention the unpopularity with which Woodrow Wilson consummated what almost until the end had been a remarkably successful political career. For the election of 1920 the Republicans nominated for president a genial conservative Midwestern senator, Warren G. Harding of Ohio, and for vice-president Calvin Coolidge, who had won some renown as governor of Massachusetts for his part in breaking the notorious police strike in Boston. The Democrats nominated James M. Cox, a progressive governor of Ohio. The Republicans swept easily to power, winning large majorities in both houses of Congress as well as in the presidential election.

Harding personally was not a reactionary, but his political instincts were conservative. 'America's present need is not heroics but healing, not nostrums but normalcy, not surgery but serenity', he had said during the campaign. As such he could sometimes show a little sympathy for progressive causes, as in 1923 when he permitted pressure to be brought on US Steel and other steel companies to abandon the twelve-hour day. Also in keeping with progressive values was the establishment of the Bureau of the Budget in 1921, to give the executive greater control over the budget-making process and replacing the traditional haphazard methods (under which each government department had separately asked Congress for funds) with a more efficient system, a measure initially called for by the Wilson administration.

But whatever administrative improvements may have been made, for the most part they served a conservative purpose. Harding's secretary of the treasury was the millionaire Andrew Mellon, who pleased the business community by containing government expenditure and securing substantial tax cuts, particularly for wealthier taxpayers. Mellon, who remained in office through the Republican administrations of the 1920s, was unable to do away with the income tax or even reduce it to pre-war levels, but he made it substantially less progressive and ended corporate taxes on excess profits. The administration also moved quickly to restore the principle of protection, the Fordney-McCumber Tariff Act of 1922 allowing rates to be raised to forbiddingly high levels. It proved less sympathetic to farmers, many of whom were suffering following the collapse of the high wartime prices.

Harding also pleased the conservatives by appointing business sympathizers to such regulatory bodies as the Interstate Commerce Commission and the Federal Trade Commission, thus largely undoing progressive attempts to police corporate America in the public interest. The Republican chair of the FTC, which was meant to enforce anti-trust legislation, redefined its mission as being a 'help to business'. Budget cuts in any case severely limited the administrative capacity of the regulatory agencies. The administration did not bring anti-trust prosecutions against large corporations, although a new merger movement was taking place. Similarly illustrative of the administration's political stance was its suspicious attitude towards organized labour. In 1922 the Attorney-General secured a sweeping injunction against picketing to end a railroad strike.

Assisting the Harding administration in its repudiation of progressive reform was the Supreme Court. Harding, remarkably, chose as chief justice the last Republican president, William Howard Taft, who told his fellow justices that he had been appointed 'to reverse a few decisions'. The modest protection from court injunctions that the Clayton Act had tried to afford organized labour was further eroded. ('That faction we have to hit every little while', Taft said of labour in 1922.) Other progressive gains were also assailed. After the 1918 decision annulling the Keating-Owen Act, Congress had passed another act to control child labour, but this too was knocked down by the Court in 1922. In 1923, in *Adkins v Children's Hospital*, the Court ruled against a women's minimum wage law introduced by the District of Columbia. Harding wittingly furthered the conservative orientation of the Court. In his less than three years of office it fell to Harding to appoint four Supreme Court justices, each one a convinced conservative.

But progressivism of a kind survived in Washington. Liaising with the business community was Herbert Hoover, who served as secretary of commerce between 1921 and 1929 and whose sensitivity to business conditions was allied to a progressive regard for the public weal and the efficient deployment of resources. Hoover did not believe in direct government intervention in the economy, but he saw it as government's job to research economic conditions and to encourage business to conduct itself efficiently. Trade associations might be formed to promote codes of fair practice (such as in humane employment policies), standardize products and sustain economic viability by adjusting production to demand. Cut-throat competition and boom-and-bust would become things of the past in this vision, and the whole community would benefit. Secretary of Commerce Hoover inspired the creation of hundreds of associational agreements and built up the expertise of his department.

Herbert Hoover enhanced his reputation, but not all of Warren Harding's appointments were well judged. Some of the friends he found jobs for proved to be less than honest, using their influence to misappropriate funds or extract bribes. Harding himself was not a party to these scandals, but evidence of misconduct was emerging by the summer of 1923 when his health was failing. 'I have no trouble with my enemies', Harding told journalist William Allen White. 'But my damned friends, my God-damn friends, White, they're the ones that keep me walking the floor nights!' He died in August, and in the ensuing months the corruption within his administration became public. Climaxing the scandals was the Teapot Dome Affair, in which Secretary of the Interior Albert B. Fall had secretly leased government oil lands to private interests in return for large 'loans'. 'To the victors', it was said, 'belong the oils.' Fall was convicted and sent to prison for bribery. Others met a like fate, while the investigations led two officials to commit suicide.

Harding's death, the succession to the presidency of the strait-laced Calvin Coolidge and the return of prosperity limited the political damage that the Teapot Dome scandal may have wrought on the Republicans. Coolidge was even more conservative than Harding, believing in strictly limited government and holding that 'the business of America is business'. He continued Harding's practice of appointing pro-business conservatives to the regulatory commissions and other government agencies.

The presidential election of 1924 illustrated the marginalization of the progressive impulse. The Republicans, keeping 'Cool with Coolidge', were able to enter the campaign claiming that the economic boom was the product of their policies, especially the tax cuts, of which they promised more. The Democrats offered a somewhat more liberal platform, although in choosing as their candidate a corporation lawyer, John W. Davis, they were hardly sending out reformist signals. Dismayed by the choice, progressives from both major parties, as well as Socialists and labour and farm representatives, met in their own convention to nominate a Progressive ticket headed by Robert M. La Follette. 'The great issue before the American people today is the control of government and industry by private monopoly', the La Follette platform bluntly began. If so, the American people did not seem to mind greatly, because Coolidge was handsomely re-elected with 54 per cent of the popular vote, while La Follette (who, unlike Roosevelt in 1912, took more votes from the Democrats than the Republicans) managed a modest 17 per cent.

True to their promises, the Republican White House and Congress made further substantial tax reductions, especially on higher incomes. With the president's encouragement, the Federal Reserve Banks expanded credit to businessmen and investors. Gross National Product leaped from $74 billion in 1922 to $104.4 billion in 1929. Not everyone fared well in these years, but the prosperity was sufficiently pervasive as to sustain the political dominance of the Republicans. In 1928 Calvin Coolidge decided not to seek another term and the party's nomination went to the successful Secretary of

Commerce Herbert Hoover. On this occasion the Democrats nominated a potent candidate in Al Smith, an urban Catholic of Irish-Italian descent and progressive governor of New York. He also campaigned against Prohibition, which the Republicans still supported despite its widespread evasion. Riding the wave of prosperity, the Republicans, as expected, won another victory, Hoover securing 58 per cent of the popular vote and Smith 41 per cent. Smith's Catholicism and identification with big city 'wets' hurt him in parts of the country, but he had improved on Davis's disastrous showing of 1924 and he won majorities in the country's twelve largest cities. A voter realignment was under way which, in due course, would end Republican ascendancy.

'I have no fears for the future of our country', said President Hoover in his inaugural address in March 1929: 'It is bright with hope.' In October share prices on the stock market spectacularly collapsed, declining on average by 40 per cent, but even that did not entirely destroy confidence in the world's leading economy. 'Things are better today than they were yesterday', boomed motor tycoon Henry Ford in November. But it was soon clear that a devastating depression was materializing, one that hit Americans far harder than the people of any other industrial nation. Over half of the drop in the world's industrial production occurred in the United States. 'The stock market crash', noted the writer Edmund Wilson, 'was to count for us almost like a rending of the earth in preparation for the Day of Judgment.'

By 1932 industrial production was down to little more than half what it had been in 1929. In 1929 there had been virtually full employment, but by 1933 official unemployment was nearly 25 per cent. If farm employees are excluded from the statistics, over a third of the country's workers were without jobs, a staggering figure in an industrial society. Even the possession of land did not mean security; one in eight farmers had lost his farm by 1933. The high and sustained level of unemployment in the United States overshadowed that of every other contemporary modern economy.

Unemployment brought fear and despair for it could mean starvation and homelessness. The suicide rate rose by nearly a quarter between 1929 and 1932, and marriage and birth rates dropped markedly as young people recoiled from the prospect of raising families. There were no welfare or dole payments for the unemployed to fall back on, except for the meagre relief sometimes available from local authorities. Only a tiny fraction – 2 or 3 per cent – of the millions of families without a male breadwinner received pensions. Private charity, the traditional American buffer against hard times and geared to limited and temporary distress, could not come close to meeting the scale of the emergency. Men roamed through the country looking for work. People slept in public parks, under bridges, even, in Arkansas, in caves. They sometimes took refuge in the shanty towns or 'Hoovervilles' that appeared outside large cities, living in packing cases and cardboard shacks. There were hunger marches and demonstrations in the early 1930s, but they were difficult to sustain and many of the unemployed soon lapsed into a bitter apathy.

The Stock Market Crash and the subsequent Depression were separate though related phenomena. The crash itself can be explained largely in terms of the extraordinary speculative bubble that had built up in the late 1920s. The prosperity of the decade had promoted the conviction that the United States possessed a resilient economy, fostered public confidence in business and political leaders and enabled many Americans to build up savings. Above all it was faith in the miracle of the money market that impelled people to speculate. Andrew Mellon's generous tax cuts meant that well-to-do citizens had even more cash to invest, and the bubble grew larger because of the practices that prevailed. Buying 'on the margin' was widespread, that is paying a fraction of the price of stock in the expectation that its price would rise, when the remaining cost could be paid off. But the whole frenetic system depended on stock market prices continuing to go up. When, for whatever reason, they ceased to do so, investors would face ruin and, in attempting to extricate themselves from the market, would likely precipitate a panic. And so it proved. The bubble itself swelled rapidly between 1927 and 1929, when the average price of common stocks soared by about 300 per cent, until something pricked it in October 1929.

A stock market crash is not necessarily followed by a deep and prolonged depression. But in 1929 it soon became evident that the economy was far from robust. As the crash ruined speculators, triggered company bankruptcies and bank failures and destroyed commercial confidence, the stock prices slid ever lower, and continued to do so year after dispiriting year, not reaching bottom until July 1932. The American economy, capitalism's proudest creation, was after all frighteningly vulnerable. The flush times of the 1920s had hidden serious economic weaknesses. As J. Kenneth Galbraith has dryly phrased it, 'the economy was fundamentally unsound'.

Scientific and technological advances – chemicals, electricity, the moving assembly line – had served greatly to boost both productivity and production in the 1920s, but consumption had not been able to keep pace. Farm incomes were disastrously low, as were those of certain industrial workers, exacerbating what was already a serious maldistribution of income. The rich grew a lot richer in these years and the poor only a little less poor. The top 1 per cent of the population seems to have increased its substantial share of the national income by over 50 per cent in the 1920s. The wealthy might throw their gains on the stock market, but consumers at large lacked the means to sustain consumption. There was not enough purchasing power in the economy to support it if the expenditures of the rich were suddenly curtailed.

This perverse distribution of income was paralleled by other systemic flaws. One was the unstable nature of American banking. The country was festooned with thousands of small and independent banks, many with inadequate reserves, and when a panic occurred they could collapse like a row of dominoes, taking people's savings with them. The Federal Reserve System, that proud accomplishment of progressive reform, in the event offered flimsy protection. The renewed combination movement had intensified another fault, the domination of the industrial economy by large companies and investment houses. The holding companies at the top depended for their profits on the supply of revenues from the operating companies beneath them, and anything that interrupted this flow could undermine the whole pyramidical structure. Also unhealthy was the pattern of foreign trade. The United States exported more than it imported, but this meant that foreign countries could maintain their purchases only through American loans. If these were reduced for any reason – such as a banking crisis – the foreign markets of American exporters were liable to shrivel, bringing the economy even lower. When financial crises finally hit Europe in 1931 they were relayed around the world, and the global depression could only intensify that of the United States. While these various structural weaknesses were long-standing features of the American economy, the practices adopted by government, such as the insouciant regulation of money market practices and the high tariffs, served more to accentuate than to alleviate them. The unsound foundations of the economy meant that it could not withstand the impact of the Stock Market Crash, resulting in a deep and prolonged depression.

It was Herbert Hoover's misfortune to preside over the United States during this débâcle, and his organizational prowess did not prove equal to the misery that engulfed the country. The key to industrial recovery, he believed, was the restoration of business confidence, and he deployed his prodigious energy in exhorting businessmen and bankers to avoid deflationary actions (like reducing credit) and stimulating private charities to feed the starving. These tactics had seemed to help the economy bounce back from recession in 1921, but the Great Depression proved more obdurate. In 1930 Congress voted money for public works, but the funds were small and state governments in any case cut their spending by even greater amounts. In January 1932 Hoover secured the establishment of the Reconstruction Finance Corporation, which tried to shore up key bank, railroad and other large companies by making loans to them. But the loans were modest and the business failure rate reached a new high in 1932. A tariff act of 1930 raised protective tariffs to their highest level ever, sparking off retaliatory action by other countries that further depressed international trade. A sharp increase in taxes in 1932, as Hoover tried to control the budget deficit, had a further deflationary effect. Few of these measures directly addressed the plight of the unemployed, despite the evident failure of private charities and municipal governments to provide for them.

Many of these measures depended for their success on the voluntary action of others – state governments in maintaining spending, farmers in reducing production, employers in sustaining payrolls. When one businessman offered a plan to allow trade associations to enforce price and production levels and unemployment insurance on employers, Hoover denounced it as 'an attempt to smuggle fascism into America through the back-door'. The federal government was to keep out of the relief business, which Hoover saw as a matter for private charities and local government.

He believed there were dangers in allowing a bureaucratic state to take over people's lives. Hoover was not heartless, but his rigid belief in self and local help and his sombre manner conveyed an impression of indifference. This impression was deepened as the 1932 election approached, when some 20,000 veterans of the First World War marched on Washington to demand the payment of bonuses they believed due to them, and Hoover allowed the army to disperse these unarmed and ragged protesters with tanks and bayonets. Hoover failed to see that traditional and voluntarist methods could not cope with the scale of the destitution that characterized the Great Depression, and he and his party sacrificed the support of millions of Americans. It would be another twenty years before more than half the electorate could again be persuaded to cast their votes for a Republican candidate for president.

Yet it is unlikely that Hoover's administration could have devised effective measures to end the Depression. The reforms of the Progressive Era had equipped the federal government with the weakest of tools. By European standards, it could almost be said, the United States still did not possess a central government. The American diplomat George Kennan once recalled of his early boyhood days in the Midwest that 'when times were hard, as they often were, groans and lamentations went up to God, but never to Washington'. The only federal agency in most towns was the post office. The routine tasks of governance were still performed by local and especially state governments. In 1929 federal expenditure represented a tiny 2.5 per cent of GNP. If Hoover had somehow contrived to decree unemployment or welfare payments, there was no government department through which to disburse them. When Hoover did agree to release surplus wheat to feed the hungry in 1932, it had to be distributed by the Red Cross. The absence of anything like the state welfare systems that were emerging in Europe meant that any attempts at social policy would be severely circumscribed. The tradition whereby communities looked after their own distressed residents had been the product of an agricultural society, when hardship could be expected to be local and temporary. The administrative structure of the federal government had simply not been adapted to the needs of an urbanized and industrialized nation. The progressives, after all, had not sufficiently modernized the American system of government.

By 1932 the economy was sinking even deeper into depression. Between 1931 and 1932 unemployment rocketed by about 50 per cent. As the election of 1932 approached, there were some 12 million Americans miserably seeking work, an awesome figure which did not have its like in living memory. There were rumbles of discontent across the country, but no organized revolt against the American economic and political system. Many of the destitute were simply worn out from years of struggle. But perhaps too the American political process offered a measure of hope. The Depression was irretrievably identified with Herbert Hoover and the Republicans. A change of government could offer a solution.

The Democrats nominated for president the ebullient Franklin D. Roosevelt, who bore a famous name and who had won plaudits as a reform governor of New York. Their platform followed conventional wisdom in speaking of the need for balancing the federal budget, and Roosevelt himself from time to time reiterated this demand. But his campaign was invested with an optimism that his gloomy rival could not match, and his pragmatism kept bursting through. Roosevelt spoke of 'distributing wealth and products more equitably, of adapting existing economic organization to the service of the people'. The means to this egalitarian end were far from clear, but Roosevelt seemed to be offering action of some sort. Where major businesses abused their power, he suggested, the state might step in. What the campaign did reveal was Roosevelt's energy and optimism in the face of national adversity. His coast-to-coast offensive effectively buried the image of a crippled body (his legs had been paralysed by poliomyelitis in 1921), and his skilful radio talks sent a note of hope into the furthest reaches of a devastated nation. His crushing victory marked the end of Republican hegemony.

Franklin Roosevelt won the election with over 57 per cent of the popular vote – the largest majority his party had ever enjoyed – and an even greater proportion of electoral votes. The Democrats' electoral success was confirmed by the congressional returns. They won a huge majority in the House of Representatives and a large one in the Senate. For the next thirty-odd years the Democrats were to be the majority party. During the inaugural parade the bands played 'Happy Days Are Here Again'. By this date the term 'New Deal' had entered the language, although it was far from clear what this meant or just how Americans could expect to exercise their inalienable right to the pursuit of happiness.

The political order presided over by the Anglo-American élite was irreparably damaged. Further, the committed progressives had not achieved many of their avowed goals. If there was a 'progressive movement' (and not all historians are prepared to dignify the mixed assortment of causes with that term), by the end of the first third of the twentieth century it had failed.

The curbs placed on machine politics may have done a little to contain corruption, but the marked drop in electoral turnout hardly testified to a robust democracy. The party machines remained in the larger cities and the Teapot Dome Affair (and the collusion of many city governments with bootleggers) hardly suggested that corruption had been driven from politics. In any case, the political influence of business remained substantial and the various antitrust measures had patently failed to contain big business. A new consolidation movement was taking place in the 1920s, unhampered by the law, and the regulatory commissions were increasingly being staffed by members more responsive to the demands of big business than to the needs of the public. A marked increase in the number of bank suspensions in the 1920s did little to increase confidence in the new Federal Reserve system, which was evidently inadequate to withstand the strains placed upon it from 1929.

Prohibition had been enacted but was doing more to incite crime and corruption than to purify urban life. Women may have had the right to vote, but by the mid-1920s it was clear that there was no distinctive 'women's vote' pressing for social betterment and 'maternalist' reforms were being lost. The labour movement had sometimes acted as an auxiliary to progressive reform, but the union growth of the first two decades of the century had gone into reverse. Abroad too the Wilsonian vision of a new world order was in ruins. It is little wonder that many progressives retreated from public life in despair in the 1920s. As Leo Wolman, a labour economist, expressed it in 1927: 'Within less than a decade those who have faith in the uses of a controlled society have seen an elaborate structure of social control disintegrate before their very eyes.'

PART

II

THE NEW DEAL POLITICAL ORDER, 1933–69

|6|

The New Deal Order
1933–69

The political system that had first begun to take shape in the 1890s rapidly crumbled after 1929. The Stock Market Crash was not the only reason for the demise of the Progressive Order – which tottered on into the early 1930s – but it represented a body blow from which recovery was all but impossible. The modernization of the machinery of government undertaken in the previous three decades had proved insufficient to save the United States from economic catastrophe. The idea of a more positive government had in some measure been legitimized, but the particular instruments introduced had been found wanting. The popular dissatisfaction with the old political order became apparent in the mid-term elections of 1930, when the Republican Party lost its large majority in the House of Representatives, but a more spectacular meltdown for the Republicans came in 1932, when a sitting president was swept out of office by over 7 million votes and the Democrats won easy control of both houses of Congress. Immigrants, industrial workers and African-Americans were among those who contributed to this rout. A new political order was in the making.

When Franklin Roosevelt accepted the Democratic nomination for president he spoke of offering a 'New Deal' to the American people. Whatever he may have meant by the phrase, it soon became identified with the domestic policies of his administration. For the most part the electorate approved of those policies, for Roosevelt was to win the 1936 election with an even greater majority, although from about 1938 further reform legislation proved elusive. But the New Deal Order, as we might call it, long outlived the New Deal itself, for the political patterns that took shape in the 1930s broadly continued to characterize American politics until the late 1960s. To a significant degree it was initially fashioned for a political society characterized by a mass urban working class, and began to come apart when a largely suburban middle class won demographic ascendancy.

One feature of the New Deal Order was the electoral dominance of the Democratic Party, which became the normal party of government.

Another was the faith put in government, especially the federal government, to manage the affairs of society, a notably greater faith than the progressives had been able to muster. For the most part, too, it was American liberals who set the public agenda through the middle third of the twentieth century. This is not to suggest that they always had their way, for powerful conservative forces could often defeat them, but both major parties came to accept the need for a mixed economy and some measure of reform. There was broad acceptance that the state had a right to intervene in the economy with a view to protecting the weak and promoting opportunity for all. And the New Deal Order possessed other characteristics as well. The consensual values of the progressives tended to be displaced by a pluralist understanding of American politics. Groups previously allowed only a subordinate political status found that they had a voice, and governing bodies became less exclusively populated by high status Anglo-Americans. The Protestant moralism that had suffused the political realm in the early decades of the century was replaced by a more secular sensibility. The American political system seemed to have arrived in the twentieth century. (Yet in some respects the New Deal Order was an aberration – religious sentiments and distrust of big government surfaced again in the succeeding era.)

The New Deal Order was in large part the product of crisis conditions. The Great Depression was a major catalyst, politicizing some Americans, effecting an electoral realignment and obliging government to assume new responsibilities. The Second World War sustained the pressure on the federal government, and on the executive in particular, to assume a directing role in the nation's affairs, and the subsequent Cold War maintained these pressures, ensuring the continuing presence of a national security state. It is arguable that neither the first third (before 1929) nor the last third of the century witnessed crises for the United States of comparable magnitude. The later part of this era may have been a 'golden age' of affluence, but even the bounty to a large extent was the product of crisis conditions.

At the simplest level, the Democratic Party became the majority party. Between 1933 and 1969 a Democrat was in the White House for twenty-eight of those thirty-six years; only the popular war hero Dwight Eisenhower broke that Democratic monopoly. In the same period, the Democrats held majorities in both the House of Representatives and the Senate for all but four years (1947–8 and 1953–4). Throughout the era of the New Deal Order nearly twice as many Americans identified with the Democrats as with the Republicans. In October 1952, just before a Republican president was elected, 47 per cent of those polled described themselves as either 'strong' or 'weak' Democrats and only 27 per cent as Republicans, and the proportions did not change greatly before the late 1960s. This was the electoral heritage of Franklin Roosevelt.

The rules of the electoral game remained much as they had been left by the Progressive Era and they were not greatly revised in the middle decades of the century. Women, of course, had been enfranchised by constitutional amendment, and by the 1920s the direct primary was in operation in all but a few states (though primarily for state rather than presidential elections). But there was one significant change and that was the partial admission of Southern blacks to the political nation. In the 1930s only 2 or 3 per cent of Southern blacks were registered to vote, but pressures associated with the Second World War, the Cold War and an emerging civil rights movement forced concessions from the white South. By 1947 some 12 per cent of Southern blacks were on the electoral rolls and by 1960 the figure had edged up to 29 per cent, though only after the Voting Rights Act of 1965 did it pass 50 per cent. The principal electoral impact of this enfranchisement came a little later, and more important for the political process of the mid-twentieth century was the continued growth of black voters in the North as a consequence of the Great Migration.

There were also signs that American politics were becoming a little more popular. As we have seen, the electoral revisions of the progressive generation had tended to diminish the active electorate. In the presidential elections of 1920 and 1924 turnout had sunk to a little below 50 per cent of potential voters, and even in the emotionally charged election of 1928 it reached only 57 per cent. But during the New Deal Order turnout staged at least a partial recovery, reaching over 60 per cent in seven of the nine elections between 1936 and 1968, the high point being 65 per cent in 1960. The great crises dominating these years perhaps did something to bestir the electorate, although of greater impact may have been the closer competition between the parties. The revival of the Democratic Party meant that more balanced two-party systems emerged in several urban-industrial states. The greater competitiveness of the party system worked to the benefit of the Democrats, for whom low-income voters, encouraged by organized labour, turned out at relatively high rates. The enhanced mobilization of the electorate, however, did not survive the New Deal Order. After 1968 turnout fell again, particularly among the working classes.

The low-income voters who helped to sustain the long Democratic ascendancy were part of a resilient electoral coalition that formed under the aegis of Franklin Roosevelt. The New Deal coalition was not created overnight in 1932, but by the mid-1930s it had taken reasonably precise form. An important element was the urban working class, a high proportion of which consisted of those of recent immigrant stock, including many Southern and Eastern European Catholics, or 'ethnics' as they would be later called. The nation's big cities had once been firmly Republican, but in the 1920s the Democratic urban vote began to rise. In 1928, indeed, many immigrants cast their votes for the Catholic Al Smith, who won a slim plurality in the twelve largest cities. By 1936 the Democratic plurality in these cities was about double that enjoyed by the Republicans in 1920. These masses of new Democratic voters, many of them Catholic or Jewish, helped to impart to the New Deal Order its distinctive urban and pluralist character, particularly as small-town and middle-class Protestants in the North and West tended to revert to the Republicans. The urban working classes were a significant element in Harry Truman's surprise presidential victory in 1948.

In part this firming up of the Democratic urban vote was the work of organized labour, which in itself became a distinctive member of the New Deal coalition. In 1936 the newly formed Congress of Industrial Organizations (CIO), casting off the impartiality of the AFL, gave organizational support and generous funds to the Democrats. Also contributing to the consolidation of the urban vote were the city machines, most of which had rallied strongly to Roosevelt when they found that New Deal programmes provided them with a new source of patronage. The progressives had tried to limit the influence of the machines, but the New Deal gave them a new lease of life. Low-income voters naturally enough responded positively to New Deal programmes, not least African-Americans, who had traditionally voted Republican where they had been able to vote at all, but who in the course of the 1930s shifted massively to the Democrats. Probably over three-quarters of Northern blacks voted for Franklin Roosevelt in 1936, and most African-Americans thereafter remained loyal to the Democrats, an extraordinary 94 per cent voting for Lyndon Johnson in 1964. Another urban-ethnic group to be strongly attracted to the new Democratic coalition were Jews, more affluent than African-Americans and sometimes with the education and public experience that enabled them to be appointed to high positions in the administration. The Democrats had made the large cities their own.

It could also be argued that intellectuals were an important part of the New Deal coalition. They may have lacked a mass constituency, but they had some access to the policy-makers around the president, and the support that many academics, writers and artists gave to the New Deal coloured its image and served to enhance its legitimacy in the eyes of some. For the most part intellectuals too remained an identifiable part of this electoral coalition until some of them began to defect in the late 1960s and 1970s. The liberal policies of Democratic administrations from Franklin Roosevelt to Lyndon Johnson were in no small measure rooted in their support from organized labour, African-Americans, Jews and intellectuals.

There were some elements of the New Deal coalition that played a restraining role. Some support was secured from members of the business and financial communities, such as certain capital-intensive industrialists and international bankers, who were relatively unconcerned about the New Deal's pro-labour laws but were interested in its turn towards free trade. By embracing such prominent businessmen as Averill Harriman, the New Deal both broadened the base of its support while introducing a limit to its economic radicalism. Harriman was still serving Democratic presidents in the 1960s. Other Wall Street investment bankers were prominent in the Truman administration, while President Kennedy recruited a higher proportion of his appointees from the largest corporations than did his Republican predecessor. The liberalism espoused by the New Deal Order may have experienced periodic friction with the business community, but it was not directed against capitalism.

Also affecting the shape of the New Deal was an even more conservative constituency, the white South. The Democratic Party had long enjoyed a near monopoly in Southern politics, and as a result the Solid South wielded considerable electoral and congressional clout. The white South helped to sustain the Democrats' ascendancy in national politics, but there was a cost to pay, and several measures of the New Deal and later Democratic administrations had to be accommodated to the racially based sensitivities of Southern chieftains. Journalist Thomas Stokes described this Southern bloc in 1940 as 'the ball and chain which hobbled the Party's forward march'. The Wall Street bankers and the white Southerners in their very different ways served to blunt the enthusiasms of the New Deal coalition's more radical members.

The constituent elements of the New Deal coalition, to the degree that they more or less cohered for some three decades, were able to further a liberal political agenda in national politics, although there were always to be limits to its liberalism. The coalition also gave the Democratic Party its split personality, for in the post-war period its Southern wing became increasingly conservative as its Northern elements proved sympathetic to civil rights.

The strange bedfellows of the New Deal electoral coalition seemed less strange as American politics came to be viewed as a pluralist exercise, or, alternatively, as a form of interest group democracy. Whereas the earlier progressive vision had seemed to imply a high-minded élite governing in the public good, New Deal assumptions about government envisaged a reasonably fair competition between legitimate interests for access to public resources. In this view, America was not an organic society possessed of an identifiable and overarching common good. It was a pluralist society operating within the institutional framework of political democracy in which a range of groups and constituencies pursued their own interests through a process of conflict and accommodation. There was little room for Victorian morality in this materialist conception of a modern democracy and some old progressives became disenchanted with the new order.

In a pluralist world well-born Anglo-Americans were simply the first among equals. Franklin Roosevelt himself once famously began an address to the Daughters of the American Revolution with the words, 'Fellow immigrants'. In 1958 John Kennedy published a book entitled *A Nation of Immigrants*: 'every American who ever lived', he pointed out, with the exception of one group, 'was either an immigrant himself or descended from immigrants'. During the course of Franklin Roosevelt's administration it became clear that Wasps could no longer claim to be the undisputed governing class. Jews figured conspicuously in the coterie of advisers close to Roosevelt, among them Felix Frankfurter, whom Hugh Johnson once described as 'the most influential single individual in the United States'. Another Jew, Henry Morganthau Jr. filled the crucial post of secretary of the treasury for over eleven years. Catholics too were prominent in the administration. Two joined Roosevelt's first cabinet, while six times as many were appointed to the judiciary than had been the case under the Republican administrations of the 1920s. The rolls of senior and middle-rank federal appointments became festooned with names of Irish, German and Italian origin. Nor were they exclusively men. Roosevelt appointed the first woman to the cabinet, Frances Perkins as secretary of labor. Succeeding administrations broadly preserved this kind of diversity. In 1960, of course, a Catholic was finally elected president, and a few years later Lyndon Johnson was to manage an impressive pair of 'firsts' with the appointment of the first African-American to the cabinet and the first African-American to the Supreme Court. Wasps remained prominent in their membership of élite institutions, but their monopoly was broken.

Franklin Roosevelt once observed, 'I am a Christian and a Democrat'. Christian he was, but the New Deal regime lacked the sense of Protestant moralism that had pervaded the previous era. One of the first measures of the Roosevelt administration was the repeal of Prohibition, swiftly passed by Congress and ratified by the states – a major reversal for the evangelical cause. Historian of religion Sidney Ahlstrom has described repeal as 'the greatest blow to their pride and self-confidence that Protestants as a collective body had ever experienced'. It could also be seen as a reassertion of the old American principle of the separation of Church and State. Protestant periodicals preferred Republican to Democratic presidential candidates in the 1930s, and a poll of the clergy in 1936 revealed that over 70 per cent were opposed to the New Deal.

The secular nature of the New Deal Order was underlined by the disaffection of the religious right. A number of fundamentalist denominations enjoyed a revival and for the most part they were deeply hostile to the heritage of New Deal liberalism. For the first time in the 1930s a number of religious messiahs with a right-wing political agenda emerged to assail the dominant political regime. One was the Baptist Gerald B. Winrod, who denounced the 'Jewish New Deal', and another was the remarkable orator who ascended through the Disciples of Christ, Gerald L. K. Smith, who was even to make common cause with the Catholic 'radio priest' Charles E. Coughlin in denouncing the 'communistic' New Deal. These nativist and anti-Semitic movements were taking up arms against a regime they saw as subversive.

It is hardly surprising that the New Deal Order met with charges of subversion, given the access it allowed to an unwontedly broad array of economic and ethnic groups, but the same strategy meant that it had to secure itself on the principle of the separation of Church and State. The Almighty could never be repudiated of course, and as the United States became locked in a cold war with 'atheistic communism' there were attempts to impute religious values to the American political system. The association of patriotism with piety created a form of what has been called 'civil religion'. Thus in the 1950s the phrase 'In God We Trust' became the country's official motto and the words 'under God' were added to the Pledge of Allegiance.

Nonetheless these rituals remained ecumenical in style, as illustrated by President Eisenhower's revealing statement: 'Our government makes no sense unless it is founded on a deeply felt religious faith – and I don't care what it is.' Sectarian passions had faded sufficiently by 1960 to allow a Catholic to be elected president, and John Kennedy's success owed something to his powerful avowal of the principle of the separation of Church and State. The Supreme Court in the 1960s used that principle to reaffirm the primacy of secular values in the public realm, prohibiting the reading of the Bible and the recital of prayers in state schools. In a sense these decisions were of a piece with the New Deal's disavowal of Prohibition in 1933, and they were no more welcome to traditionalists. In the final third of the twentieth century religious and moral issues would again invade the political mainstream.

The secular state was also an activist state. What characterized the New Deal Order above all was an unusual degree of faith in government. As one prominent liberal, Albert Gore, first elected to Congress as a Roosevelt supporter and ultimately defeated during the Nixon presidency, expressed it at the end of his career: 'it had always seemed to me perfectly logical that government should play an active role in the nation's business affairs, and I had never lost faith in the government's ability to guarantee economic justice to all its people'. Americans have traditionally been suspicious of government, but in these years there was a widespread belief that government could deliver, especially among liberals. 'Better the occasional faults of a government living in the spirit of charity than the consistent omissions of a government frozen in the ice of its own indifference', said Franklin Roosevelt. 'This administration believes in doing the greatest good for the greatest number of people', intoned President Lyndon Johnson a generation later. Even a budget-conscious President Eisenhower was prepared to endorse massive public investment, as in the great scheme for building interstate highways and the money poured into higher education. Constrained by conservative local interests, many liberals put their faith in an enlightened national bureaucracy. While there had been growth in the regulatory functions of government during the Progressive Era, much of that regulation had been through semi-autonomous agencies; under and after the New Deal the state itself held much greater sway. As Franklin Roosevelt expressed it: 'The day of enlightened administration has come.'

One indicator of the growth of government was its cost. During the 1920s, after the boost imparted by the First World War, governmental budget expenditures at all levels (local, state and federal) had accounted for about 10 or 12 per cent of Gross National Product (GNP). The emergency of the 1930s thrust such expenditure up to 18 or 20 per cent, while the exigencies of the Second World War sent it yet higher. The return of peace allowed some reduction, but the Korean War and Cold War in the 1950s pushed the figure up again to a new record, between 25 and 30 per cent of GNP. Indeed, by this measure the government's role was to continue to rise in coming decades, largely because of growing Social Security payments, themselves a product of the New Deal. Another indicator of governmental activity is the number of government civilian employees as a proportion of the civilian labour force. In the 1920s this had been around 6 per cent, but the figure jumped to over 12 per cent in the 1930s, and was still around 10 to 12 per cent in the 1950s (eventually peaking in the mid-1970s). Broadly the new political system meant a rough doubling of the proportion of government employees. But more important than these crude figures was the growth in the middle decades of the century of governmental power in the management of the economy.

The New Deal Order placed an unusual faith (for an American regime) in economic and social planning. New Deal politics was not socialistic, and compared with several other industrial economies the formal role of government remained limited. The New Deal did not aim at the creation of a large state, in the sense of the state owning the means of production or employing a high proportion of the workforce. But the state assumed a major responsibility for the economic well-being and the social security of the citizenry. The function of modern government, explained Franklin Roosevelt, was 'to assist the development of an economic declaration of rights, an economic constitutional order'. In this perspective, the political constitution, with its emphasis on individual autonomy, was joined by a new economic constitution. The Social Security Act of 1935 began the process of putting a safety net under the mass of employed Americans. The Employment Act of 1946, while it drew back from a commitment to full employment, declared that it was 'the continuing policy and responsibility of the Federal Government to promote maximum employment, production and purchasing power'. In the early 1960s the economists of the Kennedy presidency were confident of their ability to 'fine-tune' the economy and maximize its productive capacity.

Within the governmental edifice, it was the role of the federal government that was most enhanced. The New Deal system promoted the centralization of policy-making in Washington. The crisis of the Depression forced the administration into a more active stance on policies for industry, agriculture, industrial relations, banking, housing and even regional development. The growth of the scope of the federal government left little room for local economic strategies. Broadly, government became committed to a national policy of managing economic demand, and even post-war Republican administrations were to accept the responsibility of the national state in this respect. Farmers, workers, poor regions and the unemployed would no longer be subject to the full rigour of the market; women and racial and ethnic minorities would also eventually be afforded some protection.

The federal government thus came to underwrite a number of important institutions in the polity. The New Deal extended the federal regulation of banking, made the Federal Reserve Board more responsive to the federal government, and introduced the federal guarantee of bank deposits. Such measures, as well as low-interest loans, implicated the government in the process of capital formation. It also became central to the regulation of industrial relations, the Wagner Act of 1935 making it, in effect, a sponsor of industrial unionism. The welfare system too became a permanent federal responsibility. In the 1960s, both because of Supreme Court decisions and legislation to protect black voting rights, local electoral arrangements became subject to federal supervision, making Washington the guarantor of the principle of 'one man, one vote'.

There was also some reshaping of American federalism. The New Deal initiated the kind of federal–state partnership represented by the system of federal grants-in-aid. With the onset of the Depression, the Hoover administration had been reluctant to supply the states with funds for unemployment relief, but the Federal Emergency Relief Administration in 1933 provided $500 million to distribute to the states, half as outright grants, half as matching funds (the state to supply the matching amount). A more permanent federal–state partnership was established by the Social Security Act which, among other things, provided that certain needy categories (such as blind people or dependent children) be supported by state and federal monies on the matching funds principle. In a variety of programmes established in the 1930s and later, the federal government developed as a major source of state government revenues. In certain respects this enhanced the authority of the federal government, extending its influence into new areas and enabling it to lay down conditions on which aid might be granted. On the other hand the system respected the autonomy of the states and perpetuated the decentralization of government intended by the Founding Fathers. State governments could determine their own degree of participation in a programme, and for this reason there were wide variations, for example, in the provision of 'welfare' from state to state.

In directing funds towards states and local governments, the New Deal system meant that the federal government was becoming a major source of patronage. A number of city machines were revitalized by the patronage opportunities afforded as they came to administer New Deal projects in their localities, and the programmes of the Great Society of the 1960s also provided rich patronage pickings. But there was a larger sense in which the nation state was becoming an extended exercise in government by patronage. Where the progressives had used the state to regulate private interests, New Dealers and their Great Society disciples used it to confer benefits. Consumers rather than producers became the focus of government attention. The unemployed who were dependent on relief, the farmers who looked for price supports, veterans who expected to be rewarded with benefits, the elderly who depended on the Social Security programme for their pensions and on Medicare for their health needs, universities that received funding for scientific research, students who sought federal grants and loans, labour which looked to government for legal protection – a wide array of constituencies became tied to the federal government in one way or another during the middle decades of the twentieth century. The demands of these constituencies tended to swell government further. According to one sociological theory, as groups develop vested interests in governmental programmes there is constant pressure to expand those programmes. While circumstances varied greatly between different kinds of constituencies, it seems clear that at least some federal programmes expanded over the decades in this way.

As government came to confer its benefits or protections, previously underprivileged groups organized to demand their share. In the Progressive Era, blacks had looked uncertainly to the courts to secure their rights. They still did so, but increasingly looked to the federal government itself, as when their threatened march on Washington in 1941 induced Franklin Roosevelt to issue Executive Order 8802 requiring the greater employment of blacks in government jobs and the defence industries, and when the civil rights demonstrations of the 1960s spurred presidents Kennedy and Johnson to ask for desegregation and voting rights laws. Before the second third of the twentieth century was over, women, gays and others were also mobilizing to demand greater recognition.

The growth of the national state as a great patronage machine also had an impact on party and Congress. While patronage could be dispensed with party objectives, the executive could also use it to circumvent traditional party organizations and build alternative alliances. In the conferment of benefits the New Deal was creating its own constituencies (and arguably undermining the old party structures). Yet it could not be sure of always controlling its new allies. Well-organized interests lobbied not only the White House but also Congress, and in particular the relevant congressional committees. This process fostered the so-called 'iron triangles'. A particular policy might be shaped by the interaction of three elements: the interest group pursuing the benefit, the congressional committee providing the funds or scrutinizing the rules and the government bureau administering the programme. A great deal of expertise often developed within these elements, and when a triangle agreed on a strategy even a president could have difficulty diverting it. In fact, policy formation was often a messy process, with a large and changing number of participants seeking a voice. But whether influence lay with 'iron triangles' or 'issue networks', Washington and the state capitals became hotbeds of lobbyists exerting their own distracting pressures on party leaders.

A belief in the efficacy of government was allied to a respect for authority of all kinds. The progressives had introduced experts to government and the cult of the expert continued to grow. Franklin Roosevelt had his 'brain trust', Harry Truman created the Council of Economic Advisers and President Eisenhower brought scientists into the White House. The Manhattan Project (which developed the atomic bomb) and the Second World War were important in showing that experts could produce in a crisis. To formulate his Great Society programmes Lyndon Johnson established task forces composed of leading academics. Economists, sociologists, psychologists, criminologists and others enjoyed an unusual influence over the policy-making process. In the view of some, intellectuals were co-opted by the state and readily served its purposes.

And within the federal government, it was the role of the president that was most visibly expanded. During the New Deal, it is said, the 'modern presidency' was created. Franklin Roosevelt by no means had everything his own way, but during these years the old model of the presidency as a sort of executive clerkship was supplanted by one in which executive leadership became institutionalized in a system of government in which the president was the pre-eminent figure. Roosevelt was unusually active in mobilizing congressional support for his programme, extending the use of unilateral power (such as by issuing executive orders) and developing a personal bureaucracy. The primacy of the White House was to be reinforced by World War and Cold War.

One sign of the changing shape of government was the transfer of the Bureau of the Budget from the Treasury to the White House in 1939. This was to give the president more control over designing the budget and signalled, in the words of political scientist Sidney Milkis, 'the development of the presidency, hitherto a modest office, into a full-blown institution'. In the same move Roosevelt created the Executive Office of the President, an attempt to distance himself from congressional supervision. Previously he had been able to employ only four administrative assistants; by 1945 there were eleven, including the first chief of staff. This vesting of administrative tools in the hands of the president continued in the post-war period. In 1946 the Council of Economic Advisers was created to assist in the formulation of fiscal policy, and in 1947 the National Security Council was added to strengthen the president's command of foreign policy. In 1959 the Office of Science and Technology Policy was formed, and in 1964 the Office of Economic Opportunity followed (which was to be closed by Richard Nixon, though in 1969 he did create the Council on Environmental Quality). As the president thus gradually acquired an administrative apparatus of several hundred staffers directly accountable to him, he might hope to exercise greater control over the making and execution of policy. There were, of course, dangers as well as advantages in the expansion of an independent presidential power, as the Watergate and Iran-Contra affairs were later to demonstrate.

The presidency was not alone as an active player in the polity. In the early years of the New Deal the Supreme Court took action of a negative kind, striking down much of Franklin Roosevelt's innovative use of governmental power in combating the Depression. This situation changed after Roosevelt's celebrated confrontation with the Court in 1937 (discussed in Chapter 8). Thereafter he was able to appoint as many as nine justices of his own choosing, and the Court abandoned its attempts to keep the federal government out of economic life. But, partly thanks to appointments made by President Eisenhower in the 1950s, most notably Earl Warren as chief justice and William Brennan as associate justice, in the later years of the New Deal Order the Court displayed a renewed activism, this time in a liberal direction, a position it maintained for a few years after 1969 when Warren Burger became chief justice. In the two decades from 1954 the Court became a major author of public policy, most notably in school desegregation, the reapportionment of electoral districts (ensuring that they more fairly reflected the distribution of population), the overhaul of the criminal justice system (so that the rights of alleged offenders were more fully recognized), the liberalization of obscenity laws, the banning of religious exercises in state schools and the establishment of abortion rights. According to law professor Martin Shapiro: 'The Warren Court and the early Burger Court confirmed the New Deal stance of the 1930s that constitutional rights were for members of the New Deal coalition (that is, the poor, minorities, government employees, and intellectuals) and not for the New Deal's enemies (that is, the business community and the propertied).'

The ascendancy of the Democratic Party and its association with the state meant the promotion of a liberal political ideology. National liberalism to a large extent became focused on the presidency, and tended to be encouraged by the policy experts and other specialists who offered their advice to the White House. Often liberal presidents, such as Franklin Roosevelt in the late 1930s, Harry Truman for much of his term, and John Kennedy, found themselves at odds with Congress, and liberal measures were extracted with difficulty. But liberals set the agenda. The definition of liberalism itself subtly evolved in the course of the New Deal Order. In the early years it was largely associated with a modest restructuring of the economy, attacks on unemployment and sympathy for organized labour. By the post-war period it was associated with offering access to an expansive economy to everyone and extensions of rights.

A broadly liberal stance characterized these years partly because at the heart of New Deal politics was a partnership with organized labour. Though the marriage between the Roosevelt administration and the unions was slow to effect and hardly a model of harmony, by 1935 it formed the basis of a liberal style of politics. From 1936 the CIO provided the Democratic Party with organization and money. In the post-war period, there were usually 300 or 400 union members at Democratic national conventions, while the Republicans typically mustered no more than a dozen. The Democratic administrations for their part provided some protection for labour, stabilizing industrial relations and offering a modest welfare state, as they also supported policies designed to incorporate wage-earners and their families into the consumer economy.

Organized labour and other New Deal constituencies also benefited by the foreign economic policies of the United States. The decision to come off the gold standard in 1933 to an extent protected the domestic economy, as did the international monetary system arising from the Bretton Woods Conference in 1944, when foreign currencies were pegged in value to the dollar. Largely because other countries were prepared to deal in dollars, the United States now enjoyed an unusual degree of autonomy in relation to its domestic economy, and compared to Europe was able to maintain relatively low interest rates. With the dollar a universal reserve currency, at a time when countries rebuilding their economies wanted dollars, there was relatively little pressure on the American government to contract the domestic economy to correct balance-of-payments deficits, a situation that was to come to an end in 1971. Once the Second World War had lifted the United States out of depression, the New Deal Order allowed consumers to luxuriate in an unprecedented affluence.

Yet, compared to many other industrial states, the scope of American government was not especially pervasive. The New Deal showed little interest in public ownership or other forms of what Europeans would recognize as socialism. Major industries were not nationalized, and the American welfare state remained a patchwork affair, a 'semi-welfare' state by international standards. Indeed, even during Roosevelt's administration federal policy tended to move away from restructuring capitalism and towards sustaining a consumer society. 'We stand on the threshold of an economy of abundance', said the National Resources Planning Board in 1943, 'this generation has it within its power not only to produce in plenty but to distribute that plenty.' By this date New Deal liberalism was posited on an expanding economy, in which government would see to it that demand was sustained and that individuals were provided with security and equality of opportunity.

For the most part too, this liberal vision was not a parochial one. Liberal Democrats typically wanted to make the world a better place. While during the dark days of 1933 Franklin Roosevelt undermined the London Economic Conference, which had hoped to rescue the global economy, by 1934 he was taking a more internationalist stance in foreign economic policy. Roosevelt was obliged to bow to isolationist pressures for neutrality legislation in the mid-1930s, to keep the United States free from dangerous foreign entanglements, but he signed the measures unenthusiastically and by the late 1930s was seeking to circumvent them. The Second World War, of course, precipitated the United States onto the world stage, and it played a major role in restructuring the post-war world in keeping with the values of liberal capitalism. The Marshall Plan, which provided financial support for Western European economies, could be seen as an extension of the principles of the New Deal abroad, as could the various foreign aid programmes of the 1950s and 1960s.

The assumption of a major international role by the United States added greatly to the authority of Washington. With the onset of the Cold War, the New Deal state was augmented by the national security state. But this internationalist stance was also to contribute to the undermining of the New Deal Order. The eventual humiliation of the United States in the jungles of Vietnam exposed the limits of American power and fostered distrust in government, particularly as exercised by the Democratic Party. But demographic, economic and social changes at home also chipped away at the foundations of the New Deal system of politics. The replacement of depression by a long period of prosperity turned many of the beneficiaries of the New Deal into middle-class taxpayers, sensitive to the costs as well as the benefits of government. Affluence also eased the way of new issues onto the political agenda, as quality of life, cultural and lifestyle concerns came to jostle with those relating to economics and welfare. The eruption of the civil rights movement, made possible in part by the combination of prosperity, demographic change and Cold War influences, ruthlessly exposed the split personality of the Democratic Party. In these conditions Franklin Roosevelt's electoral coalition, which had underpinned American politics for over a generation, could not be sustained. By the late 1960s the New Deal Order was unravelling.

|7|

Workers and Women
1933–69

During the early years of the twentieth century women's groups had rivalled and sometimes surpassed organized labour in the influence exerted on public policy. Neither women nor workers had succeeded in making themselves into major players in the polity, but the former had fashioned a distinctive role that owed something to the relative weakness of labour. But the middle decades of the century witnessed a species of role reversal. Finally the labour movement emerged as a major political force while the gains made by the 'first wave' feminists proved largely illusory. This dichotomy should not be exaggerated, since women joined trade unions themselves and New Deal legislation facilitated the organization of unskilled women workers. Yet in some respects the New Deal Order was even more of a man's world than the Progressive Order it replaced.

The new influence of labour was partly a question of numbers. The union movement revived in the 1930s and by 1945, encompassing some 35 per cent of the non-farm workforce, was fielding big battalions. Thereafter its size began to erode as service industries and white-collar occupations grew faster than the old smokestack sectors of the economy, but the figure was still 27 per cent in 1970. During the Progressive Era the proportion of the industrial workforce enrolled in unions had peaked at a little under 20 per cent; in 1990 the figure would be down again to 16 per cent. It was in the middle decades of the twentieth century that organized labour was at its most formidable and it was then too that it penetrated high political councils. Much of the labour movement aligned itself with the Democratic Party, which served both to empower labour and reinforce the commitment of the Democrats to a liberal agenda. At the same time the movement was obliged to accept the constraints imposed on it by its allies. Harassed by the courts for so long, organized labour became enmeshed in a regulatory if protective framework as government assumed responsibility for ordering industrial relations. In addition to the federally approved collective bargaining system, this informal compact at the centre of the New Deal Order included state-subsidized economic growth and a social security system.

In the early years of the Great Depression, as employers savagely retrenched, organized labour was in retreat once more. But then the movement spectacularly revived. Between 1932 and 1939 union membership roughly trebled, from under 3 million to nearly 9 million. By 1945 over 14.3 million American workers were unionized, a quite extraordinary advance on 1932. This represented a level of organization unknown in the United States and comparable to that of Northern Europe. For the most part, in contrast to the aftermath of the First World War, these unions were largely able to withstand the post-war anti-labour reaction. And they reached into new parts of the economy. Previously unions had been concentrated mostly in construction, the railroads, mining and the needle trades, while manufacturing was largely untouched. Now there was an explosion of organizing in such vital mass-production industries as iron and steel, electrical goods and automobiles. And many unskilled and semi-skilled workers organized for the first time, in what were known as the new industrial unions, in contrast to the traditional craft unions of the AFL. The industrial unions aimed to enrol all the workers in a particular factory, whatever their job or craft.

The New Deal's first overture to the unions came in the National Industrial Recovery Act of June 1933, Section 7a holding out the prospect of collective bargaining as a right. Labour organizers soon told workers that 'the President wants you to join'. Great unionizing drives took off, and by October the AFL's William Green was claiming 1.5 million new members. But as employers resisted labour demands industrial conflict grew. By 1934 a major strike wave threatened the government's strategy; there were bitter disputes on the San Francisco waterfront, in Minneapolis and among textile workers in New England and the South. These violent confrontations left residues of dead bodies, mostly of strikers or pickets shot down by police bullets. The craft-oriented AFL was powerless to defend these workers, as was the National Labor Board under Senator Robert Wagner, established in 1933 to try to restore industrial peace. Wagner and his associates began to explore new ways of ordering industrial relations.

The Wagner Act of 1935 signalled the new orientation of American labour. It was essentially the work of the urban liberal Senator Robert Wagner of New York and his industrial relations advisers. It was fashioned not so much by labour (nor by employers) as by politicians, bureaucrats and labour relations specialists, and what gave them their opportunity was the Supreme Court's destruction of the National Industrial Recovery Act in 1935 (and with it Section 7a).

The new act was based on the bold premise that collective bargaining could avert strikes and other forms of industrial disruption. Managers and workers were to be obliged to negotiate together. The act banned company unions and certain unfair employer practices; workers could themselves choose which union would represent them, in elections administered by the National

Labor Relations Board (NLRB). Employers could no longer safely ignore or undermine unions, and workers were guaranteed specified rights. The NLRB, for example, could order the reinstatement of an unfairly dismissed worker. The unions, their legal status powerfully enhanced, could now take on the major corporations and hope to win. The Wagner Act thus shifted the focus of labour conflict away from violent confrontation at the picket lines and towards the hearing rooms of the Labor Relations boards. As Melvyn Dubofsky has expressed it, the measure transformed unions 'from private, voluntary organizations into quasi-public institutions charged with implementing aspects of public policy'. Further, the Wagner Act aimed more generally at industrial recovery based on an expanding mass consumption. If unions could be strengthened, they would keep up wage rates, and hence there would be more consumer purchasing power in the economy.

The Wagner Act aided union recruitment though there were growing pains. The growth of the militant industrial unions threatened the traditional hold of the conservative craft unions over the AFL. In 1936 the industrial unions broke away to form the separate Congress of Industrial Organizations (CIO), which forged ahead with its own drive, and in the 1936 election threw its weight behind Franklin Roosevelt. For the first time in its history, the Democratic Party received heavy financial aid from labour groups. John L. Lewis also helped to form Labor's Non-Partisan League, a kind of popular front organization active on Roosevelt's behalf in several industrial states. It held rallies in major cities, mounted nightly radio broadcasts and expended much energy in getting workers to the polls. Such labour assistance would become a familiar feature of Democratic campaigns through the era of the New Deal Order.

In 1937 the CIO demonstrated its muscle by winning stunning victories in the automobile and steel industries, which had repeatedly beaten back attempts to unionize. At the end of 1936 the Union of Automobile Workers (UAW) forced General Motors (GM) to shut down, in the highly publicized sit-down strike centring on Flint. In previous eras troops might have been sent in to break the strike, but in this instance the New Dealers in both federal and state governments made it clear that this weapon was no longer at the disposal of capital. In February the GM giant surrendered and agreed a contract. A few weeks later US Steel also capitulated. The victories over these two giant corporations touched off a wave of mass organization of unusual intensity.

Industrial unionism thus became a dynamic force in the late 1930s, sweeping up millions of mass production workers. The CIO unions took the lead in recruiting African-Americans, sometimes becoming assertive champions of their rights, and also succeeded in enrolling many immigrants. Further, unlike the AFL, the CIO unions admitted Communists, realizing that they often made good organizers. By November 1937 the CIO claimed over 4 million members and its leaders boasted that 'We are the dominant labor force in this nation'. But the AFL energetically expanded its own membership.

The labour movement even found a friend of a kind in the Supreme Court, which by the late 1930s (and in the aftermath of the 'court-packing' crisis discussed in Chapter 8) usually sustained the Wagner Act and the authority of the NLRB.

The extraordinary union growth of these years reflected a measure of class consciousness. The CIO had helped to politicize many workers, particularly ethnic workers, for the first time. They were weaned from their old neighbourhood and ethnic attachments and recruited into national unions and a national political party. A variety of influences had heightened a sense of worker commonality: the sheer hardships of the Depression, the spread of a common popular culture spearheaded by the radio and movies, the erosion of skill differences on the shop floor with increasing mechanization. Such shared economic and cultural experiences helped to promote a common working-class consciousness and spurred workers to join unions and vote for Franklin Roosevelt. Unlike workers in several European countries, they turned to an existing major party, not wishing to destroy the capitalist system but to redistribute a measure of power within it. Government and unions, they hoped, might constrain the corporations and win a better deal for labour. Yet, as Samuel Gompers had feared, in becoming part of the political order, unions risked evolving into defenders of the status quo.

Nevertheless the framework provided by the Wagner Act was there to stay, and meant that American industrial relations evolved in the direction of collaboration between modern management and centralized unions. The experiences of the Second World War abetted this process. Industrial firms anxious for defence contracts recognized unions and huge numbers of the formerly unemployed joined unions as they found work. While the government co-opted businessmen to run many of the wartime programmes, labour was also accorded a role, as in the National War Labor Board (NWLB), on which business, organized labour and government each had equal membership. Despite massive coal strikes in 1943, most unions worked hard for the war effort, in particular in trying to avert disruptions in the defence industries, promoting a 'no strike' pledge and accepting wage controls. The NWLB itself tended to push for more clearly formulated grievance procedures, so that disputes would be resolved through bureaucratic rather than industrial action. The state both protected labour and restrained it. The war, with its consequent return of full employment and a government anxious to maintain production, enabled the industrial unions to root themselves firmly in America's political economy.

With the ending of the war the prospect of industrial conflict loomed once more. Rather as in the First World War, both labour and capital had each wrung certain benefits from the crisis. The prominence of businessmen in the war effort had gone a long way to redeeming the corporate image, while the unions emerged boasting more members than ever. Business fretted not only over the Wagner Act but also the wartime concessions to labour, while the labour movement was anxious to cast off the wartime constraints, notably the no strike pledge, and to secure protection from the insistent inflation and anticipated job losses. In the six months from September 1945, a record number of American workers went on strike. Yet this great wave of industrial conflict differed from that of earlier periods, being largely free of the kind of violence traditionally seen. J. B. S. Hardman, a union official party to the labour experiences after both world wars, observed: 'One was determined and ruthless, the other circumspect and mindful of a kind of "protocol" of civilized behavior.' The authorities and employers themselves for the most part respected the rights unions had won under the New Deal. Little use was made of injunctions or strike-breakers, and the NLRB was prominent in trying to resolve these conflicts. The industrial relations innovations of the New Deal may not have averted strikes, but they made them more orderly affairs.

Some labour activists even hoped to expand the role of labour in America's political economy. In 1944 the CIO's Philip Murray remarked that: 'It is a new departure for American labor to lead ... a national movement devoted to the general welfare just as much as to the particular interests of labor groups.' Progressive CIO leaders seemed to contemplate some kind of corporatist management of the economy, rather as the NWLB – with its equal representation for management, labour and government – had helped to ease the economy through the war. The UAW strike at GM in 1945–6 demonstrated an ambitious objective. UAW leader Walter Reuther demanded a 30 per cent wage increase without any compensating rise in car prices, and also a 'look at the books' to show that the company could afford it. This was indignantly rejected as an infringement of managerial prerogatives. 'We don't even let our stockholders look at the books', riposted one executive.

After a protracted strike, GM succeeded in facing Reuther down. The books remained closed and the UAW had to settle for a more modest wage increase. Yet Reuther was not alone in his quest for a voice in management. As the novel phenomenon of collective bargaining had taken firmer hold during the war, contracts began to touch on areas previously the preserve of management. A survey of senior executives in 1945–6 uncovered a fear that the collective bargaining process would 'eventually culminate in such stringent impairment of management's freedom that it will not be able to do its job satisfactorily'. A primary concern of management at this juncture, as historian Howell Harris has shown, was to restore 'the right to manage', that is to limit labour's ability to control the shop floor. Broadly business succeeded in upholding managerial rights, but the unions for their part generally won significant wage increases. Thereafter such unions as the UAW abandoned their interest in restructuring the American political economy. Many employers for their part perceived advantages in dealing with the union leaders. Managers and union leaders would bargain face to face, often fiercely, but once a deal had been struck the union leaders would be expected to deliver their members. In return for higher wages, employers could expect stability on the shop floor.

The corporations' reclamation of management prerogatives was furthered by the reactionary 80th Congress, elected in the sour aftermath of the post-war strike wave. In 1947 the conservative bloc pushed through the Taft-Hartley Act over a presidential veto, with the objective of restoring the balance in industrial relations that the Wagner Act had allegedly tipped to labour. According to Senator Robert A. Taft, the act 'simply reduces special privileges granted to labor union leaders'. Where the Wagner Act had outlawed a list of unfair practices by employers, the Taft-Hartley Act extended the same principle to unions. Among other things, it prohibited a number of labour practices (like mass picketing and secondary boycotts), banned the closed shop (under which union members only could be hired) and required affidavits disavowing the Communist Party from union officers wishing to make use of NLRB procedures. The act cramped organized labour, which did not sustain its remarkable wartime expansion, but was not an all-out assault on it. The right to collective bargaining remained in place, as did the NLRB itself, reshaped arguably as a neutral referee.

As industrial relations became characterized by a regular bargaining process between corporate and union leaders, the bitter warfare of the 1930s receded into the past. An important milestone was the GM-UAW contract of 1950, which set a five-year term, improved cost-of-living adjustments (COLA) and wage increases and provided a pension system. In 1951 *Fortune* magazine described this collective bargaining system as a distinctively 'American' solution to the 'problems of class struggle and proletarian consciousness'. The steady work, high wages and fringe benefits that workers experienced in the post-war years enhanced their sense of security and admitted them more fully to the culture of the consumer society. Labour officials pointed to the contribution that high wages made to consumer purchasing power (and in emphasizing the economic value of a decent 'family wage' reinforced the primacy of the male wage-earner in the New Deal Order). Over half of major union contracts recognized the COLA principle by the early 1960s and 90 per cent featured a grievance-arbitration procedure, representing the consummation of what labour historian David Brody has called a 'workplace rule of law'.

As strong unions developed within a legal structure they also forged yet closer links with the Democratic Party. During the war, anxious to fend off a conservative revival, CIO leaders created the CIO-Political Action Committee (CIO-PAC), which proved its worth in the 1944 election in raising funds and mobilizing workers' votes for Roosevelt. With the advent of the Cold War and the growing perception of American radicals as agents of the Soviet Union, the CIO leadership became uncomfortable with the presence of the Communist members. Many ethnic (and Catholic) members of the CIO unions themselves developed an ardent anti-communism following the Soviet expansion into much of Eastern Europe. Further, it was clear that repeal of the hated Taft-Hartley Act would depend on powerful advocates in Congress and the White House. Only the Democrats seemed likely to furnish such allies, and the CIO leaders had powerful reasons both to disavow the Communist elements and to emphasize their loyalty to this major party.

A few radicals did break with the Truman administration in 1948 and launched a campaign for Henry A. Wallace (an ardent New Dealer and Franklin Roosevelt's former vice-president) for president as the candidate of the Progressive Party, but these defections were small. The Marshall Plan, offering aid to reconstruct the economies of post-war Europe, had its attractions for CIO leaders, with its promise of markets abroad and jobs at home. CIO president Philip Murray dismissed pro-communists from his staff and the CIO-PAC poured over $1 million into Democratic campaigns. When a few union officials nonetheless defected to Wallace, the CIO leadership concluded that the time had come to purge them. 'We can no longer tolerate within the family of CIO the Communist Party masquerading as a labor union', the CIO explained in 1949. In 1949–50 the CIO expelled eleven Communist-oriented unions.

By this date both the AFL and the CIO were regularly pronouncing on foreign as well as domestic policy issues. The AFL was an early enthusiast for American Cold War policies. The CIO was slower to endorse the thrust of the Truman administration's foreign policy, but the unveiling of the Marshall Plan made accommodation easier. In 1949 the AFL and the CIO cooperated in helping to found the International Confederation of Free Trade Unions as a counterpoise to communist-led unionism abroad. The unions and government worked together on the foreign front, the unions helping to sell government policies like Marshall Aid to European workers.

Domestic circumstances too were increasing the pressure on the unions to eschew radical experiments. The Wallace candidature performed disastrously at the polls in 1948, the débâcle demonstrating the futility of third party politics, and it became the objective of organized labour not to capture the Democratic Party but to make it reflective of the broad interests of American workers. 'The labour movement', said Walter Reuther on one occasion, 'can only be effective if it becomes less an economic movement and more a social movement.' The unions hankered after the repeal of the Taft-Hartley Act. The AFL, traditionally cautious about political activity, set up Labor's League for Political Education (LLPE) to campaign for this, and the CIO's Political Action Committee gave its usual support to the Democratic Party in the 1948 and 1952 elections. The AFL too finally endorsed the Democratic presidential candidate in 1952. The politicization of the AFL and the deradicalization of the CIO opened the way for a reunion of the two. In 1955 they became the merged AFL-CIO. Its first president, George Meany, made clear its philosophy: 'We do not seek to recast American society in any particular doctrinaire or ideological image. We seek an ever rising standard of living', by which he meant '… not only more money but more leisure and richer cultural life.' It had become even clearer that the unions were not seeking to subvert capitalism but to improve it, in particular in securing a fairer share of its benefits for the lower middle and working classes. Like other elements of the New Deal coalition, organized labour was embracing the creed of commercial Keynesianism.

By this date many workers were enjoying longer and paid vacations and a range of fringe benefits, such as life insurance, health and pension schemes (some provided by the unions themselves). In most other advanced economies, the state eased life for its citizens by developing forms of welfare. In the United States unions and employers were tending to plug the welfare gap, developing a distinctive American style of humanizing an industrial economy. Further, the labour movement constituted a major lobby for a range of social policies, such as extending the coverage of the Social Security Act. Together, the varied benefits provided by the federal and state authorities, by the unions themselves and by employers, meant that Americans enjoyed a degree of economic security never before known.

Or at least some of them did. In 1955, after all, around two-thirds of American workers were not unionized, and hazards persisted for those who did not belong to the well-organized core of the working class. The notion that economic growth supplemented by a range of social policies would raise many wage-earners to the middle class proved something of an illusion. While the material conditions of life for many did improve, economic reverses still meant layoffs. For the many workers in non-union firms there was virtually no protection against arbitrary dismissal. Rancour at poor working conditions and unfair pay scales contributed to a relatively high level of wildcat strikes in the 1950s and 1960s, and the decentralized nature of collective bargaining – firm by firm – reinforced the differentiation in rewards. The diversified patchwork of public and private provision in the United States meant that workers' experiences varied enormously. The powerful UAW in the prospering automobile industry could win generous rewards for its members. Unorganized workers in marginal industries might at best hope to hang on to their precarious jobs and pittance wages, especially in the South, where state legislation and employer hostility weakened organizing efforts.

The new relationship between capital and labour was not without other costs. As collective bargaining became ever more complex, so did the organizational structures of the unions, and power increasingly came to rest with the centre. The scale of this bureaucracy exceeded that of other countries with higher proportions of union members. By 1962 there was one full-time union official for every 300 workers; in Britain the ratio was one in 2000. A union headquarters could seem remote to ordinary workers, and occasionally union officials developed overly cosy relationships with corporate executives. The large funds that some unions controlled also carried temptations. The use of pension funds by Jimmy Hoffa, president of the International Brotherhood of Teamsters, and his suspected links with organized crime, prompted a number of investigations. The unfavourable image given to labour by exposures of union racketeering eased the passage of the Landrum-Griffin Act of 1959, although Democrats in Congress ensured that it was not too unpalatable to their labour allies. The law offered union members certain protections against their officers, obliged unions to hold regular elections and required them to make their financial arrangements more transparent.

In buying into the values of the consumer society organized labour did not lose its role as a potent force for liberal reform within the New Deal Order. The CIO-PAC and the LLPE were replaced by the Committee for Political Education (COPE). With a nationwide structure, COPE developed sophisticated campaign techniques and enlisted a huge number of volunteers at election times, becoming closely linked to the Democrats in several states. Kennedy's narrow victory in 1960, when he carried most of the industrial states, was owed in part to the labour vote in the cities. This labour energy contributed to the ascendancy of liberals in the Democratic Party. The AFL-CIO lent its weight to various Kennedy administration measures, such as area redevelopment and manpower training, as it also supported its civil rights initiative of 1963. When the Republicans nominated the right-wing Barry Goldwater for president in 1964, labour activity for Democratic and liberal candidates redoubled. In the new Congress labour believed that it had sixty 'friends' in the Senate and 248 in the House, and its support was vital to Lyndon Johnson's reform administration. Even as late as 1968, when enthusiasm for the Great Society was waning, labour support helped to secure the largest enhancement to date in Social Security benefits.

As David Brody has suggested, organized labour was more successful in securing broad reform objectives as part of the Democratic coalition than it was in defending the narrow interests of unions, as when it failed to avert the Landrum-Griffin Act or to secure the repeal of Taft-Hartley. Karen Orren has also demonstrated its key role in the shaping of domestic policy in the post-war decades. The British political scientist Vivian Vale summed up the position of labour in American politics in 1971:

> It cannot buck the political tide in any election, but in close and uncertain races it can provide the margin of victory. To retain this degree of political significance it must for the foreseeable future preserve its special relationship with the Democratic Party. As a pressure group it must seek coalitions, and the most congenial allies are usually to be found among small liberal groups outside the purely industrial arena. These circumstances oblige union leaders in the political sphere to commit themselves to a vastly wider concept of the obligations of unionism than in the merely economic. In so doing they and their followers can constitute by far the largest and most stable body supporting liberal causes in the United States today.

The commitment of organized labour to a broad agenda of economic and social reform, and its identification with the liberal wing of the Democratic Party, meant that it was more than the narrow interest group that it has sometimes been depicted as. Yet Vale's description was ceasing to apply even as it was being written, for by this date the New Deal Order was crumbling.

By 1970 the unionized proportion of the non-farm workforce had slipped. The union leadership also found it more difficult to maintain discipline.

Younger workers in the late 1960s, perhaps infected by the protest movements of the era, seemed to chafe at the old union establishment. While the CIO in the past had supported the causes of black and female Americans, and while the AFL-CIO loyally continued to press a liberal agenda on the Democratic Party, the social upheavals of the 1960s brought other actors to the fore. Increasingly a large part of organized labour seemed at odds with the reform spirit of the day.

One source of strain was African-American militancy. Although unions were better integrated than almost any other major institution in American public life, black activists had no difficulty in identifying evidence of discrimination, even in the UAW with its celebrated liberal leadership. Blacks represented over a quarter of AFL-CIO members in the early 1960s, but very few held senior positions. In Detroit in the late 1960s black workers were in virtually open rebellion against the UAW leadership, despite its proud record of progressivism. From this turmoil emerged several black workers councils, most notably DRUM (Dodge Revolutionary Union Movement). Such racial tensions weakened organized labour as well as the larger Democratic electoral coalition. The Vietnam War proved even more disruptive. As protests mounted against the Vietnam policy of the Johnson administration, the AFL-CIO remained wedded to its Cold War ideology, resolutely supporting the American military commitment. The old reform coalitions fractured. The Americans for Democratic Action, for years closely associated with labour in the broad reform front, came out against Johnson's Vietnam policy, and in 1968 the UAW walked out of the AFL-CIO, accusing it of 'failing in the broad social responsibilities it has to the total community of America'. American liberalism was coming apart, and organized labour seemed increasingly to stand for an outmoded agenda. The AFL-CIO threw itself behind Democratic presidential candidate Hubert Humphrey in 1968, but he had lost the confidence of many anti-war liberals. As left-wing Democrats sought to gain control of the party in the convulsions after 1968, the labour establishment distanced itself from them. When the insurgent candidate George McGovern won the Democratic nomination in 1972, the AFL-CIO broke with tradition by refusing to endorse him.

As organized labour became estranged from other progressive constituencies, it came to assume more the character of an interest group, concerned only with its own well-being. There was no longer a range of reforms on which liberals could agree, and it became increasingly difficult for the unions to identify their cause with the general interest. The growth of public sector unionism and its increasing militancy also served to make organized labour appear self-serving. A strike of teachers or garbage collectors seemed to make labour an enemy rather than an ally of the public interest or American consumers. As the evolution of a 'post-industrial' economy eroded the number of union members, as the protest movements of the sixties introduced their own strains into the labour movement, and as racial and foreign policy issues undermined the larger New Deal Order, the heyday of organized labour in

American politics came to an end. The alliance with the Democratic Party remained, although its value was now questionable, exposing the Democrats to the charge of being the party of 'special interests'.

While labour became intimately intertwined with the New Deal Order, women for the most part remained little more than spectators, although some did help to bring it into being. What is striking about the middle decades of the twentieth century is that women were unable to capitalize on their earlier achievements. In the Progressive Order women had been extraordinarily active in benevolent activity and were largely responsible for the hesitant emergence of a 'maternalist' welfare state. Through the Children's and Women's Bureaus they had exerted a degree of influence in the federal government, and their domination of certain areas had given them a voice in public affairs – a subordinate one, but distinctive. During the years of the New Deal Order, however, women's benevolent empire lost its cohesion, and while enough of the network survived to have some access to government, there were fewer spheres which women could claim as their preserve. Once welfare policy became central to government, men tended to take the reins. The American welfare state, limited though it was, lost its maternalist cast and was reshaped to serve the priorities of men, not least the industrial unionists aligned with the Democratic Party. While more women joined the labour market, for the most part they were used as a pool of reserve labour and very few reached beyond the lower grades of jobs. In the 1960s the feminist movement did revive, in large part a product of the frustrations of women with these constraints.

American women had entered the twentieth century among the best educated in the world, which helps to account for their early success, but this advantage tended to slip away as time moved on, partly because of government policy. In 1930 the proportion of men and women in the age group twenty-four to twenty-nine who had completed at least one year of college was the same (12 and 13 per cent respectively); by 1965 a remarkable gap had opened up, the figures being 31 per cent for men and 22 per cent for women. The absolute number of women in college had grown with the steady expansion of higher education, but the number of men at college had risen much faster, not least because of the generous educational grants accorded to Second World War veterans. Hardly surprisingly, it was men who reaped the advantage in the growing professional occupations. The proportion of employed women in professional jobs hardly increased in the forty years after 1930, but the corresponding figure for male professionals jumped by nearly 40 per cent. There were very few women in the higher paid professions during the entire era of the New Deal Order.

The enfranchisement of women had not empowered them after all. It had become clear by the mid-1920s that women did not vote as a bloc, and politicians had begun to ignore them for electoral purposes. A few women entered politics, but too few to exert much influence. The number of women in Congress increased from one in 1919 to nine in 1929. But the number was still nine in 1939 and only eleven in 1969.

The acquisition of the vote also had no discernible effect on women's employment patterns. The proportion of women going out to work rose slowly to over a quarter between the two world wars (many women remarkably found jobs during the Depression), and after 1940 increased more markedly. By 1960 the figure was 35 per cent and by 1970 nearly 42 per cent. The great surge of women onto the labour market thus resumed with the Second World War, and the advent of the Cold War helped to sustain it. Women were the solution to the labour shortage of a resurgent and expanding economy; they saw advantages for themselves and their families in employment. Further, the sort of woman at work was changing. In 1930 barely 12 per cent of wives held jobs, but the figure soared to 40 per cent by 1970, and most of the new recruits were white. At the beginning of the period, the 'typical' female worker was either young, white and single – a working-class 'girl' – or African, Mexican or Asian American. At the end of it most working women were white and married and many were middle class.

Perhaps female employment would have increased at a faster rate earlier had it not been for the Depression, when public opinion endorsed barring wives from jobs if their husbands were in work. Nonetheless more women did secure employment then, and they fought for themselves too in the bodies being revitalized by men, the industrial unions. When these gathered up the great armies of the unskilled and semi-skilled they encountered many women. While male workers often expected priority in benefits, the CIO unions enrolled more female members and a few, like the UAW, which supported the principle of equal pay for women, tried to make them welcome. The number of women trade unionists more than trebled in the 1930s, providing some links to the Democratic Party.

If a few women trade unionists won access to the Roosevelt administration, they had little impact on its welfare measures. Hitherto such labour and welfare legislation that existed had tended to be directed to the needs of women rather than men. The fashioning of America's welfare state during the 1930s, however, actually reduced the role of women in shaping public policy. Prior to the Depression, a 'social work' network, dominated by women and employing casework techniques, had enjoyed some influence in informing social policies and establishing the modest beginnings of a 'maternalist' welfare system. But in the universities and research institutes were academics and theorists, mainly men, who had been addressing the issue of poverty and, influenced by European programmes, saw social insurance as the answer. People might be insured against unemployment, ill health or old age, and claim the relevant benefits as of right. Rehabilitation and casework were irrelevant to this means of averting poverty. The trade unions, which under Sam Gompers had once been wary of state benefits, warmly supported this strategy – as they were also opposed to the Equal Rights Amendment (ERA) advanced by some feminists.

The Social Security Act of 1935, with its introduction of old age and unemployment insurance, reflected the new priorities. The crucial decision was to base entitlements on wage-earning; those in jobs covered by the act became a privileged category. But it was also agreed that the various state and local mothers' aid programmes had to be supplemented, and the result was Aid to Dependent Children (ADC), designed by the Children's Bureau. In the welfare package that emerged, the most generous benefits were attached to the 'insurance' schemes, which were designed for urban workers, that is, largely white male wage-earners. Even many working women did not benefit, since they were often in occupations not encompassed by the act. ADC, in contrast, was less well funded, and the moralistic element continued to infuse it as caseworkers decided which unhappy women to relieve. In the early twentieth century widowed mothers had been seen as a deserving group, and the plight of their children had served as the entering wedge for state welfare. During the New Deal years, as Linda Gordon has shown, the elderly supplanted fatherless children as the personification of the deserving poor, and unattached mothers increasingly became a suspect group, the undeserving supplicants for 'welfare' as opposed to the worthy citizens who had earned their 'social security'. Further, as a welfare edifice was built, it came to be run primarily by men. Women had constituted 80 per cent of social workers in 1930; by 1940 the percentage had dropped to 65. The celebrated GI Bill of 1944 conferred yet further benefits on men, since only about 2 per cent of military personnel were women. The New Deal's faith in the expert allowed no room for the spiritual contribution traditionally imparted by women.

Yet some women did succeed in carving a niche in the New Deal Order. If jobs and political office proved elusive, some women's groups threw themselves into a consumers' movement which organized boycotts to contest high prices and lobbied government for greater regulation of food and other products. The women of the National Consumers' League (NCL) helped to secure the Fair Labor Standards Act of 1938 (see Chapter 8). The activists of the older women's reform network (as well as the trade unionists) naturally gravitated towards Franklin Roosevelt's Democratic Party, and the president's wife, Eleanor Roosevelt, cherished her links with them and served as their eloquent spokesperson. A responsive president appointed the first woman cabinet member and the first woman judge on the federal Circuit Court of Appeals. Further, women's expertise was needed in the new welfare and labour programmes. Roosevelt's secretary of labor, Frances Perkins, had once participated in the settlement house movement and brought a deep knowledge of working conditions to the cabinet. From the black women's club movement came Mary McLeod Bethune, director of the Office of Negro Affairs. Another with social work experience was Molly Dewson, who developed a career within the Democratic Party, becoming the first full-time director of its women's division. By 1936 she commanded an information corps of 15,000 women preaching the merits of the New Deal around the country. This absorption of part of the older women's network into the New Deal coalition has allowed historian Tony Badger to argue that 'women played a more substantial role in government and politics then than at any time before or since', but that role soon weakened. These women were more interested in economic and social reform than in feminism. They were wary of the ERA lest it undo the network of protective laws for women that had been wrung from state and federal governments. After the economy revived, the skills of the social work nexus were less in demand and their influence in government waned.

The war nonetheless had an important impact on the lot of American women. Wartime demands not only restored the economy to full employment, but also created a labour shortage that many African-Americans, teenagers and women rushed to fill. Jobs in the major manufacturing industries hitherto had been overwhelmingly the preserve of white men; now women and African-Americans of both sexes joined them. Women went into the shipyards and the aircraft factories and trained as fitters, welders and electricians. They also replaced men as bank and sales clerks, cab drivers and accountants, and many went into the proliferating wartime bureaucracy. By 1945 there were 4 million more men in paid employment than there had been in 1940, but there were over 5 million more women, a stunning advance. Large numbers of married and older women also joined the workforce. The war jolted the older patterns of employment.

With the ending of the war, those pressures that had sent women into the workplace were thrown into reverse. Some women were happy enough to resume their traditional role, but surveys revealed that at least 75 per cent wanted to remain at work. Government was anxious to restore the returning veterans to their jobs, and union and business leaders too were anxious to propitiate male workers. 'From a humanitarian point of view, too many women should not stay in the labor force', said the head of the National Association of Manufacturers. As the war effort wound down, women were laid off in disproportionate numbers. Yet this reverse was to prove temporary. As the economy surged ahead in the post-war period, another labour shortage loomed and women again found more employment opportunities. The rise of a consumer economy and the continued growth of the white-collar and service sectors also expanded the number of jobs that were deemed suitable for women.

By 1960 the proportion of women going out to work was again at the wartime level, with married women surging onto the labour market, and by 1970 it had reached a new high at 41.6 per cent. Prejudice against hiring wives had limited their opportunities in the first half of the century, but despite traditional notions about women's role, attitudes changed in the post-war years and by the 1950s rules prohibiting their employment were generally abandoned. Many of these working wives, of course, had children, and were demonstrating the capacity to fulfil the roles of both mothers and workers.

These conditions help to explain the rebirth of feminism. Even as more women were going out to work, what Betty Friedan called the 'feminine mystique' was being vigorously promoted. There was nothing new in the idea that woman's place was in the home, but there were ideological forces at large in the immediate post-war period that served to strengthen conservative views of the family. The very fact that more women were taking jobs triggered fears about broken homes and juvenile delinquency. A wide array of authorities – educationists, psychologists, politicians – endorsed the view that women's first duty was to home and family. Popular magazines, radio, TV and films tended to promote the notion that the success of the family rested on the wife, who succoured her husband, guided the socialization of her children and effortlessly managed the household.

The domestic ideology of these years both contributed to and was a reflection of unusual family patterns. The United States has traditionally had a very high marriage rate, but it soared to new heights in the 1940s and 1950s, and what is more Americans were marrying younger. By 1956 the average age at which marriage took place was twenty-two for men and twenty for women, and one consequence of the marriage boom was a baby boom. The birth rate had generally been dropping since the early nineteenth century and had sunk to a low of under twenty per thousand in the 1930s, but in the post-war years it suddenly revived. By 1955 it had reached twenty-five before beginning to decrease in the 1960s. It was 18.4 in 1970 and thereafter continued to drop, so in the brief period after the Second World War Americans were vigorously bucking a long-term trend. With high marriage and birth rates, and relatively low divorce rates too, the 1950s could be called the heyday of the family.

The post-war affluence was probably a necessary but not a sufficient reason for the commitment to family. The disruptive experiences of depression and war for family life surely had something to do with the impulse to find security in domesticity. So did the anxieties associated with the Cold War. Many of these new families found homes in the expanding suburbs, and it should not be assumed that women were dragged kicking and screaming to what feminist Betty Friedan characterized as 'comfortable concentration camps'. In a survey of 600 couples in the 1950s, the great majority expressed themselves as happy enough with their lot. Perhaps they would say that, but the respondents repeatedly stressed the satisfaction they found in family life. The era of the 'feminine mystique' was also the era of the 'man in the grey-flannel suit', when, according to popular sociology, work was being increasingly bureaucratized and there was declining scope for individual initiative. Private rather than public life – the family home, the station wagon, the ball game – arguably offered suburban Americans of both sexes more satisfaction than the work desk.

But the domestic idyll was being fractured even as it was being celebrated. The Soviet Sputnik of 1957 precipitated an urgent reassessment of the American educational system, and some educationists pointed to the loss of the talents of the female half of the population. Groups like the National Federation of Business and Professional Women joined the tiny

National Women's Party in lobbying for the ERA. When Betty Friedan's book, *The Feminine Mystique*, was published in 1963, ferociously assaulting the ideology placing women in the home, the time was ripe for it. The middle-class women that she studied had tried to fulfil themselves as wives and mothers but they experienced instead a profound emptiness. Their capacity for personal growth had been stunted, said Friedan; they were fated to be housewives and mothers, while men had the opportunity to explore their talents and ambitions.

In many ways there was nothing new in what Friedan said, and her passionate polemic distorted women's plight. Its focus on college women, for example, slighted the experiences of working-class and minority women. But the book touched a responsive chord because there was already a tension between the conventional ideology and contemporary experience. Had the feminine mystique been as pervasive as Friedan suggested, had women passively accepted their prescribed role, it is difficult to see how her book could have become a bestseller. But women had not been performing their traditional role for nearly a generation. There were more wives and mothers at work than ever before. Those who had been made to feel guilty for leaving the home were now being told that a career was the only route by which they could find happiness and that their families would benefit as well. And in the affluent society of the 1960s there were many jobs for them to take – as typists, teachers, nurses and sales assistants. Yet college-educated women, their consciousness raised by people like Friedan, aspired to more than this.

But for the moment the new feminists were less influential than the older women's network associated with the New Deal Order, whose priority had been to improve the conditions of working women. Yet times were not easy for these either. The Women's Trade Union League had ceased to exist in 1950 and in 1953 the Democratic Party discontinued its women's division. But many such women remained Democratic activists, among them trade unionists, members of the NCL and officials of the Women's Bureau. Responding to this constituency, President Kennedy in 1961 appointed a President's Commission on the Status of Women, the first ever attempt by the federal government to examine women's position. When it reported in 1963 it called for equal pay for women, but also for special training for young women for marriage and motherhood. The implication was that women were still mothers first and workers second. The Commission disappointed many professional women in declining to support the ERA, which it felt would jeopardize the protective legislation for working women. It put its faith instead in the 14th Amendment, with its guarantee of 'equal protection' to 'any person'. The call for equal pay was formally respected in the 1963 Equal Pay Act, and in 1964 a remarkable victory was achieved with the insertion of a prohibition against sex discrimination in the Civil Rights Act.

The New Deal Order, however, was ill designed to meet the growing expectations of the women's movement, which, like the labour movement, was tending to divide between those prepared to work with government and those who were losing faith in it. The Equal Employment Opportunity Commission, whose responsibility it was to enforce the Civil Rights Act, declined to take women's claims seriously, to the fury of such activists as Betty Friedan. In 1966 Friedan and other professional women founded the National Organization for Women (NOW), which demanded 'a fully equal partnership of the sexes, as part of the worldwide revolution of human rights'. NOW soon committed itself to two main causes, the ERA and 'the right of women to control their reproductive lives', that is, abortion. The ERA had been a feminist goal since the 1920s, but suddenly young activists in the sixties embraced it. Abortion too was a radical demand and it disturbed many otherwise sympathetic women. The Women's Equity Action League (WEAL), led by professional and academic women, broke away in 1968 to concentrate on economic and legal action. But abortion had a powerful appeal to many young and educated women and NOW expanded in membership. The modern feminist movement erupted.

Many of the women joining the 'second wave' of feminism had been active in the civil rights and New Left movements (see Chapters 11 and 12), where they were daily prompted to contemplate the meaning of rights. Yet egalitarian ideals were not always observed even in these movements, as women found themselves fulfilling subordinate roles. The new feminism rebelled not only against the priority afforded to male wage-earners in an industrial society and the domestic mystique of post-war America, but also against the masculine ethos of the New Left. Women could be seen as the victims of 'sexism', a new term, much as African-Americans were the victims of racism. By the late 1960s more radical varieties of feminists outflanked liberals such as Friedan. In September 1968 some radicals commanded media attention by staging a dramatic protest at Atlantic City during the Miss America Pageant, scorning its degrading symbolism and crowning a live sheep Miss America. In 1970 Kate Millett's *Sexual Politics* offered a more sophisticated explication of this philosophy, arguing that sexism was a product of a patriarchal system that structured the whole society.

This approach implied that the policy changes and constitutional amendments favoured by NOW would be woefully insufficient to effect the liberation of women. The New Deal Order, with the privileged status it tended to accord to men, could not satisfy such radical demands. The crusading feminism of the late 1960s heralded the advent of a new political era.

At the very time that American feminism turned against the New Deal Order, one of the latter's principal pillars began to crumble. The extraordinary expansion of organized labour in the 1930s had helped give the Democratic Party its electoral majority. The CIO unions in particular had provided funds and organizational prowess for the New Deal Order and had helped to shape the broadly liberal agenda accepted by Democratic presidential candidates in these decades. But a political alliance, forged in depression and sustained by the urgent mobilization demands of World War and early Cold War, lost its potency with the changing sociology and new issues of the 1960s. Union membership eroded and class issues gave way to issues related to rights and lifestyle. Progressive coalitions became more difficult to sustain as the new political activists headed off into such discrete causes as Black Power, environmentalism, consumer protectionism – and feminism. For a long season labour had enjoyed a major role in the polity, a role that tended to relegate women to secondary status, but as the cracks in the New Deal Order widened American feminists seized their opportunity.

8

Franklin Roosevelt's New Deal
1933–45

When Franklin Roosevelt was sworn in as president in 1933 great swathes of the economy lay in ruins and over 12 million dispirited Americans were searching for work. In that year per capita Gross National Product sank to its lowest level in thirty years, just $590 (in 1929 prices). When death eventually released Roosevelt from his duties in 1945, agriculture and industry were booming, unemployment was negligible and per capita GNP was a massive $1293. Much of this transformation was owed to the Second World War, but even before the war the New Deal was reshaping both the American landscape and the nature of government. New highways, dams, buildings, forests and parks stood as monuments to the government's determination to resist fate. Industrial workers, the unemployed, children, bankers, farmers and devastated regions had been afforded some governmental protection against the vagaries of the market. 'Our government is not the master but the creature of the people', Franklin Roosevelt had insisted in 1931. 'The duty of the state towards the citizens is the duty of the servant to its master.' He was no intellectual and he never offered a sophisticated account of the role of the state in modern society, but Roosevelt did believe in the potential of government for improving the lot of humankind. That faith was central to the New Deal.

There was, of course, no absolute break between Progressive America and New Deal America, and the continuity was personified by Roosevelt himself. He was a quintessential Wasp, a member of a New York gentry family and a distant cousin of Theodore Roosevelt. In 1910 he had been elected to the New York State Senate as a Democrat, where he early displayed a progressive's distaste for bossism and an interest in conservation and labour issues. He joined Woodrow Wilson's administration as assistant secretary of the navy, and when the United States entered the First World War the formidable task of mobilizing the navy fell to him. 'He was likable and attractive,' a contemporary recalled, 'but not a heavyweight.' But Roosevelt gained experience with the machinery of government and his vitality won admirers. He was sufficiently prominent by 1920 to be chosen as the Democratic candidate for vice-president, when he cheerfully stumped for progressive causes and the League of Nations.

In 1921 the thirty-nine-year-old Roosevelt was savagely felled by poliomyelitis; he never walked unaided again. The effect of this trauma is often credited with weaning him off his patrician arrogance and perhaps enhancing his empathy with the distressed, although his humanitarian instincts had long been evident. Perhaps it helped him to address later political crises with equanimity. 'In all the years of my husband's public life', his wife Eleanor once observed, '... I never once heard him make a remark which indicated that any crisis could not be solved.' (His paralysis also served to encourage the shy Eleanor to develop a larger role in public and political life, as she learned to combine being her husband's surrogate with a distinctive career of her own.) Franklin soon returned to Democratic politics, urging on his party 'the principles of progressive democracy'. In 1928 he was prevailed on to run for the governorship of New York. In that year Al Smith as the presidential candidate failed to carry his own state, but Roosevelt distinguished himself by winning it. As governor, he sustained his reformist stance as the economy collapsed, furthering conservation principles and pioneering state aid for the unemployed. When the Democrats chose him as their candidate for president in 1932, he told the convention: 'I pledge you, I pledge myself, to a new deal for the American people.'

When Franklin Roosevelt was sworn in on 4 March 1933 the economic crisis was at its most terrifying. The number of people unemployed had been growing relentlessly since the Great Crash, and now stood at about a quarter of the workforce. Through the winter of 1932–3 the primary symbols of American capitalism, the nations' banks, had been toppling like a row of dominoes, and state governors moved to stem the disaster by calling bank holidays. By March three-quarters of the banks had closed their doors, and European governments rapidly removed money from American vaults. Hours before Roosevelt took the oath of office even the great financial states of New York and Illinois had suspended banking, and the New York and Chicago stock exchanges closed. The collapse of the banking system threatened to bring business to a screeching halt.

In his inaugural address Roosevelt called on Congress to give him 'broad Executive power to wage war against the emergency, as great as the power that would be given to me if we were in fact invaded by a foreign foe'. Roosevelt's reaction to the banking crisis illustrated something of the New Deal, at once speedy, dramatic, conservative. He did not seize dictatorial powers or seek to nationalize the banks, as some thought he might. On 5 March, his first full day in office, Roosevelt first proclaimed a national bank holiday, buying a few precious days in which to prepare legislation, and on 9 March he sent Congress his banking bill. Within less than eight hours it had been whisked through all the stages of that usually cumbersome body and had received the presidential signature. Three days later Roosevelt spoke to the nation in his first radio 'fireside chat', reassuring citizens that their money was now safe, and the next day the major banks opened their doors for business. Deposits flowed into the banks once more and the immediate crisis was over. The Emergency Banking Act established a procedure to allow banks to reopen when they showed themselves sound, provided capital where necessary for the hard-pressed and required the reorganization of weak banks. Fashioned largely by members of the banking community, the act reinstated rather than reformed the existing system. But the president had pulled off his first coup: by speedy action, conservative means and a reassuring manner, he restored confidence in the nation's banks.

These qualities were to be displayed time and again in the years ahead. Between 1933 and 1938 bill after bill poured out of the Roosevelt administration, and many of them made it into law. Few aspects of the nation's life remained untouched. The political landscape was transfigured. Yet exciting and innovative as these times were, they were hardly revolutionary. The degree of energy in Washington was unprecedented, but many of the measures introduced, seen singly, were cautious in design. Franklin Roosevelt combined boldness with conservatism, optimism with persistence.

Congress obliged Roosevelt's request for broad powers to wage war against the emergency. During the celebrated 'hundred days' of the spring and early summer of 1933 Roosevelt made fifteen proposals to Congress, all of which were adopted.

When Roosevelt took office perhaps 50 million people were in desperate poverty, and for the first time ever the federal government moved to offer succour to the unemployed. Within a month an act established the Civilian Conservation Corps (CCC) to provide work for young men, in a range of tasks from reforestation to mosquito control, a programme that proved very popular. A little later came the Federal Emergency Relief Administration (FERA), under the energetic Harry Hopkins. The FERA made direct grants to the needy, although preferred to disburse money to state and local governments to fund public projects. By the time it closed in December 1935 it had spent about $4 billion, although even this unprecedented amount seemed little more than a token given the scale of the problem. But the FERA had decisively broken with federal government tradition of staying out of relief work, and it saved many families from starvation.

Of greatest urgency (after the banking crisis) to officials in the early weeks of the New Deal was the crisis in agriculture. Overproduction followed by the collapse of markets both abroad and at home had meant precipitate drops in farm prices, unnerving farm indebtedness and countless foreclosures. Total farm income in 1932 was less than half what it had been in 1929, and in the Midwest farmers were threatening a national farm strike – withholding their produce from market. Within a fortnight of taking office, determined to boost farm incomes (and thus also increase demand for industrial products), Roosevelt sent a sweeping farm bill to Congress. The resultant act set up the Agricultural Adjustment Administration (AAA), the basic strategy of which was to try to increase farm income by the novel means of paying farmers to reduce output. Since the act went into operation after some foodstuffs like corn and pork were already in production for 1933, the yield could be reduced only by destroying the products, and thus the AAA was obliged to slaughter 6 million piglets as some Americans starved. Farm prices were to rise again after 1933, although it is questionable how far the production controls were responsible. Perhaps more helpful to farmers was the credit made available by New Deal programmes. Late in 1933 the Commodity Credit Corporation was established to provide loans on stored crops like cotton and corn; only if prices rose above a given level would the loans have to be repaid. So was inaugurated the price-support system that provided for farm stability for the rest of the century.

A month after enacting the AAA Congress passed the National Industrial Recovery Act (NIRA). Although hastily devised, this is often seen as the centrepiece of the first hundred days. As Frances Perkins was later to remark: 'In some people's minds, the New Deal and the NRA were almost the same thing.' Again the economics of scarcity were employed in an effort to stabilize industry. Businessmen were to be protected from the anti-trust laws if, within each industry, they drew up 'codes of fair competition' to limit production and maintain prices and wages. A morsel was offered to labour by Section 7a which recognized a right to collective bargaining. The National Recovery Administration (NRA) was set up under General Hugh Johnson to administer the codes. This was an attempt at cooperation between government and industry, though the marriage soon proved an unhappy one. Small businesses resented the domination of the code-writing process by big business; most big corporations detested the concessions afforded to labour; unions felt cheated of the protection they thought they had been promised; government became disillusioned by the failure of the economy to recover. The act had also established the Public Works Administration with a budget of $3.3 billion, and it was hoped that pump-priming via the funding of public works would help boost purchasing power. But, unlike Harry Hopkins and Hugh Johnson, who tried to introduce their programmes with furious speed, the old progressive Harold Ickes was determined on giving the taxpayer value for money and insisted on rigorous appraisals before approving public works projects. The money was injected too slowly to give the economy much of a boost and in May 1935, when the Supreme Court struck down the NIRA, industrial production was only marginally greater than it had been in June 1933.

More successful was another celebrated product of the frenetic hundred days, the Tennessee Valley Authority, established in May to develop one of the poorest regions in the United States, some 40,000 square miles. Progressive attempts to harness the power of the Tennessee River had for years been frustrated by conservative opposition and private power interests, but remarkably the TVA was empowered to construct and manage dams, generate cheap electricity, control flooding, prevent soil erosion and even produce nitrogen fertilizers for sale. The degree to which this public agency competed with private interests and worked with rural cooperatives provoked hostility from business conservatives, but it was to play a massive role in the economic development of several South-Eastern states. In 1933 only 2 per cent of Tennessee Valley farms had electricity; by 1945 the figure had risen to 75 per cent.

There were other measures of the first hundred days, among them an act to protect homeowners from mortgage foreclosures and the Glass-Steagall Act to reform the banking system (which among other things provided for the guarantee of bank deposits). Yet despite the furious activity, recovery did not swiftly follow. The emergency measures of the spring and summer of 1933 helped to arrest the unnerving collapse of economic activity that seemed to be occurring in Herbert Hoover's last months in office. The principal economic indicators ceased to turn down and by the end of Roosevelt's first year were looking a little stronger. But real economic recovery proved frustratingly elusive. There was more legislation passed in 1934, including the Securities Exchange Act to curb stock market abuses, putting the stock exchanges under the supervision of the Securities and Exchange Commission (SEC). This was an important step in opening up the ways of American finance capitalists to scrutiny; Wall Street was to be regulated by Washington.

As the winter of 1933–4 had loomed, Roosevelt had secured another emergency measure, the Civil Works Administration (CWA), to provide work relief for the needy, exceptionally without a means test. By February 1934 the various relief agencies – the FERA, the CCC and the CWA – were reaching over a fifth of the American population. Yet millions of people were denied relief and those that were favoured got only a fraction of the rate regarded as necessary for subsistence. Extraordinary and unprecedented though the measures of the early New Deal were, by June 1934 there were still 11 million people unemployed.

Roosevelt had never been happy about doling out relief, and the continued high unemployment induced him to think more about work schemes. A bill of May 1935 appropriated an extraordinary $4.54 billion and allowed him to set up the Works Progress Administration (WPA), again under Harry Hopkins. This would employ people rather than handing them a dole, and according to Roosevelt the work would be 'useful ... in the sense that it affords permanent improvements in living conditions or that it creates future new wealth for the nation'. The WPA survived until 1941, during which time its various critics from all parts of the political spectrum exposed its many shortcomings. It reached only about a third of the unemployed at any one time; it paid more than the FERA but less than the average private wage (and well short of the subsistence level for a family); and many of its projects were make-work, in part because it was prohibited from competing with private industry.

Nonetheless, the WPA stands as an imaginative emblem of the New Deal. It was under the WPA that the Federal Theatre Project flourished, staging theatrical productions across the country and employing thousands of directors and actors, including Orson Welles. Similarly, the Federal Writers' Project and the Federal Art Project found work for other artists, such as Jackson Pollock. Under the aegis of the WPA too was the National Youth Administration, which found part-time jobs for over 2 million students and work for another 2.5 million unemployed young people. Altogether, the WPA was responsible for over a quarter of a million projects, including building or upgrading thousands of playgrounds, school buildings and hospitals, many military bases and even aircraft carriers. Broadly, the WPA won the imagination of liberals and intellectuals and the hostility of conservatives.

Also in May 1935 Roosevelt established the Rural Electrification Administration. At this point some 90 per cent of American farms had no electricity, which was a luxury enjoyed by city folk. Over the next few years this potent form of energy was carried into the countryside, suddenly consigning to the past many of the wearisome routines of rural life. By 1941 the percentage of electrified farms had risen to 40, a steep climb which continued into the following decades. Perhaps no other single measure of the New Deal was as responsible for transforming life in the American South.

The innovations of the New Deal had been criticized from the beginning, but its conspicuous weaknesses by 1934 gave its enemies some credibility. On the right some wealthy businessmen and conservative Northern Democrats formed the Liberty League and subjected the New Deal to sustained attack for its alleged socialist proclivities. On the left some segments of organized labour voiced their chagrin, particularly with the NRA or 'National Run-Around'. Unsettling too were the large followings soon being won by a number of figures peddling their own remedies for the Depression. There was the elderly Californian doctor, Francis E. Townsend, whose proposal to give everyone over sixty a monthly pension of $200, provided it was spent within the month, won millions of supporters, particularly among those over sixty. Even better known was Father Charles E. Coughlin, the celebrated 'radio priest', who commanded the largest regular radio audience in the world in 1934, and by the following year mixed populist and anti-Semitic prescriptions with denunciations of Roosevelt. But the most formidable opponent of the New Deal was Senator Huey Long, the 'Kingfish' of Louisiana, the effective ruler of the state and leader of a 'Share Our Wealth' campaign, advocating a massive redistribution of wealth from rich to poor. By 1935 Long claimed a membership of 8 million in his Share Our Wealth clubs and demonstrated a remarkable popularity in the Plains states; one poll suggested that he might win 100,000 votes even in the supposedly sophisticated state of New York if he ran for president on a third-party ticket in 1936.

That was the possibility that some Democratic leaders feared. If Long could carry with him the disaffected followers of Father Coughlin and Dr Townsend, he might not win the White House but might siphon off enough Democratic votes to evict Franklin Roosevelt in favour of a Republican. This was part of the political context to Franklin Roosevelt's renewed reform drive in the summer months of 1935, the 'second hundred days'. The need to 'steal Long's thunder' was not the only reason for this reform offensive. The Supreme Court had begun to dismantle some of the hastily contrived measures of 1933 and they needed to be replaced. The administration had tried to engage business in some of its programmes, but business was not overly cooperative; in May 1935 the US Chamber of Commerce came out fiercely against the New Deal. The economy remained mired in depression, there was a strong economic and humanitarian case for new measures and Roosevelt could still look to large Democratic majorities in Congress. In June 1935 he determined to regain the initiative by calling on Congress to enact five major measures.

One of the most far-reaching was the National Labor Relations Act, or the Wagner Act, passed in July (more fully discussed in Chapter 7). Roosevelt himself, betraying an old progressive's unease about organized labour, initially had not favoured this attempt to strengthen the unions. But the Supreme Court had struck down the NIRA, including Section 7a, and Roosevelt finally threw his weight behind Senator Wagner's bill, ensuring its speedy passage. Thus began the New Deal's historic identification with organized labour. More than was the case in many other countries, the national government was getting into the business of regulating industrial relations. There followed the rapid growth of the CIO unions.

Another epochal measure was the Social Security Act, the federal cornerstone of the country's welfare state; its principles would govern the evolution of American welfare. In most other countries a range of social policies tended to shade the differences between the various categories of 'deserving' and 'undeserving'; in the United States the act sharpened the distinction. The first principle was social insurance; workers (and their employers) were to make contributions to establish the workers' rights to old-age pensions, and a payroll tax obliged employers to help fund unemployment benefit. The second principle was that of categorical assistance, that is relief to various worthy categories, mainly dependent mothers and children. The benefits claimed under the insurance principle, to which people felt entitled, were better than those under categorical assistance, which were often grudging and meagre.

Nonetheless even the unemployment benefit levels were modest when compared, say, to Britain, and large categories (notably domestics and agricultural labourers, who were mainly black or Latino) were excluded from the pension and unemployment benefit programmes. The act did little to redistribute income and the employee tax was regressive, but, as Roosevelt said, 'With those taxes in there, no damn politician can ever scrap my social security program'. (Later administrations found rueful truth in this remark.) As initially enacted the measure was inequitable, but its compromises ensured its survival, the economic security of many Americans was significantly expanded, and in time the main excluded categories were quietly incorporated. As previously noted, the act also represented a significant shift in the American approach to welfare. Earlier state and local programmes had been largely directed to helping mothers, but the new schemes offered rights mainly to middle- and upper working-class (white) males – those with reasonably secure incomes.

Another belated piece of 'must' legislation was the bill which became the Banking Act in August 1935. This established a permanent deposit insurance system and reconstituted the Federal Reserve Board as the Board of Governors of the Federal Reserve System, most members of which would be political appointments, and gave it power to set the rediscount rate. Essentially the act enhanced the authority of the federal government and centralized the power of the Federal Reserve System over monetary policy.

Conservatives had initially seen the banking bill as an attack on private bankers, and other measures of the summer of 1935 also seemed like an assault on business. One was the public utility holding company bill, which aimed at reducing the holding company pyramids and subjecting them to the supervision of the SEC. While the final act was a little less draconian than Roosevelt had wanted, it was a major blow at sheer bigness in business and led to the dissolution of several major utility structures. More upsetting to business interests was Roosevelt's wealth tax act of 1935. Again, conservative opposition in and out of Congress succeeded in modifying this measure, but it did increase top personal income tax rates and imposed a progressive income tax on large companies. Its effect in redistributing income was modest, but it represented an important symbolic victory over the moneyed interests.

By the autumn of 1935 the great reforming thrust of the New Deal was beginning to weaken. Never again in the Roosevelt years would Congress be subjected to the blitz that it experienced in the second hundred days. Not that Roosevelt himself wished to abandon the cause. In the election of 1936 he denounced his new-found enemies, the 'economic royalists'. The Democratic platform ridiculed the Republicans' proposals to return serious economic and social problems to the separate states, and boasted of the administration's success in 'humanizing the policies of the Federal Government as they affect the personal, financial, industrial and agricultural well-being of the American people'. After his re-election, when he won 60 per cent of the popular vote and carried every state save Maine and Vermont, Roosevelt renewed the call for reform in his inaugural address, when he pointed out that 'tens of millions' of American citizens were still denied 'the greater part of what the very lowest standards of today call the necessities of life'. The test of the nation's 'progress', he insisted, was 'whether we provide enough for those who have too little'.

Yet despite the large Democratic majorities in Congress, such 'progress' was not easily attained. A major obstacle was the Supreme Court, long wedded to the doctrines of limited government and *laissez-faire*. The Court took particular exception to what it saw as the New Deal's tendency to delegate legislative power to executive agencies. In 1935 the Court had struck down the NRA, and in 1936 it effectively killed off the AAA, and it moved against other New Deal acts too. In due course the epochal measures of the second hundred days would come before it. Feeling that the 1936 election had shown

that the Court was at odds with the popular will, Roosevelt proposed to remedy matters by asking Congress for an act allowing him to appoint a new
justice for each of those over the age of 70. The bill applied to the whole of
the federal judiciary, but six of the nine Supreme Court justices had already
reached that age. Even many of Roosevelt's supporters recoiled at this plan,
which seemed like a crude attempt to pack the Court, and it eventually failed
in the Senate. By that time, however, Roosevelt was beginning to win the
war. One justice announced his intention to retire while another began to
side with the liberals, so that the Court more consistently upheld New Deal
legislation. Soon Roosevelt was able to appoint liberal justices as the old men
retired or died, and he encountered little further resistance from that quarter. What has been called a 'constitutional revolution' was accomplished – the
Court had ceased to question the right of the federal authorities to manage
the economy, a momentous change in attitude.

But there was a heavy political price to pay. The Democrats were disastrously divided by the measure, those among them who had disliked New
Deal reform now having an issue on which they could legitimately oppose the
administration. Further, the fight overlapped with an extraordinary wave of
industrial unrest. The great sit-down strikes centring on Flint in Michigan
scandalized many by their effrontery in occupying private property. Conservatives throughout the country were appalled both by the challenge to managerial prerogatives and property rights and by the protection afforded the
strikers by leading Democratic officials. It seemed to many that Roosevelt
was condoning attacks on property at the same time as he was assaulting the
Supreme Court. Later in 1937 a sharp plunge in the economy brought further
political woes. Inevitably the administration's critics blamed the 'Roosevelt
recession' on the president and New Deal policies.

During the fight over the 'Court-packing bill' conservatives of both parties
in Congress began to make common cause, and the sit-down strikes and the
recession further aided the formation of a conservative bloc. In December
1937 members of this group issued the Conservative Manifesto, which called
for a balanced budget and reduced taxes (especially on business), and asserted
the inviolability of property rights. By this date even the vice-president,
John N. Garner of Texas, had broken with the New Deal and accorded the
conservative bloc the benefit of his prestige. Many of the Democrats elected
in 1936, it seemed, particularly those from the South, were not so liberal after
all, and the president's stumbles encouraged them to resist New Deal measures, in concert with congressional Republicans. They were not wholly successful, but Roosevelt no longer had a compliant Congress, and reform
legislation dwindled. One sign of the truculent mood in Congress was the
formation in May 1938 of the House Committee on Un-American Activities,
which soon focused its suspicious gaze on a number of New Deal agencies.

But in 1938, with the mid-term elections still looming and congressmen
wary of attacking measures that might be popular with their constituents,
reform was still possible. A new AAA law made good some of the damage

of the Supreme Court, authorizing subsidies for staple products, new marketing quotas and soil conservation. Important too was the Fair Labor Standards Act, which addressed some of the issues once the preserve of the NRA, introducing maximum hours and minimum wages for workers in industries engaged in interstate commerce and strictly regulating the use of child labour. This helped further to reduce sweatshop conditions and promptly raised the wages of hundreds of thousands of workers. If industry could not regulate itself, regulation would be imposed on it. A similar attitude was displayed in the administration's continued attempts to combat bigness in business. The president prevailed on Congress to establish the Temporary National Economic Committee, empowered to investigate price-fixing and other monopolistic practices, and Thurman Arnold was appointed to the Justice Department to head a new trust-busting drive. It was in 1938 too that Roosevelt persuaded Congress to combat the recession by resuming large-scale spending on federal projects, so that he now seemed more prepared to embrace Keynesian ideas, in contrast to his attempts to cooperate with business in 1933. These various measures, in tending to raise industrial wages and threaten both business autonomy and Southern white supremacy, further strengthened the anti-New Deal alliance between business-oriented Republicans and racist Southern Democrats.

But Roosevelt's legislative gains in 1938 were made with difficulty, and he tried to use his personal popularity to remove some of his congressional enemies, endorsing attempts during the Democratic primary elections to replace conservatives with loyal New Dealers. But the attempted 'purge' invited unhappy comparisons with Hitler's Germany and Stalin's Soviet Union, and such presidential interference aroused local resentments. Almost all the obstreperous conservatives were re-elected, and the Republicans too made a significant comeback in the mid-term elections. While the Democrats still formally held majorities in Congress, the liberals had lost control of it. Conservatives had learned that they could publicly confront the president without suffering the wrath of their constituents. Reform legislation now became the exception, and in 1939 Congress was even able to chip away at parts of the New Deal, reducing relief expenditure and terminating a few controversial programmes like the Federal Theatre Project. The greater part of the New Deal edifice remained standing, but if conservatives could not dismantle it, nor could liberals add to it.

The New Deal coalition itself was being subjected to severe strain. Since 1932, and particularly since 1935, the Democratic Party had become increasingly identified with industrial workers, the Northern cities and immigrant and black voters. Rural Democrats were less enamoured of programmes that seemed to help the urban working class than they had been of measures to help agriculture. Many Southern Democrats were perceiving in New Deal programmes tendencies that might undermine the traditional economic and racial hierarchies of the South. The minimum wage law cut against the interests of low-wage Southern industry, and the various anti-poverty measures gave Southern blacks (and poor whites) some alternative to the grudging patronage of white landlords. Several leading Democrats who drew their support from racist local élites became fiercely hostile to Franklin Roosevelt. These unreconstructed Southerners did not necessarily bolt the New Deal electoral coalition, since Democratic Party membership remained valuable to them and the Southern and Northern urban wings of the party needed one another in national elections, but they served as a powerful counterweight to the influence of the liberals.

The weakening of Roosevelt's authority was illustrated by his prolonged tug-of-war with Congress over the reorganization of the executive branch. The powers of the presidency had increased since 1932, but the frugal staffing of the White House had made them difficult to exercise effectively, while the haphazard proliferation of executive agencies meant that the structure of government defied coordination. The president had been pressing for action since 1937, but the fight over the 'Court-packing bill' had already provoked accusations of dictatorial intent on Roosevelt's part and executive reorganization sparked the same charges. The measure became known to its critics as the 'dictator bill', a sobriquet which was unhelpful at a time when the European dictators were attracting disapproving attention. The bill was lost in 1938, although in 1939 Roosevelt secured a much modified version. This at least enabled him to issue Executive Order 8248, which established the Executive Office of the President, staffed it with six assistants and brought into it the Bureau of the Budget, taken from the Treasury Department, and the National Resources Planning Board. The president was now a little better equipped to manage the extended machinery of government that the New Deal had created.

Roosevelt's growing difficulties with Congress owed something to signs that his personal popularity was not quite what it had been and that the public was finding New Deal prescriptions less convincing. A poll of June 1938 found that 72 per cent of respondents wanted the administration to be 'more conservative' for the rest of its term. Further, by the late 1930s, the president, Congress and the public at large became increasingly distracted by threats posed from abroad. In September 1939 war finally broke out in Europe, and soon American exports revived and the United States prudently rearmed.

Roosevelt insisted that he had no intention of taking the United States into the war, a promise he repeated in the presidential election campaign of 1940, when he broke with all precedent by running for a third term. No other New Deal candidate had emerged who commanded widespread support and the alarming international situation seems to have persuaded Roosevelt to make himself available for a third nomination. Popular anxiety over Europe also contributed to the Republicans' decision to choose as their presidential candidate the engaging businessman Wendell Willkie, who like Roosevelt was an internationalist in foreign policy. Both Roosevelt and Willkie favoured helping the Allies while promising that the United States would remain at peace – 'Your boys are not going to be sent into any foreign wars', Roosevelt assured American parents – and Willkie also endorsed much of the domestic New Deal. Wendell Willkie fared better against Roosevelt than his previous Republican opponents, but the country stuck with the president it knew, Roosevelt again running well in the cities and among the lower-income groups.

A year later the Japanese attack on Pearl Harbor precipitated the United States directly into the war. The Second World War accomplished what the New Deal had not, the rescue of the American economy from depression. The unemployed quickly disappeared into the factories and armed forces, farmers found markets for their products, factories throbbed day and night and company profits blossomed. Even allowing for inflation, GNP increased by 70 per cent between 1939 and 1945.

Once in the conflict, Congress extensively delegated its powers to the president, eventually creating something close to a command economy. On paper at least the president's powers were far-reaching – powers to conscript men to military service, to allocate essential materials, to direct manpower, to control prices and rents, to ration consumer goods. The New Deal had warily extended the presence of the government in the market place; now the sacred principle of free enterprise seemed almost entirely abandoned. 'It has been a long fight to put the control of our economic system in the hands of the government', reflected Eleanor Roosevelt when the war had ended.

Progress towards mobilization was slow at first, but eventually impressive results were achieved. In 1939 the United States had spent only $1.3 billion on the military; this rose to $80.5 billion in 1945. By 1944 the United States produced some 60 per cent of Allied munitions. Technically many American weapons (including the Sherman tanks) were inferior to their German counterparts, and it was the sheer quantity of the Allies' armaments that was to win the war. The demanding logistics of expanding and equipping the military were also mastered. For most of the 1930s the number on active duty in the armed forces had usually been about a quarter of a million; by 1941 the figure had ballooned to 1.8 million; and by 1945 to over 12 million. Altogether a hefty 12 per cent of the population was to wear uniform.

Putting the country on a war footing also meant improving its internal security, for which Roosevelt was prepared to tolerate some erosion of civil liberties. The most serious abuse was suffered by Japanese Americans, living mainly on the West Coast, some of them Japanese-born and technically still aliens, but 80,000 were *nisei*, or American citizens born in the United States. After Pearl Harbor an emotional distrust of this Asian presence coursed through many white Americans, particularly as Japanese forces swept across the Western Pacific early in 1942. In February Roosevelt authorized the relocation of Japanese Americans. Some 112,000 people, most of them American citizens, had to abandon their homes and possessions and suffer confinement in overcrowded camps. The policy became more difficult to justify as the Americans began to win the Pacific war and it was abandoned at the end of 1944. There was no evidence of subversive intent among Japanese Americans, and some of them in fact were released from the camps to serve in the war, one *nisei* combat unit emerging as the most decorated in the entire United States Army.

The mass of Americans were more directly affected by another wartime imperative, the need to pay for mobilization. The emergency made possible an ingenious restructuring of the national taxation system. Roosevelt's earlier attempt to impose heavier taxes on the rich had been largely frustrated, but he did find a way of tapping the bulging wage packets of wartime workers. Before the war only a small proportion of American adults paid federal income tax, less than 4 million in 1939. The Revenue Act of 1942 lowered personal allowances, bringing many more into the system, and by 1945 nearly 43 million Americans paid federal income tax. The new tax structure was broadly accepted as tolerably just, despite its sweeping extension to lower-income earners. Government revenues increased enormously. New Deal benefits had given many ordinary citizens a direct interest in the activities of the federal government for the first time; now they had another interest.

But the greater part of the war cost had to be funded by borrowing. During the Depression the national debt had grown to an unprecedented 43 per cent of GNP in June 1940, but it exploded to a phenomenal 129 per cent by June 1946. The public provided some of this by subscribing to war bonds, but increasingly important was the role of the Federal Reserve System, which administered these huge sums and whose member banks bought up much of the debt, as did private banks and other financial institutions. In short, the banking system that the New Deal had restructured largely managed these complex operations in deficit financing.

During the war such deficit spending achieved new respectability. The budget deficits that conservatives had deplored in the 1930s had reached $4.4 billion at their most extravagant in 1936, but this was dwarfed by wartime spending, the deficit reaching $54 billion in 1943. The GNP responded in the vigorous way predicted by Keynesian economics. It had been $85 billion in 1938, but in 1940 topped $100 billion for the first time since 1929, and then took off in an extraordinary way, reaching $214 billion in 1945. The war had done much to vindicate government involvement in the economy. This ebullient growth meant that unemployment all but disappeared. During the 'Roosevelt recession' of 1937–8 unemployment had risen again to over 10 million, but by 1941 it was down dramatically to 5.6 million, and by 1944 to a mere 670,000, a tiny 1.2 per cent of the civilian workforce. As the war ended the number without jobs crept up again, but only to 3 or 4 per cent, not to the terrifying figures of the Depression. Massive deficit spending had vanquished the scourge of the 1930s. Even some businessmen were converted to Keynesian economics by this extraordinary experience.

As in the early critical days of the New Deal, Roosevelt again sought to work with big business. As Secretary of War Henry L. Stimson explained: 'If you are going to try to go to war, or to prepare for war in a capitalist country, you have got to let business make money out of the process or business won't work.' In 1942 Roosevelt largely abandoned anti-trust action. Businessmen were recruited in large numbers to the mobilization agencies. Many executives remained on their company payrolls and served government as 'dollar-a-year men', infusing the public agencies with business values. Tax write-offs were used to encourage firms to switch to war production and public subsidies were made available to expand capacity. The hostility which had existed between the administration and much of the business community in the late 1930s was replaced by an ambiguous intimacy. The close relationships between government, business and the military in these years helped to forge what later became known as 'the military-industrial complex'.

The rewards accorded to big business were politically palatable because many ordinary Americans prospered too. The war both boosted wage rates and afforded more opportunities for overtime, so that for working people take-home pay increased substantially. Average weekly earnings for production workers in manufacturing industries doubled, and many homes enjoyed the experience of two wage-earners for the first time. But the war distorted consumption patterns, restrictions meaning that less was spent on such items as motor cars and recreation. Instead people hoarded their money. Total personal savings in the national economy during the Depression years had been meagre, peaking at $3.7 billion in 1937; in 1944 they reached the incredible total of nearly $37 billion. This figure fell off dramatically in the post-war period as Americans were finally able to spend their enforced savings.

The relative good times experienced by many Americans may account for the difficulty experienced by liberals in rekindling interest in reform. Franklin Roosevelt and his advisers had not abandoned their New Deal aspirations. In 1943 the National Resources Planning Board called for dramatic expansions of welfare, including medical care, and in 1944 Roosevelt proposed an Economic Bill of Rights, attacked business monopoly and made full employment a goal. But apart from the generous benefits poured on veterans by the GI Bill of Rights of 1944 (which provided millions of young men with access to higher education and home mortgages), Congress and the public at large were largely unmoved by these calls. Democratic majorities in Congress had been sharply reduced by the mid-term elections of 1942, and a conservative Congress eroded some of the surviving New Deal programmes. Asked in a Gallup poll of August 1943 whether after the war they would like to see 'many changes or reforms ... or have the country remain pretty much the way it was before the war?' some 58 per cent of respondents wanted no reform.

The historian Christopher Thorne once remarked of the Second World War that where 'most of the societies involved, to put it crudely, turned "left-wards" in consequence, American society turned further to the right ...' It might equally be said that the war served to expand the centre. The New Deal had always been more about saving capitalism than eroding it, though it had contained some people who dreamed of beating back big business, redistributing income and using government to exercise economic control. But by the 1940s the interest in restructuring American political economy was fast fading. The conservative coalition in Congress remained a block on liberal reform, while big business was rehabilitated in public confidence by participation in the war effort. The surviving radicals tended to find themselves marginalized. Further, some aspects of the wartime experience with regulation proved disappointing, while the war revived faith in the capacity of capitalism for growth. By 1945 liberals, probably including FDR himself, were less interested in directly controlling the economy and more in Keynesian-style management and growth.

But if liberals grew a little more conservative, many conservatives also moved to the centre. Republicans and businessmen had come to accept many New Deal achievements, like social security and collective bargaining, and the war helped to reconcile many of them to the greater role of government, as it also challenged the Republican Party to embrace an internationalist foreign policy. Future prosperity would depend in part on a continuing if limited partnership between big business and government in managing a consumer-oriented economy. Many of government's emergency powers would be abandoned in the post-war period, but its authority had been permanently enhanced – as illustrated by the enlarged size of the civil service – and its use of fiscal policy and its new world role could serve business ends. In the post-war years a degree of consensus on broad political and economic strategies would emerge between the major parties. The good society would be achieved by relying on the economy's increasing productivity, which would provide a surplus with which to address poverty and other ills; wealth need not be redistributed. This was the underlying philosophy that would inform government policy for the remainder of the New Deal Order. With the Democrats abandoning their more radical dreams and the Republicans acquiescing in New Deal and wartime innovations, the future of the New Deal Order was assured.

|9|

Isolation and World War
1933-45

In the aftermath of the First World War the United States had once more renounced European entanglements, and in 1933 seemed to be reverting to a yet deeper form of isolationism. Neither Wilsonian idealism nor the business diplomacy of the Republican administrations of the 1920s had succeeded in refashioning international relations according to an American agenda. The Depression was releasing frightening forces in the world, while in the United States the economic crisis was at its most terrifying as Franklin Roosevelt took office. The new administration did not see international cooperation as the answer. Within a couple of years, too, Congress was energetically enacting neutrality laws to ensure that the United States would never again be drawn into European quarrels. But true isolationism was not possible for the world's greatest economic power, and in any case technological advances were diminishing the protective value of the Atlantic and Pacific oceans. The retreat from neutrality began before Japanese planes precipitated the United States directly into the Second World War, but the war itself fatally weakened the old isolationist impulse. The war also both rescued the United States from depression and greatly enhanced the New Deal's tendency to centre power in Washington. And the Second World War made the United States unquestionably the first among nations. 'When FDR died in 1945', George Will has written, 'America was more supreme than Great Britain after Waterloo, than the France of Louis XIV, than any power since the Roman Empire.'

As Roosevelt assumed his duties as president, Adolf Hitler was taking command in Germany, and over the next few years the international situation unnervingly deteriorated. In October 1933 Hitler withdrew Germany from the League of Nations and in 1936 he illegally reoccupied the Rhineland. Mussolini's Italy was also flexing its fascist muscles. In October 1935 Italy annexed Ethiopia, and from 1936 the two fascist regimes were giving assistance to General Franco in the civil war in Spain. Meanwhile, the military had gained the political ascendancy in Japan, and intensified Japanese aggression in China. Further, these belligerent nations seemed to be reaching an accord. In November 1936 Nazi Germany and Japan signed an Anti-Comintern Pact, which Italy joined in 1937, identifying the Soviet Union as their common foe. It became increasingly difficult for the United States to ignore the rise of fascism or the prospect of a confrontation between fascist and communist totalitarianism. Further, for some the New Deal was a symbol and a test of democracy, the most promising alternative in the economic crisis of the 1930s to the systems personified by Adolf Hitler and Joseph Stalin.

The international instability to a large extent arose from the harrowing nature of the Great Depression, although initially Roosevelt was disposed to accept the view that the hard times suffered by the United States were largely of its own making. It followed from this analysis that the American government should pursue its own remedies. Accordingly in July 1933 Roosevelt withdrew the United States from the World Economic Conference, which had been convened in London to try to rescue the international economic system, an action that effectively destroyed any possibility of collaboration with other countries to combat the Depression. This left Roosevelt free to employ his inflationary policies, though as the hard times dragged stubbornly on he began to appreciate that the difficulties encountered by the New Deal did not arise exclusively from the domestic scene. 'As we plan today for the creation of ever higher standards of living for the people of the United States', he said in a radio address of October 1937, 'we are aware that our plans may be most seriously affected by events in the world outside our borders.'

Roosevelt had never been a committed isolationist, but the economic nationalism of the early New Deal was compatible with the isolationist currents that were then asserting themselves in American public life. These caused him few problems in Latin America, towards which Roosevelt developed his 'good neighbor' policy, forswearing the right claimed by Progressive Era presidents to intervene militarily if American interests seemed threatened. In 1936 he accepted that intervention in the region was 'inadmissible' for any reason. But isolationism primarily meant isolation from Europe. In 1934–5 a congressional committee, chaired by the progressive Republican Gerald P. Nye of North Dakota, probed the causes of American participation in the First World War and came to the conclusion that intervention had been largely at the behest of bankers and munitions exporters who had profited from the war. The isolationists argued that the best way to prevent a recurrence was to forbid the export of arms or the extension of loans to any participant in a foreign war, and they secured their objectives in the neutrality acts of 1935–7, measures to which Roosevelt unhappily acceded. The laws as enacted risked encouraging aggression, for they meant that a victim nation could not look to the United States for succour.

The success of Congress in dictating the terms of foreign policy in the mid-1930s owed something to Roosevelt's preoccupation with domestic issues, but by 1937 he was recognizing that the New Deal could not after all be insulated from the rest of the world. The resumption of Japanese aggression in China, at a time when the fascist powers of Germany and Italy seemed to be moving closer together, pointed up the dangers inherent in isolationism. In Chicago in October 1937 Roosevelt challenged isolationist sentiment in his celebrated 'quarantine' speech, suggesting that peace-loving nations 'quarantine' the disease of 'world lawlessness', provoking a furious isolationist response. Abroad, the international situation continued to deteriorate. In March 1938 Hitler incorporated Austria into the Third Reich, and six months later demanded that Czechoslovakia hand over the German-populated Sudetenland. At Munich Britain and France bought 'peace in our time' by allowing Hitler to dismember Czechoslovakia, and in March 1939 the Nazi dictator seized the whole of that country. Mussolini paralleled Hitler's action by seizing Albania for Italy.

Roosevelt deplored these events but was powerless to influence them. He blamed the neutrality laws for encouraging fascist aggression, but Congress was loath to amend them. In August 1939 news of the Nazi–Soviet non-aggression pact hit a disbelieving world, an accord which secretly allowed the two participants to carve up part of eastern Europe between them. Confident of the Soviet Union's complicit acquiescence, at the beginning of September Nazi Germany launched its attack on Poland, and Britain and France, which had previously guaranteed Poland's boundaries, were finally obliged to declare war.

American fears of a bloody general war in Europe had been growing for years. Americans had their sympathies but they did not want to be embroiled in foreign quarrels, and at the outbreak of the war Roosevelt could only declare American neutrality. In fact, much more than had been the case in the First World War, public opinion identified strongly with the Allied cause, although there was less accord on what the United States should actually do. Most could agree that the United States should not enter the war, but while some wanted to ensure this by a rigid application of the neutrality acts, others favoured revising them in a way that would help Britain and France. Towards the end of 1939 Franklin Roosevelt finally won from Congress a repeal of the prohibition on the export of arms, but not at the risk of American lives. In purchasing munitions belligerent countries would have to take them away in their own ships; this was the principle of 'cash and carry'.

In December Americans were deeply distressed by the Soviet invasion of Finland, but there was little they could do beyond deploring it. The early months of 1940 witnessed the continuance of the 'phoney war', as Hitler bided his time. For the moment American strategy retained some credibility. It was plausible to believe that France's vaunted Maginot Line would hold off the German columns, that Britain would retain naval supremacy and that the war would settle down to an extended stalemate, eventually perhaps to be won by the Allies if they could be sustained by American supplies. This complacent vision was shattered in the spring and summer of 1940. Norway, Denmark, Holland and Belgium quickly succumbed to German arms, and in

June France too capitulated, attacked by Italy from the south as well as by Germany from the north. The collapse of France had momentous consequences. Great Britain now stood alone, and during the late summer and autumn Nazi bombs rained down on its cities in preparation for a German invasion. The bombing of London, graphically described by American newsman Ed Murrow in regular radio broadcasts, sent home to many Americans the sickening lesson already spelled out by the remorseless German sweep across Europe. The United States was vulnerable after all. And even if an exposed America remained untouched, it could find itself standing alone in a fascist world. Congress suddenly became much more amenable to voting funds for defence.

The case for protecting the United States by assisting the Allies was becoming ever stronger, although powerful congressional forces remained suspicious of measures that might suck the country directly into war. In September Roosevelt circumvented Congress by reaching a deal directly with British Prime Minister Winston Churchill, by which fifty aging American destroyers were given to Britain in return for the gift of air and naval bases in Bermuda and Newfoundland and long-term leases to several other military bases on British possessions in the Atlantic or Caribbean. Yet this would hardly suffice. Roosevelt was well aware that the Allies desperately needed much more support if Hitler was not to prevail. But if the United States supplied weapons, how could the depleted British treasury pay for them? Roosevelt came up with an ingenious solution – 'lend-lease'. The United States would simply lend or lease weapons, food or other supplies to Britain (or other threatened countries). Such loaned items would somehow be returned or replaced after the war. This was an extraordinary pledge to one side in the European war. As Roosevelt himself described it: 'Suppose my neighbor's home catches fire, and I have a length of garden hose ... If he can take my garden hose and connect it up with his hydrant, I may help him to put out his fire.' He would not want paying, just 'my garden hose back after the fire is over'. The programme, adopted in March 1941, eventually swallowed up some $50 billion, most of it for Britain.

Lend-lease was presented as a defensive measure, but a greater commitment to the Allied cause short of an outright declaration of war could hardly be imagined. The United States had moved a long way from the proclaimed neutrality of the 1930s. It was now to wage war by proxy, or, as Roosevelt put it, to serve as 'the great arsenal of democracy'. The implementation of the policy took the United States even deeper into the conflict. For lend-lease to succeed, the British ships laden with American goods would have to be protected from German submarines while crossing the North Atlantic. Roosevelt quietly directed American warships into Atlantic waters 'on neutrality patrol', helping British shipping negotiate at least the western half of the ocean. Soon the inevitable happened. By the autumn US Navy destroyers were being torpedoed by German U-boats and American lives were lost. For the moment neither the German dictator nor the American president was prepared to declare war, although Roosevelt was able to use the incidents to secure the repeal of most of what remained of the neutrality legislation.

But American security was threatened from the east too; in July 1940 Japanese militarists finally won full control of their government. Japan was dependent on the import of oil and other raw materials, and its leaders now saw an opportunity to seize the resources it needed closer to home. In September Japanese troops marched into French Indochina, and Roosevelt retaliated by banning the export to Japan of scrap iron and steel. In July 1941 the Japanese government extended its control over the whole of French Indochina, to which Roosevelt responded by freezing all Japanese assets in the United States, one (somewhat unintentional) effect of which was to stop all oil exports to Japan. The Japanese government concluded that it must seize the oil of the Dutch East Indies, but to do that it needed first to destroy American military power in the Pacific. On 7 December 1941, without warning, Japanese planes struck at the American fleet at Pearl Harbor. On the following day the president appeared before a joint session of Congress, and the two houses declared war on Japan.

For the United States, war may formally have begun in the Far East, but since the spring of 1941 American naval operations had been assisting the Allies in the North Atlantic. The European war was dramatically transformed in June when Adolf Hitler, unable to invade Britain, suddenly hurled his armies at the Soviet Union. As Nazi divisions streaked towards Moscow, Winston Churchill urged the American president to give unstinting aid to their potential new partner. If the Red Army could hold off the Germans, Britain might be spared an invasion and Nazi strength might be seriously impaired. Soon huge supplies were on their way to the Soviets. Roosevelt went further in August, when he and Churchill met in Newfoundland and drew up the Atlantic Charter, which broadly enunciated the war aims. They asserted the right of all peoples to choose their own form of government, and identified as among their goals freedom from fear and want, a fair international economic system and the disarmament of aggressors. Here was Roosevelt formulating war aims when technically the United States was not a combatant. Churchill privately recorded that 'The President ... said he would wage war, but not declare it'.

'That day ended isolationism for any realist', Senator Arthur Vandenberg was to write of Pearl Harbor. Vandenberg had been a leading isolationist himself, but he was now converted to the internationalist view that American security demanded international cooperation. In fact isolationist sentiment was not dead, but it had been cripplingly weakened, just as from the late 1930s the experiment with strict neutrality had been progressively discredited. Neutrality in the modern world seemed an illusion, isolation a danger. A tradition dating back to George Washington was finally being irrevocably broken. Henceforth American foreign policy would be internationalist in orientation, and for as long as anyone could foresee the United States would be the biggest player on the world stage.

Prior to December 1941 the United States was conducting war indirectly, the resources of its vast economy helping to sustain Britain and the Soviet Union against Nazi might and China against the Japanese invaders. When the United States was precipitated directly into war its wealth made it the senior partner. On American insistence it was agreed that there should be a unified Anglo-American command, with senior American and British officers forming a Combined Chiefs of Staff in Washington. As it evolved, it could be said that the Second World War constituted two wars, one in Europe and one in the Pacific, and the United States alone played a major role in both. The American commitment was colossal. During the First World War the American army had only been fully engaged for the last six months; during the Second the United States entered at a low point for the Allies and was to carry the major part of the burden for nearly four years.

Nonetheless, despite the gradual increase in defence expenditures from the late 1930s, the United States, whose military was tiny by international standards, was far from ready for war in December 1941. Mobilization would take time and the prospect of stopping the Axis powers looked remote.

An early issue was where American resources should be concentrated. The United States had been attacked in the Pacific, but its allies were primarily fighting the war in Europe and North Africa. The Soviet Union, desperately fending off the Nazi invasion, wanted Britain and the United States to launch an assault across the English Channel and open a second front in France. Roosevelt was friendly to this idea but Churchill rejected it as premature, arguing instead that Anglo-American forces initiate an offensive in North Africa, where the British were already pressing the Germans and Italians and where landings could be effected on Vichy French territory. The Axis forces could be caught between an Anglo-American invasion force from the west and a British thrust from Egypt. The American military would have preferred to commit their resources to the Pacific, but Churchill persuaded Roosevelt to undertake a North Africa campaign. The British believed that Hitler's empire might best be undermined by a 'peripheral' strategy, attacking him around the edges, probing for his weak points and obliging him to divide his forces. When German strength was sufficiently depleted an invasion of the European continent could follow.

General Dwight D. Eisenhower was given overall command of the North African campaign. In October 1942 General Bernard Montgomery's British Eighth Army confronted the forces commanded by General Erwin Rommel at El Alamein and drove them out of Egypt. In the following month Allied troops landed at Oran and Algiers in Algeria and at Casablanca in Morocco, Eisenhower having made a deal of a kind with the Vichy French commander which reduced the possibility of resistance from French troops. Following the Allied invasion of Casablanca and Algeria, Allied troops began pressing east. The North Africa campaign took longer than anticipated, but in May 1943 the besieged Axis forces finally surrendered to superior firepower. The Nazis, it seemed, could be beaten after all. Two months later, from their bases in North Africa, Allied forces landed in Sicily. In September they pressed on into Italy and the Italian government quickly surrendered, although German divisions stopped the Allied advance south of Rome. Nonetheless Allied strategy thus far had been largely successful. The Germans and Italians had been removed from North Africa and Italy had been knocked out of the war.

Meanwhile Roosevelt and Churchill had met one another secretly at Casablanca in January, when the invasion of Sicily and Italy had been planned. This meant delaying the second front in Europe yet again, somewhat to the embarrassment of Roosevelt since he had promised Stalin an invasion of France to take Nazi pressure off the Soviet Union. But the president went a little way towards mollifying the Russians by announcing that the Allies would insist on the 'unconditional surrender' of Germany and Japan. There was a risk that this demand would prolong the war, but the message was that Britain and the United States would not desert the Soviet Union. The demand also reflected a determination to occupy Germany, as had not happened in 1918, to avert the possibility of yet another world war.

Ironically, the political pressures for opening a second front increased with Soviet victories. In February 1943 Soviet forces won the bloody battle of Stalingrad, capturing twenty-two German divisions. Hitler's mighty armies were forced back under Soviet advances, and by the summer it was being borne in on British and American strategists that the Soviets could reach Berlin first. The Soviet Union might be an ally, but Roosevelt and Churchill had no wish to see German domination of Europe replaced by Russian. The Americans determined on a strike across the English Channel.

Operation Overlord was to be commanded by Dwight Eisenhower. Through the first half of 1944 Allied planes repeatedly bombed German factories, ports and cities. Meanwhile massive Allied forces were gathering in England, and in June, on D-Day, the greatest amphibious attack in history was launched with the invasion of Normandy. Eventually German resistance was overwhelmed by sheer numbers. The Allied troops crossed France, and towards the end of August Paris was liberated. But months later Hitler launched a counter-offensive, diverting resources from the eastern front and sending 250,000 troops through the Ardennes and towards Antwerp in the hope of piercing the Allied lines. This assault culminated in the Battle of the Bulge of December 1944 and January 1945, in which the Germans suffered even greater casualties than the Allies. Meanwhile the Soviets took advantage of the depletion of German forces in the east to launch their own winter offensive, their massive armies quickly smashing across Poland. By February 1945 the Red Army was within fifty miles of Berlin. During the spring of 1945 American and British forces pressed into Germany from the west, and at the beginning of May Soviet troops occupied Berlin. By that time Adolf Hitler had committed suicide and what was left of the German government quickly agreed to unconditional surrender.

But the Allies were fighting a war in the Far East as well as in Europe. After Pearl Harbor Japanese forces had quickly pursued their advantage in

South-East Asia and the Pacific. The British were turned out of Hong Kong and Borneo and suffered a massive blow with the capitulation of Singapore. Burma succumbed too. By April 1942 the Dutch possessions of Sumatra and Java had also fallen to the Japanese. In a matter of months the European empires had been devastated. The Americans suffered humiliations too, as the Japanese seized Guam, Wake Island and the Philippines. The western Pacific was becoming a Japanese lake, and the Americans' uncertain ally, China, was left even more exposed to Japanese aggression. In the summer of 1942, however, the Americans were able to inflict a crushing naval defeat on the Japanese at the Battle of Midway, frustrating their attempt to win complete ascendancy in the Pacific.

With Japanese expansion in the Pacific arrested, the United States was now able to counter-attack. American troops landed on Guadalcanal in the Solomon Islands, and after prolonged resistance the Japanese eventually withdrew in February 1943. The war in the Pacific was finally turning in the Allies' favour. Allied forces could now hope to prevent essential raw materials like oil from reaching the Japanese home islands and to proceed towards Japan and the Asian mainland by seizing groups of islands in the Pacific. The resultant engagements with Japanese forces were often costly in terms of men and weaponry, but the extraordinary resources of the United States prevailed. The greatest naval battle in history was fought at Leyte Gulf in the Philippines in the fall of 1944, crippling the Japanese navy, and in the spring and early summer of 1945 the Americans moved closer to Japan by winning bloody engagements at the islands of Iwo Jima and Okinawa. Hoping to burn the Japanese into surrender, the Americans began to direct heavy incendiary bombings against Japanese cities.

But Japan did not surrender, at least not until the United States released a horrendous new weapon. In August 1945 atomic bombs were dropped on Hiroshima and Nagasaki. Massive firestorms immediately incinerated tens of thousands of people, perhaps some 150,000 in the two cities together. At the same time the Soviet Union declared war on Japan, which finally surrendered without an invasion, much to the relief of Allied troops. Whatever considerations governed the American decision to use the atomic bomb, revenge for Pearl Harbor and Japanese atrocities among them, a major one was the desire to effect a quick release from the war.

By VJ Day the era of Franklin Roosevelt was over. The president had died in April, knowing that Germany was defeated but that Japan remained defiant. For the bulk of American citizens and servicemen, not to mention the United States' allies, news of Roosevelt's death was stunning. In the same month Benito Mussolini and Adolf Hitler also died, and three months later Churchill was swept out of the premiership by the British electorate.

Franklin Roosevelt had already largely accomplished his objectives. However hesitantly, he had led Americans away from isolationism and all but ensured that the United States would play a commanding role in the new world order. In January 1941 he had told Congress that he wanted a world grounded on the 'four essential freedoms', that is the freedoms of speech and religion and freedom from want and fear. The Atlantic Charter that summer spoke of 'a wider and permanent system of international security'. One British observer in the United States in 1942 told his government of the conviction within American official circles 'that the United States stands for something in the world – something of which the world has need, something which the world is going to like, something, in the last analysis, which the world is going to take whether it likes it or not ...' In that year Secretary of War Henry L. Stimson expressed the official view in a propaganda film: 'We are determined that before the sun sets on this terrible struggle our flag will be recognized throughout the world, as a symbol of freedom on the one hand ... and of overwhelming power on the other.' The survival of American values was linked to the proper ordering of the world.

The power of the United States, as Stimson intimated, was certainly awesome. Quite apart from its nuclear monopoly, the war had massively enhanced its military capability. The North American continent may have survived the war unscathed, but the notion that the United States could shelter behind its two ocean barriers and limit itself to a small military establishment could no longer be countenanced. During the 1930s total military personnel had usually numbered between 250,000 and 300,000. At the height of wartime mobilization the figure reached over 12 million, but even after demobilization the armed forces were reduced only to about 1.5 million, before being increased again with the Cold War. In 1935 the national security and military budget had been about $711 million; in 1948, its lowest in the post-war period, it would be $11,771 million. War had had its usual ratchet effect on the military. If it so chose, the United States could continue to exercise a military presence in the world.

But with the ending of the war it was time to beat swords into ploughshares. Roosevelt's preoccupation with the post-war order had been manifest at each of the conferences he held with Allied leaders. At Casablanca in January 1943 it was made clear that the Nazi empire would be totally destroyed; there would be no place even for a repentant and diminished Hitler in post-war Europe. At Tehran in November it was agreed to establish a United Nations organization and to dismember Germany, and it was also in effect conceded that eastern Poland would remain under Soviet control. The outline of the post-war world was coming into clearer focus.

Roosevelt, Churchill and Stalin met again at Yalta in February 1945 to discuss the post-war settlement in more detail. They reached accord on the broad shape of the United Nations. Germany was to be divided into four zones, occupied respectively by the United States, the Soviet Union, Great Britain and France. The fate of Poland, the Nazi invasion of which had triggered the war, was largely determined by the brute fact that the Soviet army already occupied that unfortunate country. It was decided to defer agreement on Poland's western frontier, but Britain and the United States reluctantly agreed that Poland's government might be constituted around the Lublin

Committee, dominated by Polish-Russian Communists, although some members of the Polish government-in-exile in London were to be included. Stalin promised that a permanent government would be chosen through 'free and unfettered elections as soon as possible'. Given the military and political realities, Roosevelt felt that there was little more he could do to protect Poland. Further, he wanted and secured a Soviet promise to enter the war against Japan, which was expected to reach into 1946. 'I didn't say the result was good', reflected Roosevelt after Yalta, 'I said it was the best I could do.'

In his fourth inaugural address in January 1945 Roosevelt concluded: 'We have learned that we cannot live alone, at peace; that our own well-being is dependent on the well-being of other nations far away.' Restoring economic well-being had been the objective of the New Deal, and the president in effect now suggested that the very success of the New Deal itself would depend on the new international order that was being created. In some respects, in designing the new political and economic institutions by which the world would be governed, the Roosevelt administration could be said to be extending the New Deal to the world.

The structure of the United Nations was planned by the Allies at a conference in August 1944 at Dumbarton Oaks in Washington, DC. It was agreed that there was to be a general assembly in which every country could be represented, and a powerful security council of eleven members, in which the United States, the Soviet Union, Great Britain, France and China would each enjoy a veto power. The post-war world was to be ordered by the Allies. American influence was reflected in the very preamble of the eventual UN Charter, which echoed the American Declaration of Independence by opening with the words 'We the peoples of the United Nations ...' Other agencies to emerge from wartime discussions included UNESCO, to promote 'international collaboration in the fields of education, science and culture', and the United Nations Relief and Rehabilitation Administration, which poured assistance into countries that the war had reduced to desperate circumstances. Governmental agencies, not private charities, would ease the lot of humankind.

Roosevelt also recognized that the United States would have to act as economic guarantor of the new world order, the economic needs of which were addressed by a conference at Bretton Woods in New Hampshire in July 1944. Memories of the Depression dominated the minds of the delegates. The 1930s had seen not only many peoples of the world ravaged by poverty, but also consequent political tensions which had spawned fascism and war. These conditions the Bretton Woods planners were determined should not recur. Their objective, in the words of one of them, was to 'distribute happiness throughout the earth'. The key to this goal, it was held, was a global market place in which free trade might flourish together with international control over national monetary systems. Two international governmental agencies were established to facilitate this healthier global economy. The World Bank was to extend credit to countries to rebuild their economies and also promote the economic development of emerging nations, while the function of the International Monetary Fund (IMF) was to promote international currency stability, primarily by providing financial assistance to countries with serious balance of payments problems. It was agreed that the monetary system would rest on the US dollar and gold. The United States, in effect, would be the world's banker. Unsurprisingly, both the World Bank and the IMF soon became largely subject to the will of the American government.

After the war a Gallup poll showed that 68 per cent of respondents believed that the United States should do everything to tell other nations 'the advantages of our type of democracy for the common people of the world'. Wilsonian idealism had not died altogether. The world in 1945 was indeed being reconstituted somewhat along American lines. In Germany, Italy and Japan authoritarian regimes were removed and replaced by political systems that conformed to American definitions of democracy. In contrast to its attitude to the League of Nations, the United States became (for the time being) the foremost champion of the United Nations, and its influence was felt in the several other international institutions established to promote global stability and further the well-being of humanity. Woodrow Wilson had failed to establish a Pax Americana after the First World War. The United States had another opportunity to fashion the world after the Second. The veteran columnist Walter Lippmann reflected: 'What Rome was to the ancient world, what Great Britain has been to the modern world, America is to be to the world of tomorrow.'

|10|

Post-war Consensus:
from Truman to Kennedy
1945–61

The fifteen years following 1945 witnessed the materialization of what John Kenneth Galbraith ironically dubbed 'the affluent society'. The World War had hoisted the United States out of depression, and the high Cold War expenditures – together with considerable private consumption – contributed to the sustained prosperity. This age of opulence, however, was also for the most part an age of political stalemate. Liberals found that they could not revive the reform momentum of the New Deal, while conservatives found that they could not dismantle the constructions of Franklin Roosevelt. Harry Truman as president offered an array of proposals to Congress relating to full employment, public power, civil rights and other issues, but few of them survived the attention of congressional conservatives. Dwight Eisenhower as president had little love for the innovations of the New Deal but recognized the political folly of leading his party back to an unreconstructed conservatism. The political consensus that is often said to characterize these years was for many founded on a sense of resignation rather than conviction. Looming over domestic politics and contributing to the deadlock was Cold War, which did occasion the expansion of federal government (as in its sponsorship of an interstate highway system in the name of national security). The unnerving foreign crises could not but preoccupy the attention of the Truman and Eisenhower White Houses, and also promoted a conservative temper in Congress and the country at large. In any case, the gratifying experience of an unmatched prosperity suggested that the economic and social systems were not in urgent need of attention.

The New Deal Order survived, though its liberal guardians were shifting somewhat to the right. Impressed by the stunning wartime experience, many liberals were less interested in overhauling the economy and more in exploiting capitalism's capacity for growth. Economic growth, sustained – as Keynesian theory advised – by the government's fiscal powers to tax and spend, would both heal class wounds and provide government with the revenues needed to finance social policies (not to mention massive Cold War armaments). Direct intervention in the economy could be kept to a minimum. Such ideas informed the policies of the Truman administration and would resurface in the Kennedy White House. Expanding consumption, not redistribution, was the focus of this strategy. The government did its part. Such measures as the GI Bill, tax incentives for home ownership, public health care and environmental reform served to promote what historian Samuel P. Hays has called a 'social service state for the benefit of the mass middle class'.

Roosevelt's death in April 1945 finally removed 'that man' from the White House. Into his place was precipitated Harry S. Truman, the former Missouri senator who had served as vice-president for less than three months, during which time he had not been fully privy to the decisions being made in the White House. Only after he became president did Truman learn of the atomic bomb being developed by the Manhattan Project. Nonetheless he was determined to uphold Roosevelt's legacy. 'I'm trying to do what he would like', he would explain to visitors early in his term. In a message to Congress in September 1945 he called for the enactment of Roosevelt's Economic Bill of Rights and other reform measures.

Truman's first major domestic responsibility was to oversee the massive demobilization of the military and the economy. Bowing to insistent public demand, Truman brought home servicemen as fast as he could. The 12 million military personnel on active duty in June 1945 were reduced to 3 million a year later and subsequently to about 1.5 million (still about six times the pre-war size). Yet more daunting was the task of reconverting the economy to peacetime production. The millions of Americans discharged from the armed services were hitting the job market at the same time as government was cancelling war contracts. There were widespread fears that the United States would revert to a traumatizing depression after the manner of the 1930s. This nightmare was not realized. During the war wage-packets had fattened and savings had risen, and with the return of peace Americans embarked on a joyous consumer boom. Further, while federal government expenditure declined it was much greater than it had been before the war. This private and public spending averted the anticipated depression.

Yet reconversion hardly proceeded smoothly. As wartime controls were withdrawn prices rose steeply, and attempts by the president to reimpose them encountered obstruction in Congress. Price ceilings were placed on meat in the summer of 1946, but farmers withheld produce from the legitimate market and disposed of much of it on a flourishing black market. The failing offensive against inflation was linked to another protracted struggle, that with the unions. Having for the most part observed a no strike pledge during the war, the unions were itching for substantial wage increases to compensate for rising prices. A great strike wave shook the autumn of 1945, and intense industrial action continued through 1946, when the sheer number of strikes hit a new record. Most disputes were resolved more or less peacefully, but the Truman administration became embroiled in fierce confrontations with the

United Mine Workers under John L. Lewis, resulting in the government assuming formal control of the mines, and with the railroad unions, leading Truman both to seize the railroads and, more alarmingly, to ask Congress for power to draft railroad workers into the army. The settlement of the strike averted this outcome.

While Truman's stand against 'Big Labor' aligned him with public opinion, his general performance in 1945–6 did little to establish public confidence. The liberal constituencies in the New Deal coalition were further distressed when several prominent New Dealers, including Frances Perkins and Henry Wallace, left the Truman cabinet. But two historic measures secured in 1946 were in accord with New Deal prescriptions. One was the Atomic Energy Act, which placed the development of nuclear energy under the control of an Atomic Energy Commission, a government agency composed of five civilian appointees. Fissionable material was to be in government hands alone – the public, not the private sector. The other was the Employment Act, which created the Council of Economic Advisers, and while congressional conservatives nullified its commitment to full employment the act did vest responsibility for maintaining prosperity in federal hands.

The industrial unrest and the uncertain handling of reconversion, however, created a public impression that Harry Truman was out of his depth and in the mid-term elections of November 1946 the Republicans overturned the large Democratic majorities in both houses of Congress. The two years 1947–9 constitute the only period during the entire era of the New Deal Order when a Democratic president faced a Republican-dominated Congress. The relationship was one of mutual hostility, as each branch sought to frustrate the designs of the other. Truman's hopes of securing further reform legislation were all but dashed and to a large extent Congress seized the political initiative. Its Republican leadership interpreted the outcome of the 1946 elections as an invitation to give a rightward thrust to public policies and it eagerly embraced the opportunity to try to arrest the direction taken by the federal government since 1933. A major priority was to cut taxes and a tax reduction bill was eventually passed in 1947, over Truman's veto. Broadly congressional changes to the tax codes during the Truman administration made them less progressive, serving the cause of consumption rather than redistribution (and also tending to privilege the male breadwinner).

Similarly close to Republican and business hearts was a determination to strip organized labour of the advantages afforded it by the New Deal. The strike wave of 1945–6 had made unions distinctly unpopular, and several anti-labour bills were introduced. The legislation which eventuated in mid-1947 was the Taft-Hartley Act (discussed in Chapter 7). Truman, mindful of his need to restore his credibility with labour after his bitter quarrels with the miners and railroad workers, vetoed the bill in a ringing message, but Congress easily overrode his veto.

Yet the Taft-Hartley Act represented the only significant modification of a New Deal policy. The 80th Congress may have contemptuously refused to act on the president's requests for new reform measures, but the major legislative accomplishments of the New Deal remained in place. Occasionally measures were secured that the Roosevelt administration had favoured. The most significant was the National Security Act of 1947, which brought the army, navy and air force together under a new Department of Defense. It also established a National Security Council (NSC) to harmonize defence and foreign policies, and a Central Intelligence Agency (CIA) to develop a coordinated intelligence-gathering capability. The location of the NSC in the Executive Office of the President (rather than the Pentagon) gave the White House another instrument with which to formulate policy, although its influence did not become marked until the Cold War deepened.

In 1948 some liberal Democrats were still toying with finding a new presidential candidate, but the national convention nominated Truman on the first ballot. Still, given the Republican triumph in 1946 and persisting doubts about Truman's ability, 1948 was widely expected to be a Republican year, and when the Republicans nominated Thomas E. Dewey, the governor of New York, Dewey soon led in the opinion polls. Confident of victory, Dewey kept a low profile in the campaign. Harry Truman took a different tack. The Republicans had in fact inserted some reform planks into their platform, and Truman announced to the Democratic convention that he was calling a special session of Congress on 'turnip day' and challenging it to pass the promised bills. (In Missouri, it seemed, farmers sowed turnips on 26 July.) When Congress failed to enact any significant measure Truman embarked on a 'whistle-stop' campaign, making over 350 speeches and energetically lambasting the 'do nothing' Congress as the 'worst' in American history.

Even so the odds against Truman seemed enormous since the Democratic Party was splitting into three (as it was to do again more fatefully in 1968). On the left were radicals who felt that Truman was betraying the promise of the New Deal, particularly in his strongly anti-Soviet foreign policy, and they seceded to form a Progressive Party ticket, headed by the former vice-president Henry A. Wallace, to whom the Communist Party also lent support. On the right were conservative Southern Democrats dismayed by Truman's initiatives on civil rights and particularly by the strong civil rights plank thrust on the national convention by Northern liberals. A group of them walked out of the convention and formed a States Rights – or Dixiecrat ticket – headed by Governor Strom Thurmond of South Carolina. Both the Wallace and the Thurmond candidacies threatened to siphon off votes from the Democrats. On the eve of the election the public opinion polls showed Dewey ahead by about five points, and on election night the *Chicago Tribune* confidently went to press with the headline 'DEWEY DEFEATS TRUMAN'.

It was actually Truman who was a few percentage points ahead in the popular vote. Wallace's campaign faltered badly, partly because he was red-baited by the two major parties, and he salvaged little over 1 million votes. Thurmond fared as badly in the popular vote, and while he carried four deep Southern states his intervention did not throw any state to the Republicans.

Truman did well in the big cities and carried much of the industrial Midwest. The greater part of the South remained loyal to the Democrats and, more surprisingly, most Western states went for Truman too. It seemed that farmers had been none too happy with the 80th Congress's apparent indifference to sliding farm prices.

The unexpected outcome of the election has been attributed to a number of features, among them Dewey's complacent campaigning, Truman's spirited fightback, the recapture of the Midwestern farm vote and an electoral tendency to close ranks behind the president at a time of serious foreign policy crises (most notably the Communist coup in Czechoslovakia early in the year and the Soviet blockade of Berlin in the summer). The Democrats won too because after the hiccups of 1945–6 the economy was thriving. Fundamentally, however, Truman won because – in contrast to 1968 – the New Deal coalition held together, and elements of it, especially organized labour and African-Americans, probably made the difference in key states. The 1948 presidential election was the first in twenty years in which Franklin Roosevelt was not a candidate. Truman's victory, together with Democratic majorities in both houses of Congress, in a sense represented the confirmation of the New Deal style of politics. The personal qualities of Franklin Roosevelt may have attracted many urban voters to the Democrats in the first place, but 1948 showed that the Democrats could retain their majority position without him.

Elected president in his own right Truman called for a new reform offensive, including civil rights and national health legislation, stressing his programme's continuity with the New Deal by dubbing it the Fair Deal. But he was unable to make much headway, Southern Democrats often siding with Republicans in Congress to obstruct liberal measures. An act to support the building of low-income housing did pass in 1949, since it won the support of the Republican leader Senator Robert Taft, and in 1950 Roosevelt's Social Security Act was significantly broadened, mainly to embrace self-employed people.

By this time Truman's popularity was sagging once more, rendering the enactment of a reform programme even more remote. No great groundswell of public opinion had emerged to give buoyancy to the Fair Deal. Americans seemingly had no wish to undo the New Deal but they had no stomach for a new reform crusade either. Indeed, by the late 1940s reform proposals were being regarded with some suspicion. The intensifying Cold War enabled conservatives to impute socialist tendencies to programmes that would further enlarge the scope of government. The American Medical Association, for example, spent large sums in mobilizing opposition to Truman's plan for a national system of health insurance. As the relationship of the United States with the Soviet Union deteriorated markedly during Truman's second term, fear of Communist subversion came to overshadow other domestic concerns.

The Red Scare of 1919–20 had illustrated the potential of anti-communist sentiments, which began to mount again in the late 1930s. They found expression in the establishment of the House Un-American Activities Committee (HUAC) in 1938 and the passage in 1940 of the Smith Act, seeking to outlaw conspiracy to overthrow the government by force. That 'little red scare' was cut short by the Second World War, when the Soviet Union was an ally, but after it red scare politics revived. Many Democratic voters, among them working-class Catholics from immigrant families, turned strongly anti-communist as the Soviet Union extended its control over their former home-lands. The Truman administration made containing international communism its primary foreign policy objective, assuming a highly visible ideological stance, but the Republican 80th Congress happily used the communist issue to embarrass the administration. It was in this congressional session that HUAC became a household name through its celebrated hearings on the Communist infiltration of Hollywood in the fall of 1947, although it also paid attention to the major labour unions and popular front groups like the Southern Conference for Human Welfare, that is to those constituencies associated with the leftward edge of the New Deal coalition.

The Truman White House responded to congressional harassment by trying to make security issues the preserve of the executive. In March 1947 the president announced an historic turning point in American foreign policy, the Truman Doctrine offering aid to those 'free peoples' of the world menaced by communist aggression. The domestic counterpart was a federal loyalty programme, under which existing or prospective government employ-ees would be screened for 'disloyalty'. It is doubtful that Truman, bent on pre-empting the Republican Congress before it fashioned more draconian legislation, appreciated the crudeness of the programme's procedures. In 1948 the administration strengthened its anti-communist stance by deploy-ing the Smith Act against twelve Communist leaders, charging them with conspiring to organize the Communist Party (CP) as a body advocating the violent overthrow of the government.

The outcome of the 1948 presidential election left the United States poised on the brink of an intensive red scare. The weakness demonstrated by the Communist Party (via the Progressive Party) in the 1948 election rendered it exceedingly vulnerable, for even labour leaders were drawing the conclu-sion that association with it was a distinct liability. And Republican Party leaders, seething at their unexpected defeat, saw in the communist issue a weapon that could be turned against the Truman administration.

By 1950 the United States was succumbing to its second major red scare. In that year Senator Joseph McCarthy began brandishing his lists of alleged Communists in the State Department; the Internal Security Act was passed over Truman's veto; and Republican candidates appeared to profit consid-erably in the November elections from red-baiting tactics. What really gave the Republicans the opportunity to crucify the administration for being 'soft on communism' was the evolution of the Cold War itself, with the 'fall' of China in 1949 (the result, allegedly, of an incompetent or disloyal State Department), the surprise Soviet explosion in the same year of an atomic bomb (perhaps American secrets had been leaked) and the onset in 1950 of the Korean War in which American boys were soon dying.

It was the Hiss case that allowed Republicans to implicate the reigning Democrats in the communist conspiracy. A former senior official in the State Department, Alger Hiss in 1948 was named as a Soviet spy by ex-Communist Whittaker Chambers. Hiss had been with Roosevelt at Yalta – where right-wingers believed that the United States had been sold out to the Soviet Union – and was ideally cast to personify the Republican charge that Communists had penetrated to the very heart of the New Deal. In 1949 Hiss went on trial, and when he was found guilty in January 1950 the conspiracy theory seemed vindicated. The certitude that the Soviet Union had had access to American secrets was corroborated in February 1950, when Klaus Fuchs, a British scientist who had worked in Los Alamos during the war, admitted in London that he had spied for the Soviets. The unexpected reverses in post-war foreign policy were now explained to the satisfaction of right-wing Republicans.

By February 1950 Republican speakers across the country were laying into the administration for harbouring Communists. One such speech was given by an obscure senator from Wisconsin, Joseph R. McCarthy. It was in Wheeling, West Virginia, that he flourished his imaginative 'list of names' of 205 Communists in the State Department, which next day in Denver became '207 bad risks' and in Salt Lake City '57 card-carrying members of the Communist Party'. Whatever the number, here was a United States senator claiming to possess a specific list of Communist employees. The press was electrified and within a few months McCarthy became the personification of American anti-communism. That summer war broke out in Korea and Julius and Ethel Rosenberg were arrested as spies, further evidence that Communists had successfully breached American security. Better than anyone, partly because he was not inhibited by the facts, McCarthy was able to tap the vein of suspicion that there were traitors in government. The Republican leadership encouraged McCarthy in his thuggish assaults on the Truman administration. He was sometimes criticized for his reckless falsehoods by fellow senators, but when some of his critics lost their seats at the elections of 1950 and 1952, McCarthy's electoral clout reached mythic proportions.

The Korean War provided the backdrop for the prolonged red scare known as McCarthyism. In September 1950 the conservative bloc in Congress demonstrated its contempt for Truman's loyalty programme by passing the Internal Security Act over a presidential veto. This required Communist and Communist-front organizations to register with the government. Truman's loyalty programme had been focused on federal employees; the new act subjected private associations and individuals to political surveillance. The trustworthiness of Communists at any point in American society was being questioned, legitimizing the emerging purges of 'subversives' in Hollywood, education and private industry. HUAC continued on its marauding way, and the Senate in 1951 set up its own body, the Senate Internal Security Subcommitee (SISS), so that senators too could win Communist scalps.

While Joe McCarthy and the Republicans had ratcheted up the communist issue, the Truman administration had been seeking to remove Communists from public life since its adoption of the loyalty programme. The Smith Act defendants were convicted in 1949, and after their convictions were upheld by the Supreme Court in 1951 further indictments followed. Dozens of local Communist leaders were soon on their way to prison. The anti-communist drive of the Justice Department was sensationally illustrated in 1951 by the trial and conviction of Julius and Ethel Rosenberg for conspiracy to commit espionage. The judge vouchsafed the opinion that the Rosenbergs were part of a 'diabolical conspiracy to destroy a God-fearing nation', had given the Soviet Union the atomic bomb and so brought on the war in Korea, and sentenced them to death.

The Republicans sought to extract maximum advantage from the communist issue in the 1952 presidential election. Even presidential candidate Dwight Eisenhower, who detested McCarthy, told a campaign meeting that a Republican administration 'will find the pinks, we will find the Communists, we will find the disloyal'. The Republicans promised to be even more vigilant than the Democrats in rooting out Communists, and their victory ensured the continuance of the anti-communist cause.

The FBI and various government departments were soon energetically discharging their patriotic duty in dismissing, prosecuting and deporting the Communists they thought they discovered. In 1953 President Eisenhower established a new federal programme that expanded the criteria under which employees would be dismissed as security risks. The administration soon boasted of the multitude being severed from federal employment. Many of these held lowly offices in the federal bureaucracy, but occasionally a major figure was netted. The most celebrated was J. Robert Oppenheimer, whose popular front associations before the Second World War had not precluded his directing the atomic bomb programme during it. The security community had never been entirely happy about Oppenheimer, and his criticism of Cold War defence strategy earned him further enemies in the military. By the 1950s he had returned to academic life, but he remained a consultant of the Atomic Energy Commission until 1954, when a review board concluded that he was a security risk because of 'his past associations with persons known to him to be Communists'.

The Republican electoral victories of 1952 also enabled Senator McCarthy to assume chairmanship of a committee, the Committee on Government Operations, along with its investigative subcommittee authorized to scrutinize 'government activities at all levels', of which he took personal control. It was his junketings in 1953 that greatly increased his public recognition. By the end of the year McCarthy was probing army radar laboratories, while, coincidentally, his aide Roy Cohn was applying intense pressure on the army to obtain favourable treatment for his close friend David Schine, who had been drafted. The relationship between the army and the McCarthy subcommittee deteriorated as each nursed grievances against the other.

But in taking on the army McCarthy overreached himself. His contemptuous behaviour towards senior army personnel ultimately pitted him against the Commander-in-Chief, President Eisenhower, who was furious at the treatment of his old service. Eisenhower was paying the price for his political timidity during the campaign of 1952, when he had failed to come to the defence of his old patron, General George Marshall, who had been viciously attacked by McCarthy. The president's stand in 1954 was hardly more edifying, although arguably it was effective. Deciding that he was not going to dignify the senator by confronting him personally, Eisenhower kept in the background while using others to try to bring him down. Vice-President Nixon went on radio to condemn McCarthy's methods, and in the Senate fellow Republican Ralph Flanders delivered a devastating attack on him for 'doing his best to shatter' the Republican Party. Some of McCarthy's allies deserted him as he fell out with the Republican administration.

As these forces mobilized against McCarthy, the army released a report on Roy Cohn's harassment of the army to secure privileges for Schine. With the army and McCarthy each levelling charges at the other, the investigative subcommittee determined to hear both sides as McCarthy yielded the chair to Senator Karl Mundt. Millions watched the televised hearings that opened in April 1954, mesmerized by McCarthy's endless points of order and bullying demeanour. The dramatic high point came when McCarthy gratuitously smeared a young lawyer, allowing the army's counsel, Joseph Welch, to transfix his audience with the rejoinder: 'Until this moment, Senator, I think I never really gauged your cruelty or your recklessness.' By June McCarthy's Gallup poll ratings had turned distinctly 'unfavourable', and in July Senator Flanders demanded his formal censure. In the past McCarthy's fellow Republican senators had generally protected him from serious political injury, but they had little reason to do so now there was a Republican administration. In December 1954 the Senate voted to 'condemn' him. Further, the Democratic successes in the November elections ended Republican control of the Senate and deprived McCarthy of his prized chairmanship. Increasingly a loner, he attracted little further attention until his death in 1957.

The destruction of McCarthy did not put an end to the harassment of radicals, but eventually the tide turned. McCarthy had given anti-communism a bad name and the larger crusade lost some of its dynamic. The evolution of the Cold War seemed to make nuclear holocaust less imminent. It was increasingly seen as a long struggle for the minds and hearts of the peoples of the world, making imperative the display of the finer qualities of American civilization. Leading public figures spoke out more boldly in upholding civil liberties and the Supreme Court began to dismantle the official anti-communist machinery. The Court delivered its most devastating blows in June 1957, when it handed down decisions that narrowed the investigative scope of congressional committees like HUAC and eviscerated the Smith Act. Anti-communist impulses did not die, but the McCarthyite red scare was over.

Whether McCarthy had contributed much to the Republican success in the 1952 election is doubtful. Ardent McCarthyite candidates, in fact, had not fared particularly well and McCarthy himself had trailed the Republican field in Wisconsin. But use had been made of the communist issue, as when Karl Mundt defined the Republican platform as 'K_1C_2 – Korea, Communism, Corruption,' and the nomination of the moderate Dwight Eisenhower for president had been balanced by giving the vice-presidential slot to Richard Nixon, whose rise to the Senate had owed something to judicious red scare tactics.

The explanation for the Republican victory rests primarily elsewhere. Truman's personal standing had reached another low point, partly because of corruption charges that had been levied at some of his aides. More importantly, the Korean War had dragged on dispiritingly into its third year and had become exceedingly unpopular. Truman himself, recognizing the immense obstacles that would attend his own candidacy, had decided not to run again and the Democratic nomination had gone to the eloquent governor of Illinois, Adlai Stevenson. But Stevenson's wit was no match for the charisma that the adored hero of the Second World War brought with him, and Eisenhower's offer to go to Korea to end the war was the message that many Americans wanted to hear. Eisenhower swept the country, Stevenson retaining the loyalty only of the Democratic Deep South and a few border states.

Yet the Republican victory did not overthrow the New Deal system of politics. Eisenhower's coat-tails did provide Republican majorities in both houses of Congress, but only narrowly. And Eisenhower had made clear in the campaign that he did not intend to revert to the narrow political economy of Herbert Hoover. If necessary, he promised, government would use its powers to combat a depression. He would also follow Roosevelt's lead in maintaining the internationalist stance of the United States. In fact the New Deal coalition stood up well enough to provide Adlai Stevenson with more popular votes than Truman had won in 1948. The industrial cities, organized labour, African-Americans and most of the rural South remained in the Democratic column. The New Deal coalition lived to fight another day.

'When it comes down to dealing with the human in this country ...' President Eisenhower once reflected, 'the people in this administration believe in being ... liberal, and when we deal with the economic affairs of this country, we believe in being conservative.' The new president's political instincts were fairly conservative, and privately he had had little affection for Franklin Roosevelt and his works, but he possessed common sense and was temperamentally drawn to accommodation. He was appalled by the posturing on the far right of the Republican Party and saw little point in pulling down the structures associated with the New Deal. The Social Security system was safe with him, as was the minimum wage. 'Should any political party attempt to abolish social security and eliminate labor laws and farm programs', he told his brother, 'you would not hear of that party again in our political history.' To his cabinet he admitted his wish to sell the TVA while ruefully conceding that 'I suppose we can't go as far as that'. Eisenhower did want to balance the budget, and at a time when Keynesian economics was becoming the new orthodoxy his fiscal prudence could seem like a reversion to an earlier economic order, but when recession loomed he was prepared to countenance some – modest – government spending. It could be said that the Eisenhower administration fortified the New Deal state by accepting it, though that is not an epitaph he would have cherished.

Eisenhower nonetheless liked to think of his political style as 'dynamic conservatism'; other labels have also been applied, such as 'Modern Republicanism'. Historian Robert Griffith has used the term 'corporate commonwealth' to define Eisenhower's vision. There was a sense in which Eisenhower did hark back to traditional values, and that was in his assumption that the public good was indivisible and it was the responsibility of men of good will to subordinate their private interests to those of the country. He feared the conflicts in modern society, especially the destructive potential of class conflict, and believed rather that classes and interests were interdependent and that it was the duty of government to try to resolve the differences. In his view, 'no prosperity for one economic group is permanently possible except as all groups prosper'. This vision reached into the wider world. Unlike some of his Republican fellows, he was committed to the internationalist stance that the United States had assumed since the Second World War and he believed that it should play a role in promoting a stable world order.

To his administration Eisenhower sought to recruit men (and a few women) who shared his attachment to disinterested public service. It could be said that he was clothing the New Deal state in progressive values. He turned to corporate America for its expertise, particularly to the 'corporate liberals' who accepted the presence of organized labour and a modest welfare state though wanted no more New Deal reform. His cabinet was said to consist of 'nine businessmen and a plumber'; his secretary of defense was Charles E. Wilson, president of General Motors, who embarrassed the administration by explaining that 'what's good for General Motors business is good for America'. The plumber was a union official, Secretary of Labor Martin Durkin, though he lasted less than a year and was replaced by a business executive. Eisenhower did not believe in handing favours to business, but he sought a cooperative relationship with it. Broadly he agreed with the business community that government intervention in the economy should be minimal and that the powers of the state should not be further extended. Ideally he would have liked to reverse the trend towards big government.

Central to Eisenhower's efforts was his determination to balance the budget. As he later expressed it: 'The Budget is not designed for special interests; the real purpose is to promote the good of all America.' Soon after assuming office he reduced appropriations for foreign aid and defence, and the ending of the Korean War allowed further cuts. By the fiscal year 1956 the overall budget was actually in surplus, a feat Eisenhower was to achieve twice more as he kept a tight control on defence expenditure and trimmed Democratic programmes where he could. This exercise in prudent housekeeping was deplored by some economists but was remarkable in the light of the budget deficits that had been the norm since 1931. Eisenhower was helped by a mostly growing economy, but the Cold War was also at its height and the pressures for more defence spending were intense. Repeatedly this former NATO commander saw off the demands of the military. As he observed in 1956, 'some day there is going to be a man sitting in my present chair who has not been raised in the military services and who will have little understanding of where slashes in their estimates can be made with little or no damage'.

Eisenhower's caution on the budget was matched by his insistence on shedding the responsibilities of the federal government where practicable to the states or to private business. While he was prepared to sustain the limited welfare commitments inherited from the New Deal he had no intention of initiating new programmes; welfare he considered the responsibility of the states. Where possible too he encouraged the replacement of public provision with private enterprise.

The Truman administration had held to the view that the offshore lands off the Gulf Coast, known to be rich in oil, belonged to the federal government, much to the irritation of the states and oil companies. Eisenhower sided with states' rights and the business community and in 1953 secured the Tidelands Oil Act, which transferred the oil deposits to the states, mainly Texas and Louisiana, which were expected to allow commercial exploitation. Similarly, rather than proceed with a large federal dam on Idaho's Snake River, the administration instead approved three smaller dams built by private companies. In 1954 it rebuffed the TVA, the symbol of publicly provided electricity, by giving a contract for an immense new electricity plant near Memphis to a private power syndicate, though congressional opposition killed the deal. Eisenhower also wanted to limit government involvement in agriculture. He tried to reduce price supports for farmers, though with modest success. He did abandon the federal monopoly of the development of atomic power, securing legislation to permit private companies to build and operate atomic reactors for electricity under the authority of the Atomic Energy Commission. In these various instances the thrust was to reduce federal responsibilities or place services in private hands. The business community was also kept happy by the appointment of pro-business members to such regulatory bodies as the Federal Trade Commission and the Interstate Commerce Commission.

Many businesses also benefited from the Interstate Highway Act of 1956, which provided large subsidies for the construction of a network of freeways across the nation, or as Eisenhower himself put it, 'the biggest peacetime construction project ... ever undertaken'. The cost was to be shared with the states, and Eisenhower's concern for financial prudence was propitiated by a provision raising revenue for this mighty enterprise through increased taxes, including a petrol tax. The act was to have profound implications for the American transport system in particular and the economy in general, among other things promoting further suburbanization.

While Eisenhower wanted to curb government costs and provide an environment in which business could flourish, he had no intention of restoring the political economy of Herbert Hoover. Indeed, in 1954 and 1956 he agreed with Congress to broaden the reach of Social Security, bringing 10 million new workers into the system, and the minimum wage was also raised. The costs of these changes fell more on business than on the federal government. Eisenhower also showed some flexibility when recessions loomed, promising in 1954 that the government would step in if unemployment rose seriously. In fact, partly because of Eisenhower's fear of stoking inflation, government action was fairly minimal in the recessions of 1953–4 and 1957–8; as Iwan Morgan has commented, Eisenhower was 'at best a passive and half-hearted Keynesian'. What perhaps is surprising is the degree to which New Deal structures remained intact in spite of an economic conservative in the White House.

One reason why Eisenhower failed to roll back the New Deal was that he rarely commanded the support of Congress. The Republican majorities in that body were slender during his first two years and they disappeared altogether for the rest of his administration. The Democratic Congress frustrated some of Eisenhower's initiatives, although it showed little interest in liberal reform measures itself. Southern Democrats often sided with Republicans in support of fiscal discipline.

Whatever the success of the Democrats in congressional elections, however, Eisenhower's personal popularity was insurmountable in presidential elections. For the election of 1956 the Democrats again fielded Adlai Stevenson, but he won fewer popular votes than in 1952. The avuncular Eisenhower was aided by foreign policy crises (notably the Soviet suppression of an uprising in Hungary and the Anglo-French confrontation with Egypt over its seizure of the Suez Canal), while the buoyant economy meant that there was no serious discontent with the administration. Yet the Democrats retained control of both houses of Congress. Eisenhower might be trusted to keep the peace, but it may be that voters had no wish to imperil the gains of the New Deal by allowing Republicans to dominate Congress. A substantial part of Eisenhower's energy during his second term was spent resisting the attempts of congressional Democrats to increase spending.

He was also obliged to give rather lukewarm attention to civil rights. The civil rights movement was gathering strength and the president did recognize the constitutional right of African-Americans to the franchise, while Republican strategists still hoped to win back more black votes. In 1957 Eisenhower requested a law to protect voting rights, a demand that would normally be frustrated by Southerners in the Senate, though on this occasion the Democratic majority leader, Lyndon Johnson, persuaded the Southern leadership to withhold a filibuster on the understanding that the bill would be a mild one. The Civil Rights Act of 1957 was an historic measure as the first such act of the twentieth century, though its effectiveness was limited. It established a Commission on Civil Rights to investigate abuses and authorized the Justice Department to seek injunctions against denials of voting rights. Anyone indicted under the law, however, would be accorded a jury trial, an important provision for Southern senators who knew that Southern juries were unlikely to convict a white man. Another civil rights act in 1960 slightly strengthened the modest protections afforded to African-Americans wanting to vote.

Eisenhower's belief that federal authority should not be deployed more than necessary was illustrated in his attitude towards racial integration in schools. He had no liking for the Supreme Court's *Brown* decision of 1954, calling for school desegregation, publicly made no comment on it and showed no eagerness to use federal influence to enforce it. Massively resisted in the Deep South, integration proceeded very slowly even in the border states. As discussed in Chapter 11, however, the school board of Little Rock, Arkansas, tried to introduce gradual desegregation at the Central High School, a process which was frustrated in September 1957 by a hostile state governor and an angry white mob. Obliged to uphold federal authority, and sensitive to the harm being done to the American image in the Cold War world, Eisenhower reluctantly sent in paratroopers and the children were admitted to the school under guard. In other Southern states too the white authorities resisted school integration, which made barely token progress during the rest of the Eisenhower administration. Like many others, the president believed that social attitudes could not be legislated. In 1958 the Arkansas governor, Orval Faubus, was identified in a Gallup poll as 'one of the ten most admired men in the world'.

Shortly after the Little Rock crisis came the Sputnik crisis, when in October 1957 the Soviet Union became the first power to succeed in putting an artificial satellite into space. Another Sputnik containing a dog went up in November. When the United States attempted to emulate the Soviets in December the Navy Vanguard rocket exploded on its launching pad. This shattering evidence of Soviet technological superiority precipitated an intense debate in the United States over the adequacy of the American educational system and prepared the way for the National Defense Education Act of 1958, which poured federal money into the study of science, mathematics and foreign languages, including undergraduate and graduate programmes. Not since the land-grant college act of 1862 had the federal government offered significant financial support for higher education. Already expanding fast, American colleges and universities were boosted further, albeit in the name of national security. Nonetheless there was no quick fix to the 'space race' (which Eisenhower regarded as a low priority anyway), and the continuing success of the Soviet Union in space generated suspicions that it also enjoyed an advantage in nuclear missiles. Democratic critics of the administration made much of the so-called 'missile gap', particularly as the 1960 election loomed.

The personal popularity of Dwight Eisenhower had enabled the Republican Party to overcome the electoral advantages of the Democrats in the presidential elections of 1952 and 1956, but in 1960 Democratic hegemony was restored – just. The closely contested campaign aroused voter interest and the turnout was unusually high at 65.4 per cent. The main elements of the New Deal coalition – several big industrial states, a substantial part of the South, urban-ethnic, trade-unionist and African-American votes – reasserted themselves to place John F. Kennedy in the White House. The youthful Kennedy, skilfully using the medium of television, projected an image of vigour, identified himself with a rather mild New Deal liberalism and, above all, promised action. His Republican opponent, Richard Nixon, like Kennedy offered economic growth at home and the containment of communism abroad, but it was Kennedy's graceful and energetic image that won the day, although the popular vote could not have been narrower. With a lead of only 0.17 per cent, Kennedy could barely claim a mandate, and the Democratic majorities in Congress were trimmed as well.

But the New Deal coalition had restored Democratic ascendancy in both the executive and the legislative branches of government. While the Cold War still exercised its sobering impact on domestic politics, McCarthyism was in the past and just possibly the age of political stalemate was over. The liberals in the Democratic Party looked to some kind of a revival of New Deal reform, though in this age of affluence the liberal agenda was turning more to the extension of rights than the underpinning of economic security. Black Americans were among those who saw reason for optimism.

|11|

The African-American Challenge
1933–69

The middle third of the twentieth century did not deliver equal rights to African-Americans, but it did witness a major transformation of race relations. The Progressive Order had, in effect, placed African-Americans firmly beyond the pale. In 1933 the great majority were still legally the subjects of a segregation that rigorously excluded them from the 'normal' opportunities of American life. Outside the South there were fewer formal barriers to the ambitions of black Americans, but they generally lived on the fringes of the economy and enjoyed negligible political influence. Racial prejudice was endemic. As late as 1944 only 45 per cent of whites thought blacks should 'have as good a chance' as themselves 'to get any kind of job'. By the late 1960s, however, the condition of African-Americans had changed profoundly. Jim Crow had formally ended, and blacks and whites were using the same public facilities even in the Deep South, where blacks were also casting votes in unprecedented numbers. The old attachment of African-Americans to the party of Lincoln had been severed, for they had been incorporated into the Democratic Party as part of the New Deal coalition. In the Progressive Era the few black Republican voters had been too marginal to the political process to carry any weight; during the New Deal Order black voters could determine the outcome of presidential elections. White attitudes had apparently softened too. By the early 1970s almost all whites – 97 per cent – said that blacks should have the same opportunity as whites for a job. By 1970 there were ten blacks in Congress, a figure that suggested that there was still a mountain to climb, but an advance on the lone black congressman of 1930.

Demographic upheaval accounted for much of this change. With the collapse of the Cotton Kingdom in the South and the ending of large-scale European immigration to the United States, African-Americans streamed northward to supply the industrial states with workers. Nearly 80 per cent of black Americans still lived in the South in 1930, but by 1960 the figure had fallen to below 60 per cent; over a third now resided in the North and others in the West. This massive redistribution of African-Americans reflected the continuing impact of the Great Migration. Although it slowed somewhat during the depressed 1930s, it accelerated again with the huge demand for labour during and after the Second World War. Between 1940 and 1960 over 3 million African-Americans left the South. The massive decline of cotton farming and the subsequent mechanization of Southern agriculture in these decades destroyed huge numbers of jobs, while in 1950 a young black man could earn over 50 per cent more in the North than in the South.

As important as the relocation of African-Americans was their urbanization. In 1930 the census classified most whites as urban and most blacks as not; by 1960 the proportion of urbanized blacks was greater than that for whites. In the former year, about 70 per cent of Southern blacks lived in rural areas, but within the South too blacks were moving into towns and cities, and by 1960 the proportion in urban areas had almost doubled. Outside the South by 1960, a stunning 93 per cent of blacks were living in what officials defined as metropolitan areas. This swift environmental revolution held profound implications for socialization, education and collective action. For one thing, it meant that millions of non-voters were being turned into voters. But it did not mean an end to segregation. Southern whites were still slowing the integration of their school systems, while *de facto* segregation in the North increased as blacks moved to city centres and whites took refuge in the suburbs. Nonetheless, the 'typical' black American had swapped the captivity of the Southern soil for the uncertainty and opportunities of urban life.

Changing economic conditions had powerful implications for black Americans. The Great Depression imperilled their livelihoods and even their lives, but also created the circumstances that allowed them to secure new political allies. The succour offered by the New Deal persuaded many to embrace the Democratic Party, which in turn meant that they were finally able to escape from their historic state of political impotence. Then the Second World War opened unusual employment opportunities, a feature sustained by post-war growth. The median annual income of black men was a mere 41 per cent of that of white men in 1940; by 1970 it was 59 per cent. A modest black middle class emerged, the proportion of black males in professional occupations jumping from 1.8 to 7.8 per cent. These gains meant that African-Americans were better placed to provide resources and leadership for organizations devoted to their cause. Further, the larger environment had changed in their favour, since the World War and Cold War not only greatly enhanced demand for their skills but also obliged government to pay greater heed to American democratic ideals.

But these better times could not be glimpsed in 1933. The Great Depression hit black Americans disproportionately hard. Millions of black sharecroppers, tenant farmers and farm labourers in the South, many of them already suffering from malnutrition, faced starvation following the precipitous collapse of cotton and other farm prices. Those that could escaped to the cities, although prospects were scarcely inviting. As a black sociologist observed in 1932, in a phrase that was destined to be endlessly repeated, the African-American was 'the surplus man, the last to be hired and the first to be fired'. By that date about half of black adults were unemployed in such cities as Chicago, Detroit and New York, perhaps twice the rate for whites. But desperate though these times were they were significant in allowing African-Americans an entry to the political system.

Franklin Roosevelt's New Deal never directly confronted the race issue, but its attitude to the needy won over many African-Americans. The fact that blacks constituted a high proportion of the unemployed meant that many benefited from the New Deal programmes. 'Let Jesus lead you and Roosevelt feed you', Chicago blacks were told. In the South federal relief payments to blacks were much less than those for whites, but the fact that they were made at all contrasted with the previous indifference of American government. Some New Deal agencies betrayed traditional racist attitudes, but others made attempts to channel to blacks a fairer share of resources. As many as a million African-American families were sustained by the Works Progress Administration in 1939, a remarkable figure at a time when the number of black households was little over 3 million. Government at last was holding out a hand to American blacks, even as its other hand was firmly clasped by self-regarding whites.

Other bonds were also forged between the New Deal and African-Americans. The Wagner Act was welcomed by the NAACP for the strength that unionization promised for blacks, and particularly significant was the New Deal's alliance with the CIO. Many black Americans were in unskilled and semi-skilled jobs in parts of the economy subject to the drives for industrial unionism. Spotting the potential for new recruits, CIO leaders established a Committee to Abolish Racial Discrimination. By the early 1940s there were 400,000 African-Americans in trade unions, and the CIO unions played their part in lining black voters up behind the Democrats. New Deal legislation served to strengthen the Brotherhood of Sleeping Car Porters, the black union headed by A. Philip Randolph, who became a black leader of national stature. The Roosevelt administration also offered unprecedented numbers of jobs to African-Americans. Roosevelt appointed the first ever black federal judge, and the proportion of blacks in the federal civil service more than doubled between 1933 and 1941. Mary McLeod Bethune, the daughter of a sharecropper, made a significant impact as director of the Office of Negro Affairs.

As late as 1932 about two-thirds of black voters still opted for the Republican presidential candidate, but by 1934 they were changing sides. Conscious of this expanding electorate, Democratic candidates began to campaign in black neighbourhoods, and civil rights activists constantly reminded their constituents of Roosevelt's promise that for him there would be 'no forgotten men and no forgotten races'. Further, more African-Americans were turning out to vote. 'In no national election since 1860', remarked *Time* magazine, 'have politicians been so Negro-minded as in 1936.' Franklin Roosevelt won over three-quarters of Northern black votes in that year. Black Americans were beginning to recognize too that the federal government could be an ally in contesting the local power structures that had for so long kept them in a state of subjection.

African-Americans thus acquired a modest leverage in the Democratic Party. Chicago, with its heavy black population, had sent a black Republican to Congress in 1928, but in 1934 it elected a black Democrat to succeed him. By 1946 there were over two dozen blacks in the Northern state legislatures. In the competitive two-party systems that tended to characterize the urban-industrial states the black vote could be decisive. These states wielded great influence in presidential elections, and the black voters in them were to prove crucial in delivering the elections of 1944, 1948 and 1960 to the Democratic candidates. National Democratic politicians could no longer ignore this constituency, even if their need not to alienate the white South meant that they were tempted to woo black voters with words rather than actions. Even symbolic recognition, however, gave the African-American cause an enhanced legitimacy.

As demographic and political currents brought some relief to African-Americans, civil rights groups took heart. The NAACP, which had been primarily a Northern organization in its early years, made substantial inroads into the South, over 70 per cent of new chapters being located there in the twenty years after 1930. It came increasingly to emphasize litigation rather than legislation, and in 1939 created the separate NAACP Legal Defense Fund to pursue rights through the courts. The National Negro Congress appeared in 1936 to try to coordinate black organizations, though Communist influence within it eventually limited its appeal. Southern liberalism displayed a remarkable vitality in the Southern Conference for Human Welfare, formed in 1938 to contest racial discrimination and the poll tax. A major objective at this time was a federal anti-lynching law, but neither the black electorate nor the civil rights groups could compete with the entrenched power of the white South in Washington. Then the outbreak of global war reconfigured the larger environment.

The Second World War followed by the Cold War brought a long period of economic growth and a labour shortage that blacks could hope to fill. In moving into cities they had access to better educational facilities, more varied occupational opportunities and better conditions for organization. Black churches, colleges, clubs and civil rights groups flourished more readily in urban environments, where blacks were somewhat less subject to white intimidation than in the countryside. When Southern states in the 1940s moved to pre-empt the Supreme Court by spending more on the black school systems to sustain the pretence that they really were equal, they were helping to create more sophisticated students, and the proportion completing high school increased dramatically. The 1940s alone witnessed a doubling of Southern black college enrolments; by 1950 about 4.5 per cent of blacks of college age were in higher education, far short of the white percentage but one that compared not unfavourably with the youth of other advanced countries. Expanding too was the number of African-Americans in professional jobs (though mainly in lower-paid professions, like social work and nursing). Very soon black organizations in Southern cities would be strong enough to mount challenges to the white power structures.

The new geopolitical circumstances also gave African-Americans hope. The United States had abandoned its traditional isolationism in favour of the role of 'free world' leader, first against fascist aggression and then against Communist 'slavery'. American political leaders could be acutely embarrassed in their conduct of foreign policy by the evidence of second-class citizenship at home. In the aftermath of the Second World War the European powers began to withdraw from their colonial empires, and as the Cold War evolved the United States was obliged to pay some heed to the increasing number of non-white nations. The maintenance of Jim Crow did not sit easily with its new global responsibilities, particularly as the reputation of racial theories in general reached a new low in the light of Nazi atrocities.

The outbreak of the Second World War seemed to presage major changes in American race relations. The war for the 'Four Freedoms' helped to raise the political consciousness of many African-Americans. The NAACP exploded from a membership of 54,000 in 1939 to an extraordinary half a million in 1945, and the Congress of Racial Equality (CORE), a Northern group interested in direct action, was established in 1942. Remembering the First World War, when W. E. B. Du Bois' advice to 'close ranks' in the war effort had not produced rewards, the NAACP and other groups determined on a 'Double V' campaign, to fight for democracy both abroad and at home. An early test came in 1941 when Roosevelt was busily turning the United States into 'the arsenal of democracy'. A. Philip Randolph elaborated a plan for a march on Washington to force the president to outlaw discrimination in government jobs and the military, and the idea caught the imagination of the black masses. Randolph had anticipated 10,000 marchers, but soon there were reports that 100,000 were preparing to participate. Roosevelt yielded and issued Executive Order 8802 banning discrimination in federal employment and the defence industries and establishing a Fair Employment Practices Committee (FEPC) to monitor its implementation. The march was called off and the black triumph seemed momentous. For the first time in history the federal government had capitulated to African-American pressure.

But Randolph's victory was more symbolic than substantive. The Executive Order was widely evaded and the administration made little attempt to enforce it, largely because of white intransigence. The influx of black Americans into urban America and the military was accompanied by racial stress and the growth of discrimination outside the South. The most vicious eruption was the 1943 race riot in Detroit, the heart of the defence industry. Hundreds of thousands of poor whites and blacks from Appalachia and the South had arrived to compete with the city's immigrant groups for jobs, overwhelming the housing supply and accelerating the physical deterioration of other public facilities. While the Detroit riot was the most destructive, with the deaths of twenty-five blacks and nine whites, riots and racial attacks also occurred in other cities, and there were several examples of racial violence on military bases. Also suffering from racial abuse were Mexican Americans, similarly drawn by the war demand for labour in the South-West and California, and some of whom were victims of the 'zoot suit riots' in Los Angeles in 1943, so-called because of the clothing then fashionable among young black and Latin males.

The war jolted but did not overthrow the caste system that had held so many black Americans in place. The labour shortage had an impact on employment patterns: the share of jobs for African-Americans in the defence industries rose from 3 per cent in 1942 to 8.6 per cent in 1945 and the number in the federal bureaucracy trebled. The services remained segregated, but the war introduced African-Americans to different parts of the country and service overseas. Black demands met with some response. In 1942 the Justice Department initiated an investigation of a lynching for the first time. In 1944 the Supreme Court, in *Smith v Allwright*, declared the white primary in Texas to be unconstitutional, opening the possibility of blacks becoming incorporated in Southern voting. Registration of black adults in the Southern states jumped from a tiny 3 per cent in 1940 to 12 per cent in 1947, mainly in urban areas like Atlanta. But civil rights progress was precarious. Some of the gains of the war years were soon reversed. In 1946 white Southerners secured the abolition of the FEPC and black unemployment rose again.

Jim Crow proved remarkably resilient. In the post-war decades the tension between the Southern white power structures and national administrations became palpable. The former were determined to maintain segregation and white supremacy, while the latter were increasingly conscious of the growing black electorate and world opinion. The Democratic Party struggled agonizingly to keep together its electoral coalition of conservative Southern whites and Northern labour, liberal and black constituents. Republican strategists also hoped to win back black voters, even as they weighed the prospects of winning support in the white South. These divided impulses within the major political parties simultaneously gave hope to African-Americans while placing limits on what they could expect.

The heightened salience of civil rights early became evident in the Truman administration, shaken by increased racial tension in the post-war South. Black GIs had been returning from the war and demanding the vote. 'After the close of hostilities', said one black soldier, 'we just kept on fighting.' A number of Southern states resisted by tightening registration procedures and imposing insurmountable literacy tests. A series of violent incidents in 1946 prompted Truman to establish the President's Committee on Civil Rights in December, and its report in 1947 called for an extension of federal authority to attack racial discrimination throughout American life. For the first time a presidential administration threw itself behind the civil rights cause when Truman responded to the report by asking Congress for laws to combat segregation. In 1948, an election year, Northern liberals inserted a strong civil rights plank in the Democratic platform, precipitating a split in the party as some Southern Democrats broke away to run a rival States' Rights candidate for president. Anxious not to alienate yet more Southern whites, Truman did not emphasize the plank, but during the campaign he did order the desegregation of the military (the only recommendation of the President's Committee to be implemented).

De facto discrimination still persisted in many areas in the North, but a combination of black agitation and embarrassed state governmental legislation substantially eroded it in the post-war years. Yet for the South the political environment again turned against black expectations. After 1948 foreign policy issues dominated the national agenda, and the increasingly anti-Soviet tone of American foreign policy was matched by a suspicion of radicalism at home. The civil rights movement itself was subjected to vicious red-baiting, and its organizations tended to be disrupted by disputes over whether to allow Communists to be members. Still, the Cold War ensured that the federal authorities themselves displayed some sympathy for black Americans, not least because racial outrages in the United States were a staple of Soviet propaganda.

There was little to be expected of Congress, in which Southern Democrats had the power to block civil rights bills, but court action offered a way forward, and the Justice Department now regularly lent its support to suits brought by civil rights groups. The NAACP had been challenging segregation in the courts for years, and since the late 1930s had been moving from a strategy of trying to secure genuinely equal treatment in separate facilities to one of denying the very constitutionality of the old separate but equal doctrine. The Supreme Court proved reasonably receptive to this thrust. In 1938 it had ruled that Missouri could not deny blacks admission to the white school in the absence of a black law school; in 1950, its *Sweatt* decision determined that a separate law school for blacks hurriedly created by Texas was not equal to the white school.

The NAACP's strategy of court action was vindicated in May 1954 in the historic *Brown v Topeka* decision. The Supreme Court unanimously concluded that 'in the field of public education the doctrine of "separate but equal" has no place. Separate educational facilities are inherently unequal'. Segregation, it determined, was an unconstitutional violation of the 14th Amendment and the South should end the practice. Yet the decision was not quite as dramatic as it first appeared, for it did not lay down a timetable for integration. A year later the Court ruled that integration should proceed 'with all deliberate speed', seeming to invite local school boards to integrate at their own pace. But local NAACP chapters in the South had begun to petition their school boards to comply with *Brown*.

If the Court hoped to appeal to moderate leadership in the South, its strategy misfired. 'Massive resistance' mounted, as local and state officials made clear their determination to defy the *Brown* ruling. In 1955–6 angry whites formed Citizens' Councils in many Southern cities, often composed of local businessmen, farmers and lawyers. Their intention, according to an Alabama member, was to 'make it difficult, if not impossible, for any Negro who advocates desegregation to find and hold a job, get credit, or renew a mortgage'. There was failure at the national level too. President Eisenhower clearly disliked the *Brown* decision, and while he did not publicly criticize it his silence allowed Southern racists to gain the initiative.

The South's few moderate politicians found the political tide sweeping against them. One former moderate to cleave to the white supremacist position was Governor Orval Faubus of Arkansas. In the town of Little Rock the gradualist school board had decided to comply with a federal court order and integrate the Central High School. But in 1957 Faubus was fighting an uphill battle for re-election and he decided to play the race card, despatching national guardsmen to the school to prevent nine black children from enrolling. Thereafter a large white mob surrounded the school. President Eisenhower reluctantly sent in army paratroopers, not so much to uphold civil rights as to restore order. Nonetheless, the intrusion of federal bayonets both enraged the racist white South and suggested to African-Americans what resistance could achieve. For the first time in living memory federal authority was protecting Southern blacks from the furies of those around them.

For the first time too television covered a major racial disturbance. Audiences around the world watched in bemusement the flickering images of a heaving white mob spitting abuse at a few little black children, and the experience left its mark on American opinion. Polls revealed that 90 per cent of white Americans outside the South supported the decision to send in troops. Nonetheless, if Washington fretted about the international reputation of the United States, the will of the Eisenhower administration was not behind integration, which continued to make minimal progress. This was again illustrated in Little Rock, for the governor ordered the city's high schools closed in 1958, and not until 1959 did black children gain entrance to Central High – just three of them!

Meanwhile, with the fading of red scare politics and the easing of international tensions after the ending of the Korean War, African-American communities gradually supplemented the NAACP's litigation strategy with their own direct action campaigns. Church groups in particular emerged at the forefront of local actions, particularly in contesting bus segregation.

There was a bus boycott in Baton Rouge in 1953, but it was a campaign in Montgomery, Alabama, in 1955–6 that won widespread attention. In December 1955 a black seamstress, Rosa Parks, was arrested for sitting in the white section of a Montgomery bus. Local African-Americans mobilized on her behalf and most of the local black churches joined the cause. These clerics and activists formed the Montgomery Improvement Association (MIA), which organized a boycott of the city's buses. A young Baptist minister, Martin Luther King Jr., was persuaded to accept the chairmanship of the MIA, a position that catapulted him to national celebrity. Race relations in the city deteriorated as its white Citizens' Council grew in size and blacks, in turn, determined to keep the city's buses empty. Boycott participants were harassed and King's home was bombed. Local blacks also challenged bus segregation in the courts, and in November 1956 the Supreme Court confirmed that it was unconstitutional. Just before Christmas, Martin Luther King and his black and white friends rode together at the front of a Montgomery bus.

While Montgomery did not immediately inspire a large wave of protests, some communities witnessed bus boycotts, usually sustained by black church groups, and in several cities local blacks created protest organizations fashioned after the MIA. These ventures enabled Martin Luther King and other black ministers in 1957 to organize the Southern Christian Leadership Conference (SCLC), the first civil rights group led by black Southerners and dedicated to ending segregation. As Adam Fairclough has written: 'The SCLC transferred the religious fervor of black Christians ... from the church to the Civil Rights Movement.' Black ministers were relatively secure economically, and their churches offered the means of reaching the mass of Southern blacks, providing activists with meeting places and raising funds. King himself travelled and spoke widely. In 1958 he met President Eisenhower.

The SCLC's technique of peaceable direct action allowed a role for ordinary blacks and represented an alternative to the NAACP's reliance on the slow-moving judicial process. King, an admirer of Mohandas Gandhi and his use of passive resistance against British rule in India, came to possess a deepening belief in non-violence, both as a matter of religious conviction and as a tactic. He wanted action now, yet he also told the angry blacks that gathered outside his home after it had been bombed: 'We must love our white brothers no matter what they do to us.' King's blend of convictions pointed to a potent strategy. 'We will soon wear you down by our capacity to suffer,' he explained to the oppressors, 'and in winning our freedom we will so appeal to your heart and conscience that we will win you in the process.'

As the decade ended, however, it was students rather than ministers who precipitated an extraordinary explosion of black protest across the South. One Monday in February 1960, four well-dressed black youths sat down at the whites-only lunch counter in a Woolworth store in Greensboro, North Carolina, and politely asked to be served. They were ignored but they persisted and in the following days other black and some white students joined them; by Friday over three hundred awaited service. Their example was promptly followed by students in other Southern communities. Buoyed by media publicity, sit-ins at lunch counters, restaurants and theatres took place even in the Deep South. Many were complemented by boycotts and for the most part they were successful as local businessmen reluctantly yielded. In the post-war period, as historian Lizabeth Cohen has observed, the political and economic virtues of America's consumer society had been so widely lauded that the moral right of black Americans to be consumers too could hardly be denied. During 1960 hundreds of sit-ins occurred, involving perhaps some 70,000 people, black and white. From out of this activity there emerged the Student Nonviolent Coordinating Committee (SNCC), formed by militant young blacks.

To a large extent the sit-ins represented the spontaneous action of Southern black youth, growing impatient with the cautious ways of their elders. Unlike boycotts, the sit-ins, however peacefully conducted, were confrontational, and there was no assurance that court rulings on the integration of public services had any applicability to private businesses. The participants were mostly well-educated young blacks from the growing urban communities of the South. While they risked beatings and jail, in many cases they did not have jobs to lose or families to support. They were uniquely placed to express the moral anger of black America, and they had an electric effect on black Americans across the country.

The sit-ins consummated the recent restiveness of Southern black communities. The petitions for school desegregation by NAACP chapters, the boycotts of segregated transportation by church groups and the sit-ins were primarily actions by local organizations or individuals, even if national figures sometimes intruded. In the 1960s 'the civil rights movement' emerged more clearly as a national presence, with new organizations – SCLC, SNCC and a resuscitated CORE – assuming leadership positions along with the NAACP. The church and student groups remained a part of the equation, often co-opted by the formal organizations in campaigns that had twin targets, ending segregation in particular Southern communities and forcing action from the national authorities.

The NAACP had not been idle as black communities developed their campaigns. Despite the severe harassment of its chapters throughout the South, it had pressed ahead with court action and lobbying Congress for civil rights laws. Partly as the result of its efforts, two civil rights acts were passed in 1957 and 1960 (discussed in Chapter 10), far weaker than the NAACP had wanted but an uneasy acknowledgement by the white power structure of the growing expectations of African-Americans. It was this nervousness within the political establishment that the civil rights bodies sought to exploit during the first half of the 1960s. The election of John Kennedy in 1960, on a platform containing a strong civil rights plank, strengthened the sense among African-American leaders that a unique opportunity now existed for overthrowing Jim Crow.

The first major campaign of the new phase was the Freedom Rides, organized in 1961 by James Farmer of CORE. Southern bus stations had always been racially segregated, with separate waiting rooms, bathrooms and eating places. The Supreme Court in December 1960 had already declared against such segregation, without much practical effect, but the ruling provided CORE with an opportunity to act knowing that ultimately the law was on its side. An interracial group of 'freedom riders' was to embark on a bus journey through the South, insisting on sharing the facilities. Farmer anticipated that the riders would be arrested, and he hoped to fill up the jails until the South was forced to abandon segregation, as he also hoped to pressure the Kennedy administration into decisive support for civil rights. The Freedom Rides represented a shift from local action to 'cutting across state lines', as Farmer put it.

The riders set off in two buses in May. Cities in the Upper South desegregated their terminals to greet them, but as they descended further the atmosphere grew uglier. One bus was firebombed outside Anniston, Alabama, and in Birmingham the riders on the other were savaged by whites. CORE was obliged to discontinue the protest when no willing drivers could be found, but then SNCC assembled a new group, which set out from Birmingham for Montgomery. A worried Kennedy administration sent two officials to Alabama in the hope of discouraging violence, but when the riders arrived in Montgomery a mob again attacked and one of the emissaries was himself beaten unconscious. And still the riders pressed on, with buses now prepared to proceed under the guard of federal marshals that the Justice Department had finally despatched. Other Americans scrambled to join the rides, and hundreds were arrested.

The Freedom Rides were a stunning public relations success, with pictures of the burnings and beatings relayed across the world. As James Farmer later explained, 'we were counting on the bigots in the South to do our work for us'. Attorney-General Robert Kennedy prevailed on the Interstate Commerce Commission to ban segregation in interstate travel. But CORE was less than enamoured with the Kennedy administration, which had been stirred to limited action only after the riders had been attacked. The White House also proved reluctant to intervene a year later, when a black student, James Meredith, attempted to enrol in the University of Mississippi. Only after a riot broke out in which two people died did President Kennedy despatch US Army troops to restore order and protect Meredith.

Meanwhile the SCLC was developing its own strategy for destroying Jim Crow, having been bettered in a campaign it had joined in 1961–2 in Albany, Georgia. One reason for the failure was the canny conduct of the Albany police chief, who successfully prevailed on his officers to refrain from overt violence. Martin Luther King and Ralph Abernathy, in the latter's words, at one point were 'thrown out of jail' so that they would not become martyrs. Since order in the city was largely preserved, a relieved federal government denied that it had the authority to intervene, enabling Albany officials to ignore the demands to integrate. Only 'tension and crisis', reflected the SCLC's Wyatt Walker, 'forces a resolution of the dilemma'.

King then determined to force a crisis with a bold campaign for the desegregation of Birmingham, Alabama, probably the South's most racist city, a reputation personified by the hardline police commissioner, Eugene 'Bull' Connor. The object was to force the Kennedy administration into a more vigorous commitment to civil rights. King was arrested in April 1963 and from his cell issued his moving 'Letter from Birmingham Jail'. When the supply of black adults willing to go to jail began to thin, their place was taken by children, hundreds of whom offered themselves to the disconcerted police. As Connor's exasperation grew, his officers showed less restraint, and they finally used powerful fire hoses and Alsatian dogs on the demonstrators. Television and newspaper pictures showed savage police dogs lunging at children. The local business community finally buckled in May. Public opinion in the country at large and continuing presidential pressure ensured a grudging desegregation of public facilities. The lingering hate in the city was shown in September when four little black girls were killed in a bomb attack on their Sunday school. (Eventually, in May 2001, a former member of the Ku Klux Klan was sentenced to life imprisonment for this outrage.)

Birmingham was a major turning point, raising public consciousness in a way that nothing else had. In the early spring, before Birmingham hit the headlines, an opinion poll had reported that only 4 per cent of respondents designated 'racial problems' as the country's most important issue; in October the figure reached 52 per cent. The SCLC success in the city unleashed a tidal wave of black protest across the South. Perhaps a thousand demonstrations – sit-ins, marches, boycotts – illustrated the new activism of Southern blacks during the tense summer of 1963. Some remained peaceful and several towns integrated their public facilities, but in others protesters were clubbed and tear-gassed. Between April and November there were nearly 15,000 arrests arising from racial demonstrations, in which perhaps 100,000 people participated. The civil rights cause had become a mass movement. To many the country seemed to be teetering on the edge of race war. Little wonder that the White House was now giving civil rights its most urgent attention.

In June (as discussed in Chapter 12) the full weight of the presidency was finally put behind civil rights as Kennedy took to television to insist that blacks could no longer be appeased with 'counsels of patience'. A week later he sent to Congress a civil rights bill designed to drive segregation from the South. To encourage Congress to pass it, the civil rights groups cooperated in the great March on Washington in August, mobilizing 200,000 blacks and 50,000 whites. This was a massive show of unity along a spectrum of moderate, liberal and radical organizations, consummated by Martin Luther King's celebrated speech anticipating the day when 'all God's children ... will be able to join hands and sing in the words of the old Negro spiritual: "Free at last ... Thank God Almighty, we are free at last".' His wife later observed: 'At that moment it seemed as if the Kingdom of God appeared. But it only lasted for a moment.'

Despite public support for the bill, the white South's unreconstructed representatives in Congress were determined to defeat it, if necessary with a filibuster in the Senate. Only a two-thirds majority could impose cloture. But fate took a mordant hand with Kennedy's assassination in November. The popular wave that developed in favour of sustaining the programme of the martyred president, together with the parliamentary skills of his successor, helped to make it possible to override the filibuster after the longest congressional debate in American history. The civil rights bill became law in July 1964. Jim Crow had finally been outlawed.

The act struck primarily at segregation in public places, such as hotels, restaurants, cinemas and swimming pools, though also reinforced *Brown* in authorizing the withholding of federal funds from public programmes (such as education) in which discrimination persisted. Another provision more generally prohibited racial and gender discrimination in public and private employment and established an Equal Employment Opportunity Commission to promote this goal. To the surprise of many, the integration of public facilities in the South proceeded fairly swiftly, but the attack on Jim Crow did not end discrimination. The act made only a modest attempt to guarantee voting rights, and segregation obdurately persisted in the school systems.

The Kennedys themselves had done something to encourage voter registration, which initially seemed less confrontational than sit-ins and freedom rides. In 1962 they endorsed the Voter Education Project, which channelled philanthropic funds to civil rights groups for voter registration drives. Intrepid SNCC and CORE activists had already penetrated the very citadel of Jim Crow, the notoriously 'closed society' of Mississippi, in 1961. As their drive took off, its perilous nature became clear but, determined to demonstrate their staying power to local blacks, the activists pressed on through arrests, beatings and shootings. With national public sympathy for civil rights growing in 1963, SNCC persuaded CORE, the SCLC and the NAACP to join it in the formation of a Council of Federated Organizations and a sustained attempt at voter registration in Mississippi. When white students joined the campaign it was noted that they attracted media attention. In 1964 SNCC announced a major registration drive, 'Freedom Summer', and it encouraged white students to participate. As one organizer later starkly explained, the 'death of a white college student would bring on more attention to what was going on than for a black college student getting it'. Hundreds of black and white students from the North (more whites than blacks) poured into Mississippi, entreating dubious rural blacks to register and offering their children a fresh form of American history and civics in 'freedom schools'. There were many violent incidents, and thirty-seven black churches were burned in Mississippi that summer. But commanding the headlines and a CBS news special were the horrific murders of three volunteers, two of them white Northerners.

The Johnson administration could not ignore these atrocities, and the FBI for once made a determined effort to identify the perpetrators, but the White House had also been exasperated by the dangerous nature of the Mississippi project. It took another campaign led by Martin Luther King fully to establish the moral urgency of voting rights. In the spring of 1965 he orchestrated a voter registration campaign in Selma, Alabama, pushing his philosophy of non-violent resistance to its limits as he successfully preserved peaceful behaviour among the protesters while provoking violence by whites. King's colleague, Hosea Williams, told a group of marchers that 'We must pray, in God's name, for the white man to commit violence, and *we must not fight back*!' An obligingly belligerent police chief deployed electric cattle prods against the protesters. The violence climaxed on 'Bloody Sunday', 7 March, when state troopers and mounted deputies charged at peaceful marchers. After the television networks relayed these stunning scenes several thousand other Americans hastened to join the protesters. Both black and white activists died during the Selma campaign. Within two weeks of Bloody Sunday a Gallup poll revealed about three-quarters of Americans in favour of a voting rights act.

King's Selma campaign impelled Lyndon Johnson to plead with Congress for the Voting Rights Act, which passed both houses with large majorities. It proved effective, particularly because of a provision to send federal registrars if necessary into the South to do the registering. In 1960 only 29 per cent of eligible Southern blacks had been registered as voters. The campaigns of the early 1960s helped to raise the proportion to 42 per cent in 1964, and then the Voting Rights Act boosted the figure to 67 per cent in 1970.

The Voting Rights Act in a sense marked the climax of the civil rights movement, which had focused on the constitutional rights of the individual and the integration of blacks into American society as equals. 'There is no more civil rights movement', reflected Martin Luther King, 'President Johnson signed it out of existence when he signed the voting rights bill.' Thereafter the movement lost force as the principal civil rights organizations headed in different directions and the larger political environment increasingly proved less receptive to black aspirations.

The various organizations had never found it easy to work together. Some SNCC members had come away from the March on Washington bitter at the way in which their spokesman John Lewis had been pressured into moderating his speech. Black activists in Freedom Summer, who had helped found the Mississippi Freedom Democratic Party to rival the state's white Democratic Party, had been incensed when King and other liberals failed adequately to support their demand to be seated as the state's official delegation at the 1964 Democratic national convention. When King abided by an agreement with the president to turn around a march at Selma rather than again confront state troopers, some blacks felt betrayed. While the SCLC tried to keep open channels of communication with the Johnson White House, by 1965 SNCC and CORE leaders were antagonizing it by criticizing its Vietnam policy. If the civil rights movement had remained united enough to win its major legislative goals with the acts of 1964 and 1965, the struggle had also served to radicalize many black activists, who were losing faith in the political system and were growing impatient with the pacifist philosophy of Martin Luther King.

There always had been some black radicals who had held aloof from the civil rights movement. Strands of black nationalist aspiration had survived the Garveyism of the 1920s, and in the 1930s the Nation of Islam took root in Northern black ghettos, promoting notions that blacks were God's chosen people and that Christianity was a white man's creed foisted on blacks to control them. The Black Muslims, as they were dubbed, were led by Elijah Muhammad and enjoyed particular success among the rootless urban underclass. Members embraced an austere lifestyle, abjuring drugs, alcohol and tobacco and working hard. One minor criminal captivated by this faith was Malcolm Little, who, reborn as Malcolm X, quickly became one of the

Nation's most eloquent leaders. Scorning what he saw as the accommoda-
tionist strategy of the civil rights movement, Malcolm offered a separatist
vision with a rhetoric that hinted at violence. In 1964 the charismatic
Malcolm quit the Nation after a breach with its reclusive leader and that summer formed the Organization for Afro-American Unity. A visit to Mecca
inspired him to espouse the equality of all races, including whites. By this
date, still lacking a clear strategy, Malcolm's support among African-
Americans was very limited, but early in 1965 he was assassinated. In his
martyrdom he bequeathed to American blacks not a coherent ideology but
a powerful vision of black pride, one rooted in an African rather than an
American heritage. His posthumously published *Autobiography* sold 1.5
million copies in its first year.

Malcolm X was a voice from the black ghetto rather than the black South,
and the cities were already beginning to rumble. In July 1964 blacks in
Harlem and Rochester took to the streets, the first of the 'summer riots'. A
few days after Lyndon Johnson signed the Voting Rights Act in August 1965,
the Watts district of Los Angeles experienced week-long turmoil that left
thirty-four dead. Televised images of black mobs running amok to the cry
of 'Burn, baby, burn', sent very different tremors among whites to those
imparted by Martin Luther King's transcendent rhetoric. In 1966 racial violence erupted in Chicago, Cleveland and elsewhere, and in 1967 in Newark
and Detroit. In the Detroit riot forty-three people died and the army drove
tanks into the streets to restore order. In April 1968 riots flared across the
nation as news of Martin Luther King's assassination reached black communities. In Washington over 700 fires burned. Nearly 300 people died in the
course of the 'long hot summers' of 1964–8, close to nine in ten of them black.

The riots were more or less spontaneous affairs, a product of baulked
expectations and growing awareness among blacks of their collective plight.
The civil rights movement had focused on destroying Southern segregation,
and its agenda had been of marginal relevance to the expanding black ghettos of the North, where conditions were often deteriorating. There was no
easy way of channelling this discontent, but the emergence of urban rage
coincided with the growing militancy of SNCC and other activists disillusioned with conventional politics and white allies by their experiences in the
Deep South.

From out of this frustration came 'Black Power', a cry taken up in 1966
by student leader Stokely Carmichael. That year James Meredith had
embarked on a lone march across Mississippi, and when he was wounded
other civil rights leaders continued the protest. Carmichael used the march
to break with the old civil rights leadership. Rather than seeking integration
into the existing society, his call for Black Power implied separatist strategies as it also seemed to repudiate King's philosophy of non-violence. But
the term was ambiguous. Although for some the slogan implied a revolutionary challenge to the existing structure, to many blacks it came to mean
a call for racial solidarity in the struggle against discrimination. At the very

least it promoted black consciousness, encouraging African-Americans to be proud of their heritage and to cherish the notion that 'black is beautiful'.

The old civil rights coalition fell apart as the more militant groups, mesmerized by Black Power, careered into a rhetorically violent nationalism. Revolutionary theories were also being injected into the public arena by young whites rebelling against corporate America, disrupting the liberal alignments of the New Deal Order. SNCC leaders had recoiled from reform alliances after the 1964 Democratic Convention, with its failure to seat the black Mississippi delegates. In May 1966 it elected Stokely Carmichael chairman and in December its executive committee expelled its white members. By 1967 H. Rap Brown was SNCC's chief spokesman, and in that riotous summer he advised: 'Meet violence with violence.' CORE followed a similar trajectory, the black nationalist Floyd McKissick replacing James Farmer as director in 1966. But white liberals (not least New York Jews) had helped these groups financially, and their funding dwindled as their exclusivity and militancy grew.

Also calling for a revolutionary reconstruction of American society was the Black Panther Party for Self-Defense, founded in September 1966 in Oakland, California. The Panthers' black berets and their open display of guns captured press attention, and by 1969 they claimed chapters in several large cities. Their philosophy was Marxist, albeit 'a Yankee-Doodle-Dandy version of socialism', according to leader Eldridge Cleaver. In order to build local support the Panthers engaged in community programmes, such as providing free breakfasts for poor children. As socialists they also accepted the need to forge class alliances with other groups, including whites.

The various black militant groups commanded abundant media coverage but little support. In a 1968 survey of black Northerners, Stokely Carmichael and Rap Brown each secured only 14 per cent approval ratings, while the disapproval figures were 35 and 45 per cent respectively; Martin Luther King, by contrast, was approved by 72 per cent. Only 15 per cent of these urban blacks held that violence was 'the best way for Negroes to gain their rights'. The impoverished radical groups were also subject to police harassment and subversion by FBI moles. The threat of violence seemingly legitimated the use of repression by the FBI and police authorities in the late 1960s. In 1969–70 several Panthers died in shoot-outs and others went to jail. By the early 1970s the militant organizations were collapsing. SNCC had gone out of existence, CORE was a tiny sect and the Black Panthers had all but disappeared.

The mainstream civil rights groups survived, but there was no longer an agreed focus. The demands of the radicals and the ghetto riots intensified a white backlash against the aspirations of African-Americans generally, and the Vietnam War increasingly commanded the attention and resources of the Johnson administration. Civil rights opportunities were diminishing in this changing environment.

Distressed by the ghetto riots, in 1966 Martin Luther King did turn his attention northward, moving to Chicago – home of more blacks than Mississippi – with a campaign for improved community services and open housing. But the SCLC's limited resources were no match for the size of the city. Systemic racial discrimination was much more difficult to confront than the Jim Crow kind, and there was little hope of bringing the pressure of the federal government to bear against the city's powerful Democratic machine. But the experience deepened King's understanding of urban conditions, and by the late 1960s his analysis of the race problem was not so different from some versions of Black Power. He was questioning the nature of the capitalist economy, contemplating massive government programmes to provide jobs and redistribute wealth. King knew that such goals would remain elusive as long as resources were poured into the bottomless pit of Vietnam. When he condemned the war in 1967, his frayed relationship with the Johnson White House was finally severed.

King now determined to move the issue from civil rights to poverty, developing a plan to bring thousands of poor people of all races to Washington, where they would camp until the government acted. In April 1968 he told a black audience in Memphis: 'I may not get there with you, but I want you to know tonight that we as a people will get to the promised land.' He was assassinated the next day. In the dispirited aftermath the SCLC went ahead with the Poor People's Campaign, but order was difficult to maintain and turnout was disappointing. Civil rights as a coherent movement seemed to be petering out. The optimism that had once buoyed black protest activity waned in the face of growing white antipathy.

The veteran civil rights leader Bayard Rustin argued in 1965 that African-Americans should move 'from protest to politics', building their strength within the Democratic Party. A majority of black voters, of course, had swung to the party during the New Deal, but from the presidential election of 1964, when 94 per cent voted for Lyndon Johnson, their vote was overwhelmingly Democratic. The Voting Rights Act brought many more blacks to the polls in the South, while the increasing concentration of blacks in the inner cities in the North enhanced their electoral power in local politics. Yet in being so fully absorbed into the New Deal Order, blacks also inadvertently threatened it. Some white ethnics came to resent the benefits that Democratic administrations seemed prepared to offer blacks and began to desert the party. Republican strategists, for their part, were soon calculating that there was little point in wooing black voters and more advantage to be gained by courting the white backlash. As African-Americans elected more of their own to office and consolidated their position in the Democratic Party, the party lost the political ascendancy that it had enjoyed for over a generation. Barely recognized in the polity in 1933, by 1969 American blacks occupied a conspicuous place in it, but their very presence served to destabilize the New Deal Order.

|12|

New Frontier and Great Society: from Kennedy to Nixon
1961–9

Many former New Dealers initially looked askance at the presidential candidacy of John F. Kennedy. The Massachusetts senator had not been notably associated with liberal causes and he was the son of Joe Kennedy, the wealthy businessman who had served as ambassador to London before turning against Franklin Roosevelt and befriending Joe McCarthy. Cool and pragmatic rather than earnest and ideological, and apparently propelled by family ambition, John Kennedy was evidently more interested in foreign than domestic affairs. But by the time of his election his articulacy had largely dispelled the liberals' doubts, and he had succeeded in revitalizing much of the broader New Deal coalition. In their platform the Democrats had identified themselves as the 'Party of Hope', ready to wrest control of the nation's affairs from the 'Party of Memory', and there were at least some reasons for believing that a more liberal age was at hand. As it happened, the New Deal coalition was to achieve a much greater electoral victory in 1964, and the powerful reforming thrust of the Lyndon Johnson administration did invite comparisons with the New Deal. But it was also in the Johnson years that the New Deal Order began to come apart. The electoral coalition that had given the Democratic Party its majority status since the 1930s unravelled, and there were emerging doubts about the capacity of government to manage a complex society. Disillusionment with liberal prescriptions was paralleled by a disheartening realization of the limits of American power abroad.

To a degree the problems of the Kennedy and Johnson administrations were occasioned by success. A generation of unprecedented growth had created a wondrously affluent society. Between 1869 and 1948 the annual rate of growth of GNP per capita had been 1.7 per cent; between 1947 and 1973 it was a heady 2.2 per cent, making possible a hefty defence build-up, an array of domestic programmes and increased private spending. The industrial working class of Franklin Roosevelt's day was being displaced by a mass middle class, generated by the expansive economy and consumer-oriented government policies, such as measures that promoted home ownership. This enlarged middle class was far from homogeneous and its demands were varied, but its expectations of government focused less on economic survival and more on the quality of life. Significant parts of it too were uneasily aware that the affluent society had not embraced all Americans, and that more needed to be done if the trumpeted national goal of equality of opportunity was to be achieved.

The theme of John Kennedy's 1960 campaign was the need to get the country 'moving again'. Whatever he meant by that, his youth and élan suggested that change was imminent, and most of the elements in the New Deal coalition came to invest their hopes in him. From his Massachusetts background he brought ties with the labour movement, and he had cultivated the traditional city bosses like Mayor Daley of Chicago. He had been a prominent critic of the existing immigration laws, particularly the racist national origins quota system, giving him an identification with white ethnics. In selecting the Texan Lyndon Johnson as his vice-presidential running mate he had sent assurances to the South. He had pleased black voters during the campaign by phoning Coretta King when her husband, Martin Luther King, had been jailed in Georgia. Harvard scholars Arthur Schlesinger and Kenneth Galbraith testified to his appeal to intellectuals. Kennedy, in short, had touched base with each of the principal constituencies of the New Deal coalition and just enough had voted for him to make him president. As William Leuchtenberg has written, 'he ran well in many of the sorts of districts that had given their ballots to Roosevelt'. Nonetheless, as Kennedy pointed out, the 1960s were not the 1930s, and what he called the New Frontier 'holds out the promise of more sacrifice instead of more security'. He had barely polled more popular votes than his Republican opponent, and in Congress Democratic majorities had actually been reduced.

Kennedy had not promised Americans a life of ease. His invocation of the New Frontier at the Democratic convention was a call for self-sacrifice: 'Beyond that frontier are uncharted areas of science and space, unsolved problems of peace and war, unconquered pockets of ignorance and prejudice, unanswered questions of poverty and surplus.' The times demanded imagination: 'I am asking each of you to be pioneers on that New Frontier.' This summons to service attracted many. Eisenhower's rather conservative policies had conveyed the impression that domestically it was an administration's first duty to preserve an environment favourable to business. Kennedy's rhetoric, however, combined with his youth, suggested other priorities. Many young people were moved by his call, and saw in the New Frontier an opportunity to enlist in a cause of some worth. An early symbolic measure was the establishment of the Peace Corps, which sent young (and some older) Americans to help in community projects in developing countries.

Action did not mean radicalism. The Kennedy men were impatient with what they saw as the torpidity of the Eisenhower administration, but this did not mean that they favoured peace initiatives abroad or socialistic solutions at home. They were members of their generation, brought up on the Cold War, in which they wished to regain the initiative. In economic policy, they looked to adopt the lessons of Keynes in managing the economy, and while this implied a more active role for government it did not imply disturbing the basic structure of corporate capitalism.

The shuffling of New Deal politics towards what has been called 'commercial Keynesianism' had begun in the Roosevelt and Truman administrations, as they came to deploy fiscal methods of managing the economy in place of more regulatory techniques. Liberal Democrats concluded that liberal goals might best be pursued by accepting corporate capitalism and using government to maintain high consumption, thus promoting full employment and bulging wage packets, and increasing tax revenues that could be used for social programmes. But commercial Keynesianism was no radical creed; it did not look to a fundamental economic restructuring. One way of stimulating the economy would be through tax cuts that put more money in the hands of consumers.

Kennedy himself did not immediately embrace the 'new economics', which hardly sat well with his call to Americans for self-sacrifice. His first tax changes involved depreciation allowances and investment tax credits, much to the pleasure of business. In June 1962 he did publicly question the conventional wisdom about the need for balanced budgets and urged the priority of promoting growth. Finally, in January 1963 Kennedy called for tax reforms and submitted a budget incorporating a cut of $10.2 billion. In the event most of the reforms were removed by Congress, but it was the massive tax cut that the president wanted most, and by October 1963 the House of Representatives had agreed to it.

In one sense the tax cut was conservative economics. The stimulus to the economy was not to be given by greater government spending but by leaving money in the hands of individuals and corporations. The cut was to provide a precedent for future administrations, and indeed budget deficits became the norm until the end of the century. On the other hand, in 1963 Kennedy was flying in the face of fiscal orthodoxy, and the measure required vigorous drives to win over Congress and business. None of his predecessors had called for a large tax cut when the budget was already in deficit and the economy not in recession. After the measure passed in 1964 economic growth did speed up. In fact the cut accelerated rather than triggered a boom, but by 1965 the growth rate was a remarkable 6 per cent and Kennedy's supporters could claim that he had got the economy moving again. That year *Time* magazine's nomination for man of the year was John Maynard Keynes.

Through 'fine-tuning' it was believed that economic growth could be secured without inflation, and among the techniques used to contain the latter were wage and price guidelines. The 1950s had witnessed a great merger movement, as smaller firms were taken over by larger. Business consolidation no longer worried liberals as once it had, but they worried about price-fixing, when a large corporation acted as price 'leader', setting a price for its products that other producers followed. Kennedy's wage and price 'guideposts' illustrated his intent on more active economic management. These were not 'controls', but the message was that any increases should not exceed productivity gains. In practice, the guideposts meant that government officials would try to exhort union and corporation leaders into exercising restraint. The test came in steel, and discussions with the interested parties resulted in an understanding that any wage increase would be absorbed without a price increase, or so the White House thought. In April 1962 US Steel signed a contract with the union in which the wage increase was well within the guidepost. The administration was delighted, but four days later the company announced a price hike, and others followed suit. Kennedy was furious. 'My father always told me that all steelmen were sons of bitches', he fumed. The White House went on the offensive, including a televised address by the president, and forced the steel companies to cancel their increase. This was the low point of Kennedy's relationship with business, and a dive in the stock market exacerbated it. Happily the share slump proved short-lived and the White House worked hard to improve its relations with business. The experience may have done something to push Kennedy towards embracing the tax cut.

One reason why Kennedy wanted to spur the economy to greater activity was to generate revenue for his expensive spending programmes, not least defence. National security was also a consideration in his determination to put the United States ahead in the conquest of space. American prestige had suffered a serious blow with the Soviet Sputnik of 1957, and another when Yuri Gagarin became the first man to orbit the earth in April 1961. In May Kennedy told Congress that it was time for 'this nation to take a clearly leading role in space achievement'. Whether the cause of science would best be served by sending a man to the moon and back was questionable, but this is precisely what Kennedy asked for 'before the decade is out', despite estimates of an astronomical cost of $30 or $40 billion. Eisenhower had resisted the idea when it was put to him, and the Apollo mission became one of Kennedy's abiding legacies.

What Kennedy's budgets did not do was provide much in the way of new domestic spending. One of his early measures was a minimum wage bill, which in raising the rate and especially bringing many more workers within its aegis, was intended to do something for the low paid without direct costs to the Treasury. A bill did become law, although only after Congress had severely narrowed its scope. A new housing programme in 1961 made it a little easier for the poor to secure mortgages. An important measure of 1963 was designed to improve mental health services and reduce the numbers incarcerated in large state mental institutions. Kennedy could also claim to have taken the first steps towards the War on Poverty. The 1961 Area Redevelopment Act provided for federal monies for regions of high unemployment, and the Manpower Development and Training Act of 1962 was largely designed to help people into jobs by providing them with training. Further, at the president's behest, the Council of Economic Advisers began a study of the nature of poverty.

Given Congress's long-standing lack of interest in liberal legislation, Kennedy's record on the domestic front was respectable enough. But he was disappointed in failing to secure some of his favoured measures, most notably federal assistance for public (that is, state) schools and medical insurance for the elderly. These social or welfare measures were in the tradition of the New Deal, but Kennedy also showed some sensitivity to the newer liberal emphasis on rights. In 1961 he established the President's Commission on the Status of Women. And he could not ignore the mounting demands of black Americans.

The Democratic platform of 1960 had actually placed the civil rights section last, and had emphasized executive action rather than legislation (although it recognized that new laws might be necessary). It spoke of a new Attorney-General 'vigorously' invoking the powers invested in him by existing law. 'Above all, it will require the strong, active, persuasive, and inventive leadership of the President of the United States.' The stress on executive action, of course, jibed with Kennedy's conception of an active presidency. In any case, Kennedy could not see how an ambitious civil rights bill could pass Congress. The conservative bloc in Congress was still capable of exercising its veto and Southern Democrats remained strongly entrenched in Congress, not least as chairs of major committees.

Kennedy saw little point in expending political capital in a probably fruitless confrontation with Congress over civil rights in 1961. But he did take executive action, more than any previous president. Part of this was symbolic, such as increasing the number of African-Americans in honour guards on ceremonial occasions. Part was more significant. Kennedy appointed more blacks to office than any of his predecessors, in his first two months appointing over forty African-Americans to senior posts, and in September Thurgood Marshall, the NAACP's leading lawyer, was named to the federal judiciary. The difficulty of securing civil rights legislation from Congress was pointed up when the senate judiciary committee delayed Marshall's confirmation. Kennedy issued an executive order to establish the President's Committee on Equal Employment Opportunity, under the chairmanship of Vice-President Johnson, which prodded government departments and companies with federal contracts to improve job opportunities for blacks. More belated was Kennedy's executive order to end discrimination in federal housing facilities, which had been promised in 1960 but was delayed until after the mid-term elections of 1962.

Enforcing civil rights legislation was the responsibility of the Justice Department, and it is one that Robert Kennedy as Attorney-General took seriously. He had no wish for public confrontations with Southern governors and worked hard behind the scenes to secure their voluntary compliance with the law, but his urgency in securing enforcement contrasted with the previous Justice Department. Where there was Southern resistance, as in recognizing black voting rights, he regularly secured court orders. The Eisenhower Justice Department had initiated only six suits against the denial of voting rights to Southern blacks; Robert Kennedy initiated fifty-seven.

He also assisted in the establishment of the Voter Education Project, an enterprise by a number of civil rights groups to register Southern blacks to vote.

There were tensions between the Kennedy administration and the civil rights leadership, which had hoped for faster progress, but for the most part the principal civil rights groups felt that the administration was an ally, a novel situation in itself. The story of the civil rights movement is told in Chapter 11; the following account focuses on the role of the White House, which was being increasingly and rather unhappily obliged to react to the pressures bearing in on it. In May 1961, to the irritation of the administration, the Congress of Racial Equality launched the Freedom Rides, the bus journeys into the South to challenge the continued segregation of bus stations. 'Tell them to call it off! Stop them!' demanded John Kennedy after the riders met with brutality in Alabama, angry at the distraction as he was preparing to meet Soviet Premier Khrushchev in Vienna. But his brother Robert was forced to send federal marshals to protect the riders, who ignored his plea for a 'cooling-off' period. CORE's use of direct action thus forced a reluctant if limited federal intervention, and the Interstate Commerce Commission, at the Attorney-General's behest, ordered the integration of Southern terminals.

Another confrontation that the administration had not sought was the 'Battle of Ole Miss' in 1962. Air force veteran James Meredith was determined to study at the all-white University of Mississippi, and with the aid of the NAACP secured a court order requiring his admission. The Justice Department was responsible for enforcing the order and again was obliged to intervene, directing a force of 500 marshals to protect Meredith. They were insufficient and the situation quickly deteriorated as white students and locals protested and mob violence broke out. Two people died and the president was forced to deploy troops. Meredith registered and completed his studies under protection. The reputation of the Kennedys in the Deep South sank to a new low, and was not redeemed in the following year when they faced down Governor George Wallace at the University of Alabama, where two black students were enrolled under federal protection though without violence. Wallace's attempt to block the schoolhouse door brought him over ten thousand letters of congratulation.

But there had been violence in Birmingham, Alabama, where in May 1963 Martin Luther King deployed his non-violent tactics to secure the integration of public places in this most segregated of cities. The atmosphere there was further poisoned by George Wallace's racist rhetoric, and civil rights sympathizers suffered bombing attacks. President Kennedy himself condemned the 'shameful scenes' on the television screens of police brutality directed at demonstrators. The head of the Civil Rights Division in the Justice Department was sent to try to negotiate an agreement and federal troops were mobilized in case they were needed. The administration had never previously been so active in helping the civil rights movement. Desegregation was secured, inspiring civil rights campaigns across the South.

By this date the White House was determined on a major initiative to regain its authority. In February 1963 Kennedy had asked Congress for a limited civil rights act, but the turmoil in Birmingham convinced him of the need for more. In a televised speech on 11 June 1963 he said that federal legislation was essential 'if we are to move this problem from the streets to the courts'. It was a moral issue: 'We preach freedom around the world ... but are we to say to the world, and much more importantly, to each other that this is a land of the free except for the Negroes; that we have no second-class citizens ... except Negroes?' The administration submitted a sweeping civil rights bill to Congress and stretched every nerve to build support for it. The civil rights groups mobilized the March on Washington in August in support of the measure. John Kennedy had been primarily interested in foreign affairs when he was elected, but in the summer of 1963 the civil rights issue commanded his attention.

If Kennedy had been slow to respond to the pressures of the civil rights movement, he could claim that by the summer of 1963, when racial violence simmered across the land, he was offering responsible leadership. His rhetoric had served to raise expectations, so he carried some responsibility for the civil rights activity. But as he worked to achieve a measure of justice for African-Americans, using television addresses at crisis points to mobilize public opinion behind administration policy, he also tried where possible not to alienate Southern officials. The White House spent prodigious energy bargaining with the representatives of the white South, reinforced by hints of legal pressure. Sometimes concessions were made to white interests and civil rights leaders were often offended by the compromises. Some African-Americans became embittered at the failure of the Kennedy administration to afford them the degree of support they believed had been promised, engendering in them the distrust of liberal reform that was to become the premise of the Black Power movement. But most African-Americans concluded that, whatever their failings, the Kennedys were more friends than foes of the civil rights cause and there is little doubt that had John Kennedy lived to contest the 1964 election he would have won the overwhelming support of black voters.

In November 1963, as the civil rights bill was still before Congress, John Kennedy was assassinated. The Warren Commission, which was established to investigate the murder, determined that it was the work of a lone gunman, the unstable Lee Harvey Oswald. That conclusion has often been challenged, but no alternative account of the assassination has won general acceptance by scholars. But shocking as it was, the murder interrupted rather than arrested the cause of liberalism. Lyndon Johnson pressed Kennedy's appointees to remain at their posts and he committed himself to delivering the promises of the slain leader.

The persona of the new president contrasted sharply with that of his predecessor. A massive Texan, he was overbearing and desperately insecure, insisting that he wanted aides who would 'kiss my ass on a summer's day and say it smelled of roses'. Yet the contrast with Kennedy was mainly in personality. Like Kennedy, Johnson's reputation was as a centrist Democrat. Like Kennedy, he believed in action and he saw the presidency as an office in which leadership should be asserted. But he brought to the presidency attributes of his own. He had spent twenty-three years in Congress, consummating his career there as majority leader in the Senate, and Johnson knew the corridors of congressional power as no one else did. The vice-presidency allowed only limited scope for Johnson's ambitions, but Kennedy's death precipitated into the presidency a man of extraordinary energy. His commitment to reform, largely hidden during his Senate years, also proved stronger than Kennedy's, for Johnson had been a keen supporter of the New Deal, and if he saw himself as the legatee of the Kennedy programme, he also saw himself as the heir of his hero Franklin Roosevelt.

As he assumed command Johnson threw his energies into securing the enactment of the two major pieces of legislative business left over from the Kennedy programme, the tax cut and the civil rights bill. With some modest adjustments Johnson was able to clear the way for the unorthodox tax cut and he signed the bill in February 1964. He was even more determined to see the civil rights bill through Congress without weakening amendments, and it finally became law in the summer of 1964. Johnson was aided by the way in which public opinion rallied behind Kennedy's programme in the aftermath of his murder, but his consummate legislative skills also ensured that these measures were not fatally compromised in Congress.

Kennedy's aides had also been considering measures to attack poverty, although no clear proposal had been formulated. Told of these discussions, Johnson responded: 'That's my kind of programme. We should push ahead full-tilt.' An anti-poverty crusade meshed with Johnson's New Deal values and offered him an opportunity to put his own imprint on history. 'This administration today, here and now, declares unconditional war on poverty in America,' he said in his State of the Union address in January 1964. Johnson named the energetic Peace Corps Director Sargent Shriver to head the War on Poverty, and by March Shriver had a bill ready to present to Congress. The hastily contrived act passed in August, creating an Office of Economic Opportunity (OEO) to oversee the diverse measures and providing a budget of nearly a billion dollars. Several distinct programmes developed out of it. One provided education and job training for ghetto youngsters, who were to be recruited to a Job Corps; Head Start was to offer nursery education for deprived children and Upward Bound sought to make it possible for them to reach higher education; another initiative was the Volunteers in Service to America, a domestic equivalent of the Peace Corps. The most controversial part of the package, and central to its philosophy, was the Community Action Program (CAP), which reflected the belief that the poor themselves should have some say in their own salvation and which was designed to encourage local communities to undertake their own programmes. This was a concept that shared something with the emerging New Left, some of whose student activists were already entering the ghettos in attempts to mobilize the poor into local pressure groups. The War on Poverty, said *Nation* magazine, originated in 'an almost mystical belief in the infinite potentials of American society'.

It also originated in Johnson's limitless ambition. By May 1964 the War on Poverty had expanded into the Great Society, which, said Johnson, 'demands an end to poverty and racial injustice .... But that is just the beginning'. It was also a society where 'every child can find knowledge to enrich his mind', where 'leisure is a welcome chance to build and reflect', where 'the city of man serves not only the needs of his body and the demands of commerce but the desire for beauty and the hunger for community'. Johnson was dramatically extending the tradition of New Deal reform from an economic agenda to one focusing on the quality of life. Prosperity, he said, 'is not enough', almost as if he had been listening to the New Left. Johnson's utopian vision both raised expectations and invoked cynicism. For a couple of years his bills tumbled through Congress. The 1964 elections not only gave Johnson personal legitimacy but also large Democratic majorities in both houses of Congress, overwhelming the conservative bloc that had obstructed reform legislation for decades.

The most important measures came in 1965, when Johnson was at the height of his authority. Franklin Roosevelt's New Deal and Harry Truman's Fair Deal had been unable to offer much protection to the sick, but that year Johnson secured Medicare, to his considerable satisfaction: 'No longer will older Americans be denied the healing miracle of modern medicine.' As well as this programme for the elderly, the act established Medicaid for the poor.

In 1965 too came the Elementary and Secondary Schools Act, designed to channel federal money into schools in poor neighbourhoods. This expansion of the federal government into school education was a major innovation, since the school systems had previously been the preserve of the states. 'He was a nut on education', recalled Vice-President Hubert Humphrey. 'He felt that education was the greatest thing he could give to the people.' A separate Higher Education Act included provision for scholarships and loans for students. A new immigration law overrode the National Origins Act of 1924; immigration remained restricted but was no longer to be based on racial or national quotas, a system that had become an embarrassment in the ideological struggles of the Cold War. Just as racism was being rooted out of other public policies, so future recruitment to the American population would not be determined by race or national origin. In 1965 the Department of Housing and Urban Development was created, yet another federal bureaucracy dedicated primarily to the underprivileged, with funds to promote urban renewal and low-rent public housing; and environmental reform surfaced as a liberal cause and was furthered through highway beautification and water quality and clean air acts.

Civil rights was still on the agenda too, commanding national attention by Martin Luther King's campaign in Selma to force the local authorities to register black residents. It was also designed to bring pressure to bear on Washington for a voting rights bill. The civil rights act of 1964 had been focused on desegregation, but in many Southern states blacks were still largely excluded from the voting registers. It was up to local courts to enforce the existing voting laws, but the new act would make it possible to override local officials and have federal registrars register voters. Johnson appeared personally before Congress to call for the bill, punctuating his speech by raising his arms and proclaiming the rallying cry of the civil rights movement: 'We *shall* overcome.' In August 1965 he signed it into law.

Over a hundred bills followed in 1966 and Johnson secured passage of most of them, although they were less consequential than the historic 1965 measures. One created a Department of Transportation to coordinate the country's various transport agencies. Other bills expanded environmental standards. The Model Cities programme was designed to help major cities overcome urban blight and renovate their environments, but as an urban renewal measure it spread aid too thinly.

Johnson's legislative accomplishments were awesome. 'Johnson has outstripped Roosevelt, no doubt about that', observed Senate Majority Leader Mike Mansfield. Like Roosevelt's innovations, Johnson expected his programmes to grow over time. 'I figured when my legislative program passed the Congress that the Great Society had a real chance to grow into a beautiful woman', he recalled in 1971.

> And I figured her growth ... would be as natural and inevitable as any small child's. In the first year, as we got the laws on the books, she'd begin to crawl ... And when she grew up, I figured she'd be so big and beautiful that the American people couldn't help but fall in love with her, and once they did, they'd want to keep her around forever, making her a permanent part of American life, more permanent even than the New Deal.

Some although not all of the Great Society programmes did survive, and statistics were to show that poverty in the United States appreciably declined, partly because of the programmes and partly because of the powerful economic boom of the mid-1960s. Like the New Deal, the Great Society won mixed verdicts. A few programmes, such as Head Start, seemed reasonably successful; others, such as the Job Corps, proved disappointing. Medicare and Medicaid became permanent if expensive parts of the American welfare state, while the Civil Rights and Voting Rights acts were lasting memorials to the Johnson presidency. But some measures quickly encountered resistance. The local CAPs met with complaints from influential senators and big city mayors, particularly when they accorded a role to black activists.

The Great Society was also evolving in other ways that strained alliances. When in 1965 Johnson spoke of African-Americans as being entitled to equality of outcome he was departing from the traditional ideology of equality of opportunity. He was seeking to align himself with the new political currents of the 1960s, expressed in the demands for community action, consumer protection, environmentalism and feminism as well as civil rights. But the exponents of the 'new politics' consorted uneasily with the veterans of the old. Johnson could not align himself with the peace movement, and by the end of his administration his commitment to the war in Vietnam had turned most proponents of the 'new politics' against him.

But in 1964, when Lyndon Johnson grandiloquently committed himself to an audacious programme of liberal reform, he seemed at one with the temper of the times, and the New Deal Order was at its most formidable. Johnson was looking to the election to the presidency in his own right, coveting a massive vote of confidence from the American people. For the election the Republicans fielded the right-wing senator from Arizona, Barry Goldwater, who worried many voters by hinting at nuclear escalation in Vietnam and suggesting curbs on New Deal programmes, such as Social Security. Portraying Goldwater as a trigger-happy extremist, Lyndon Johnson won the 1964 presidential election with a landslide, securing 61 per cent of the popular vote, and his coat-tails helped to increase Democratic majorities in both houses of Congress. This was the Last Hurrah of the New Deal coalition. Organized labour had rallied to Johnson, low-income voters generally were overwhelmingly for him, as were Catholics and Jews. So were an extraordinary 94 per cent of African-American voters, with whom Johnson proved more popular than Franklin Roosevelt or John Kennedy. The big city states were strongly for Johnson, the surviving urban machines performing their time-honoured role. And Johnson carried much of the traditionally Democratic South.

But stunning though the size of the victory was, there were signs of cracks in the imposing New Deal edifice. Most obviously, Goldwater (who had voted against the Civil Rights Act) carried five states in the Deep South, which also broke with its own past by returning a handful of Republican congressmen. He had shown Republicans that the banner of a racially tinged conservatism could break the Democratic majority. There were also flickers of dissatisfaction elsewhere, as some Irish, Italian and Polish Catholic wards in urban areas showed less than their customary enthusiasm for the Democratic ticket.

The Johnson landslide in 1964 meant that these defections could be shrugged off, but signs of a backlash against Great Society policies began to grow. The ghetto riots that had erupted in 1964 proved not to be a passing phenomenon. There were more serious riots in 1965, most fearfully in Watts in Los Angeles when thirty-four people died, and more unrest in 1966. Yet Johnson was loath to desert the ghetto blacks. Influenced by *The Negro Family*, a report of Assistant Secretary of Labor Daniel Patrick Moynihan that urged the need for policies that would allow 'roughly equal results' for black Americans, Johnson in a major speech in June 1965 called for 'equality as a fact and equality as a result'. African-Americans, it seemed, were entitled to policies designed to assist them in overcoming centuries of discrimination. In an Executive Order in September Johnson required that companies with federal contracts 'take affirmative action to ensure that applicants are employed'. This was more an exhortation than a programme, but it was the first step towards the use of racial quotas with which affirmative action would later become identified. The War on Poverty became directed towards the ghettos.

The ghetto malaise disturbed Americans of all races, and some white citizens cooled towards programmes designed to give benefits to African-Americans. In February 1964 only 28 per cent of Northern whites had thought that the Johnson administration was pushing racial integration 'too fast'; the figure rose to 52 per cent by September 1966. In June 1966 one columnist observed of Great Society reform that 'the alliance of labor, Negroes, middle-class white liberals, and machine politicians upon which that strength was based is coming apart'. The Republicans did well in the mid-term elections of 1966, gaining forty-seven seats in the House and four in the Senate. This was more than their losses of 1964, an unusually high setback for the Democrats. When Johnson presented his State of the Union message in January 1967 he maintained the reform rhetoric, but the caution in his words suggested that he now had little heart for further expanding Great Society programmes.

If Johnson's domestic policies were encountering resistance on the right, his foreign policy was under attack from the left. Anti-war sentiment was emerging strongly, as illustrated by the celebrated 'teach-in' on Vietnam at the University of Michigan in March 1965, soon followed at other campuses. It was in February that Johnson had initiated the bombing of North Vietnam and by July he was embarking on the massive escalation of troops in Vietnam. In September 1965 the respected chair of the Senate Foreign Relations Committee, Senator William Fulbright, broke with the administration over Vietnam policy. Broadly public opinion still backed Johnson on Vietnam, but it was not clear how solidly.

Foreign policy was driving a wedge between the administration and many Americans previously sympathetic to the thrust of liberal reform. In 1965 the SDS (Students for a Democratic Society) began to attract national attention when it organized the first large demonstration against American policy in Vietnam. The SDS had been formed in 1960, when it seemed to position itself on the liberal edge of the Democratic Party, but within a few years it became the nucleus of a loose-knit New Left, which embraced SNCC and CORE and several campus groups. The New Left came to regard liberalism as a front for corporate America, bent on maintaining the business order through policies of 'repressive tolerance' at home and imperialism abroad. Lyndon Johnson's celebrated War on Poverty, in this perspective, was little more than a series of gestures to camouflage the essential inequalities of capitalist society. By 1965 many New Leftists were speaking of 'the system' on the one hand and 'the movement' on the other. This radical rejection of the New Deal Order appealed only to a minority, but it was highly articulate and put many liberals on the defensive. The sense that a growing number of young people were alienated from the mainstream was heightened by the emergence of the counter-culture, with its associations with recreational drugs, sexual experimentation and communal living. Lyndon

Johnson's rise to power had been rooted in an unsurpassed understanding of the psychology of his fellow politicos, but the psychology of the 'flower children' was beyond him. The New Left and the counter-culture (which overlapped but were not synonymous) mocked by their very presence the legitimacy of the conventional political system.

As Lyndon Johnson's support drained away Congress became recalcitrant and the demands on the budget imposed by his domestic and foreign policies became acute. He was obliged to propose a temporary 10 per cent tax surcharge, but it met a cool reception and the continued racial tensions exacerbated his problems. The ghettos flared up yet again in the summer of 1967, most agonizingly in Detroit in July, when forty-three people died. Republican leaders issued a statement warning that 'We are rapidly approaching a state of anarchy'. Between May and August eight 'major disorders' (requiring the use of federal forces) and thirty-one 'serious disorders' (dealt with by state police) were recorded, mainly in cities of 250,000 or over. In these blood-spattered months hippies in San Francisco were celebrating 'the summer of love'. Johnson almost despaired. He felt – with some justification – that he had done more for African-Americans than any previous president, and he could not see how he could offer more. And apart from the backlash, the continued drain of Vietnam limited his scope for action. Former friends doubted whether Johnson could sustain both the War on Poverty and the war in Vietnam. 'Each war feeds on the other', remarked Senator Fulbright, 'and, although the President assures us that we have the resources to win both wars, in fact we are not winning either of them.'

The embattled president still struggled for solutions. Suspecting that the ghetto tensions might have more to do with miserable living conditions than lack of jobs, Johnson urged Congress to look to measures to improve housing. He sent another signal to black Americans when he nominated Thurgood Marshall to the Supreme Court. At a time when spiralling crime rates and black unrest dominated the headlines and a white backlash was growing, Lyndon Johnson named the first African-American to the country's highest court. (Explaining to an aide why he appointed the well-known Marshall rather than a less controversial black judge, Johnson said: 'When I appoint a nigger to the bench, I want everyone to know he's a nigger.')

Johnson boasted that the appointment would lose him votes, and his slippage in the opinion polls certainly continued. An increase to record levels of the number of US troops in Vietnam, the call for the 10 per cent tax surcharge and the destructive race riots, all concentrated in the summer of 1967, did his administration irreparable harm. An approval rating of 52 per cent in June had slumped to 38 per cent by October.

The pressure never let up. Opposition to the war grew both in Congress and in the country at large in the second half of 1967. Administration claims that the United States would prevail were contradicted by reports in the press. 'Victory is not close at hand', concluded an authoritative account in the *New York Times* in August. 'It may be beyond reach.' By this time prominent

figures like Robert Kennedy, now Senator from New York, regularly criticized government policy. A Gallup poll in October showed 57 per cent disapproving and only 28 per cent approving Johnson's 'handling of the war'.
That month nearly 100,000 people descended on Washington in a two-day
anti-war demonstration.

By the end of 1967 Johnson wondered whether he could win re-election.
Given the dissatisfaction within the party, particularly on its liberal wing, he
knew also that he might well face competition for the Democratic nomination,
and there was speculation in particular that Robert Kennedy would declare
himself a candidate. And Johnson's position continued to weaken. The insistent defence budget forced him to impose significant cuts on his cherished
Great Society programmes, and in the New Year the Viet Cong's shocking Tet
offensive wrecked the credibility of his military policy and intensified a run
on the country's gold reserves. Johnson repeated his request for a 10 per cent
tax hike, to which Congress eventually agreed as a major financial crisis
loomed. Neither the military nor the financial imbroglios enhanced public
confidence in the White House.

A rival for the Democratic nomination in fact emerged in the liberal form
of Senator Eugene McCarthy of Minnesota. McCarthy had announced his
candidacy in late November, promised disaffected youth an 'entrance back
into the political process', and sought to mobilize a variety of dissident groups
behind an anti-war banner. He came a disturbingly close second to Johnson
in the New Hampshire primary in March with 42 per cent of the vote. Soon
after Robert Kennedy announced his own candidacy. By this time Johnson's
approval rating had fallen to 36 per cent and disapproval had risen to 52 per
cent, and close to two-thirds of those polled disliked his policy on Vietnam. On
31 March 1968 he announced his withdrawal from the presidential election.

The Democratic Party was being pulled in three directions. On the left
were anti-war Democrats, mostly liberals and radicals and some close to the
campus New Left, who wanted to get the United States out of Vietnam and
extend the social reform agenda in the direction of the 'new politics'. In the
centre were those who remained loyal to the Johnson administration, whose
new champion was to be the vice-president, Hubert Humphrey. On the right
were those who had had enough of the Great Society and seemed to hanker
for a strong hand to smite the Communists abroad and to discipline the rioters and disobedient students at home. By 1968 this tendency seemed to be
on its way out of the party. In 1967 George Wallace, whose belligerent defence
of white supremacy in Alabama had given him a national profile, had founded
the American Independent party in order to run as a third party candidate for
president, and he hoped to recruit 'white backlash' voters to his cause. Wallace
was no longer a single-minded segregationist, pitching to a broader constituency hostile to street demonstrators and 'pointy-headed intellectuals'.

Robert Kennedy won the California primary on 5 June, and for a moment
looked as if he might just win the Democratic nomination, but that night he
became the second Kennedy to be assassinated, just two months after the

murder of Martin Luther King. The angry passions coursing through American politics spectacularly erupted at the Democratic convention in Chicago that August. Hippie, Yippie and peace demonstrators staged noisy protests outside the convention hall, and inside the Johnson forces ruthlessly pushed through Hubert Humphrey's nomination. Johnson also ensured that the platform endorsed administration policy on Vietnam. Both the tempers in the hall and the violence on the streets (as police clubbed and tear-gassed young protesters) were vividly conveyed by television and did the Democratic cause immense harm.

Tied to the Johnson presidency, Humphrey found it difficult to mount an effective campaign. The central issue between the major party candidates became who was best able to free the United States from Vietnam. The Republican presidential candidate, Richard Nixon, implied that he had a 'secret plan' to end the war, though he was probably assisted more by the sheer unpopularity of the Johnson administration. Johnson finally announced a bombing halt on 31 October, but if this helped Humphrey it came too late. A wide variety of discontents were bubbling up, some of them personified by George Wallace. Polls in the autumn suggested that he could win as much as a fifth of the popular vote, a remarkable proportion for a third-party candidate. In November Richard Nixon was the victor with 43.5 per cent of the popular vote, just topping Humphrey's humiliating 42.9 per cent. Wallace garnered an impressive 13.5 per cent and carried five Southern states. Since Johnson had achieved over 61 per cent just four years earlier, the reversal for the Democrats was colossal. The party of reform had been repudiated, as the majority of voters opted for the two varieties of conservatism in the presidential race. (The Democrats retained control of Congress.) As a Republican report put it at a point when the Humphrey candidacy was stumbling badly, 'the Democratic coalition, forged in New Deal days of the big city vote, manual workers, Catholics, labor union members and the Negroes, fell into brief disarray'. But the disarray would not be so brief.

The South's long identification with the Democratic Party was fatally wounded. Apart from Lyndon Johnson's Texas and the border states of West Virginia and Maryland, the South had gone for Nixon or Wallace. Democratic presidential candidates could never again count on the South to deliver them a substantial bloc of electoral votes. Elsewhere, not only blacks but most other members of the New Deal coalition remained faithful to the Democrats, but some Northern ethnics and working-class Catholics voted for Nixon or Wallace. Union leaders reported difficulty in dissuading members from defecting to Wallace, and 9 per cent of Northern manual workers voted for him. In 1960 John Kennedy had won 61 per cent of the votes cast by white unskilled or semi-skilled manual labourers; in 1968 Humphrey managed only 38 per cent. In the 1930s the New Deal had offered working people of this kind some relief; by the 1960s many of them were taxpayers, and some did not care to see their tax dollars thrown at students and blacks and the shiftless poor. As Richard Scammon and Ben Wattenberg observed, in 1968 the New Deal coalition was 'shaken loose from its moorings'. The Republican task in the 1970s, they concluded, was 'to shake loose more of this vote and to see to it that more of it goes to the Republican side'.

Gallup polls sent a similar message: between 1963 and 1969 the proportion of respondents identifying themselves as 'liberal' dropped from 49 to 33 per cent. In his inaugural address in January 1969 President Nixon cast his eye back over the years of the New Deal Order: 'In this past third of a century, government has passed more laws, spent more money, initiated more programs, than in all our previous history.' The administration, of course, would continue to pursue the public welfare: 'But we are approaching the limits of what government alone can do.' The kind of liberalism represented by the New Deal and the Great Society no longer commanded the confidence of a growing number of Americans, and the political structures to sustain it were irreparably damaged.

|13|

Cold War and Vietnam
1945–69

'The United States stand at this moment at the summit of the world', observed Winston Churchill in 1945. American policy-makers were well aware of the towering stature of the United States at a time when much of Europe and Asia lay devastated. They recognized that the United States could not withdraw into isolation, although they were uncertain about the particular role that the country should assume. Franklin Roosevelt had stressed the need for a system of international security, sustained by cooperation between the wartime Grand Alliance of the United States, Britain and the Soviet Union. Before he died Roosevelt's faith in Soviet goodwill was eroding, and almost as soon as the Second World War was over a chilling Cold War began replacing it. The new threat to American well-being and world peace, so it seemed, lay in an expansive Soviet Communism. The rather sudden fracturing of the world into East and West was rendered the more frightening because humankind now lived in the shadow of nuclear destruction. Assigning to itself the historic role of champion of 'the free world', the United States erected a mighty military state, fashioned a fistful of military alliances and scanned the globe for fell communist activity. This anti-communist persuasion became the key principle of American foreign policy in the post-war decades and was eventually to lead the United States into the jungles of Vietnam. There it was brutally revealed that there were limits to American power, a humiliation that hastened the end of the New Deal Order.

The notion that peace might be preserved by a network of international institutions was soon dashed. By 1946 the Grand Alliance was a thing of the past. While the United Nations had come into being, the Soviet Union had decided not to ratify the Bretton Woods Agreements, thus destroying hopes of a truly global economic system. The ambiguous agreement at Yalta over the government of Poland quickly frayed as the promised 'free and unfettered elections' failed to materialize. The governments established in Rumania and Bulgaria similarly reflected Soviet design. In Germany the wartime Allies continued to occupy their respective zones.

The relationship during the war between the United States and the Soviet Union had been less than cordial, as illustrated by the exclusion of the latter from the secret Anglo-American development of the atomic bomb. The ending of the war with Japan, of course, had exposed this fearful weapon to the whole world, and in 1946 there were discussions at the United Nations about the possibility of placing the development of nuclear energy under the authority of an international body. The Americans professed to favour this solution, but their Baruch Plan envisaged continued American influence in the monitoring process and accord could not be reached. The impasse presaged the arms race that was to dominate much of the rest of the century as each major power turned to the development of its own nuclear weapons.

The frontier atmosphere taking hold was pointed up in March 1946 by Winston Churchill's celebrated speech in Fulton, Missouri, when he spoke of an 'iron curtain' being imposed by the Soviets to cut off Eastern Europe from the West. The administration had already received a 'Long Telegram' from an official in the US Embassy in Moscow warning of the futility of 'compacts and compromises' with an insecure Soviet Union. George F. Kennan expanded on his notion of an alternative policy of 'containment' in the *Foreign Affairs* journal in July 1947. The Soviet Union, he argued, regarded the United States as an enemy, did not believe that permanent coexistence was possible and assumed that its own survival depended on undermining American power. Thus the Soviets needed to be confronted 'with unalterable counter-force at every point where they show signs of encroaching upon the interests of a peaceful and stable world'. Kennan's analysis fitted neatly with the recent exasperating experience of the Truman administration in dealing with the Soviet Union, and also with the conservative turn of American politics. In the 1946 mid-term elections the Republicans won majorities in both houses of Congress, bringing with them greater suspicions of Soviet actions abroad and red subversion at home. The containment of Soviet Communism became the new guiding philosophy of American foreign policy.

In the perception of the Truman administration the Soviet Union was coming to replace Nazi Germany as the epitome of totalitarian expansionism, and when the British government found that it could not maintain its presence in Greece and Turkey, Truman had to decide whether the United States should assume the responsibility for resisting communism in those areas. This was a momentous decision. Not only was it the first expression of the new doctrine of containment, but it also represented the final abandonment of the American tradition of isolation from the Old World. Never before had the United States been militarily implicated in Europe in time of peace, and when Truman asked Congress for military and economic aid for Greece and Turkey in March 1947, he sought to mobilize public support by conjuring a new battle for freedom. 'I believe that it must be the policy of the United States to support free peoples who are resisting attempted subjugation by armed minorities or by outside pressures,' he said, and he accepted Senator Arthur Vandenberg's advice to 'scare hell out of the American people' by dwelling on the totalitarian alternative that somehow threatened even the United States. The peoples of the world were being invited to choose between the American and Soviet models of governance. Like Wilson during the First World War, Truman was faced with potentially crippling domestic opposition, and he was resorting to ideological pressures to create a new foreign policy consensus. Many liberals were dismayed by the belligerent tone of the Truman Doctrine, which, as well as being fiercely anti-communist, allowed no role for the United Nations.

If the Truman Doctrine put the United States on course to combat Soviet influence by military means if necessary, the Marshall Plan offered a different approach to the Cold War. It was an economic rather than a military strategy that was first deployed. In a speech at Harvard in June 1947 Secretary of State George C. Marshall announced that the United States would provide resources to help the European countries rebuild their devastated economies. This, as Republican critics pointed out, could be regarded as an attempt to export the New Deal to Europe. The Truman Doctrine and the Marshall Plan, as Truman put it, were 'two halves of the same walnut'. It had become clear that the plight of the European economies was desperate, and France and Italy in particular, which possessed large communist parties, were thought to be faced with serious political instability. In principle aid was to be offered to all European countries, including the Soviet Union, but since the conditions set by the Americans meant opening economies to outside inspection it is doubtful whether American officials seriously expected the Soviet bloc to participate. The Soviet delegates angrily stalked out of the preparatory conference in Paris.

Helping to mobilize American opinion behind Marshall Aid was the Communist takeover in Czechoslovakia in February 1948. In the following month the European Recovery Plan sailed through Congress, and by December 1951 the United States had made available $12 billion for European reconstruction, the greatest shares going to Britain, France and West Germany. By the early 1950s the Western European economies generally were prospering and their communist parties held little influence. Ostensibly offered initially as a means of uniting Europe, the effect of the Marshall Plan was to deepen the divide between East and West. After the Soviets had rejected it they announced the Molotov Plan to develop trade within the Soviet bloc. Europe was dividing into separate armed camps.

The British and Americans merged their zones of occupation of Germany in 1947, and in 1948 agreed to strengthen the Western German economy by introducing a new currency (an improvement on the Lucky Strikes cigarettes that often served as cash). This looked like the prelude to the creation of an independent West German state, but Berlin had been partitioned in the same way and was located within the Russian zone. The Soviets responded in the spring of 1948 by blocking road and rail access to western Berlin. The Truman administration was faced with a major test. It refused to abandon Berlin but it found a non-military solution. A massive airlift carried supplies of food and raw materials to the West Berliners, with planes landing every sixty-two seconds. The Soviet Union dared not attack American planes and after a year abandoned the blockade. The division of Germany, still said to be temporary, was formally marked in 1949 with the respective creations of the Federal Republic of Germany and the Soviet-dominated German Democratic Republic.

The major Western powers had cooperated in the Berlin airlift and a more formal alliance was not far away. The North Atlantic Treaty Organization (NATO), launched in April 1949, was the military counterpart of the Marshall Plan, finally committing the United States to the military defence of Western Europe. But no sooner had it been formed than the international situation deteriorated. By the end of 1949 China had 'fallen' to the Communists and the Soviet Union had exploded its first atomic bomb, years ahead of American predictions. These successive crises prompted an intensive review of American defence policy, consummating in April 1950 in the seminal National Security Council Paper No. 68, more simply known as NSC-68.

This apocalyptic report observed that for centuries the normal pattern in international relations had been for power to be distributed among a number of nations, but that in the aftermath of the Second World War power had gravitated to two centres, the Soviet Union and the United States. Thus constructing the world in bipolar terms, NSC-68 argued that the Soviet Union was 'animated by a new fanatic faith' and sought 'absolute authority over the rest of the world'. Containment was the appropriate response, but given the fast-growing military strength of the Soviet Union the military posture of the West urgently needed to be strengthened. Only the United States could offer the necessary leadership. NSC-68 went beyond Kennan's containment assumptions in envisaging the eventual collapse of the Soviet Union if sufficient pressure were applied. Implementation of NSC-68 meant a massive military build-up, of both conventional forces and nuclear weapons. In the words of historian Ernest May, NSC-68 'provided the blueprint for the militarization of the Cold War from 1950 to the collapse of the Soviet Union at the beginning of the 1990s'.

As it happened it was Communist expansion in Asia rather than Europe that triggered new defence expenditures. China had long held a special place in the foreign and commercial relations of the United States. After the Second World War the Americans hoped to re-establish their influence in this vast but troubled land, where Chiang Kai-shek and the nationalist Kuomintang struggled for control against Mao Tse-tung's Communists. The Truman administration tried to secure a truce between the nationalists and the communists and offered some aid to Chiang, but his disregard of American advice and his incompetence exasperated the State Department. Chiang found that the Truman administration was not willing to provide the massive support needed to sustain his regime, and Mao's armies finally established control of mainland China in 1949. Chiang Kai-shek retreated to the island of Taiwan (Formosa), where he claimed to lead the legitimate government of China.

Truman was exposed to Republican accusations of 'losing' China to the Communists, and the bipolar world took more ominous shape. In February 1950 Mao Tse-tung signed a treaty with the Soviet Union. Those two vast countries, Russia and China, were now aligned, and the Communist bloc stretched from Central Europe right across Asia.

There were also disturbing signs that it was probing for weaknesses in the American strategy of containment. After the ousting of the Japanese in the Second World War, Korea had been left with Soviet and American armies occupying different zones, separated by the 38th parallel. The division was meant to be temporary, but during the political instability of the late 1940s a Communist regime under Kim Il Sung emerged in the North and a right-wing government under Syngman Rhee in the South. US and Soviet troops withdrew and in June 1950 Kim decided to secure reunification by launching a surprise strike on the South. American policy-makers, taken aback by this aggression, assumed that it was yet another example of Moscow-inspired Communist expansionism. (Soviet documents were later to reveal that Stalin had agreed to the initiative reluctantly, in part to stop Kim looking to Mao for backing.) The Truman administration immediately authorized military action; Soviet aggression, as it was perceived, had to be stopped. Since the Soviet Union was boycotting the UN Security Council at this time, Truman was able to secure UN condemnation of the invasion and American troops were despatched as part of a UN force.

UN forces under General Douglas MacArthur quickly drove the North Koreans back, raising the prospect of a reunification of Korea on American terms. At this point the administration seemed to be going beyond the policy of containment and toying with the concept of 'roll-back', reducing Communist territory. But as MacArthur advanced northwards beyond the 38th parallel China threatened to intervene. When he neared the Chinese border China duly responded, despatching hundreds of thousands of troops as 'volunteers' (not wanting to be formally involved in a war with the United States). MacArthur itched for an offensive against China, but by April 1951 Truman decided that he could not risk escalating the war and recalled his restive general. The war continued wearingly around the 38th parallel. Eventually, in 1953, a truce was agreed, and North and South Korea remained divided from one another by the 38th parallel – and by contrasting economic and political systems.

The Korean War was a critical event. It reinforced perceptions of a bipolar world and promoted greater solidarity within each of the two power blocs. It demonstrated that the United States was committed to deploying military force if necessary to contain Soviet expansionism. It served greatly to enhance the McCarthyite pressures in American politics and it persuaded the administration and Congress to carry through the recommendations of NSC-68. The draft was reinstated and the number of Americans in uniform reached record numbers by peacetime standards. Around 1.5 million in the late 1940s, military personnel swelled during the war and still numbered 2.8 million in 1957, four years after it had ended. Before the Korean War, annual federal spending on the military had been about $12 billion; it was $39 billion in 1957. Yet again crisis conditions had ratcheted up the military establishment.

Some of the money was being spent on building a nuclear arsenal, and the first hydrogen bomb was tested in 1952. (The Soviet answer came a year later.) Partly to curb the military budget, President Eisenhower emphasized nuclear arms. The number of nuclear warheads multiplied from 1000 to 18,000 during his terms, while expenditure on conventional weapons and personnel was tightly contained. This was the 'new look' in defence policy, or, as it was otherwise phrased, 'more bang for the buck'. The Soviet bloc was to be contained by the threat of 'massive retaliation'.

Further, as foreshadowed by NSC-68, American forces were deployed in strategic locations around the globe. By the end of 1952 NATO had built up large army and air forces in Europe, and in the years ahead would considerably enhance them – by 1974 NATO had 29.5 divisions in Western Europe, compared to thirty-one Soviet divisions in Eastern Europe. In the Far East and the Pacific too the United States sought to strengthen 'free world' security. The American occupation of Japan formally ended in 1951, although the United States was granted military bases in the islands. This recent enemy was being developed as the hub of American interests in the Pacific. The United States was also providing resources to help the French in Indochina against the nationalist Vietminh forces of Ho Chi Minh. Not everyone applauded the build-up of the military and the accompanying American commitments abroad. By the end of the 1950s George Kennan was referring to the 'overmilitarization of thought' about the Cold War.

In the aftermath of the Korean War, with the nuclear superpowers wary of direct confrontation, the globe became a kind of chessboard. In Europe, as NATO and the Warsaw Pact bleakly stared at one another across the Iron Curtain, a kind of stalemate had been reached, but the unstable regimes of the Third World attracted both interest and suspicion. With the election of Dwight Eisenhower to the presidency it seemed for a time as if American policy might become more aggressive, since the Republican platform of 1952 had expressly attacked the 'futile and immoral' policy of containment, and more ambiguously looked to policies that would 'revive the contagious, liberating influences which are inherent in freedom'. But Eisenhower was reluctant actually to send American forces into combat. The Republican talk of 'liberation' may have done something to encourage local risings against Soviet rule, as in East Berlin in 1953 and Hungary in 1956, but the rebels received no American aid. Characteristic of the Eisenhower presidency too was its use of what has been dubbed the 'hidden hand', which in foreign policy meant a willingness to use covert action. Thus the CIA was deployed to help the Shah of Iran secure control of his country in place of the nationalist Mosaddeq regime in 1953 (although it was unsuccessful in an attempt to overthrow the popular Sukarno regime in Indonesia in

1959–60). But a little more than the hidden hand was needed when Soviet influence was feared in Indochina, the Middle East and Latin America.

Since the Second World War France had been trying to reassert its authority in Vietnam, where the nationalist Vietminh under Ho Chi Minh had proclaimed independence. But Ho was also a Communist, and by 1954 the United States was paying for 80 per cent of the French military effort against his forces. In that year the French suffered a major defeat at Dien Bien Phu and the war soon ended. At the Geneva Conference it was agreed that Vietnam should be divided along the 17th parallel prior to reunification following elections to be held in 1956. The United States, wary of the popularity of the Vietminh, declined to be a party to these accords and continued covert operations against the Ho regime in the North, as it also financially backed the Ngo Dinh Diem government in South Vietnam. But Diem never secured public support and was unable to defeat the Vietminh when fighting broke out again in 1960. Eisenhower resisted calls for direct military intervention, although he had apparently committed the United States to protecting South Vietnam from Communism.

The Middle East was another danger spot. In Egypt in 1956 President Gamal Nasser seized the Suez Canal, in which the British and French owned stock and which was crucial for the West's supply of oil. Israel also regarded the Nasser regime as a threat to its own security. The Israelis, French and British colluded secretly and in October 1956 Israel suddenly invaded Egypt. Britain and France then intervened with their military forces, ostensibly to separate the combatants, and did so without forewarning the United States. To a furious Eisenhower the Anglo-French action looked like old-style European imperialism, and he feared that it might push the Arab countries towards the Soviet Union. He forced the British and French into a humiliating withdrawal. But the United States was not prepared to allow the Soviets access to the region. Early in 1957 the administration announced the Eisenhower Doctrine, offering economic assistance to Middle Eastern countries and aid against Communist aggression. But it was Arab nationalism rather than Communist subversion that made the region unstable, and only the Lebanon was prepared to take the suspect American money. Eisenhower despatched marines to protect the Lebanese regime when it felt threatened in 1958.

The deepening of the Cold War also increased American unease about the prospect of subversion in the affairs of the impoverished Latin American nations. When a reform government seized land in 1954 from an American company in Guatemala, in which a communist movement was emerging, the secretary of state, John Foster Dulles, persuaded the Tenth Inter-American Conference to condemn 'international communism'. In the event the Eisenhower administration secretly deployed the CIA to help overthrow the Guatemalan government.

But it was in Cuba that the United States espied the greatest Communist threat. At the beginning of 1959 the incompetent regime of Fulgencio Batista was overthrown by revolutionaries led by the young Fidel Castro.

Some Americans welcomed the Cuban Revolution as a liberating phenomenon, and the Eisenhower administration quickly recognized the new government, in which Castro denied there was Communist influence. But the executions of his opponents, his intimations of a desire to promote revolution throughout Latin America, and the economic reforms he introduced disturbed the United States. When Castro took over the oil companies in 1960 the Eisenhower administration responded by closing the vital American market to Cuban sugar, a major blow to the Cuban economy. This gave the Soviet Union an opportunity to step in with purchases of its own. Eisenhower decided to ask the CIA to prepare plans to overthrow Castro, and in January 1961 the United States severed diplomatic relations with Cuba.

Locked in its fortress mentality, the United States tended to magnify evidence of Soviet influence in the 1950s, whether in Vietnam, Cuba or elsewhere. It is hardly surprising that there were few sustained attempts at directly improving relations with the Soviet Union, although occasionally an opportunity gleamed. With Stalin's death and the ending of the Korean War in 1953 there did seem some prospect of a thawing of the Cold War. President Eisenhower welcomed the idea of a 'summit conference' of the leaders of what were known as the 'great powers' – the United States, the Soviet Union, Britain and France – and the four duly met one another at Geneva in 1955, the first such meeting since 1945. The 'spirit of Geneva' resulted in expressions of goodwill though no concrete agreements, and by 1956 – which saw both the Suez Crisis and the brutal Soviet repression of a revolution in Hungary – East–West relations deteriorated again. Festering too was the issue of Berlin. Soviet Premier Nikita Khrushchev resented the presence of West Berlin inside Communist East Germany and in 1958 he insisted that the Western powers leave the city. Eisenhower had no intention of permitting such a retreat, but he invited the Soviet premier to talks in the United States, which proved reasonably cordial if inconclusive. Eisenhower intended to return the visit after a summit meeting in Paris in 1960. But shortly before it opened an American observation plane was shot down over the Soviet Union. The Soviets exposed the American pretence that it was an off-course weather plane and an embarrassed Eisenhower accepted personal responsibility for the spy flights. Khrushchev launched a highly bitter attack on the president at the opening of the summit, effectively aborting it. As the Eisenhower presidency ended the Cold War was as glacial as ever.

The failure of the United States, with all its resources, to establish clear supremacy in the Cold War was deeply frustrating for Americans reared to believe that they were the guardians of freedom. The immediate post-war reverses had been attributed by McCarthyites to traitors in American government, a charge indignantly denied by American liberals, but by the end of the 1950s some liberals were beginning to believe that government was at least partly at fault. Within the Democratic Party a growing body of opinion held that the Eisenhower administration had been too passive in its conduct of the Cold War, particularly in the arena which was assuming greater importance in that ideological conflict, the Third World. The Democratic platform of 1960 began with a promise to restore American pre-eminence, and John Kennedy's victory brought to office a regime that believed that an opportunity existed to reassert American leadership.

'Let every nation know ... that we shall pay any price, bear any burden, meet any hardship, support any friend, oppose any foe to assure the survival and the success of liberty,' said Kennedy in his inaugural address, affirming his vision of the United States as a beacon for mankind. One White House security aide claimed that the move from Eisenhower to Kennedy represented 'a shift from defensive reaction to initiative'. An early symbol of the administration's intentions was the establishment of the Peace Corps, composed of American volunteers equipped with educational, agricultural or health skills and despatched to Third World countries to assist community development.

During the 1960 campaign the Democrats had made much of the 'missile gap', yet another illustration of the Eisenhower administration's sluggishness, but on coming into office they discovered that the 'gap' was in favour of the United States. Still, Kennedy was uneasy about the degree to which the Eisenhower strategy had depended on the deterrence of nuclear weapons, and local tensions around the globe suggested that what was needed was a more 'flexible response'. He launched an arms build-up, defence expenditures increasing by 13 per cent during his presidency. Flexible response meant that the United States was less dependent on threatening the use of nuclear weapons and conventional capability was accordingly enhanced, although the implication was that military intervention abroad would increase. But Kennedy wanted nuclear superiority too; he doubled the number of Intercontinental Ballistic Missiles (Minutemen) and enlarged the fleet of Polaris submarines. Yet what had been started could not easily be stopped. The Soviet Union could not allow its rival to gain an overwhelming superiority and threw itself desperately into producing more missiles of its own, obliging the United States in turn to increase its commitment. The Democratic criticism of Eisenhower for tolerating a missile gap helped to precipitate an unnerving arms race.

The new president was determined to stand up to the Soviets. 'I have to show him that we can be as tough as he is,' he said of a prospective meeting with Soviet Premier Khrushchev. The two met in June 1961 in Vienna, where Khrushchev's belligerence shook Kennedy, warning of supporting 'wars of national liberation' in Third World countries subject to Western control. Khrushchev reiterated the Soviet demand that the Western powers quit West Berlin (through which refugees from the Communist East streamed), which would become part of East Germany. Kennedy returned home determined to stand firm: 'All Europe is at stake in West Berlin.' In the event the Soviet Union found a solution to the crisis – in August the Berlin Wall was built to shut the East off from the West, thus stopping the embarrassing flow of refugees. The United States tacitly accepted the continued division of Germany.

But it was in the Third World that Kennedy anticipated the greatest Cold War challenge. He had criticized the Eisenhower administration for paying too little heed to the way in which European decolonization was changing global configurations of power. Nonetheless such gestures as the Peace Corps were hardly sufficient to combat the economic desperation that could breed communism. For Latin America, at least, Kennedy believed he had an answer. In his inaugural address he had offered a 'special pledge' to the region for 'a new alliance for progress – to assist free men and free governments in casting off the chains of poverty'. One possible strategy for a United States worried about Castro's boast of exporting revolution was to extend economic aid to Latin American nations and encourage them to develop democratic institutions. In August 1961 the Alliance for Progress was established with this objective, with the United States promising vastly increased financial aid in return for internal reforms. To Kennedy this was a programme 'which I believe can successfully counter the Communist onslaught in this hemisphere'.

The Castro regime also provoked a more direct response. President Eisenhower had authorized the CIA to prepare a force of Cuban exiles to invade the island, in the hope of triggering a popular uprising against Castro. Kennedy permitted the invasion to go ahead in April 1961, though – deciding that US forces should not be directly involved – withheld air cover. The Bay of Pigs operation was a disaster as the invaders were quickly defeated, a humiliation that made the Kennedys even more determined to destroy Castro. Operation Mongoose was secretly launched, involving sabotage attempts on Cuban property and plots to assassinate Castro.

The harassment of Castro served to push Cuba closer to the Soviet Union, which in 1962 tried to seize the advantage by provocatively installing medium-range missiles on the island. In October US reconnaissance planes photographed a missile launch pad under construction. The presence of Soviet missiles in Cuba would not much alter the balance of power, but Kennedy would have difficulty in persuading the American public of this, and in any case considered it dangerous to display weakness to the Soviet Union. 'This is reprise on the Bay of Pigs business and this time there will be no charges that somebody weakened at the crucial moment', one government official noted. The momentous confrontation took place. Kennedy took to television and starkly warned the Soviet Union that any nuclear missile launched from Cuba would provoke a full response by the United States directly on the Soviet Union. Kennedy's military advisers favoured an air strike on the missile bases, but he decided on a naval blockade of the island to prevent Soviet ships from getting through. At the critical point the Soviet vessels turned back. Kennedy further publicly demanded that the Soviets dismantle the missiles, and Khrushchev was privately given to understand that US missiles in Turkey would be soon removed. The Soviet premier bowed to Kennedy's public demand and the threat of nuclear war was averted.

Kennedy emerged from the Cuban missile crisis with considerably enhanced stature, at least in the United States. But his need to demonstrate his toughness both to the American public and to Khrushchev had taken the world to the brink of nuclear war. And the crisis weakened the Western alliance, suggesting to European leaders that the United States would pay them minimal attention when it had its reasons for acting.

Having looked over the brink, John Kennedy turned to ways of easing US–Soviet tensions. Both the Soviet premier and the American president began to show greater interest in a ban on nuclear testing, and in a speech in June 1963 Kennedy stressed that the United States did not want 'a Pax Americana enforced on the world by American weapons of war'. He suggested that conflict with the Soviets was not necessarily inevitable and looked to an ending of the arms race. Kennedy suspended atmospheric nuclear tests and in August the two powers signed the nuclear test ban pact, renouncing testing above ground level.

But the competition for the allegiance of the Third World precluded any real chance of détente. In his inaugural address Kennedy had referred to 'those peoples in the huts and villages of half the globe struggling to break the bonds of mass misery', pledging them American help 'to help themselves', not 'because the Communists may be doing it ... but because it is right'. But Communist activity in the Third World certainly disturbed Kennedy, particularly in South-East Asia. The Truman administration had been seriously damaged by the 'loss' of China to the Communists, and ever since the United States had been anxious to contain further Communist advances in the region. It had become an axiom among American policy-makers that the 'fall' of Indochina would lead to the Communist control of the whole of South-East Asia and, in due course, of India and even Japan too. The 'domino theory' required the protection of the most exposed domino.

At the time of Kennedy's accession there were 685 US military advisers in South Vietnam, sustaining the regime of Ngo Dinh Diem in the face of rebellion from the National Liberation Front (NLF) or Viet Cong, which was aided by the North Vietnamese leader, Ho Chi Minh. To Secretary of State Dean Rusk the Diem regime in the South was the victim of aggression instigated by Communist North Vietnam, which in turn relied on China. Vietnam, he warned, must not become another Munich. There was little likelihood of Kennedy abandoning Vietnam. He thought he had the means of turning the situation round. He believed that Eisenhower had been unable to respond adequately to Soviet moves because the United States had become too dependent on the nuclear deterrent; Kennedy's favoured 'flexible response' included a capacity to wage guerrilla warfare. The insurgency that the Soviet Union seemed to be encouraging in the Third World could be seen off by counter-insurgency.

Kennedy's interest in counter-insurgency was illustrated by the attention he paid to the American Special Forces units, or Green Berets, which he expanded fivefold. This was an élite corps equipped with the latest technology. With such American expertise, local forces would be trained and, together with political and social reforms, the threat of Communist rebellion would be contained. Kennedy increased aid to the Diem regime. By November 1963 there were 16,700 US military personnel in Vietnam, though the president resisted military requests for combat troops.

In that month Diem was the victim of a military coup, one acquiesced in by the United States, which had become impatient with the ineffectiveness of the South Vietnam government. A few weeks later Kennedy himself was assassinated. It is possible, as some of his advisers later claimed, that had he lived Kennedy might have found a way of disengaging from Vietnam before the American commitment became massive. But his successor by temperament was unlikely to lead a voluntary retreat. 'I am not going to lose Vietnam', insisted Lyndon Johnson. 'I am not going to be the President who saw Southeast Asia go the way China went.'

Vietnam became the defining foreign issue of his presidency, but the Cold War was a global phenomenon. Like other American leaders of his generation, Johnson was wary of communist encroachments wherever they might seem to impinge on the 'free world'. He took particular interest in Latin America (where Kennedy's Alliance for Progress was faltering by 1963) and came to use it as a vehicle for encouraging private business investment and supporting anti-communist governments. The most serious Latin American problem to confront him concerned the Dominican Republic. In April 1965 an uprising threatened the pro-American regime there and Johnson sent in the marines, ostensibly to protect American lives on the island. But he also feared a Castro-style coup, in a television address talking of 'communist leaders' taking 'increasing control' of the rebel forces. Eventually the Organization of American States sent in a peacekeeping force, and a pro-American government was elected in 1966. Public opinion generally supported Johnson's policy, although it became clear to close observers that he had exaggerated the communist threat. 'It suddenly occurred to me that maybe they weren't telling the truth in Vietnam either', recalled a Peace Corps official of the invasion of the Dominican Republic.

More challenging was the situation in the Middle East, where for years there had been border friction between Israel and its Arab neighbours. The Johnson White House worried about Moscow's machinations in the more radical Arab states and the dependence of Western Europe on oil from the Persian Gulf. In 1966, hoping to stabilize the region and counter Soviet influence, the administration began supplying military equipment to the 'moderate' Arab countries of Iran, Saudi Arabia and Jordan, and increased military supplies to Israel. But in June 1967 the Six Day War broke out between Israel and the states of Egypt, Jordan and Syria. Israeli forces quickly established superiority and took the Sinai, the West Bank of the Jordan, east Jerusalem and the Golan Heights. Johnson, worried that backing Israel might lead him into a confrontation with the Soviet Union, pressed for a ceasefire, and the State Department announced that the United States would be 'neutral in thought, word and deed'. This did little to placate the Arab governments, a number severing relations with Washington. The Soviet

Union threatened to intervene and the administration eventually prevailed on Israel to agree to a ceasefire. With Israel hanging on to its territorial gains, the situation in the Middle East remained tense. Johnson feared another explosion there, but his influence in the region was limited and American resources were being increasingly swallowed up by Vietnam.

During Johnson's first several months in office the war in Vietnam dragged on frustratingly, with the unstable South Vietnam regime unable to strike effectively at the Viet Cong, and with Johnson both unwilling to withdraw and unwilling to commit American combat forces. In August 1964, however, North Vietnamese torpedo boats opened fire on US destroyers in the Gulf of Tonkin (or so the rather murky evidence suggested). Characterizing the incident as open aggression against the United States, Johnson asked Congress for a resolution giving him authority to take 'all necessary steps' to protect South Vietnam. Johnson wanted congressional endorsement for any escalation of the war, and the vital resolution was passed unanimously by the House and with only two dissenting votes by the Senate.

In the early months of 1965 Johnson finally lost patience with the apparently endless policy of propping up ineffective governments in Vietnam. He had hitherto resisted advice to strike at the North while there was an unstable regime in the South, but he now calculated that increased pressure on Hanoi might serve to stiffen South Vietnamese resolve. In February a two-month bombing campaign, 'Rolling Thunder', was launched without announcement. As columnist James Reston put it, the United States had embarked on 'an undeclared and unexplained war in Vietnam'. Johnson doubted whether the bombing would do much to deter Hanoi, but he hoped that it would help avert a collapse of the South Vietnam government. 'Light at the end of the tunnel', he growled to an aide. 'Hell, we don't even have a tunnel.' There were still only 23,000 military advisers in Vietnam, an increase on the number Johnson had inherited but hardly overwhelming. Johnson did agree to send marines to guard the American air base at Denang, although not to send them into combat. But American commitment was almost imperceptibly growing. Johnson soon expanded the bombing, increased the number of military advisers, sent another couple of marine divisions and, more significantly, by early April allowed the marines to shift to offensive operations. And with the bombing emerged increasing liberal criticism, to the surprise of the White House, which had previously been more subject to criticism from the right.

In a major speech in March Johnson defended his policy, insisting that the American presence was vital to containing Communism in Asia. Hanging over the conflict, he insisted, was 'the deepening shadow of Communist China'. But he also called on the North Vietnamese to enter peace talks, promising that if Hanoi guaranteed the independence of South Vietnam, the United States would pour a billion dollars into the area: 'The vast Mekong River can provide food and water and power on a scale to dwarf even our own TVA.' Like Roosevelt and Truman before him, Johnson had a vision of carrying the New Deal to the world. Hanoi was not interested, but the broadly favourable public response to the speech helped to steel him to further action.

Reports from Vietnam indicated that the US Marines were inflicting far greater damage on the Viet Cong than the Vietnamese forces had ever achieved, suggesting that only the deployment of American ground forces could produce success. By mid-June 1965 US forces in Vietnam had reached a total of 82,000, although offensive operations other than the bombing remained limited. Yet pressure for a more aggressive strategy mounted. The bombing campaign had not brought the desired results; the Vietnamese forces were reeling before the Viet Cong; and the South Vietnam government again seemed on the verge of collapse. The head of the US military mission in Vietnam, General William Westmoreland, wanted his troops more than doubled so that he might 'take the war to the enemy'. By July Johnson decided that he had little alternative to escalation. A continuation of the existing strategy would bring only a slow defeat, while withdrawal would mean surrender to the Communists, with all the fateful consequences this would have for American prestige, the stability of South-East Asia and the viability of the Johnson presidency. At the end of the month Johnson announced that US troops would be increased to 125,000.

Lyndon Johnson was deeply agonized during the summer of 1965, not wanting to risk American casualties in Vietnam but unable to accept defeat there. He realized only too well that the United States could be sucked ever deeper into the quagmire, which he also knew could wreck his cherished Great Society programmes. His wife Lady Bird later told historian Robert Dallek of her husband's torment over the war: 'It was just a hell of a thorn stuck in his throat. It wouldn't come up; it wouldn't go down ... It was just pure hell and did not have that reassuring, strong feeling that this is right, that he had when he was in a crunch with civil rights or poverty or education.'

The administration hoped that the intensified force would persuade Hanoi that it could not win. By October there were 200,000 US troops in Vietnam. The press and public opinion broadly supported Johnson's policy. Nonetheless American commitment was growing with little explanation by the White House. There were those who distrusted the news management by the administration and Johnson's 'credibility gap' began to show.

Step by step the American military commitment in Vietnam grew ever larger. The nearly 200,000 US troops there at the end of 1965 grew to 450,000 a year later. Little over a year again there were 500,000. By early 1968 an estimated 220,000 Viet Cong soldiers had been killed, but it was the body bags being shipped home that most distressed the American public. By the middle of 1967 nearly 70,000 Americans had been wounded or killed; by the end of 1968 the figure had reached 130,000. (There were ultimately to be over 58,000 American deaths, compared to over 2 million Vietnamese.) A greater weight of bombs was dropped on Vietnam between July 1965 and December 1967 alone than the Allies dropped on Europe during the entire Second World War. As US commitment and casualties mounted, the White

House continued to insist that the United States would not abandon its South Vietnam ally. By the end of 1967 Johnson desperately wanted a peace, but not at the cost of a unilateral withdrawal. 'I'm not going to be the first American President to lose a war', he told a newsman.

At the end of January 1968 the Viet Cong launched the massive Tet offensive, striking not only at Saigon but also at five of South Vietnam's largest cities and three dozen provincial capitals. Even the US embassy was invaded. In fact American firepower ensured that Tet resulted in defeat for the Viet Cong, who lost perhaps 50,000 soldiers. But the relatively large scale of American losses at the hands of an allegedly exhausted enemy did the White House great political harm. The 500,000 US troops had been unable to protect the country. After an initial patriotic rallying to the president's position, the American public's support for the war dropped. Early in March a poll showed 49 per cent of respondents saying that sending troops to fight had been a mistake; 41 per cent supported the policy.

By this time even Secretary of Defense Robert McNamara had despaired of a satisfactory outcome to the war and had been replaced by Clark Clifford. Johnson remained loath to beat a retreat. 'We shall and we are going to win', he declared in March. But a request from the Joint Chiefs for another massive troop escalation shook the White House, which after all had claimed to have won the Tet encounter. Clifford seized the opportunity to encourage a change of direction. He arranged a meeting with the 'Wise Men', veteran foreign policy experts who in the past had broadly endorsed Johnson's wishes but who now urged disengagement. 'These establishment bastards have bailed out', a bitter president was reported as saying. Johnson, whose personal standing had been falling in the polls and who faced raucous anti-war protests, could no longer push out of his mind the need for a change of strategy. At the end of March he went on television to announce a partial bombing halt and a willingness to enter peace talks. He also announced that he would not be a candidate for re-election.

The remaining months of the Johnson presidency dragged on without disengagement from Vietnam being secured. Johnson sent representatives to preliminary peace talks in Paris in May, and at the end of October announced an end to all bombing of North Vietnam. But the damage his policies and events had inflicted on his party was already too great. The Democratic presidential candidate, Hubert Humphrey, was narrowly defeated by the Republican Richard Nixon, who had vaguely talked about a 'secret plan' to end the war.

In fact there did not seem to be much of a 'secret plan'. Richard Nixon realized that the United States could not win the war, but he was no more willing than Johnson to lose it. 'I will not be the first President of the United States to lose a war', he said in 1969, repeating a now familiar presidential mantra. His military solution proved to be 'Vietnamization', replacing American troops with Vietnamese, amply resourced by the United States and supplemented by massive bombing campaigns. But these tactics had not worked before and not until January 1973 was Nixon able to achieve his 'peace with honor' and complete the withdrawal of American forces. Defeat had to be masked as victory of a sort.

Disengagement may have been difficult and protracted, but by 1969 it was clear that the United States had little alternative. Vietnam had exposed the limits of American power and humiliated the United States as never before. The post-war generation's policy of containment had been found seriously wanting, while some Americans were questioning the very premises of the Cold War. No less than the chair of the Senate Foreign Relations Committee, Senator William Fulbright, had censured American policy for displaying 'the arrogance of power' and had told American leaders that they were not qualified 'to play God'. The Vietnam experience demonstrated that the United States did not have the capacity to manage the course of world events. The new sense of limits was expressed in the Nixon Doctrine, promulgated in the middle of 1969, which gave notice that in future the United States might help threatened countries with economic and military aid but would not send combat troops. The Cold War was not over as far as Washington was concerned, but a new strategy had to be found for conducting it. The expansive foreign policies of Democratic presidents from Franklin Roosevelt to Lyndon Johnson no longer commanded wide consent.

PART

III

THE DIVIDED POLITICAL
ORDER, 1969–2000

|14|

The Divided Order
1969–2000

The political landscape associated with the New Deal Order did not survive the convulsions of the 1960s. The long years of Democratic ascendancy came to an end, and faith in the efficacy of government was severely eroded. As the Democratic Party faltered the Republicans experienced a modest revival, although never achieved clear ascendancy. This loss of political coherence was related to a weakening of the party system itself, which was less able to impose order on the governing process. In the final third of the twentieth century public esteem for party politicians sank to a dispiriting low, and crucial decision-making on public matters often seemed to fall to bodies outside the conventional realm of electoral politics. Broadly speaking, conservatism enjoyed a new respectability while big government liberalism tended to retreat, although many liberals found alternatives in more focused campaigns like feminism and environmentalism. Division and confusion characterized the American polity in the closing decades of the century.

In a sense the New Deal Order had done its work, fashioning a liberal capitalist state in which government invested heavily in education, welfare and health care for an industrial working class and a growing middle class, easing the class tensions of an earlier generation. But as suburbia outgrew the city, politicians became more responsive to the concerns of middle-class taxpayers than of urban workers. Many Democrats remained fiercely committed to the New Deal system, though their stance seemed increasingly defensive as they fought to preserve their creation at a time when demographic change was subjecting it to increasing strain. The number of Americans receiving Social Security benefits, for example, rose from 26 million in 1970 to over 40 million in 1991. In Roosevelt's day the elderly could expect to collect their pensions for no more than five years before death intervened; two generations later they were surviving for ten years and more. New Deal institutions creaked under the growing demands, and liberals were vulnerable to charges that their programmes had brought inflation and fiscal crises in their wake and were stifling entrepreneurial vigour through high taxes and excessive government. Further, the New Deal experience had broadly separated voters on economic and social policies, but lifestyle and cultural issues now cut across the old party allegiances. The liberals' enthusiasm for rights was charged with abetting a permissive culture defined by rising crime rates and disintegrating family life. But conservatives were no more able to articulate a vision that commanded general support.

A diverse range of analyses of the American condition towards the end of the twentieth century emphasized the themes of discord and disintegration. From a post-industrial perspective, sociologists John Urry and Scott Lash argued that the American political economy had moved from a form of 'organized capitalism' to one of 'disorganized capitalism', characterized by population movements away from the old industrial cities, a deconcentration of capital, the wider dispersal of industry, a weakening of the nation state and a decline in class politics. Some analysts focused on cultural discord, the heightened awareness of ethnicity triggered by the civil rights movement having promoted a perception of the United States as a multicultural society. When pride in cultural identity descended into the so-called 'culture wars' that erupted in the late 1980s, historian Arthur Schlesinger was moved to protest at *The Disuniting of America*. An excessive and unchecked emphasis on racial and ethnic differences, he warned, risked bringing about 'the fragmentation, resegregation, and tribalization of American life'. Conservative social historian Gertrude Himmelfarb in 1999 considered division of another sort in *One Nation, Two Cultures*, arguing that the experience of the 1960s had poised an essentially permissive culture against a traditional moralistic culture.

The dual backdrop to this uncertain era was a mostly sluggish economy at home and the disappearance of Cold War simplicities abroad. The United States was embarked on a trajectory that was to take it into a new global economy and the information age, but there were perilous uncertainties on the way. Growth did not disappear, but the exceptionally buoyant economy of the post-war decades gave way to more troubled times in the 1970s, and the straitened circumstances persisted, relieved only by a burst of prosperity at the very end of the century. In the expansive 1960s Gross Domestic Product (GDP) had increased (in constant dollars) by 51 per cent; expectations had declined by the 1980s, when growth slowed to 37 per cent. The real income of most American workers even declined from $315 per week in 1973 to $278 in 1995. A generational study of fathers and sons between the 1970s and 1990s found that upward social mobility actually decreased. The downward trend in the size of poverty brought about by economic growth and Great Society programmes came to an end, and poverty tended to creep up from the late 1970s, the rate peaking at 15.1 per cent in 1993, the highest of any industrialized country. It had become evident that American resources were limited; the panacea of endless and rapid economic growth was no longer there to perform its magic. As President Jimmy Carter observed in 1979, 'we cannot afford to live beyond our means'. In the following year, Lester

Thurow's *The Zero Sum Society* became a best-seller, arguing that the economy could no longer produce a surplus for social spending.

Uncertainty about the economic future was matched by confusion over the place of the United States in the world. The bipolar perceptions of the early Cold War seemed outdated before the 1960s were over, with the emergence of new nations in Asia and Africa, the creation of the European Community and the schism between the Soviet Union and China. The trauma of Vietnam provided a shocking lesson on the limits of American power and called into question the degree to which the United States should seek to impose its will in distant lands. It was also less evident that it had the capability to do so. In 1950 the American economy had represented 50 per cent of world GDP; by 1990 its share was down to 25 per cent, still formidable but not dominant, while at the same time it was more exposed to the unsettling forces of globalism. The eventual ending of the Cold War, while celebrated as an American 'victory', introduced a world for which Americans were ill-prepared. The United States had less reason than it had in the 1940s and 1950s to close ranks against a foreign foe.

The most conspicuous symptom of the divided political order was the tendency for one party, usually the Republicans, to be in possession of the White House, and the opposing party to command majorities in Congress. And division took other forms too. As foreign policy reverses and domestic scandals weakened the presidency, Congress sought to reassert its authority, competing with the president for control over public policy. But neither the White House nor Congress always seemed in sure command of the governing process. Some analysts argued that interest groups were assuming power. Others pointed to the way in which significant decisions seemed often to be made through bureaucratic processes, by anonymous officers of federal agencies. Yet other scholars drew attention to the politicization of the judiciary. As the executive and legislative branches lost the capacity to manage public policy, it sometimes seemed, major issues were resolved by the courts (rather as had been the case at the end of the nineteenth century). Whatever the respective balance between them, in the post-New Deal system the political influence of each of these elements – interest groups, the federal bureaucracy and the judiciary – was enhanced, although divisions within each also militated against a clear sense of direction. What the three had in common was that their personnel were not elected. Not only was political power dispersed, but it tended to slip away from the chosen representatives of the people. Whether or not because of a sense of powerlessness, many voters were disengaging from the political process.

The demise of the New Deal Order was signalled by the presidential election of 1968. The decline in the popular vote for the Democratic presidential candidate was the greatest the party had suffered in the twentieth century, and the humiliation of the Democrats was completed four years later when Richard Nixon won re-election by a landslide. Yet throughout his presidency the Republican Nixon faced Democratic majorities in both houses of Congress. This was a condition that characterized the rest of the century. In most years Republican presidents faced Democratic Congresses, although the situation was reversed from 1995 when a Democratic president faced a Republican Congress. Only in 1977–81 and again in 1993–5 did the same party 'control' both the White House and the two legislative houses. It was in the mid-1970s that the term 'gridlock' was first used in relation to the American political process. Such was the impasse between a Democratic White House and a Republican Congress over the federal budget in late 1995 that the government actually shut down on two occasions for lack of funds. No party enjoyed hegemony in this divided political order. Scholars applied such terms as 'split-level government' or the 'interregnum state' to this state of affairs.

The Democratic Party experienced its most serious reverses at presidential level, losing six of the nine elections held between 1968 and 2000. (It fared rather better in electing state governors and better still in winning majorities in state legislatures.) The convulsions within the national party triggered by the Vietnam War and the unease of many Americans over the welfare and racial policies it had adopted in the 1960s eroded some of its core constituencies. It had lost the mass support of the white South. Organized labour, long a vital element of the New Deal coalition and an influential force for a liberal domestic agenda, tended to lose members with the decline of traditional industries. The unionized proportion of the non-farm workforce had been slipping since its post-war high of around a third; in 1970 it was down to 27 per cent and by 1991 to only 12 per cent. Further, some working- and middle-class urban-ethnics deserted the Democrats over what they perceived as unnecessarily indulgent attitudes towards black Americans and 'law and order'. The Democratic Party by the 1970s even found that it could no longer count on the loyalty of the intellectual community. It risked being seen as a party of special interests such as blacks, feminists and a shrunken organized labour, rather than the mass of the people.

Changes in the electoral environment further worked to the disadvantage of the Democrats. As had been the case in the early twentieth century, the electorate itself underwent significant change. A major transformation occurred in the South, where African-Americans were finally registered to vote in unprecedented numbers. In seven Deep Southern states the proportion of blacks eligible to vote doubled from 30 per cent in 1964 to 60 per cent in 1969. But as black voters exerted greater influence within the Democratic Party and elected some of their own to office, for the most part white Southerners turned to the Republicans – and more of them registered to vote too. The emergence of a two-party system in the South meant that the region was not the Democratic stronghold that it had been for the greater part of the twentieth century. By 1994 a majority of Southern congresspersons and governors were Republicans, a remarkable change from 1960, when 94 per cent of the old Confederacy South's House and Senate seats had been Democratic.

It is possible to describe this process as the 'nationalization' of Southern politics, as party politics in the South came to look more like that practised elsewhere. One effect of the incorporation of blacks into the body politic was to encourage Southern white Democratic politicians to embrace more liberal attitudes. But some scholars prefer to speak of the 'Southernization' of national politics. Some white Northerners too had been deserting the Democrats since the mid-1960s. In every presidential election in the last thirty years of the twentieth century white voters nationally cast more votes for the Republican than for the Democratic candidate. The Republican Party, which had once contained a significant proportion of liberals, became relatively conservative on civil rights and related issues. (Thus each party became more unified internally, as the Democrats lost their reactionary Southern wing and the Republicans lost Northern liberals; this meant that the ideological division between the two widened, intensifying their mutual animosity.) The Republican Party did not condone overt racism, but something of a racial divide opened up between the major parties. Over six in every ten white male voters cast their ballots for Ronald Reagan in his successful presidential bids; about nine in ten black voters opted for his opponents. The disparity persisted. In the mid-term elections of 1994 some 63 per cent of white males voted Republican and 37 per cent Democrat; 91 per cent of African-Americans voted Democrat. The presidential election of 2000 produced similar figures.

This racial imbalance would have helped the Republicans more had it not been partially countered by a gender imbalance. Women at last were turning out to vote in greater numbers (perhaps because more were going out to work), and in the last quarter of the twentieth century tended to favour the Democrats. In 1976 men and women voted Democrat in about equal proportions, but in 1980 exit polls indicated that only 36 per cent of males did so compared to 45 per cent of females; in 1988 the figures were 41 and 49 per cent respectively. In the 1994 congressional elections, when white men flocked to the Republican colours, women – of all races – preferred the Democrats by a margin of 53 to 47. Working and single women in particular showed a preference for the Democratic Party, with its greater sympathy for abortion rights. They helped to re-elect President Clinton in 1996, and nearly delivered the 2000 presidential election to Al Gore, preferring him to George W. Bush by 54 to 43.

While the Democratic Party suffered some electoral haemorrhage, the Republican Party was invigorated by new currents. These were not simply the product of Democratic defections. As Lisa McGirr and others have demonstrated, middle-class suburbanites in the West and the South, both anti-government libertarians and Christian social conservatives, had long been working to place their own kind in government, and from the mid-1960s their concern over law and order and the traditional family allowed them to subordinate their doctrinal differences to a common assault on a permissive modern morality. Some Democratic voters did switch to the Republican column. Yet the loss of regular Democratic votes, what political scientists call 'dealignment', was not accompanied by a significant 'realignment'. Defecting Democrats seem rather to have joined the 'independent' voters. The Republicans thus failed to become the dominant party, although they did move to the right.

The conservative revival was furthered by the harsher economic times. For a generation Keynesian ideas had been the orthodoxy among leading economists, and most public figures had accepted some sort of management role for government in economic and social matters. But the high unemployment and inflation rates of the 1970s undermined confidence in Keynesian economic and 'big government' solutions. The Chicago economist Milton Friedman gained a wide audience for his ideas, arguing that government spending and budget deficits encouraged inflation and disrupted the free market. Another set of ideas, 'supply-side' economics, argued that economic recovery could be achieved by a major tax cut, which would leave consumers with greater purchasing power with which to generate greater production, an approach that was to dominate the 'Reaganomic' experiments of the 1980s. Supply-side economics again implied a reduced role for government, once the tax cut had been effected.

Even before monetarist ideas became popular, some intellectuals were moving away from the big government ideas associated with New Deal reformism. The failure of the Great Society to deliver on its promises, together with the rising inflation and slowing economic growth, cast doubt on the capacity of government to manage a highly complex society. These intellectuals, several of them Democrats, became known as 'neo-conservatives'. While many insisted that they remained liberals, they stood against the New Leftist and counter-cultural fringes of the Democratic Party, questioned the degree of social engineering in Great Society programmes, championed traditional cultural values, and insisted on maintaining Cold War vigilance abroad. With ready access to the media, the neo-conservatives helped to promote a change in the intellectual climate.

In time these former liberals were joined by scores of defiantly conservative intellectuals, several of whom found refuge in the flourishing research institutes, such as the Heritage Foundation and the American Enterprise Institute. Scholarly institutes had long existed, but from the 1970s there was a proliferation of highly partisan 'think tanks'. By the mid-1990s there were over a hundred in Washington, many of them handsomely supported financially by business corporations and rich entrepreneurs. Conservative journals, like the *American Spectator*, were also thriving. The free-market conservatism boosted by such sources not only excoriated the New Deal but also the compromises made with liberalism by moderate Republicans. During the heyday of the New Deal Order many intellectuals had identified with the liberal wing of the Democratic Party, but the Republican right now came to draw on considerable intellectual resources.

The right-wing think tanks could be seen as part of the New Right, an informal collection of conservative organizations that emerged by the late 1970s. Groups like Howard Phillips' Conservative Caucus and Terry Dolan's National Conservative Political Action Committee aimed to mobilize grassroots support for right-wing candidates and target liberal office-holders. They cultivated conservative single-issue groups such as the National Rifle

Association and anti-abortion organizations, and sought to circumvent the traditional media (with its alleged liberal bias) through direct mailing campaigns. Following the methods of entrepreneur Richard Viguerie, direct mailing proved critical in communicating with and mobilizing conservatives across the country, allowing the New Right groups to function independently of the Republican Party. It had been leftist Democrats that had been largely responsible for democratizing the national parties, as in insisting on the use of primary elections, but the destruction of the old party machines ironically worked to the benefit of the right, which had the resources to target voters directly.

The New Right embraced anti-government libertarians, traditional hard-line anti-communists and enthusiastic groups of religious moralists. Among the latter was Jerry Falwell's Moral Majority, formed in 1979 to promote a range of 'pro-God, pro-family' causes. In 1988 the Christian Coalition was created, and by the mid-1990s was a formidable force in about half of the state Republican parties. A renewed faith in the free market invigorated some of the groups in the New Right, but what most distinguished it from more traditional forms of conservatism was its emphasis on cultural and moral issues, a reaction to the causes associated with the New Left and the counter-culture of the 1960s. New Right activists were generally hostile to abortion and gay rights, to judicial judgments favouring bussing and opposing school prayers and to permissive attitudes regarding sexual morality and personal freedom. This cluster of concerns was often characterized by the phrase 'family values'.

The New Right drew some of its vigour from an energetic religious revival. In 1977 one survey found that over one in three adults identified themselves as 'born-again' Christians. Protestant evangelicals expanded the number of local TV and radio stations they controlled, and several 'tele-vangelists' won massive followings. They fashioned an unlikely alliance, mobilizing both urban Catholics and small-town, evangelical and fundamentalist Protestants against such causes as abortion and the Equal Rights Amendment (ERA). Public debate took on a moral and religious colouring to a degree that had been unusual in the rather secular politics of the mid-twentieth century. And many Democrats as well as Republicans sought to align themselves with the new religiosity. In 1976 the Democratic Party nominated the avowedly 'born-again' Christian Jimmy Carter for the presidency, and when Bill Clinton's sexual conduct in the White House occasioned scandal he hastened to surround himself with religious figures and prayed for forgiveness. But the Republican Party was the chief political beneficiary of this evangelical awakening, as in the case of the conservative elected governor of Florida in 1994, who began his victory speech by saying 'First, I want to thank God.' The Republican 1984 national convention closed with a prayer by Jerry Falwell, who spoke of the party's candidates as 'God's instruments in rebuilding America'. In 1988 some 81 per cent of white born-again Christians cast their presidential ballots for George Bush, and by 1995, according to one observer, 'the religious right is moving toward center stage in American secular life'.

The relative strengthening of conservative currents in American politics also reflected demographic trends, most notably the rise of the Sunbelt, that is the states of the South and the West. The population of the South grew from 30.9 per cent of the national total in 1970 to 35.2 per cent in 1997; that of the West jumped from 17.1 to 22.2 per cent. Together these sections thus came to represent a majority of the American people, and the proportions of the North-East and Midwest correspondingly declined. During the years of heady defence expenditure occasioned by the Vietnam War, the rate of capital formation and income growth in the Sunbelt reached twice that of the North-East. Traditionally, the older industrial areas had wielded considerable political clout, but as their economies flagged some residents fled to the booming Sunbelt cities, where entrepreneurial values flourished. The population shifts promoted a redistribution of political power. The old nostrum that a Southerner could not be elected president was disproved by the election of Jimmy Carter in 1976, and the power of the West was illustrated by the election of Ronald Reagan in 1980. No presidential candidate from outside the Sunbelt made it to the White House for the rest of the century.

A major conservative objective was the roll-back of the state. The disillusionment with big government was not confined to the Republicans. Many Democrats too were influenced by neo-conservative ideas and were embarrassed by the failure of some Great Society programmes. With the decline of the labour vote Democrats also became increasingly conscious of the need to secure electoral support from the suburban middle classes, for whom a 'tax-and-spend' philosophy held limited appeal. Some liberals too retained something of a New Leftist antipathy towards an impersonal bureaucracy, preferring to look for solutions in local community action. Leading figures in both major parties agreed that the 'big government' liberalism of the New Deal Order had had its day, and that government, particularly the federal government, needed to be reined in. In 1996 a Democratic president told Congress that 'the era of big government is over', a belief Clinton illustrated by tearing up 16,000 pages of bureaucratic regulations. The extraordinary burgeoning of federal activity that had characterized the middle decades of the century did come to an end, although the size and cost of central government tended to level off rather than decline. Federal spending as a proportion of the GDP inched up from 19.3 per cent in 1970 to a peak of 23.5 per cent in 1983 (when it had been boosted by Reagan's defence build-up), and thereafter eased down again, to 18.2 per cent in 2000. Federal employment as a proportion of total employment was successfully contained. There were actually slightly fewer federal civilian employees in 2000 than there had been in 1970 (although the number of full-time employees of state and local governments had increased by about 40 per cent). The federal preoccupation with budget-cutting and the general consciousness of limits exacerbated the discordant temper of American politics in these years. Constituencies and interest groups were fighting over pieces of a pie that was no longer growing as once it had.

The quarrelsome and fragmented nature of the polity in the late twentieth century was furthered by the weakening of the party system itself. The erosion of party forms had begun earlier, but was becoming pronounced. One symptom was the apparent decline of popular interest in party politics. During the New Deal Order voter turnout had been relatively high by twentieth-century standards, reaching a post-war record in the presidential election of 1960, when 65.4 per cent of the potential electorate had voted. The next two elections saw modest erosions before a marked drop to 57 per cent in 1972, after which turnout remained in the mid-50s before falling to a miserable 50 per cent in 1988. In many Western European countries turnouts of over 70 per cent were quite common. In non-presidential elections the record was even worse; in the House of Representative elections of 1990 only a third of the voting age population went to the polls. Political scientist Walter Dean Burnham remarked that 'the shift toward voting abstention since 1960 is by far the largest mass movement of our time'. The turnout of manual workers in particular dropped markedly (to the advantage of property-owning voters). The party machines and labour unions no longer mobilized the electorate to the degree they once had. The divided nature of the political order may have contributed to this voter disillusion. As one congressman observed in 1987: 'Basically, people are smart about things, and their political inaction reflects the fact that politics simply does not matter.'

Some Americans appear to have been disenchanted with the traditional parties rather than uninterested in public affairs. The shrinkage of the electorate was accompanied by vigorous grass-roots activism outside the arena of conventional party politics. If the civil rights and youth movements of the sixties had peaked by the early 1970s, a host of causes was pursued by other groups. Women's organizations, many of them locally based, remained active through the rest of the century, as did a wealth of environmental, health, anti-poverty and ethnic groups. Grass-roots activity was not the monopoly of the left. In the 1970s Phyllis Schlafly conducted a remarkable campaign against the ERA, deftly deploying neighbourhood bodies, and in California retired businessman Howard Jarvis spearheaded Proposition 13, a tax-cutting measure that won voter approval in 1978, lighting similar grass-roots crusades in other states. Causes could often be better pursued through community and single-issue bodies than through the major parties. But this did not make for an orderly political system.

The weakening in party organization was reflected also in the growing practice of split-ticket voting. In the heyday of the New Deal Order most Americans voted the straight party line, voting for the same party in presidential, congressional and state elections. In 1960 only 14 per cent of voters voted different ways in presidential and congressional elections, but in 1972 the proportion suddenly jumped to 30 per cent before settling at around 25 per cent. The increased domination of presidential campaigns by television probably encouraged ballot splitting, given the preference of the cameras for focusing on individual candidates rather than party tickets. At the same time voters ceased to identify with particular parties with the intensity they once had. In 1960 some 75 per cent of the electorate identified themselves as either Republicans or Democrats; 23 per cent claimed to be 'Independent'. By 1988 the first figure had fallen to 63 per cent and the Independent figure had risen to 36 per cent. Voters were also proving less loyal. In 1996 some 63 per cent of those asked stated that they had 'voted for different parties for president' in past elections, more than twice the figure of a similar survey in 1952. One reason for the governmental gridlock that regularly emerged in the late twentieth century was that those Americans who could bring themselves to vote often seemed in more than one mind.

As Everett Carl Ladd has commented, 'a growing segment of the electorate really doesn't belong to any party'. Falling turnout and increased split-ticket voting reflected a remarkable distrust of the political process. In 1958 some 78 per cent of those polled had indicated positive feelings about government in general; in 1980 it was only 33 per cent. The conspicuous failures of American government in the quarter-century after 1965 contributed to this disregard, as did political scandals, which became a leitmotif of public life. The control of one branch of government by the Republican Party and the other by the Democrats meant that each had an interest in discrediting the other, and the Senate in particular regularly resorted to investigating committees to probe governmental activity. The lack of comity in public debate, the contemptuous terms in which each branch treated the other, itself contributed to the erosion of public confidence. Political scientist Morris Fiorini observed in 1989 that 'divided government encourages a full airing of any and all misdeeds, real and imagined'. Between the early 1970s and the mid-1980s the number of indictments brought by federal prosecutors against national, state and local officials multiplied ten times. The political temper hardly improved thereafter. The *Washington Post* considered the 1993–4 session as 'perhaps the worst Congress – least effective, most destructive, nastiest – in 50 years'; yet there were further depths to be plumbed before the century was out. The Clinton presidency, in the view of journalist Joe Klein, marked 'an unprecedented escalation in the levels of partisan enmity and journalistic fecklessness in Washington'. During the election campaign of 2000 surveys found that over 60 per cent of regular voters regarded American politics as 'generally pretty disgusting'.

Party organization weakened noticeably after the Democratic Party almost tore itself apart in 1968. In the aftermath of the traumatic Chicago convention the party's nominating process was overhauled to make it more representative, primarily through the widespread use of primary elections. In 1968 the party chieftains had been able to impose a candidate who had not entered a single primary on the Democratic convention; thereafter the primary contests became the main route to the nomination, to be formally ratified by the convention. The low turnouts in primary elections tended to give a disproportionate influence to the voting middle classes, and increasingly Democratic politicos recognized the importance of cultivating the suburbs. The Democrats' resort to primaries encouraged the Republicans to follow suit.

By 1988 over 80 per cent of delegates at both Democratic and Republican conventions were chosen through primary elections, more than double the proportions of 1960. The influence of the traditional managers was thus much reduced, while that of the media and interest groups was enhanced, for they carried messages about the candidates to the electorate. Candidates increasingly had to emphasize their personal qualities rather than their party labels, and the ubiquity of television put a premium on personality.

The tendency for elections to become candidate-centred meant also that candidates were obliged to raise funds themselves, rather than from party chests, and the 1970s and 1980s witnessed the rapid multiplication of Political Action Committees (PACs), through which interest groups channelled funds to politicians. The number of PACs increased phenomenally from 113 in 1972 to 4,178 in 1989. Congressional candidates received just $8.5 million from PACs in 1974 and $151 million in 1988. Parties were not well placed to control candidates. Both congressional and presidential candidates have been likened to independent entrepreneurs, running their own campaigns and making their own direct appeals to their constituents.

The growth of PACs reflected the proliferation of single-interest groups (whose influence was enhanced by the dwindling of the active electorate). Congress and the state legislatures tended to become forums in which organized interests pursued their highly specific goals, colliding and colluding with one another. Thousands of lobbies – from the National Rifle Association to the National Pasta Association – campaigned for their chosen issues. The number of registered lobbyists in Washington more than doubled to 7,200 in the ten years after 1975, and according to one estimate nearly 90 per cent of them worked for business, commercial and professional bodies. The business lobbies, it sometimes seemed, were becoming the primary shapers of public policy, usurping the role of parties and elected officials. Yet interest groups rarely presented a united front. During the New Deal Order, the American Medical Association had been the dominant interest group affecting health policy; in the late twentieth century hospital associations, medical schools, insurance companies and drug companies all claimed a voice. Significant legislation required the laborious piecing together of a coalition, a different one for each issue. The 'iron triangles' which analysts once believed to be the true makers of public policy (interacting interest groups, congressional committees and federal agencies) became less stable. Political scientists suggested new terms, such as 'issue networks' or even 'sloppy hexagons', to characterize this more diffuse state of affairs.

The public's suspicion of politicians extended to those attempting to manipulate governmental decisions. From the late 1960s liberals concerned with such matters as consumer protection and the environment were active in public interest or citizen groups that sought to hold business accountable, trying to develop the means to scrutinize the conduct of both business corporations and government agencies. Their numbers were modest – only 4.1 per cent of the thousands of lobbyists in Washington represented consumers and the public interest, according to a 1984 study. If the public interest movement could not match the resources of corporate America, at least it furnished lobbies of its own and was sometimes successful in exposing abuses.

If interest groups often competed with one another, so did Congress and the White House, the rivalry between them intensified by their tendency to be controlled by opposing parties. Franklin Roosevelt had largely identified the federal government with the presidency, but from the late 1960s, thanks to Lyndon Johnson's celebrated 'credibility gap' and Richard Nixon's abuses, distrust of the Oval Office grew. A Harris poll of 1976 showed that a tiny 11 per cent of respondents had 'great confidence' in the executive branch; in 1966 the figure had been 41 per cent.

Congress, determined to wrest back power for itself, introduced reforms that broadly had the effect of energizing congressional committees with new personnel and expanding resources so that members were better able to interrogate the presidential agenda. An act of 1970 curbed the powers of committee chairs and increased the number of subcommittees. Between 1973 and 1985 the number of congressional staff increased from about 11,500 to over 24,000, equipping Congress with thousands of ambitious people eager to make their mark on public policies. To secure greater influence over the federal budget in 1974 Congress established a Congressional Budget Office, which acquired a formidable staff of nearly 200 economists and other specialists, and its budget estimates often came to carry more authority than those of the White House. 'One can trace from the time of the New Deal … a clear, gradual, perceptible increase in presidential power relative to the legislative branch', Jimmy Carter aide Stu Eizenstat was to observe: 'The creation of the CBO began to redress the balance of power. It did that in one fundamental way – it ended the president's monopoly on information, on budget forecasts, on economic forecasts.' The enhancement of congressional resources and the multiplication of subcommittees, however, did not make for coherent policy-making. Individual members were tempted to tack ever more minor amendments to pieces of legislation. If Congress was trying to become a kind of alternative government, it was also subject to strong centrifugal pressures. 'Being in the Senate', grumbled one member, 'is like getting stuck in an airport and having all your flights canceled.'

Congress sought also to limit presidential authority in the conduct of foreign affairs, emboldened by public disenchantment with the Vietnam War. The Case Act of 1972 responded to the tendency of recent presidents to circumvent the Senate's treaty-making powers by reaching executive agreements with foreign governments; now such agreements were to be submitted to Congress for approval. In 1973 the War Powers Act put limits on a president's power to conduct war without the prior approval of Congress. A president might commit military forces in an emergency, but was obliged to secure congressional approval within sixty days.

The legal curbs put on the executive were to a large degree the work of congressional liberals, an ironic development given that under the New Deal system the presidency, together with the expanding executive agencies, had tended to be the focus of liberal aspirations. Liberals had looked to the White House to take the initiative in promoting a progressive agenda, but the new domination of the presidency by the Republicans rendered this strategy obsolete. Some turned to another approach, attempting to give public interest groups more muscle. Groups or lobbies committed to such causes as consumer protection and the environment sometimes sought an alliance with sympathetic bureaucrats and congressional subcommittees to champion liberal programmes. In the 1970s the Democratic majorities in Congress enacted laws providing subsidies for public interest groups in certain situations (such as paying a group's legal fees) and for the representation of 'average citizens' in the proceedings of federal agencies. Liberals for several years thus looked for succour from an enlightened federal bureaucracy and judiciary rather than the White House. When President Reagan left office, he attributed his failure to balance the budget to an 'iron triangle' composed of 'parts of Congress, the media, and special interest groups' that he thought largely controlled the government.

Reagan's frustration owed something to a sense that the White House had lost control of the bureaucracy. The decline of the New Deal Order had been accompanied by a wave of regulation on a scale not equalled since the Progressive Era. The relationship between government and business was extensively redefined between 1964 and 1975, as federal agencies were empowered to probe into the details of the production and marketing of goods and services. The Civil Rights Act of 1964 created the first important regulatory agency, the Equal Employment Opportunity Commission, which after a slow start began ferreting into the practices of public and private bodies to root out discrimination in employment. Old agencies were also overhauled, the Federal Trade Commission for example becoming a sturdy champion of consumer protection in the 1970s. Minimum standards laws proliferated. The new laws differed from Progressive Era legislation in their emphasis on pan-industrial regulations, such as on health and safety matters, covering all industries rather than specific industries like the railroads. The regulatory impulse transcended party lines. Fiscal conservatives in some circumstances accepted regulation because, compared to programmes offering new services, the cost to government was relatively slight. Thus the drive was pushed further by the Nixon administration, with the establishment of such bodies as the Environmental Protection Agency in 1970 and the Consumer Product Safety Commission in 1972. Direct federal spending on regulations increased fivefold between 1970 and 1975. While a reaction against regulation set in by the 1980s, the Reagan administration was unable to undo many of these constraints.

It seemed to some that government had come to rest in the hands of bureaucrats and administrators, who often enjoyed great latitude in the elaboration of rules that in effect determined public policy. When the regulatory agencies acted in concert with congressional committees, presidents sometimes deemed it prudent to acquiesce. As historian Hugh Davis Graham has shown, the formulation of affirmative action policies owed much to strategically placed bureaucrats. The regulatory agencies, of course, monitored public as well as private enterprise, and different parts of government were often pitted against one another. This may have made for more honest government, though whether it furthered coherence is open to question.

The courts too assumed considerable responsibility for public policy in the last third of the twentieth century. In large part this was a consequence of the 'rights revolution' that coursed through American public life during and after the 1960s. The civil rights movement had raised consciousness about rights generally, helping to spur other groups to make claims, and in time a wide array of Americans, from gays to greys, from prisoners to hunters, also articulated rights. The growth of rights consciousness also owed something to the decisions of the Supreme Court, which under Chief Justice Earl Warren had forcefully expanded the area of individual rights guaranteed by the Constitution. Criminals, pornographers and atheists were among those whose liberties the Court was protecting, or so it seemed to its critics. 'We don't have a sick society, we have a sick Supreme Court', raged George Wallace during the 1968 campaign. Earl Warren retired from the Court in 1969, but his fellow liberal justices did not immediately lose influence. In 1971 the Court permitted school bussing and in 1973 the celebrated *Roe v Wade* decision prohibited states from banning early abortions. The rights culture flourished as it was argued that groups as well as individuals had rights.

The growth of rights consciousness encouraged Americans to turn to the courts to establish their rights. Several civil rights and public interest groups saw the judiciary as more likely to effect a desired policy change than Congress or the president. Further, Congress often delegated extensive rule-making powers to executive or regulatory agencies, in effect law-making powers, and also framed laws that were ambiguous, so that it fell to the courts to define public policy. In many other countries public policy over such issues as abortion, affirmative action, capital punishment, gay sex, censorship and gun possession would be formulated by the elected branches of government; in the United States the Supreme Court was often the decisive actor. The Court, of course, had always claimed the right of judicial review, but in the late twentieth century, when the White House and Congress were often at loggerheads, its role became unusually conspicuous.

The critical place of the judiciary in the polity, the presence on the bench of several liberal justices in the aftermath of the New Deal Order, and the Republican possession of the White House for most of the late twentieth century together created a potentially explosive situation. Republican presidents faced with a hostile Congress were tempted to further a conservative agenda by making right-wing appointments to the bench. In a sense it was the Republican failure to establish a clear party ascendancy at all electoral levels that led to the politicization of the judiciary.

During the 1968 campaign Richard Nixon charged that the Supreme Court had gone 'too far in weakening the peace forces as against the criminal forces of this country', but his attempts in 1969 to appoint conservatives to the Court were twice frustrated by a Senate appalled at his nomination of anti-civil rights Southerners. Nonetheless in time he was able to make four successful nominations to the bench, including the highly conservative William Rehnquist, who was to become Chief Justice during the Reagan administration. President Reagan's nomination in 1987 of a conservative anti-abortion candidate provoked another furious confirmation battle in the Senate, which denied approval. But Reagan did succeed in naming four Supreme Court justices of conservative disposition, and Presidents Ford and Bush together named three. The Republican attempts to move the judiciary to the right were not confined to the highest court. The Reagan administration screened judicial appointments at all levels with great care, and by the time he left office Reagan had appointed over half of the federal judiciary. As Reagan's Attorney-General Edwin Meese put it, the intention was 'to institutionalize the Reagan revolution so it can't be set aside no matter what happens in future presidential elections'.

Yet if the Republican administrations pined for a Supreme Court that would set a conservative course as boldly as the Warren Court had set a liberal course, they were to be disappointed. The suspicious screening that the Senate gave to partisan nominations meant that the Republican presidents had often to settle for moderate conservatives. The liberal justices, for their part, clung tenaciously to their seats. William O. Douglas hung on into senility, William Brennan had served for thirty-four years before his retirement in 1990, and Thurgood Marshall, determined to protect the egalitarian heritage of the Warren era, vowed that he would only leave the Court 'feet first'. He eventually resigned in 1991 at the age of eighty-three. Under Chief Justice Warren Burger, between 1969 and 1986, the Court did back away from the activism of the Warren years, but it conducted no constitutional counter-revolution. The very divisions in the Court – between liberals, conservatives and moderates of differing jurisprudential philosophies – militated against clear-cut rulings. In the *Bakke* case of 1978, in which a 5-4 ruling prohibited certain affirmative action devices but favoured others, the nine justices offered five different opinions between them. Even after a fairly consistent conservative majority emerged in the Court in the late 1980s, its decisions remained cautious. It did something to erode earlier positions on a range of 'social-civil rights' issues such as abortion and affirmative action, but embarked on no crusade.

Beset with contrary opinions, respectful of the legislative will and reluctant to become embroiled in party politics, the Court under both Burger and Rehnquist often determined a case on the narrowest of grounds, a minimalist strategy which militated against decisions having a major impact on public policy. The divided government and litigious culture of the final third of the twentieth century may have thrown more responsibility on the judiciary, but the judiciary illustrated rather than resolved the divisions and confusion of the American polity.

The journalist and historian Godfrey Hodgson characterized the American political system of the mid-twentieth century as one governed by a liberal consensus. This is not a term that could readily be applied to the political order of the last third of the century. With the White House and Congress usually occupied by opposing political parties, with the permissive values unleashed by the counter-culture combated by powerful fundamentalist currents sustaining family values, with discrete parts of the bureaucracy pulling in different directions, with myriad interest groups competing for the ears – and pockets – of elected politicians, and with a Supreme Court often at odds within itself, order and harmony were hardly the defining features of American politics. Nor was the kind of liberalism associated with the New Deal and the Great Society much in evidence, as confidence waned in the capacity of the state to manage public affairs. 'We have learned that "more" is not necessarily "better," that even our great Nation has its recognized limits', observed President Jimmy Carter, 'and that we can neither answer all questions nor solve all problems.' This implied consensus of a sort, on reducing the federal bureaucracy, containing 'welfare', offloading some governmental functions to the states and indeed maintaining American military strength. The centre of gravity of American politics had moved to the right, and progressive-minded activists tended to press their causes in separate campaigns rather than within a broad party coalition.

The conservatism of the late twentieth century could not do much to dismantle the heritage of the New Deal Order. Many of the institutional structures remained in place – the Social Security system (only the 'welfare' parts of it revised along conservative lines), Medicare, the financial and banking structures, the labour relations system, farm price supports, pan-industrial regulations, as well as the civil and voting rights acts. While voters could hardly confer with one another, it sometimes seemed that they returned Democratic majorities to Congress to protect social and economic legislation and put a Republican in the White House to disavow the permissive values of the 1960s and maintain American dignity abroad. (The pattern was reversed for much of the Clinton presidency.) Divided government was largely a product of the attenuation of party forms, which also served to expand the middle classes as a proportion of the electorate. Responding to suburban constituencies and well-resourced lobbies, elected politicians were tempted to formulate policies that broadly favoured the rich and well-to-do. Not entirely coincidentally, in these same decades the income gap between rich and poor Americans widened. But sustained policy-making of any kind was difficult in this fragmented order, and many of the issues that agitated the political waters bore on legal rights and were fought out in the courts. It is little wonder that about half of American citizens stayed at home on polling days. A poll of voters in 1992 found that 73 per cent agreed with the statement: 'The entire political system is broken. It is run by insiders who do not listen to working people and are incapable of solving our problems.'

|15|

Workers and Women
1969–2000

The New Deal Order had been shaped in part by a measure of class conflict. Organized labour had lined up with the Democratic Party and had helped to provide its electoral majorities. But in the 'golden age' of the post-war years, as an affluent consumer society assuaged economic wounds, new issues revolving around rights, lifestyle and culture invaded party politics. Class politics as traditionally conceived came to exert a diminishing influence in the late twentieth-century polity, but other issues gained in salience. Feminism – in a variety of guises – acquired an unprecedented importance, as did the forces hostile to it. Such causes as the Equal Rights Amendment, federal child-care provision and abortion rights deeply divided Americans, cutting across the economic and welfare issues that had once helped to impart order to the American party system. The Christian right, with its fierce commitment to family (some would say anti-feminist) values, came to enjoy an influence in the Republican Party comparable to that once held by organized labour in the Democratic Party.

The irony of the shrinking role of class politics was that economic stratification markedly increased in these years. During the era of the New Deal Order inequality in family income had tended to decline, as Jeffrey G. Williamson and Peter H. Lindert have shown, but after 1968 it rose again. The real wages of about 80 per cent of workers fell while the salaries of their bosses rose. Increased international competition meant downward pressures on labour costs even as higher salaries were paid to supposedly talented executives to retain their services in these beleaguered times. The income gap between the average worker and the average Chief Executive Officer increased by 340 per cent between 1974 and the mid-1990s. Similarly, the proportion of the nation's income received by the poorer families contracted while the wealthy prospered. The share of the national income for households with incomes of under $10,000 a year (measured in 1997 dollars) fell from 13.4 per cent in 1970 to 11 per cent in 1997, while the share of those receiving

$75,000 and over more than doubled. To a degree wealth was being redistributed upward. The wealthiest 1 per cent of families owned about 22 per cent of all wealth in 1975; by 1995 their share had rocketed to 42 per cent. During the years of the New Deal Order there had been some attempt to recruit a significant part of the workforce into the consumer society through relatively high wages, but this strategy was abandoned as the economy came more to depend on high levels of consumption by the upper middle classes.

The yawning income gap between rich and poor might have been camouflaged had rapid economic growth brought compensations for low-income groups. But though the economy still expanded it ceased to perform miracles. This was evident in the levelling-off of productivity. Economist Wallace Peterson has identified a 'silent depression'; his calculations indicate that while in the quarter-century before 1973 the productivity of American workers had grown pretty healthily by about 2.5 per cent a year, between 1974 and 1991 the average annual rate of growth was an anaemic 0.7 per cent. Most Americans could no longer look forward to an assured improvement in living standards, which was one reason why more wives joined the workforce – to maintain the family's income. Another set of figures told a similar story. To stay in the same place Americans had to try harder. By 1989 workers were putting in about 160 hours more a year than they had been twenty years earlier.

These austere experiences were the product of a number of conditions. The slowing of economic growth reflected the erosion of competitiveness and profitability of American business. As companies were assailed by foreign competition while simultaneously struggling with inflation-boosted costs, they searched for strategies for curbing union power and pinching wages and fringe benefits. Their allies in the political realm in both major parties (though especially Republicans), also found ways of limiting the benefits of the welfare compact inherited from the New Deal Order. Yet the harder times experienced by many workers and the growing class divide in the economic and occupational structures were not translated into a lower-class political insurgency. If anything, to judge from the decline in voter turnout among wage-earners, political apathy tended to increase. In 1976 only a quarter of the unemployed cast votes. The recurrent paralysis in the system of government perhaps detached many Americans from politics, and cultural and social issues, such as abortion or affirmative action, edged some workers to the right. Several tiny radical groups had emerged in the aftermath of 1960s protest, but the troubled economy and right-wing thrusts of the 1970s and 1980s proved inhospitable to their revolutionary ambitions.

The historical weakness of organized labour in the United States had always been in part related to the divisions within the wage-earning classes. The resumption of large-scale immigration in the late twentieth century, particularly Hispanic and Asian, accentuated the ethnic diversification. The growing obsession with cultural identities worked against lower-class solidarity.

Structural economic change also had a centrifugal impact on American workers. In a high-tech economy those with skills were paid more and those without found their work casualized or their wages squeezed. Wage differentials within the working class increased, at times quite markedly, further undermining any sense of commonality. The rise of the service sector provided more employment for women, although gender stereotyping tended to place them in different jobs to men and they were usually less unionized. Many modern industries – such as fast-food – made substantial use of ill-paid part-time workers. By the 1980s McDonald's boasted a larger workforce than the basic steel industry. The decline of the large conurbations and the dispersal of industry into smaller plants and rural areas allowed employers to recruit more non-union labour. During the 1960s and 1970s, according to one analysis, nearly 90 per cent of the new jobs created had paid middle-income wages; by the 1980s little over a third did so. The 'segmentation' of the workforce increased in these years – between unionized and non-unionized, between male and female, between whites, blacks, Hispanics and immigrants, and between full-time and part-time workers. These divisions militated against class solidarity.

And although economic growth slowed, it did not stop. Americans may have struggled to maintain middle-class lifestyles, but most were not confronted by penury. Poverty had become the lot of a relatively small minority (albeit a larger one than obtained in other advanced societies). In the 1990s about 13 per cent or so of the population was below the poverty line, a slight increase since 1970, but the overwhelming majority of Americans were judged to receive at least adequate incomes. The poverty rates for blacks and Hispanics were disproportionately high, usually close to 30 per cent each, but, inequitable though this was, these figures represented fractions of minority groups. In short, the most impoverished citizens were themselves isolated and scattered, and too few in number to stand against the forces of the 'contented majority', as J. K. Galbraith dubbed the bulk of voting Americans. Both Democratic and Republican administrations could be accused of wooing middle-class voters at the expense of minorities, but the strategy was perhaps best characterized by President Reagan's celebrated 1981 budget. According to the *San Francisco Chronicle*'s columnists: 'The budget cuts, which fall hardest on low-income Americans and Blacks especially, have been swallowed in large part because there is hope among middle-income Americans that, coupled with Reagan's tax cut, they will make life easier – for them.'

Whether most wage-earners were contented is questionable. As the American dream faded for workers the response of many was to cling to what they had rather than to turn against the political order. Organized labour, which had enjoyed some influence in the polity since the 1930s, found itself on the defensive as the precarious balance in industrial relations tipped against it. In 1978 Doug Fraser, the UAW president, charged the business community with conducting a 'one-sided class war' against working people. With the NLRB now slow to process complaints about unfair practices, employers increasingly flouted the law in sacking union members or ignoring collective bargaining procedures. Unions were obliged to protect the interests of their members first rather than act as lobbies for a broad progressive agenda. This preoccupation also meant that they were often less than zealous about recruiting from the fast-growing numbers of semi-skilled female and immigrant workers. In 1983 left-wing sociologist Stanley Aronowitz complained that the AFL-CIO had 'abandoned the organization of the working poor'. The ascendancy of the Republican Party in presidential politics in these years meant that organized labour could expect little sympathy in that quarter. Reagan appointees in the 1980s chipped away at regulations designed to protect workers.

The haemorrhage of union membership, particularly after 1978, reflected the growth of a 'post-industrial' economy focused on the service and high-tech sectors (often in non-union firms), and the 'de-industrialization' of swathes of the North as manufacturing jobs were relocated to developing countries. For the non-farm workforce, for which the proportion of union members had peaked in 1945, the figure fell from 27 per cent in 1970 to 12 per cent in 1991, less than in any other advanced industrial economy. By 1998 the number of private-sector workers who were in unions had dipped below 10 per cent. As the pool of non-unionized workers grew, employers made more use of them, thus eroding wage levels. Total union membership would have been even lower had the unions not made gains among service workers. Beginning in the 1960s organized labour made significant inroads into the public sector, such as among teachers and government workers, but when such employees went on strike, as many schoolteachers did during the school year of 1972–3, it could seem that unions were poised against the public interest. As public sympathy for unions became strained, employers and government more readily turned against them. Both government and the courts afforded less protection to labour than had been the case in the heyday of the New Deal Order. In the 1970s and 1980s unions were less successful in National Labor Relations Board elections than once they had been, and the Board itself became less accommodating. In 1985 its Reagan-appointed chairman remarked that 'collective bargaining frequently means … the destruction of individual freedom and the destruction of the market-place'. Ten years later an AFL-CIO official lamented that 'Today, the only defense of the NLRA [Wagner Act] comes from the business community'.

The erosion of organized labour weakened its leverage in the Democratic Party. If labour leaders had once claimed to speak for the mass of ordinary Americans, the claim rang hollow in the late twentieth century. Labour's diminished status enabled its opponents to dismiss it as a vested interest. Walter Mondale apart, Democratic presidential candidates in these years, sensitive to the middle-class vote, did not identify themselves strongly with their union allies.

The relationship between organized labour and the Democratic Party had come under strain in the dying days of the New Deal Order. The AFL-CIO, reflecting the patriotism of many of its members, had strongly supported the Cold War policies of the Democratic administrations, including the war in Vietnam. It resisted the party reforms that followed the notorious Chicago convention of 1968, and when the party nominated George McGovern for president in 1972, in a campaign in which he became fatally associated with New Left and anti-war currents, the AFL-CIO refused to endorse him in a dramatic break with a twenty-year tradition. It condemned the new liberals who wanted 'to take over the Democratic Party, even if it means throwing out the labor movement'. The recapture of the party by the moderates in 1976 and the nomination of labour supporter Walter Mondale for vice-president brought the AFL-CIO back on side, but the Carter administration disappointed it. Although there were Democratic majorities in Congress, there was no return to the liberal legislation of the 1960s. One mark of labour's weakened position within the Democratic coalition was its failure to secure reform of the National Labor Relations Act in 1977–8, an attempt designed to restore labour rights that had been eroded over the years. Some Democrats seemed to be listening more to business than to labour lobbies. Fifteen years later the AFL-CIO was unable to deflect the Clinton administration from its determination to pass the North American Free Trade Agreement, which could cost the jobs of American factory workers. Organized labour's alliance with the Democratic Party was proving to be of questionable utility.

In 1980 a former union leader was elected president of the United States, but Ronald Reagan proved no friend to organized labour. In 1981 the air traffic controllers went on strike. They had been employed on a no-strike contract, and here again a public-sector union could be represented as turning against the public interest. Only seven months into his presidency, Reagan was determined to assert his authority and swipe at a New Deal symbol. He summarily fired the strikers, imposed a lifetime employment ban on them and used supervisors and military personnel to keep the planes flying. The strikers were a group of skilled middle-class employees, represented by the Professional Air Traffic Controllers Organization. The union was wrecked and Reagan's message was unmistakable. He won the public relations battle and other employers felt encouraged to use similar tactics. 'Reagan made it respectable to bust unions', said labour lawyer Robert M. Baptiste. A number of unions lost strikes as their members were displaced by permanent replacements, a feature that obtained of about 20 per cent of strikes in the second half of the 1980s. When Greyhound drivers went on strike in 1990, the company quickly trained hundreds of new drivers. The courts too, increasingly filled with Republican appointees, sometimes imposed heavy compensation fines on unions.

Subjected to this barrage, and with little support from public opinion, unions grew wary of strike action. In 1970, a tumultuous year, there had been 381 major work stoppages; in 1980 the figure was down to 187 and by 1995 to a tiny thirty-one. 'In America, it's mostly legal to go on strike', said journalist Alexander Cockburn: 'It's simply illegal to win one.' But if union muscles had wasted, the role of organized labour in the polity had been marginalized rather than eliminated. In 1996, for example, when the Democrats fought to recover from their slaughter in the mid-term elections of 1994, the AFL-CIO found $35 million to conduct campaigns against selected Republicans in Congress, and it claimed to help unseat eighteen Republican members of the lower house.

Organized labour had contributed to the Democratic ascendancy through the middle decades of the twentieth century, as it had also generally been an influence for liberal policies, and its subsequent attenuation was one of the conditions for dividing American government. Class interests did not disappear from American life, but large corporations and the wealthy élite were better placed to influence public policy than the fragmented and harassed mass of American wage-earners. The large tax cuts inaugurated by the Reagan administration accentuated the tendency of a post-industrial and globalized economy to widen the distance between rich and poor. In the 2000 presidential election Ralph Nader, the candidate of the Green party, argued that both major parties had been captured by corporate interests. This populist appeal won for Nader only 2.7 per cent of the popular vote. The great majority of ordinary Americans, although not enjoying a steadily increasing standard of living after the manner of their parents, were content enough to cast their votes for the status quo – if they cast them at all. For some modest wage-earners the dynamic religious right, with its distrust of the state, now held more appeal than old-fashioned trade unionism. Among the emotions driving the New Right was a passionate opposition to the demands being made by American women.

In the late 1960s, as the New Deal Order broke down, the women's liberation movement gathered force. 'Sisterhood is Powerful' became the rallying cry. At a time when black nationalist groups were succumbing to division and repression, and when the power of organized labour was being eroded, it was women who seemed to hold the greatest potential for transforming American political society. In January 1968 young feminists staged the 'Burial of Traditional Womanhood' at Arlington Cemetery, suggesting that only by casting off the submissive role could women effectively counter the aggression of men: 'We have new men as well as a new society to build.'

Feminist sentiments coursed through American politics in the late twentieth century, though fell short of revolution, partly because anti-feminism also emerged as an influential force. The largely male-oriented welfare state fashioned in the New Deal era was successfully shorn of much of its gender bias. But women were to have greater impact in cultural and occupational spheres – seeking to transform the social order from within – than in traditional party politics. Women's consciousness rose dramatically, although significant numbers remained resistant. In 1970 only 37 per cent of white women favoured greater efforts to improve the status of women; by 1985 some 72 per cent did so. Black women, reflecting their experience of deprivation and their greater participation in the workplace and the civil rights movement, registered 60 per cent support for the proposition in 1970 and 78 per cent in 1985. In 1972, however, just 33 per cent of men strongly supported equal roles for the two sexes; as late as 1990 only 40 per cent did so. A majority of men and a minority of women remained wary of feminism, a feature that contributed to its uneven success.

An extraordinary wave of activism swept across the country between 1969 and 1973. Consciousness-raising groups mushroomed as women explored their own experiences, coming to a greater understanding of the various constraints that governed their lives. Women picketed major businesses over degrading advertising campaigns, invaded radio stations and newspaper offices to demand that they hire more women, harassed college administrations with calls for courses in women's studies and disrupted all-male bars and clubs with sit-ins. The eruption of radical groups like the Redstockings and the Radicalesbians in 1969 made even the professional women of NOW more militant, as they joined abortion speak-outs and other forms of direct action. On 26 August 1970 there were demonstrations in almost every large city in support of Women's Strike for Equality, as working women called for equal opportunity in education and employment, abortion rights and access to child care. The magazine *Ms* was launched in 1972 and within a year boasted 200,000 subscribers. Reacting to the strong cult of domesticity that had pervaded post-war America, the women's movement acquired a crusading edge.

It seemed for a time that the male world of politics was anxious to accommodate this feminist awakening, perhaps for fear that it could be translated into electoral force. In 1967 NOW had identified the Equal Rights Amendment (ERA) and abortion rights as its principal demands, and by the early 1970s these goals seemed within reach. By March 1972 Congress had endorsed the ERA and sent it to the states, which were soon busily ratifying it. In the same year the Equal Employment Opportunity Act prohibited sex discrimination in employment. By this date a number of states had also begun to liberalize their abortion laws, and in 1973 the Supreme Court handed down its historic *Roe v Wade* decision, effectively establishing a woman's right to abortion. While radical feminists were committed to more fundamental change, the formal barriers to women's liberation appeared to be toppling.

These halcyon days were not to last. By the mid-1970s an anti-feminist backlash gathered strength and for the remainder of the century women's groups engaged in grim contests with their conservative foes. The confrontations over the feminist agenda illustrated the divided state of the larger political system. Female activists quickly learned the rules of interest group politics and they became a force in the polity, but so did their opponents, an influential element in the growing New Right. The battle-lines between them were to inch back and forth for the rest of the century.

But women were everywhere. Feminist ideology was capable of taking an almost infinite number of forms and many women eschewed conventional politics. Some explored the meaning of feminism in literary and artistic expression. Female academics challenged the conventions of their disciplines, often subverting and transforming them. Young women surged into the professions and turned their energies to changing attitudes and practice. The women's health movement launched a major assault on the medical system, with its male doctors and arrogant sexism. The tendency in American politics for public policies to be pursued by single-interest groups was reflected among feminists by their division into discrete movements, such as those concerned with battered women, pornography and lesbian rights. These fissile tendencies could hardly have been avoided since American women were never a homogeneous constituency. The variety of paths taken militated against the mobilization of women as a coherent political force, but was evidence more of diffusion than of weakness. In the decades after 1970, as custom and culture were challenged on many fronts, far-reaching changes in public thought and behaviour were effected. It could almost be argued that women's liberation demonstrated the irrelevance of the political system.

Radical feminism peaked in the early 1970s. Radicals tended to shun the major national organizations in favour of local, women-centred action, such as establishing rape centres and self-defence classes. One ideological strand insisted that men were the enemy and that heterosexual relationships were oppressive. The Feminists, a New York group, advocated abolishing marriage and raising children communally; they fly-posted the subways with the message 'Fuck Marriage, Not Men'. Another group, the Radicalesbians, reached the conclusion that only lesbianism offered true liberation. But by about 1973 the more radical groups were weakening. Suspicion of organization and leadership limited the effectiveness of some. Sixties radicals, committed to an egalitarian and participatory ethic, were loath to entrust authority to selected individuals. They also suffered from the attentions of the FBI, whose infiltration of the movement (of liberal as well as radical groups) sowed mistrust.

But feminists of many kinds proliferated through the 1970s, and those interested in changing public policy did work through formal organizations. A loose network of women's groups, presses, labour bodies, credit unions and law and health centres spread out across the land. Black, Chicana, Asian and other minority women, while initially often wary of women's liberation as a distraction from their various fights against racial discrimination, formed groups to express the distinctiveness of their own situations. A symbolic high point occurred in 1977, when over 2000 women from a remarkable array of racial, ethnic, occupational and age constituencies (including conservative groups) met at a National Conference on Women in Houston to call for the fashioning of a society in which, in Maya Angelou's words, each member would be 'equally employed and equally rewarded'.

Such activity helped to bring about a sea change in women's values. As late as 1968, according to poll evidence, about 65 per cent of girls aged fifteen to nineteen said that they wanted to be housewives when they were thirty-five years old. About two-thirds of these teenagers, it seemed, planned lives as wives and mothers. In 1978 only 25 per cent of this group possessed the same aspiration. Other surveys told a similar tale. In 1970 only 21 per cent of female students specified preparing for a career as the main objective of their college education; by 1980 the figure had nearly doubled to 40 per cent (almost reaching the male figure of 43 per cent). Older women – which these students soon became – also developed new perspectives, some 56 per cent of American women claiming to regard themselves as feminists by 1986. The female baby boomers of the post-war era seemed determined to have jobs and careers; the women's movement had released their ambitions.

The heightened feminist consciousness encouraged some women to enter politics. One landmark was the National Women's Political Caucus (NWPC), formed in July 1971 at a meeting of some 300 activists, many of them members of NOW. They wanted 'to awaken, organize and assert the vast political power represented by women', although progress towards this visionary goal proved hesitant. Other groups followed. The Congresswomen's Caucus was founded in 1977, renamed in 1981 as the Congressional Caucus for Women's Issues. In 1974 the first national Political Action Committee for women appeared, the Women's Campaign Fund, to help finance campaigns and provide technical assistance.

The NWPC urged women to seek electoral office, and a few did. Diane Feinstein succeeded to the mayoralty of San Francisco in 1978 on the murder of the incumbent, and was elected in her own right in 1979, as was Jane Byrne in Chicago. By 1992 there were female mayors in nineteen of the country's hundred largest cities. In New Hampshire in 1974 Ella Grasso became the first woman to be elected a state governor in her own right (occasionally women had replaced husbands who had been prevented from serving by death or ineligibility). Washington State elected a female governor in 1976, three more states did so in the 1980s, and another three in 1990. Women were also being elected to other state and local offices. They represented just 10 per cent of state-wide elected officials in 1975 and 18 per cent in 1992. Some women sought national office. In 1968 a mere twenty women across the country had been major party candidates for the two houses of Congress; in 1990 there were seventy-eight. The 1970 election produced twelve female members of the House of Representatives and thereafter numbers rose, to nineteen with the 1980 election and forty-seven in 1992, when it was speculated that women had finally made a critical 'breakthrough'. In that year too women first made an impact on the Senate. Previously there had been only one or two women senators at any one time; in 1993 (after a Texas by-election) there were seven of them. By 1995 there were fifty-five female members of Congress.

Voters became more receptive. In the 1950s and 1960s, when Gallup had asked, 'If your party nominated a woman for president, would you vote for her if she were qualified for the job?' the percentage indicating a willingness to do so had been in the 50s, with around 40 per cent returning a formidable 'no'.

In the 1970s opinion shifted markedly, with 76 per cent saying 'yes' and 19 per cent 'no' in 1978. By 1991 the figures had moved to 86 and 9 per cent respectively. There had been a major change of attitudes in the course of a generation.

Nonetheless, given that there were slightly more women than men in the American population, a figure of around fifty in Congress was hardly impressive. Many feminists did not see political action as a priority. They might enjoy more success by investing their energies in professional careers, as many did. The murky, stalemated world of party politics was not necessarily the route to liberation. For those who took to the stump, local office might be attainable, but obstacles such as campaign costs multiplied as they looked higher. Also incumbency was a strong advantage in securing re-election, so men were not easily unseated. In some European countries parties on occasion were persuaded to adopt a quota of female candidates. The biggest increase – 172 per cent – in the number of women in the British parliament came after the general election of 1997, for which the Labour Party ensured that a proportion of its candidates were women. This was not an acceptable option to American parties. Perhaps only 9 per cent of voters by the 1990s did not like the idea of a woman as president, but that could be enough to deter a major party from nominating one.

The paucity of women in elective office helps to explain the difficulty of securing priority for women's issues on the national political agenda. Many feminists were disappointed when the Democratic national convention of 1972 failed to adopt an abortion rights plank. By 1980 women represented about half of the convention delegates and an abortion resolution was adopted, to the dismay of presidential candidate Jimmy Carter. But if Democratic sympathy for feminist demands was unreliable, the Republican Party was increasingly hostile. The 1976 Republican platform called for a constitutional amendment to ban abortion. The resolution was adopted again in 1980, when the platform also insisted that only anti-abortion people be appointed to the federal judiciary. The party also dropped the formal endorsement of the ERA that it had maintained for forty years. In the 1980 election only 47 per cent of women voters opted for Reagan, while 55 per cent of men did. This sudden appearance of a gender gap may have reflected concern over the New Right's hostility to the ERA and abortion, though significant too was suspicion of Reagan's intentions towards welfare.

The gender gap remained a feature of American politics and at least encouraged the major parties to appoint women to high office, such as to the Supreme Court or the cabinet, though substantive changes in public policy proved elusive. In 1986 women's votes helped the Democrats regain control of the Senate. Middle-class women in particular seem to have become something of a swing vote, and they contributed to Bill Clinton's presidential victory in 1992. Ever sensitive to the political winds, Clinton gave over a third of his first 500 appointments to women. In the 1996 presidential election, when men split fairly evenly between Clinton and Republican candidate

Bob Dole, female voters ensured the former's re-election, the gender gap widening to 11 per cent. Yet even after the exposure of the gap, women activists – like black politicians – were often frustrated by party leaderships that seemed most solicitous of the votes of white suburban and working-class Americans, who were assumed not to be especially supportive of feminist issues. The gender gap was not a feature of politics in most European countries. Perhaps the combination of a strong consciousness-raising feminist movement and the Republican right's suspicion of women's issues had opened one in the United States.

The limited role established by women in the political system was one reason why the goals of such bodies as NOW were imperfectly realized. The ERA had been a feminist objective since the 1920s, and it had won the nominal endorsement of the major party platforms, but it was not until the late 1960s, as a new generation of women became sensitive to their rights, that the cause gained momentum. Through the 1970s the ERA was the dominant demand of the women's movement.

The objective was to give precisely the same constitutional rights to men and women. Democratic Congresswoman Martha W. Griffiths secured a floor debate on the ERA in 1970, and eventually, after intensive lobbying, the two houses of Congress agreed to it by March 1972. 'I've never seen anything like it in all my years here', gasped one veteran senator at the feminist bombardment. 'Father, forgive them for they know not what they do', prayed Senator Sam Ervin, the measure's most obdurate opponent, on the Senate floor. The consent of three-quarters of the states was needed to ratify the amendment, and again the measure seemed popular, several states approving almost immediately. Even the AFL-CIO, traditionally committed to protective laws for women, threw its support to the ERA. By 1973 some thirty-six states had accepted it. The support of only six more would secure the amendment, which seemed unstoppable.

But stopped it was, eventually only three states short of the three-quarters majority, in no small part because it had triggered the anxieties of a significant number of women. Leading the counter-attack was Phyllis Schlafly, a sometime Goldwater activist, who in 1972 established the National Committee to Stop ERA. To Schlafly, ERA activists were 'a bunch of antifamily radicals and lesbians'. Many women rallied to her side, such as the conservative feminists of Mothers on the March, who aimed 'to preserve and strengthen the home'. Targeting the state legislatures, Schlafly fanned a grass-roots resistance by emphasizing the dangers to women of becoming legally identical to men. They would be subject to the draft and sent into combat, working women would be stripped of protective laws and even toilets would become unisex. Above all, motherhood and the family would be threatened. Men would not be obliged to support their wives and children and homosexuals might marry one another. Schlafly also pointed out that marriage and divorce laws would be determined by Congress rather than the state legislatures. Many local and state governments already resented the loss of autonomy arising from court-enforced bussing and other federal directives aimed at ending racial discrimination; the ERA seemed to promise even more intrusion from Washington. Like bussing, which denied parents the right to choose schools, the ERA could be seen as an attack on the family, for it could allow men to spurn their parental duties and perhaps throw the raising of children onto an unfeeling state. Sentiment in the legislatures against ERA hardened, and after 1977 no more states endorsed it. Congress extended the deadline for ratifying ERA to June 1982, to no avail.

By this date even some radical feminists were questioning whether the two sexes should be treated as if they were identical. There were, after all, biological differences, and the values of the white male hardly represented the ideal. Many feminists came to emphasize the distinctive and positive in women's experience, and to argue for equitable treatment rather than stark equality. In fact the equal rights decisions of the courts and the affirmative actions initiatives of the federal bureaucracies had already enhanced women's legal status. Many of the specific changes that the ERA would have mandated, such as equal treatment in schools and the military, and in property and divorce proceedings, came about in the 1970s and 1980s. Legislators, bureaucrats and the judiciary each played roles in this. In 1971, for example, building on civil rights precedents, the Supreme Court handed down a number of decisions ending gender discrimination in such areas as Social Security benefits and unemployment insurance.

The civil rights measures of the 1960s had given rise to such enforcement agencies as the Equal Employment Opportunity Commission, and by the 1970s, responding to pressure from women's groups, they upheld equal-opportunity policies for women as well as racial minorities. One major corporation challenged by the EEOC was the American Telephone and Telegraph Company, which eventually agreed to an affirmative-action programme that would end racial and sexual stereotyping in occupational categories – telephone operators, for example, need not be women and engineers need not be men. Under EEOC pressure other public and private employers prudently developed similar policies. Some single-sex colleges opened their doors to students of the other gender. More women were recruited to the police forces, some became construction workers and others found their way into such traditionally male jobs as typesetters and insurance agents. (At the same time, traditionally female positions, such as nursing and telephone operating, slowly employed more men.) It has been estimated that occupational segregation declined by about 10 per cent between 1970 and 1980, a modest enough change but unprecedented in the twentieth century.

Women activists also maintained pressure on Congress for changes in the law, working with the small number of female politicians. 'We put sex discrimination provisions into everything', recalled Representative Bella Abzug. This was an exaggeration, but Congress proved relatively sympathetic to such demands in the early 1970s. In 1972 it outlawed sex discrimination in federally aided education programmes and health profession training.

Women were admitted to fuller membership of the consumer society with the Equal Credit Opportunity Act of 1974, barring discrimination in the provision of bank loans, mortgages and credit cards. A Child Development Act also passed in 1972, to establish a national system of day care, but was vetoed by Richard Nixon, who believed that it would 'diminish both parental authority and parental involvement with children'. Nonetheless a Democratic Congress containing a core of determined women could sometimes prevail over a more conservative White House, and liberal women's groups became effective lobbies.

The lobbies chipped away at the legal and social structures that served to disadvantage women. One group to arouse concern were the so-called 'displaced homemakers', that is women who through divorce, desertion or widowhood had lost their husbands' support but had few work qualifications of their own. The Older Women's Liberation championed these 'older' women (those over 30!), succeeded in 1980 by the Older Women's League, which campaigned for job training, education and health care. 'For men, they created retirement plans, medical benefits, profit sharing and gold watches', read one poster. 'For women, they created Mother's Day.' In the 1980s the Congressional Caucus for Women's Issues helped to secure a series of economic equity acts designed to strengthen the economic position of women, as in provision of pension plans.

By the 1980s too there was growing support among women's groups for governmental backing for maternity leave and child-care centres, although Republican administrations, committed to traditional family values, remained unsympathetic. In a 1987 decision the Supreme Court upheld a California law requiring employers to provide maternity leave, but in 1990 President Bush vetoed a federal bill providing for parental leave. By the early 1990s the United States was the only industrialized country in the Western world that did not guarantee maternity leave, as it also lagged well behind most others in public support for child care.

The greater recognition of women's constitutional and legal rights afforded some compensation for the failure of the ERA. But women's groups dared not relax their vigilance at a time when the New Right sought to erode feminist gains, and by the 1980s abortion had became a major political battleground. Abortion rights had emerged as a major demand of the women's movement in the 1960s, and had been recognized by the Supreme Court in *Roe v Wade* in 1973, but opposition to the decision was immediate.

The abortion issue raised fundamental questions about what it meant to be a woman, ranging 'pro-life' groups against what came to be designated 'pro-choice' activists. Women at large were deeply divided. Surveys tended to show that working women generally supported abortion rights, while opposition came from women who had committed themselves to home and family and perhaps saw children as one means of impressing on their husbands their breadwinning obligations. The National Right to Life Committee – largely Catholic in composition – formed in 1973, and, in due course, the evangelical Protestants of the Christian right also mobilized to win reversal of the Court decision.

The pro-life forces hoped to win over public opinion and secure more supporters in the three branches of the federal government. Well-financed lobbies applied considerable pressure to national and state legislators, and in 1978 and 1980 poured money into campaigns against pro-choice senators, with some success. And public opinion was hardly unambiguous. While the great majority of Americans were clear that abortion was legitimate if the mother's life was in danger, attitudes were distinctly cooler where the mother simply did not want a child. Only a minority positively favoured abortion on demand (which, more or less, was the *Roe v Wade* position). Representative Henry Hyde, an Illinois Republican, in 1976 secured a congressional ban on the use of Medicaid funds for abortions, a position upheld by the Supreme Court in 1980. Welfare mothers did not elicit much public sympathy.

With the election of Ronald Reagan pro-life activists looked to the White House to further their agenda, as in nominations to the judiciary. As more conservatives were appointed to public office and the courts, government agencies formulated regulations militating against the practice of abortion. In *Webster v Reproductive Health Services* in 1989, the Supreme Court upheld a Missouri law forbidding institutions receiving state funds from practising abortion, unless the woman's life was in danger, a ruling that gave greater discretion to the states in determining access to abortion. In 1992 the Supreme Court endorsed a regulation introduced by the Reagan administration forbidding publicly funded clinics from counselling women about abortion. (President Clinton later lifted this 'gag rule'.) Another major ruling of that year upheld a Pennsylvania law imposing a number of restrictions on abortion, such as a twenty-four-hour delay to enable pro-life arguments to be presented. *Roe v Wade* survived, but in narrowed form.

Moderate Republicans, however, anxious about losing female votes, were wary of the abortion issue. The more zealous pro-life activists, impatient with the equivocations of politicians, resorted to direct action campaigns, aping the left-wing tactics of an earlier generation. In 1987 Operation Rescue, formed by an evangelical car salesman, Randall A. Terry, carried out its first 'rescue' when it blockaded a New Jersey abortion clinic. Others were similarly inspired to picket abortion clinics and harass the medical personnel and patients entering them. In March 1993 a Florida physician was shot dead outside a clinic by a member of Rescue America, whose director denied responsibility but excused the act by saying that it had saved 'quite a number of babies' lives'. In 2001 it was reckoned that seven abortion doctors had been murdered in the previous ten years. Unsurprisingly the number of abortion centres had declined, and many doctors who continued to practise in them had taken to wearing disguises and bulletproof vests.

Feminist gains remained vulnerable at the end of the century, but in many respects the position of women had been transformed. Quite apart from the accomplishments of feminism in effecting a sea change in the values of many women, and in reinvigorating cultural forms and academic disciplines, a host of federal and state laws and regulations had been put into place to challenge gender bias. Public policies fashioned in the New Deal era had tended to favour male wage-earners, but much of the discrimination against women was removed.

A major demand of women's groups around 1970 had been for equal employment and educational opportunities. In these areas the women's movement, combined with a variety of economic and sociological changes, did have a significant effect. After gradually invading the workplace for decades, the number of women in paid employment came to rival that of men. The feminization of the workforce was the product of a number of conditions. One was the continued expansion of white-collar and pink-collar jobs. The new consciousness of 'liberated' women spurred many to demand education and careers. Affirmative-action policies assisted in the process, though – as black and Hispanic Americans might have attested – they tended to confer greatest advantage on the middle class. The erosion in real wages also pushed women into the workplace, so that many wives sought a second income to maintain the family's standard of living.

In 1970 women had constituted 38 per cent of the civilian labour force; by 1998 they had reached over 46 per cent. Work had ceased to be identified primarily with the male gender. In 1970 some 43 per cent of American women held jobs; by 1998 the figure was 60 per cent. The figure for single women was 68.5 per cent, only a few points less than that for single men. The surge of married and older women into the workplace, which had manifested itself in the middle decades of the century, continued strongly and was particularly marked for the well educated. (As it became 'normal' for women to work and pay taxes, public suspicion of poor women who did not work – 'welfare mothers' – tended to increase.) There were also striking educational accomplishments; by some indices, women overtook men. The proportion going on to college rose inexorably. Women had accounted for only 35 per cent of bachelors degrees in 1960; by 1982 they had closed the gap, and by 1996 led with 55 per cent. The advance in professional degrees was even more spectacular, since women had represented only 3.6 per cent of such graduates in 1965 but by 1996 were a remarkable 42 per cent. While it would take time for them to reshape the professions, reshaping them they were. Law had once been overwhelmingly a male preserve, but women began to enter it in larger numbers in the 1960s and by 1970 represented 4.9 per cent of lawyers; by 1990 it was 21 per cent. In the same years the proportion of women physicians doubled. Women may not have been storming into politics, but they were effecting subtle social change as they began to feminize the major professions.

Women were developing careers rather than taking jobs (or staying at home), and some prospered. A few of them – like a few African-Americans – joined the socio-economic élite. It could be said that, apart from women who inherited large fortunes or became rich through their talents in the various arts (such as popular novelists or actresses), women joined the affluent in their own right for the first time. But it remained difficult 'to have it all'. Many opted for careers rather than family. Earlier in the century professional women had tended to remain single – only 12 per cent were married in 1920. This tradition of the single career woman remained remarkably strong in the United States. A 1985 study found that while 96 per cent of male executives were married, only 59 per cent of female executives were.

But paralleling the energetic rise of some women in the professions was the feminization of poverty. Generally speaking, of course, women had always been poorer than men. The overall proportion of Americans in poverty grew only slightly in the decades after 1970, but the ratio of poor women to poor men tended to increase.

The feminization of poverty was a long-term process. In 1950 some 54 per cent of all poor adults were women; the figure was 62 per cent in 1970; and by 1989 about two-thirds of adults living below the poverty line were women. Family structures had been changing and the feminization of poverty was related to the increase in the proportion of female-headed households. In the early 1950s over 70 per cent of American families included a father who was employed and a mother who remained at home; by 1980 only 15 per cent of families adhered to this traditional form. Poverty was by no means confined to young women struggling to bring up children on their own, but it was disproportionately concentrated on them.

In some respects the 'permissive' trends of the 1960s and after contributed to the impoverishment of women. Accepting that unhappy marriages were best terminated, several states, led by California in 1970, enacted simple no-fault divorce laws, enabling a marriage to end when one partner testified that it had experienced 'irremediable breakdown'. The rising divorce rate reached 5.2 per thousand by 1980, or one for every two marriages – much the highest in the world. If easier access to divorce liberated some women, it harmed many. As no-fault divorce reduced the element of penalty in a divorce proceeding, the amount of alimony tended to decline. By the mid-1980s only 14 per cent of divorced women secured alimony (though the figure had never been very high). According to one estimate, a man's standard of living rose by 42 per cent after divorce, while that of his wife and children dropped by 73 per cent. Child-support payments from the father were notoriously difficult to collect. A 1980 study in Denver showed that men were more likely to keep up the payments on their cars than those for their children! The Family Support Act of 1988 went some way towards obliging fathers to provide financial support for their children, but in effect 'liberated' women in the no-fault era were expected to fend for themselves and their children.

The frustrating resilience of the wage gap also handicapped women. Between 1950 and 1980 the median weekly wage for women remained stuck at around 60 per cent of the male wage. Thereafter there was some improvement (largely because of the loss of well-paid blue-collar jobs for men), and by 1990 women's earnings were about 70 per cent those of men. Yet American women compared unfavourably with working women in several European countries, who tended to receive between 75 and 85 per cent of men's wages by the 1980s, although their educational achievements did not match those of their American cousins. (What had been put into place in many European countries were substantial state supports for women, such as provision for maternity leave, child support and child-care centres.) It also took time for those surging into the professions to reach the top, their progress impeded by a suspected 'glass ceiling'. In 1985 women were reckoned to constitute about a quarter of the professionals working in investment banking, but only 1 per cent of partners and managing directors.

Women were not alone in experiencing diverging fortunes in these years. From the early 1970s to the end of the century the income levels of the richest American families and individuals increased more rapidly than those of the poorest, which at times declined. But for women the disparity was particularly pronounced. The disintegration of the traditional family structure condemned many to poverty, while the strengthening of women's legal and constitutional rights increased opportunities for the educated, talented and privileged.

American feminists were sometimes accused of an excessive focus on equal constitutional rights, leading them to downplay gender differences and neglect the needs of working women. One woman trade unionist in the mid-1970s observed that a feminist leader like Gloria Steinem, the founder of *Ms*, was 'fighting for women like herself, professional women, and that she's not thinking of women in the whole sense, just part of them'. In fact NOW campaigned on behalf of poorer women and child-care centres from its foundation, and in the 1970s a variety of groups emerged to lobby on behalf of the most vulnerable women. But it is hardly surprising that American feminists took inspiration from the American individualist tradition, which had served other movements well. Further, their social context differed from that of European women. The latter were often able to work with labour organizations to advance the interests of working women, but organized labour in the United States was relatively weak and lost further ground in these years. Women's groups and labour organizations often did cooperate but they hardly constituted an irresistible force.

It may be that American activists were less prepared to work with the major political parties than their European counterparts, but given the deadlock between the elected branches of government it was plausible that the feminist cause was better pursued in the professions and through the courts (until conservatives eventually gained the ascendancy in the latter). What the focus on the ERA and abortion rights did do, partly because of the distorting lens of the press, was to disturb a significant minority of American women, who could be mobilized in defence of traditional family values. This conservative reaction was associated with the emergence of a vigorous religious right, which had no close equivalent in other advanced industrial societies. The majority of American women may have sympathized with feminist positions by the end of the century, but they faced the determined resistance of some women and many men and unsympathetic Republicans in government. The women's movement had done something to hasten the demise of the New Deal Order, as it also became a significant presence in late twentieth-century politics, but its very presence had called forth a powerful opposition and had thus contributed to the dividing of the political order.

|16|

African-Americans, Immigrants and Ethnics
1969–2000

During the middle decades of the twentieth century the 'race issue' for most Americans had meant the relationship between blacks and whites. 'Race has exploded to swallow up all other distinctions', observed Daniel P. Moynihan and Nathan Glazer as that era ended. But the issue soon assumed more complex form. For one thing, the black revolt stirred other minorities to assert their identities. In the wake of Black Power came 'Red Power' and 'Brown Power'; ultimately there would be those who championed 'White Power'. While only a very few pushed these slogans to militant conclusions, they reflected a heightened ethnic awareness among the groups whose claims they signalled. Americans more generally had been taught by the racial and counter-cultural struggles of the 1960s to value ethnic diversity, an understanding that was reinforced by an unexpected phenomenon, the return of mass immigration. Not since before the barriers went up in the 1920s had such huge waves of peoples swept into the United States. The proportion of the foreign-born in the American population had been declining since 1910, but after 1970 it rose again. While this alien influx generated tensions and some strident prophesies of doom, the nativist reaction was less pervasive than in the 1920s. For the most part American security was not held to be seriously imperilled. Many Americans accepted more readily than an earlier generation that the United States was a multi-ethnic society. 'Our diversity is a strength, not a weakness', President Clinton liked to say.

The growth of ethnic awareness complicated public policies. Programmes that had been devised primarily to accord citizenship rights to African-Americans had to be adapted to the claims of other groups. Yet while American society became more heterogeneous, the political impact of the heightened cultural diversity was limited (though the growing New Right sentiments owed something to a reaction against the Democrats' identification with minority rights). There were flaming controversies over such matters as the content of school curricula, yet the American polity was not reshaped. Black activism had helped to undermine the old New Deal Order, but the newer ethnic strains reinforced rather than accounted for the divided nature of the late twentieth-century political system. African-Americans did establish a stronger political identity, but millions of newcomers remained outside the arena of active politics. Their presence sparked uneasy speculation about a future in which (non-Hispanic) white Americans might constitute a minority of the American population, but for the moment their political significance remained latent.

In his last speech Martin Luther King had promised his followers that 'we as a people will get to the promised land'. In some respects African-Americans could draw satisfaction from their experience in the last third of the twentieth century. The racial caste system had clearly been left behind, as illustrated not only by integration in educational institutions, the workplace and public places, but also by a dramatic decline in the racial prejudice of white Americans, at least as measured by social surveys. Affirmative action replaced integration as the primary civil rights goal, and more African-Americans appeared in senior positions in government, universities, law firms and other businesses. Yet only some prospered. The income gap between rich and poor blacks widened. The proliferation of black officeholders was not followed by a transformation of the socio-economic lot of the most impoverished blacks. African-Americans did establish a vocal presence within the Democratic Party, but in national campaigns the party was increasingly heeding the key suburban vote, and in any case was no longer the power it had been. In a sense, African-Americans were successfully integrated into the political system, but as a minority group – around 12 per cent of the population – could hardly dictate to government. Even if racial prejudice had not still lurked somewhere in the undergrowth, the accumulated consequences of centuries of economic, social and educational deprivation could not be vanquished magically by a few dozen black Americans in Congress.

The Great Migration, which had done so much to prise open political opportunities in the Northern states, came to an end, but demographic change was still exerting a political impact. Having moved to the cities, the proportion of African-Americans living in city-centre areas grew, while white citizens often relocated elsewhere. This black urban concentration facilitated the election of black politicians and promoted an amorphous Black Power sensibility. Most black leaders sought to work within the existing political system, but increasingly did so through black rather than integrated groups. In this sense the nationalist vision of Malcolm X was as influential as the integrationism of Martin Luther King. Even in the venerable civil rights organizations, the NAACP and the Urban League, which had been avowedly bi-racial, leadership positions became confined to African-Americans. Similarly black politicians formed their own caucuses in state legislatures and in Congress. Other specifically black organizations proliferated too, from the National Conference of Black Mayors to the National

Association of Black Manufacturers. But other forces were at work to fragment the black community and undermine this solidarist vision.

The moderate civil rights movement was in disarray by 1969. Local struggles continued and some African-Americans sought to further their rights by exploring forms of black cultural identity. But the sense of a cohesive direct action movement, which Martin Luther King had brilliantly imparted, was lost. The SCLC itself crumbled, its staff numbers plummeting from 125 in 1968 to 17 in 1973, and King's lieutenants scattered. Hosea Williams in 1970 founded Hosea's Feed the Hungry and Homeless charity, which by the end of the century was providing over 35,000 meals at Thanksgiving and Christmas. Andrew Young turned to politics and was elected to Congress in 1972. Jesse Jackson broke away from the SCLC in 1971 and founded Operation PUSH, which developed as a national organization pressing industry to employ more African-Americans. Ralph Abernathy resigned from the SCLC leadership in 1976, when, as he later observed: 'The civil rights movement was no longer as fashionable as it once had been.'

Direct action had depended on provoking a usable response from authority. Whatever had powered the early civil rights movement, its success, as Cornell West has observed, 'required white liberal support in the Democratic Party, Congress and the White House'. From 1969 the Democratic Party was no longer the party of government and the civil rights movement could not normally look to a friend in the White House. The expectations of black Americans declined. In 1963 some 70 per cent of blacks surveyed believed that there would be a 'solution' to the problem of relations between blacks and whites; in 1993 only 44 per cent shared that hope. These conditions were less conducive to protest activity and pointed to a return to conventional political behaviour, that is litigation in the courts and lobbying in Washington. But another resource was also available, the growing black vote in the cities and the mass enfranchisement of Southern blacks.

For the first time electoral politics became a major strategy. This had been the advice of veteran leader Bayard Rustin in his 1965 article 'From Protest to Politics'. The recent legislation had removed the legal barriers to black progress, he argued, and such goals as an end to poverty and access to decent education could be accomplished only by wielding political power, using the tools that the new laws provided. In the late 1960s the number of black mayors and congressmen began to grow, and in 1970 the black sociologist Kenneth Clark observed that 'Negro elected officials have, in a significant sense, become the new leadership of the civil rights movement'.

As the Black Panthers died of police bullets or were thrust into jail, scores of African-American moderates worked instead to make use of the voting rights that had now been guaranteed, building their own organizations and fielding their own candidates. White leaders became less acceptable to black communities. The Voting Rights Act brought more blacks to the polls in the South, while the increasing concentration of blacks in the inner cities elsewhere enhanced their electoral power in local politics. Slowly the number of elected black politicians increased, bringing with them their own priorities. Where blacks won local office there were often material gains, such as improved street paving and lighting and better garbage collection. In 1964, according to one calculation, there were only 103 black elected officials in the United States; by 1994 there were 8,406.

Black mayors first appeared in Northern cities, beginning with Cleveland and Gary in 1967. By 1970 there were forty-eight across the country and by 1996 some 405. In such cities as Detroit, Newark and Atlanta, with their black majorities, black mayors became the norm. The traditional Democratic machines were tending to crumble and were unable to keep African-Americans in subordinate positions. Symbolic was the election of the black Harold Washington as mayor of Chicago in 1983, triumphing over the divided remains of the Daley machine. Black mayors were also being elected in cities with a majority of white voters, and the same sometimes obtained of other offices. When Douglas Wilder became the first African-American to be elected a state governor in Virginia in 1989 he secured 40 per cent of the white vote. White voters became less wary of black politicians. In 1957 a poll had shown that 63 per cent of whites would not support a well-qualified black candidate for president, but in 1994 the figure was only 10 per cent. The number of African-Americans in the two houses of Congress grew from 10 in 1970 to 40 in 1995. Claiming to represent black Americans generally was the Congressional Black Caucus, organized in 1971 and constituting the most progressive faction in the national Democratic Party.

Overall the proportion of black office-holders remained far short of the black share of the American population, partly because of its geographical location. In the South the registration of black voters precipitated an increased registration of whites, many of whom transferred their allegiance to the Republican Party, which became the dominant party in the section by the end of the century. This served to check the political influence of the enfranchised African-Americans. Northern blacks too encountered political frustration. Heavily concentrated in urban areas and overwhelmingly Democratic, many black votes in the North were in a sense 'wasted', providing large majorities in a limited number of contests. There was the further irony that as the number of elected black office-holders increased, policy decisions on many issues were being taken not so much by governments as by the courts.

By the 1980s some black leaders were growing impatient with the failure of the black vote to deliver rewards. African-Americans had long been among the Democratic Party's most loyal supporters, but the national party was tempted to take them for granted and woo suburban voters instead. Jesse Jackson determined to challenge the Democratic Party to do more for its black and other minority constituents by seeking its presidential nomination. He won the Louisiana primary in 1984 and a number of Democratic Southern primaries in 1988, deploying what he called his 'rainbow coalition' of black, Hispanic, Native and Asian Americans and sympathetic white Americans.

In some measure Jackson succeeded in mobilizing fellow blacks, and also a few middle-class whites, but his candidacy revealed little or no support among lower-class whites, and support from Latin and Asian Americans was spotty. The National Rainbow Coalition was formally constituted as a national organization in 1986, when its mobilization of black voters contributed to the Democratic recapture of the Senate, but after 1988 it evolved as little more than a letterhead for Jackson.

Also testing the political waters was the Nation of Islam, which underwent a series of convulsions following the death of Elijah Muhammad in 1975. Eventually Louis Farrakhan emerged as the leader of a reconstituted Nation, which began to dabble in politics. Much of the cultural ideology of the Nation, as in the strict code of personal conduct, was retained, but Farrakhan placed less emphasis on such notions as a separate black nation and supported Jesse Jackson's presidential campaign in 1984 (although not in 1988 when some anti-Semitic remarks made Farrakhan a less welcome ally). By 1990 the Nation of Islam supported voter registration drives and permitted its members to run for political office. It had traditionally recruited support from the black underclass, but now lower middle-class blacks and students were also attracted by its nationalist ideology. The Nation of Islam kept alive something of the black radical tradition.

While Farrakhan acted as a gadfly to mainstream black politicians, more important to them was a loose-knit civil rights coalition, if only because of the limitations of the electoral strategy. The SCLC may have decayed, but the NAACP and the National Urban League, with decades of experience of lobbying and litigation, proved more resilient as these older techniques regained favour at the expense of direct action. Also enjoying a revitalized role was the Leadership Conference on Civil Rights, which had been formed in 1950 as a Washington-based lobbying group by the NAACP and the CIO, and which by the early 1980s embraced 165 different organizations.

The civil rights coalition carved out a niche for itself in a polity in which lobbies were arguably overshadowing traditional party organizations. The multiplication of black politicians strengthened its links with the Democratic Party, which generally remained in the ascendancy in Congress. This alliance played a role in frustrating Richard Nixon's attempt to appoint a conservative Southerner to the Supreme Court in 1969–70, as it also resisted later conservative nominations to the judiciary, with varying degrees of success. The Leadership Conference on Civil Rights cooperated with congressional Democrats in securing the renewal of the Voting Rights Act in 1970, and fought off Nixon's attempt to weaken its application in the South. Another victory was the closing in 1974 of a loophole allowing the infringement of UN trade sanctions against the white regime in Rhodesia. The civil rights lobby also helped win the Humphrey-Hawkins bill of 1978, intended to boost black employment. It even exacted gains during the unsympathetic presidency of Ronald Reagan, who publicly blamed Democratic programmes for creating 'a new kind of bondage' among African-Americans. The lobby won a symbolic victory with an act making a public holiday of Martin Luther King Jr. Day and a significant one in securing sanctions against white South Africa. However undramatic, the alliance between the civil rights movement and liberal political leaders still held and ensured that the legislative gains of the 1960s were not lost. President George Bush in 1990 did veto another major civil rights bill (designed to counter recent Supreme Court decisions making it difficult to prove job discrimination), but he bowed to a compromise measure in 1991. Martin Luther King's widow observed in 1995 that her late husband's ideals had become 'deeply embedded in the very fabric of America'.

While the civil rights coalition was successfully institutionalized, critical support for many years also came from parts of the federal bureaucracy and the judiciary. Administrators and judges played a major role in shifting the primary issue from integration to affirmative action. The Civil Rights Act of 1964 had been designed explicitly to prohibit racial discrimination, but within a few years it was argued that in such areas as education and employment it was legitimate to deploy policies that gave preference to blacks or other minorities. The urban riots and the growth of Black Power from the mid-1960s did something to persuade the authorities to find a faster solution to the race problem. The rationale for affirmative action, called for in an executive order of Lyndon Johnson in 1965, was that the profound injustice inflicted on black Americans by slavery and Jim Crow was so far-reaching in impact that a colour-blind policy would simply perpetuate an inherited inequality.

One area subjected to judicial or administrative decree was school integration, which had proceeded at a glacial pace after the *Brown* decision of 1954. Initially desegregation apparently meant ending the allocation of pupils according to race. As long as schools were officially open to both races, however attendance worked in practice, there could be no objection. Gradually, however, because of the frustrating delaying tactics in the South, federal agencies and the courts began to expect Southern school districts to make positive efforts to integrate. The test came to be whether the racial balance in the schools approximated that obtaining in the district. Finally, in *Alexander v Holmes County* in 1969, after the new Republican administration had countenanced delay in school integration, the Court insisted that school districts should desegregate 'at once'.

After some hesitation, the Nixon White House determined on compliance, and desegregation proceeded more or less peaceably as officials worked quietly with local leaders to that end. But in large districts, in which blacks and whites lived in different areas, a racial balance in schools could be achieved only by transporting pupils across neighbourhood lines, and bussing became a highly charged political issue. Nixon made public his own opposition to it, but powerful forces were arrayed against him. The earlier civil rights and Great Society legislation had spawned such enforcement agencies as the Equal Employment Opportunity Commission (EEOC) and the Office of Federal Contract Compliance (OFCC). As Hugh Davis Graham has shown, such bodies became locked together in 'iron triangles' with sympathetic congressional committees and the regular government departments, their expertise generating policy pressures which even the White House found difficult to resist. When they were joined by the courts they became a yet more formidable alliance. Finally in April 1971, in *Swann v Charlotte-Mecklenburg Board of Education*, the Supreme Court decided that the equal protection clause of the Constitution legitimated the use of bussing to overcome racial imbalance in schools. The White House gracelessly accepted the ruling. The proportion of black children going to segregated schools in the South dropped markedly from 68 per cent in 1968 to 8 per cent in 1972.

In the 1970s the integration of Southern schools proceeded apace. By 1980 the proportion of Southern black students in a school in which at least a quarter of the pupils were white reached 65 per cent, higher than in the North-East and Midwest. The *de facto* segregation in Northern areas was indeed an issue, with inner-city schools often predominantly black and suburban schools white. In 1973 the Supreme Court told Denver to find a way of integrating its schools, which meant bussing. While the suburbs often escaped such orders, several dozen cities outside the South, including Boston, San Francisco and Minneapolis, were instructed to devise ways of achieving reasonable racial balances in their schools. Yellow buses plied the cities, carrying children in the required direction, often away from their own neighbourhoods. For whites, bussing was massively unpopular. In a 1972 poll, only 13 per cent of whites supported bussing for desegregation purposes, while the figure was 56 per cent for blacks. A bussing plan provoked violence in Boston in the mid-1970s as working-class Irish Catholic wards defended their neighbourhood schools against liberal policy-makers whose own children were allegedly not affected. There was more to their opposition than racism, though racism was hardly absent. As a white student expressed it, 'nobody's bussing me just so some niggers can get a better deal'. Many residents voted with their feet and moved to the suburbs or put their children in private or parochial schools. The proportion of white children attending public schools in several cities subjected to bussing plans dropped markedly between the 1970s and the 1990s.

The return of large-scale immigration complicated the story. The desegregation strategies of the 1960s and early 1970s tended to be based on the assumption that for practical purposes school authorities and other public agencies had to deal with either blacks or whites. By the 1990s Hispanic and Asian children in many schools rivalled black in number. It was unclear just what constituted an 'integrated' school. By this date the Supreme Court was moving away from the social engineering schemes it had previously endorsed and was giving some support to the return to neighbourhood schools. Some bussing schemes were discontinued, and this, combined with the tendency for different racial and ethnic groups to reside in different locations, meant that school resegregation intensified.

A strategy of affirmative action was even more explicitly pursued in such areas as employment and university admissions. The 1964 Civil Rights Act had sought to outlaw discrimination in hiring practices, but it did not require employers to make positive efforts to employ minorities. Nonetheless governmental agencies like the EEOC and the federal courts came to judge an employer's policy by impact, expecting it to provide information on the racial and gender make-up of its workforce. Federal administrators, some of them black Americans, wrote many of the regulations, almost imperceptibly producing shifts in public policy. It was easier to check whether firms were apparently discriminating against hiring African-Americans by monitoring their employment statistics than by investigating individual complaints, and affirmative action became identified with racial or gender quotas (which might have the effect of 'reverse discrimination' against better-qualified applicants). Companies which could not demonstrate a reasonable racial balance risked losing federal contracts. Federal quotas made an appearance under Richard Nixon and covered some 300,000 companies by 1972. In *Griggs v Duke Power Co.* in 1971, the Supreme Court upheld the principle of affirmative action in employment, arguing that the 1964 act was designed to regulate the consequences of hiring practices, which should not have a 'disparate impact'. Affirmative action thus meant that discrimination was to be tested by effect rather than by intent, a remarkable change in legal theory.

Affirmative-action programmes became widespread, sustained by civil rights lobbies, the courts and influential federal bureaucracies (and were also increasingly applied to women, the handicapped, the elderly and language minorities). The Democratic Congress gave the EEOC greater authority in 1972 to enforce its prescriptions, and the courts proved amenable to the notion that without such a strategy historic disadvantages would never be overcome. Businesses, public agencies and universities developed ways of employing or admitting more minorities, although wary of the Supreme Court's decision in the *Bakke* case of 1978, which disallowed the use of rigid quotas although not of other tools of affirmative action. On that occasion Justice Harry Blackmun spoke of the country going through a period of 'transitional inequality' and hoped that 'within a decade' affirmative action would no longer be necessary. The flood of new immigrants was also serving to undermine the rationale for affirmative action. About 80 per cent of these newcomers could claim benefits initially intended for African-Americans, although they had not been the victims of discrimination within the United States. In certain programmes, such as the contracts supervised by the Small Business Administration, the proportion going to blacks tended to decline as Asians and Hispanics increased their shares.

Affirmative action became part of American public policy more in spite of than because of public opinion. The pressure groups, bureaucrats, courts and politicians that fashioned them do not appear to have been responding to public demand. In a 1988 poll, some 80 per cent of whites opposed the idea that blacks should receive preference in college admissions and jobs; 50 per cent of blacks were also opposed, as against 40 per cent in favour. But equally revealing was a finding that 55 per cent of whites favoured affirmative-action programmes that did not have rigid quotas; it was explicit preferential treatment they disliked. Only a few whites reported that they had experienced reverse discrimination personally, suggesting that popular fears of affirmative action were exaggerated, perhaps, as Orlando Patterson argued, because of media preoccupation with race and its exploitation by politicians and pundits.

By the end of the 1980s a conservative majority had emerged on the Supreme Court, and it was less supportive of race-conscious laws in the area of employment. In 1989 it placed the burden on the employee to demonstrate racial bias. The civil rights lobby turned for redress to Congress, and the Civil Rights Act of 1991 largely reversed the recent Court rulings. But public and élite opinion was growing against policies based on racial criteria, although the Clinton administration vigorously defended federal affirmative-action programmes. In 1995, in *Adarand Constructors v Pena*, the Supreme Court further restricted the use of racial and ethnic criteria in contracting and presumably hiring decisions. In 1996 the voters of California endorsed a constitutional amendment prohibiting racial and gender preferences by the state government, and the massive University of California followed suit. Within five years black undergraduate enrolment had declined by a third.

The defection of the University of California indicated that the resistance to affirmative action was not confined to conservatives. There was a widespread public view that such policies were no longer necessary in a less prejudiced age, and some critics argued that they were socially divisive and destructive of morale for people of all races. The resilience of the civil rights coalition ensured that affirmative action remained a central part of public policy even after other government programmes had been whittled down, but by the 1990s some supporters were being given pause by the disappointing results. Affirmative action, it had been said, was a temporary strategy that could be abandoned after the disadvantages of inherited discrimination had been removed. But a generation after its adoption black poverty had barely diminished. In 1996 political scientist Robert C. Smith argued that the evidence demonstrated 'the irrelevancy of black politics in producing in the last twenty-five years benefits for most blacks, especially the imperative to reconstruct and integrate the ghettos into the mainstream of American society'.

Affirmative-action programmes seemed to work best for the better educated and skilled workers, and perhaps did something to widen the gap between those who succeeded and the many who did not. Some blacks made impressive educational and economic advances. In the early 1960s a much higher percentage of young whites had completed four years of high school than young blacks, but by 1995 the proportion was virtually the same. At the level of higher education a gap did remain, but it had narrowed dramatically. With better education, African-Americans eased their way up the income scale. In 1970 the median income of black men was 59 per cent that of white men; by 1995 it had risen to 67 per cent. Most of the improvement was experienced by the middle class.

The black middle class had been growing through the twentieth century and the process continued. In the twenty years after 1970 there were significant gains in the 'higher' professions. The proportion of black physicians rose from 2.2 to 4.5 per cent and that of lawyers from 1.3 to 3.5 per cent. By 1997 some 36 per cent of black households were in receipt of incomes of at least $35,000, while those with incomes of under $15,000 represented 32 per cent. By this measure, the black middle class outnumbered the poor. In these years too the suburbanization of blacks proceeded at a faster pace than that of whites. One consequence was a growing distance between the ghetto blacks and the black middle class.

The proportion of blacks in poverty did ease down after 1970, though at a much slower rate than earlier. In 1970 some 33.5 per cent of blacks were below the poverty line, falling to 29.3 per cent in 1995. At the same time the proportion of whites in poverty inched up, from 9.9 per cent to 11.2 per cent, still far below the black proportion but an indication perhaps that economic forces were beginning to prevail over racial discrimination.

But if economic forces were eroding the position of low-income whites, they were not doing much to assist low-income blacks. This was evident in the statistics on child poverty, which indicated that despite the educational advances many black children were barely assisted by public policies. In 1969 some 40 per cent were in poverty and 42 per cent in 1995 (although the economic boom of the final years of the century helped to reduce the figure to 30 per cent in 2001). In 1960 over two-thirds of black children had lived in families with both parents present; by 1995 the proportion was only one-third (which was not the experience of most white children). Large numbers were dependent on the uncertain income of one parent. It was not easy for unmarried mothers either to escape poverty or to prepare a child to compete in the modern world. Parental responsibility for many males was made difficult by joblessness, which remained higher for blacks than for whites, increasingly so for young black men, partly because many were marooned in ghettos. African-Americans had been drawn to the booming industrial belt in the 1940s and 1950s, but the decline of heavy industry left them densely concentrated in these cities. For those young African-Americans who were able to forge skills and stable relationships there was the chance of a good material life. For families with both parents present, in 1995 the median income of the black family was 87 per cent of that of the white, a striking improvement on the 1967 figure of 68 per cent.

The persisting poverty of inner-city African-Americans, as well as of some struggling in areas of rural and small town decline, testified to the limitations of Great Society and affirmative-action programmes. Social isolation meant political disadvantages too. Inner-city blacks were a minority within a minority – only about a fifth of African-Americans in 1990 lived in urban ghettos. Voter registration was low in these areas and political parties were better attuned to the demands of the voting middle classes. The black community was fatally fragmented. A poll in 1997 found that 74 per cent of blacks were satisfied with their standard of living, a marked improvement on the 45 per cent figure of 1973. But while many blacks made their way into the mainstream, and a few joined the economic élite, a large minority remained condemned to lives of deprivation. By the end of the century – partly because of a penal policy that jailed increasing numbers for non-violent crimes – there were more black men in prison than in college. Black activists had called for racial solidarity, but the dynamic of an entrepreneurial economy served more to separate blacks than to bring them together.

In the age of the rights revolution other minorities were also ready to explore their roots. In the South-Western states a Chicano Liberation Movement emerged to stake the claims of Mexican Americans. One manifestation was La Raza Unida Party, originating in California in 1969 before spreading to other states. Native Americans and Puerto Ricans articulated their own nationalist philosophies and were joined by such groups as Irish Americans and Italian Americans. In 1970 over 50,000 Italian Americans gathered in New York to demand 'Italian Power'. If the more radical demands of these various liberation movements were rarely met, at least they encouraged a public recognition that the United States was a multicultural society. In 1972 Congress passed the Ethnic Heritage Studies Program Act, a tribute to 'the heterogeneous composition of the nation'. In an awkward (and unscientific) adjustment of government policies to this diversity, the federal bureaucracy in 1977 settled on its 'ethno-racial pentagon', a classification system which, as historian David Hollinger puts it, 'replicates precisely the crude, colloquial categories, black, yellow, white, red, and brown'. The 1980s witnessed the eruption of the so-called 'culture wars', as rival racial and ethnic groups rather sharply defined their identities and insisted on recognition of their distinctive traditions, precipitating fears that American society was becoming tribalized. But the differences – at least between those groups of European descent – had long been declining (and increasing numbers of young Asian, Hispanic and African-Americans too were engaging in 'mixed' marriages by this period). By the end of the century the culture wars had somewhat abated. Some analysts were looking forward to what Hollinger called a 'postethnic' nation, in which the ethno-racial element in identity was less pronounced and individuals were free to choose their own identity.

As with African-Americans, representatives of other minorities did appear in greater numbers in legislatures and boardrooms. During the New Deal Order, Italian and Polish Americans had begun to secure election or appointment to high political office. It was Ronald Reagan who named the first Hispanic to the cabinet, while Bill Clinton in turn was eager to appoint an administration that 'looked like America'. His cabinet nominees included a number of Latinos (as some Hispanics prefer to be called) and African-Americans as well as women, and just below cabinet level he appointed a former Red Power activist to head Indian Affairs. In 2001 President George W. Bush appointed an even more ethnically diverse cabinet.

Red Power protests had emerged in the wake of the 1960s, with Native Americans sometimes occupying sites to which they claimed ancestral rights. Unity was not easy among a people divided into hundreds of tribes, but broadly they sought control of their own affairs and resuscitation of their cultures. Their demands were separatist – 'Integrity, Not Integration' – although in fact many Indians were leaving the reservations for the cities. In 1971 the American Indian Movement held its first national convention. The federal government had already begun to move away from assimilationist policies, and Richard Nixon in 1970 more clearly avowed the new goal of Indian self-determination. But that promise was never adequately supported by material aid, slowed it was said by 'white tape', and protests mounted, most graphically in the armed Indian invasion in 1973 of Wounded Knee, the South Dakota site of the last Indian massacre. School programmes on the reservations were strengthened during the Nixon administration, and the new policy was elaborated in the Indian Self-Determination and Education Assistance Act of 1975, designed to enhance tribal sovereignty and economic self-sufficiency. Yet from 1978 Supreme Court decisions tended to chip away at tribal self-government, at least in the areas of civil and criminal jurisdiction. As the political climate grew more conservative, Indians, like other groups, turned to the law. The Native American Rights Fund became a major instrument in the pursuit of Indian rights, inspiring an explosion of litigation. Several groups in the 1970s and 1980s secured federal recognition as tribes or were successful in winning land and claims to fishing rights. Less helpful was the squeezing of federal funding for reservation projects during the presidencies of Ronald Reagan and George Bush, who believed in promoting tribal capitalism (soon illustrated by legal gambling operations on several reservations). Indian activism, together with some court decisions, had brought some modest gains for the tribes, but nonetheless the role of Native Americans within the American political system remained barely visible. They represented less than 1 per cent of the population, and by 1990 nearly two-thirds of them lived off reservations, dispersed across the immensity of urban America.

Further contributing to the salience of ethnicity was both the resumption of large-scale immigration and its novel composition, as it shifted dramatically away from Europe and towards the Third World. The Immigration Act of 1965 had abolished the National Origins Quota System, making entry easier for people outside Western Europe. Immigration had been creeping up since the Second World War and it rose to 5.6 million in the 1970s, to 8.8 million in the 1980s, and to an extraordinary 13.5 million in the 1990s. This last figure was well in excess of the record numbers of the first decade of the century, although a smaller proportion of the total population. Many immigrants were Hispanics (the census classification for Latinos), fleeing the poverty and political regimes of Mexico, the Caribbean and parts of South America, often arriving without documents and contriving a shadowy existence in low-wage jobs. But a high proportion were Asians, around 40 per cent by the 1980s, particularly Vietnamese, Koreans and Chinese, thanks in large part to American involvement in South-East Asia. The political instability in the Middle East also served to augment the Moslem population of the United States. For the most part these newcomers settled in the expanding Sunbelt states of the South and the West, most notably California, though some found their way to the urban North-East, especially New York. The ethnic heterogeneity of American cities was once more refreshed. Many city centres were already decaying, and tensions sometimes flared between groups competing for housing and jobs. A high proportion of these immigrants also found that they were eligible for some affirmative-action programmes, a feature that irked poor whites (who could not claim such benefits) and American-born minorities. Simmering conflicts between whites, blacks, Latinos and Asians had been noted in Los Angeles well before a major race riot broke out there in May 1992.

The direct impact of this new immigration on American politics remained limited, partly because business and civil rights groups afforded them some protection. Experienced professionals (like the skilled craftsmen of an earlier day) were fairly readily absorbed, while the legions of poor immigrants, many unable to speak English, were fragmented, and the illegal aliens among them reluctant to draw attention to themselves. These scattered newcomers, further riven by ethnic rivalries, were hardly in a position to mobilize politically. Many were not citizens, and those who were often did not find their way to the voting booth. In the 1980s Jesse Jackson failed to extend his 'rainbow coalition' much beyond his black constituents.

Latinos had always been present in several Sunbelt states. In California César Chávez, committed to non-violent action, was catapulted to prominence as the leader of Chicano and Filipino farm workers protesting against exploitation, notably in a series of grape and lettuce boycotts between 1965 and 1972. In the late 1960s the Brown Berets stalked the streets of East Los Angeles, and subsequently the more moderate League of United Latin American Citizens was formed. Like African-Americans, some Latino activists turned to conventional politics, and in the ten years from 1978, according to one calculation, the number elected to public office grew by over 100 per cent. Nonetheless their political representation never adequately reflected their numbers. Even in Los Angeles, where a third of the population were Chicanos, just one was on the city council in 1986.

The fast-growing (and racially diverse) Hispanic peoples meant that issues of race and ethnicity could no longer be reduced to the black-white dichotomy. Affirmative-action programmes structured on the assumption that integration meant the mingling of blacks and whites had to be revised, and eventually some were abandoned as impracticable. But even if integrated into 'white' schools, Latino children were at a disadvantage. Their poor command of English meant that they were often held back, generating a demand that they be taught in Spanish at least until they learned English. In California Governor Ronald Reagan backed a state bilingual education bill in 1967. A modest federal bilingual programme was initiated in 1968, and was thereafter expanded by sympathetic federal administrators loyal to the court ruling that outcome rather than intent was the test of civil rights policies. The principle of non-English speakers being taught in their own language had a wide application and was upheld by the Supreme Court in 1974, sparking an explosion of bilingual education and ensuring its survival as a contentious political issue. By 1980 bilingual programmes, designed as much to perpetuate the different subcultures as to socialize children, were conducted in eighty different languages. Again bureaucrats and the courts, prodded by ethnic lobbies, had pressed a policy beyond anything envisaged by elected politicians.

The great waves of newcomers once more raised the question of the capacity of the United States to absorb foreign peoples. While authentic refugees were often willingly admitted, many others simply contrived to secure entry without documents, particularly impoverished migrants from the Caribbean and Latin America. By the mid-1980s there were estimated to be between 3 and 5 million illegal aliens in the United States, and they were variously accused of undercutting American labour, burdening welfare programmes and smuggling in drugs. Eventually the Simpson-Rodino Act of 1986 made it an offence to employ undocumented aliens, while amnesty was given to illegal immigrants who had arrived before 1982. In 1990 another act liberalized the quotas and accorded greater priority to those with skills needed by the American economy. But undocumented immigrants were not stopped, an estimated 9 million arriving in the 1990s. President Clinton's administration got off to an embarrassed start when it was discovered that his nominee for Attorney-General had employed illegal aliens as home help.

The focus on ethnicity also did something to raise white consciousness. Some white ethnics resented the federal programmes offering benefits to African-Americans, Hispanics and others; their own families, they might intimate, had made their way by hard work. It was among such people that Richard Nixon hoped to win recruits for his new Republican majority, and the Democrats did lose some traditional supporters. Such groups as the Italian Civil Rights League and the Polish American Congress insisted on more support from government and the media for the nationalities they represented, and the Ethnic Heritage Studies Act of 1972 offered financial aid for programmes encouraging the distinct ethnic cultures. The privileged status apparently accorded to ethnic identity also bothered some of those whose ancestors had reached American shores generations before. By the 1980s such organizations as U.S. English were campaigning to have English declared the country's official language. More disturbing was the revival of white supremacist or separatist groups. Among them was the National Association for the Advancement of White People, which, as its name suggested, seemed to take inspiration from the African-American struggle.

During the 1996 presidential campaign a supporter of Patrick Buchanan, the right-winger seeking the Republican presidential nomination, told a meeting: 'Whites must assert our identity and our solidarity, and we must do so in explicitly racial terms through the articulation of racial consciousness as whites.'

While White Power groups remained on the fringes, they were a mark of the fractious temper that was so pervasive in American politics in the late twentieth century. Arthur Schlesinger attributed the cult of ethnicity to a waning optimism in the American future in an age of straitened circumstances. Each group, perhaps, sensed the need to fend for itself. Demoralized ghetto residents in particular chafed at the seeming unresponsiveness of the economic and political systems, and racial and ethnic hostilities on occasion flared into violence. Miami blacks vented resentments against Cuban refugees in 1980 in riots that took eighteen lives. Over fifty people died in the Los Angeles riot of 1992, precipitated by the acquittal of white policemen accused of beating a black American, although Korean shopkeepers were among those whose property suffered and Latinos constituted a high proportion of those arrested.

The removal of formal barriers and the broad decline of racial prejudice may have allowed a few members of minority groups to join high political and economic councils, but the impact of an increasingly globalized economy was ambiguous. The bifurcation that black Americans experienced was the fate both of other minorities like Hispanics and of the white majority too. A growing economic stratification in the closing decades of the twentieth century tended to pull rich and poor apart, a process furthered by the manipulation of the tax system. The share of the national income of the richest fifth of American families increased by 7.8 per cent between 1973 and 1990; all other segments suffered a decline, with the bottom fifth losing most. These tendencies were reinforced during the economic boom that ended the century. This put more money into the pockets of most people in absolute terms, but the proportion of total income received by the poorest households tended to edge down, especially for poor blacks and Hispanics, while households receiving $75,000 and over a year gained most. It may not have been of much comfort to Hispanic and African-Americans to know that their socio-economic profiles had come to look a little more like that of other Americans, who had always been divided between an affluent few and a struggling many.

The electoral power of black and other minorities proved limited at a time when the political initiative tended to lie with conservative Republicans and when government in any case was often divided against itself. Affirmative-action programmes and an increasingly high-tech and consumer economy, in distancing the upwardly mobile from what came to be seen as an underclass, also perhaps militated against effective political mobilization. This is not to denigrate the role of minority politicians and civil rights activists, who were often effective in protecting past gains and even exacting modest victories, although their major goals remained frustratingly elusive. Occasionally populist voices suggested that the way forward was a class alliance, uniting the poor of both genders and of all ethnicities and races in a common cause. But this too was a chimera. In sociologist Todd Gitlin's view, multiculturalist preoccupations had shattered working-class solidarity. Organized labour, a declining force in the polity anyway, deserted George McGovern when he attempted to ignite a 'new politics' crusade as the Democratic presidential candidate in 1972, and few outside the African-American community responded to Jesse Jackson's call for a 'rainbow coalition' in the following decade. When environmentalist candidate Ralph Nader attempted to mobilize ordinary Americans against the corporate interests dominating the two major parties in the 2000 presidential election, he won less than 3 per cent of the popular vote. Many minority citizens had been successfully absorbed into the American political order. Indeed, in October 1995 some 67 per cent of American blacks claimed that they still believed in the American Dream. But social isolation, division and fragmentation condemned disproportionate numbers of racial and ethnic minorities to second-class status. The census of 2000 confirmed that metropolitan areas were more racially and ethnically segregated than ever, with African-Americans remaining the most highly segregated minority in the United States.

Yet, despite increasing residential segregation, the demarcations between the various racial and ethnic groups were increasingly complex. Black–white marriages, though unusual, tripled in the quarter-century after 1967, and by the 1990s over a third of young Latinos born in the United States were marrying non-Latinos. African, Native American, Caucasian and Asian genes all contributed to the charisma of golf star Tiger Woods. There seemed to be signs too of the growth of other inter-racial relationships. As Latina scholar Elizabeth Martinez noted in 1998: 'For a group of Korean restaurant entrepreneurs to hire Mexican cooks to prepare Chinese dishes for mainly African-American customers, as happened in Houston, Texas, has ceased to be unusual.' One day at the end of the twentieth century Jesse Jackson watched a multi-racial crowd in a poor Mississippi district awaiting a speech from President Clinton, and noticed something new. He had seen multi-racial crowds before, he told journalist Joe Klein, 'but now they're *talking* to each other', adding as a joking aside: 'And you know what else, they're *sleeping* with each other, too.' Whether Jackson's observation represented anything more than wishful thinking would become clearer in the twenty-first century.

|17|

The Seventies:
from Nixon to Reagan
1969–81

In July 1969 an American spaceship landed on the moon. Senator Clinton Anderson recalled that the decade had begun – in the aftermath of the Sputnik – with the widespread expectation that the future would lie with the Soviets, but the lunar landing had redeemed the international reputation of the United States, which was now 'without peer in power and influence'. Perhaps the walk on the moon's surface of Neil Armstrong and Buzz Aldrin did something to salve the wounds on the American psyche inflicted by Vietnam and the turmoil in the cities. 'You've been drunk all summer ...' said Norman Mailer to his counter-cultural comrades, 'and *they* have taken the moon.' But conservative patriotism was not yet in the ascendant.

The presidential election of 1968 may have signalled the decline of the New Deal Order, but it was not an unambiguous victory for conservative politics. Old-time New Deal Democrats were still a force in the land, the 'new politics' leftists enjoyed their own constituencies, and there were still liberal politicians in the Republican Party. The Democrats retained their majorities in Congress, the federal bureaucracy was filled with Democratic appointees and liberals remained influential in the Supreme Court. That the broad course of American politics would be to the right could not be safely predicted in 1969. Indeed, the Nixon administration itself displayed a number of liberal characteristics, while the Democratic Carter administration a few years later exhibited conservative features. Through the 1970s conservative and liberal strands were confusingly interwoven. But in 1980 conservatives finally claimed an unequivocal victory in national politics.

The election of Richard Nixon owed more to disenchantment with the Johnson administration than it did to his own personal appeal. While the liberal consensus for which Lyndon Johnson had yearned had been fractured, the return of a Republican to the White House was not a triumph for the right. Nixon appreciated that forging a majority meant winning some votes from the centre, and his stance was that of a moderate. He displayed little interest in the old-fashioned *laissez-faire* conservatism of Barry Goldwater; his instincts were to equate the Republican Party with the middle class. During his first term he embraced a number of policies that might attract low-income voters – in furtherance of his strategy to build a new Republican majority – and also some that could be labelled progressive, although his instinct was to hide them under conservative rhetoric. 'Brilliant opportunist that he was,' historian Michael Kazin has observed, 'the president talked like a grass-roots conservative while often governing like a liberal.' He could be relatively liberal on matters relating to the economy and welfare, but on socio-cultural issues like law and order and abortion he made clear his conservative credentials. (The new breed of Democrats that emerged in the 1970s tended to display the reverse pattern.)

It was his essential political pragmatism that allowed Nixon to entwine conservative and liberal strands in his early policies, although ultimately perhaps he could never escape the conservative implications of the stance that he adopted in his bid for the presidency. The 1968 campaign had witnessed the first sighting of Nixon's 'Southern strategy', as he grasped the potential for further Republican inroads into the traditionally Democratic South. An important tactic was the selection of Spiro Agnew, the Governor of Maryland, as his running mate. As a resident of a border state Agnew should be acceptable to conservative Southerners, but important too was his image as a strong 'law and order' figure following his denunciation of urban rioters. To him, the black leaders were 'Hanoi-visiting ... caterwauling, riot-inciting, burn-America-down type of leaders'. Some disenchanted Democrats in the North might even be drawn to him. To capitalize on the anti-Johnson sentiment, Nixon had kept his campaign short on specifics, but his scorning of the Great Society's 'knee-jerk reaction of government program' poised him against big government, while his call for a 'war on crime' implied a criticism of both the Supreme Court and fashionable liberalism. A believer in the Protestant work ethic, Nixon insisted that his priority was to provide jobs rather than welfare. Further, while he deprecated George Wallace's demagoguery, he refused to make overtures to African-Americans. 'I'm not going to campaign for the black vote at the risk of alienating the suburban vote', he told a friend. In 1960 Nixon had apparently secured nearly a third of the African-American vote; unsurprisingly, in 1968 his share dropped to 12 per cent or even less.

The gauche Nixon had long been reviled by liberals as driven by a self-serving ambition that would lead him to pander to any base popular emotion. But he was also politically shrewd and his lower-class origins had not left him without some empathy for the poor. His gracelessness had served him badly in his presidential contest with John Kennedy in 1960, but the two had more in common than was often recognized. Neither possessed a highly articulated political philosophy and their policy positions as presidential candidates remained vague. Both thought the presidency could be an instrument of change, and there were interesting similarities of temperament in their approach to government. Where Kennedy wanted to be 'tough', Nixon boasted that he thrived on 'crisis'. Where Kennedy believed in an 'active' executive, Nixon was drawn to the 'big play'.

Nixon opened his administration by parading his cabinet members on television, but the cabinet was not destined to play a major role. To a large extent power was concentrated on the White House and its residents – notably Chief of Staff Bob Haldeman and Domestic Adviser John Erlichman wielded an unusual degree of influence. This was the 'German wall' that protected the president. If Nixon wanted to redistribute some services to the states, this was to reduce the power of the federal bureaucracy rather than the authority of the White House, and he sought ways of centralizing administrative control in the presidency. This impulse could lead him to stretch the law and the Constitution.

During his first year as president Nixon avowed that he would 'begin a decade of government reform such as this nation has not witnessed in half a century'. An early theme was the so-called New Federalism, unveiled in August 1969 as the administration searched for ways of reducing Washington bureaucracy and congressional interference. One dimension was to return federal revenue to the states so that some programmes, particularly the provision of services like education and health, could be managed locally. Nixon had long held a conservative's contempt for bureaucracy, but he also knew that federal offices were stacked with people suspicious of his administration. In 1970, according to one study, some 47 per cent of senior career civil servants in Washington were Democrats and only 17 per cent were Republicans. A frustrated Nixon once fumed to an aide: 'We have no discipline in this bureaucracy! We never fire anybody ... We always promote the sons-of-bitches that kick us in the ass.' This was one reason why the administration found it difficult to escape from some of the policy lines laid down in the 1960s. Under the New Federalism, where possible, the running of social programmes was to be turned over to state capitals and city halls, which could be supplied with federal revenue for the purpose. Congress proved uncooperative with a strategy that would erode its capacity to determine how money was spent, but a revenue-sharing bill was eventually signed into law in 1972.

But not all areas of public policy were readily susceptible to decentralization, such as environmental and energy matters. These Nixon hoped to make subject to executive rather than congressional direction. With the onset of divided government and Democratic majorities in Congress, ironically Nixon's instinct was to follow his New Deal predecessors in enhancing presidential power, particularly in strengthening the White House's administrative capability. The number of employees in the White House bureaucracy increased dramatically from 570 in 1969 to over 6000 in 1972. Nixon's attempts to concentrate power in his own hands drew charges that he was fashioning an 'imperial presidency', a criticism that also invoked his taste for pomp, as in dressing the White House guards in resplendent uniforms.

Nixon's particular combination of decentralization and centralization would together serve to enhance control from the White House and circumvent federal bureaucracy.

One area held to be a federal rather than a local responsibility was welfare. 'Poverty must be conquered without sacrificing the will to work', said Nixon, 'for if we take the route of the permanent handout, the American character will itself be impoverished.' These were pretty traditional sentiments, though the president's particular solution was not. Lyndon Johnson had hoped that his War on Poverty would put an end to welfare payments, but the number of Americans on public assistance had jumped from 7.8 million in 1965 to 11.1 million in 1969. The Great Society programmes had also added to the complexity of welfare arrangements, some 1152 distinct governmental units now participating in the distribution of welfare. One reason for the growth in welfare rolls was the huge movement of poor and mainly rural Southern blacks to the Northern cities. Another was the greater awareness of poor people of their entitlements and a greater willingness to claim them. Sorting out the 'welfare mess' was to be a priority for the administration. 'We hoped to cut down on red tape, and before long to eliminate social services, social workers, and the stigma of welfare', the president later explained.

The Family Assistance Plan (FAP) would provide every American family with a guaranteed annual income. Strikingly, people in employment as well as those on welfare would be eligible, so that 'those who work would no longer be discriminated against' and families could retain part of any earnings. The novel approach was that of a negative income tax, an idea that had both liberal and conservative roots. Some liberals liked the idea of a guaranteed income, while certain kinds of conservatives could applaud the prospect of sweeping away the confusing array of relief programmes and the welfare bureaucracy while increasing work incentives.

But many Americans were suspicious of what looked like giving benefits as a matter of right. Presidential aide Charles Colson thought that even organized labour was opposed to FAP, which could be 'counterproductive politically to our efforts with the average middle-class working man and the labor movement'. Further, the support of some prominent liberals for FAP did nothing to dispel conservative suspicions, and by the end of 1970 the measure had foundered in Congress. Ironically, with the failure of this reform Nixon endorsed the national introduction of uniform standards in the food stamp programme and automatic cost-of-living increases in Social Security payments; these and other adjustments to welfare measures meant that spending on domestic programmes continued to spiral during his administration. Attuned to the mentality of ordinary white Americans, Nixon was not averse to extending the benefits of the New Deal state if it brought him blue-collar and middle-class votes.

The president's bold attempt at welfare reform has been labelled 'Nixon's good deed'. If virtue is associated with the progressive end of the liberal-conservative spectrum he could claim more of it. Bowing to public and congressional pressure, Nixon agreed to the establishment of the Environmental Protection Agency in 1970, and a number of pieces of environmental legislation, aimed particularly at curbing pollution and protecting endangered species, were adopted in his first term. If it came to 'a flat choice between jobs and smoke', however, Nixon insisted that jobs came first. Following the energizing example of the civil rights movement, Native Americans had become increasingly militant in their own claims for rights, and the administration responded with some sympathy. In 1970 Nixon announced that the aim of federal policy would be tribal self-determination, a reversal of the previous integrationist strategy. Congress allowed the Bureau of Indian Affairs budget to increase by over 200 per cent during the Nixon years. It was less cooperative in Nixon's attempt to secure a comprehensive health service through a mixture of public and private provision. His National Health Insurance Partnership proposal of 1971 fell foul of the powerful American Medical Association – which deemed it too radical – and liberals who objected that it was inadequate.

Nixon trod warily in areas that had popular support and many Great Society programmes continued, but they were not untouched. As noted, he hoped to spin off some of the services to the states, and he sensed a public reaction against big government and the grandiose ambitions of Lyndon Johnson. The Great Society's primary institutional emblem, the Office of Economic Opportunity (OEO), suffered in particular. Job Corps centres were cut back and the Corps was transferred to the Labor Department. Some training programmes were put under local government control. Head Start was switched to the Department of Health, Education and Welfare, and it grew at a slower pace. The OEO was reduced to a shell.

A mingling of conservative and liberal stances similarly characterized other aspects of Nixon's first term. His need to fend off George Wallace, still chasing his presidential ambitions, and to build on Republican gains in the South (and among certain urban groups) meant that his attitude towards civil rights was at best ambiguous. As far as the Nixon White House was concerned, building a 'new Republican majority' meant (among other things) securing the allegiance of Southern whites without repelling centrist voters. Civil rights gains would not be torn down, but further assaults on Southern white sensibilities would be discountenanced.

The new Republican Justice Department at first permitted delays in school desegregation but, after the Supreme Court decreed in October 1969 that desegregation should proceed 'at once', the administration decided to cooperate with Southern officials in implementing the decision, reasoning perhaps, as Attorney-General John Mitchell did, that the courts would get the blame. As observed in Chapter 16, the president was less statesmanlike over the contentious issue of bussing, used by some districts to integrate schools. When the constitutionality of bussing was upheld by the Supreme Court in April 1971, a surly president told his aides: 'Do what the law requires and not one bit more.' After George Wallace won the Florida Democratic primary in March 1972 with a campaign focused on bussing, Nixon took to television to call for a 'moratorium' on court-ordered bussing to allow time to consider other ways of addressing the problem. On desegregation as such Nixon had felt that his office obliged him to comply with the Supreme Court's ruling, but on 'forced bussing' he came close to inciting people to disobey the law of the land.

Nixon did not regard himself as a racist. He could point to his Minority Business Enterprise programme, launched in 1969 to provide loans to help African-Americans and other minorities to establish small businesses. The Philadelphia Plan of 1969 also testified to his belief that the provision of jobs offered the most constructive route to racial equality. It required unions working on federal contracts in the construction industry to admit a quota of African-American apprentices to full membership, and was later extended to other industries. Hence originated the controversial practice of 'affirmative action' as governmental policy. Critics suspected that the initial intention was to disrupt white–black relations in the labour movement and thus weaken the Democratic Party, and Nixon later attacked affirmative-action ideas when the Democrats embraced them.

Whatever benefits Nixon offered to black Americans, he was not to be deflected from his Southern strategy. His commitment to it was displayed in 1969, when he tried to fill a Supreme Court vacancy with a South Carolinian, Judge Clement F. Haynsworth, Jr. But Haynsworth's record on the bench revealed some anti-civil rights and anti-labour positions, and opposition to him erupted in the liberal community and among Democrats, still in command of the Senate that confirmed nominations. Nixon obstinately persisted with Haynsworth, who was eventually denied confirmation, with seventeen Republicans voting against their president's nominee. Nixon then named G. Harrold Carswell, a Florida judge, but his record proved to be mediocre and even more in sympathy with white supremacy than had Haynsworth's, and he too was rejected by the Senate (despite the argument of one Republican senator that mediocre Americans were entitled to a representative on the Court!). A furious Nixon denounced the Senate as biased against men who were 'born in the South'. The president embarrassed liberals in his own party, but the imbroglio earned him a lot of credit in the white South. His aide Harry Dent concluded that: 'No action by the president did more to cement the sinews of the southern strategy.'

Yet (as noted in Chapter 14) Nixon did have some influence on the composition of the Supreme Court, eventually appointing three moderate conservatives as well as the right-wing William Rehnquist. These changes were not enough to induce the Court to go to war on Great Society legislation, but it gradually backed away from the activism associated with the Warren years.

Nixon's conservative instincts were also evident in his determination to champion 'law and order', not least in his disdain of student activism and his pursuit of the radical left. By the late 1960s the New Left itself was fragmenting into a host of squabbling groups, and a few of its shreds spun towards violent philosophies. The Nixon administration was happy to add to the radicals' problems. In 1969 it brought conspiracy charges against prominent New Left leaders associated with the demonstrations at the Democrats' Chicago convention, the celebrated 'Chicago Eight', even though the Attorney-General at the time of the disturbances was prepared to speak up for the defendants. (They were found guilty but their convictions were later reversed.) While the trial was taking place the Weathermen staged their disorderly 'Days of Rage' in Chicago and were in turn arrested. In 1970 the surviving members of this tiny violent group went underground.

Other radicals too suffered from governmental, FBI and police attention. Among them were the Black Panthers, whose offices were frequently raided in 1969; several were arrested and some died in police shoot-outs. In December the American Civil Liberties Union concluded that the 'record of police actions across the country against the Black Panther Party forms a prima facie case ... that law enforcement officials are waging a drive against the black militant organization resulting in serious civil liberties violations'. When a massive anti-war demonstration gathered in Washington in November 1969, 9000 federal troops were moved in and the Deputy Attorney-General confessed: 'We just can't wait to beat up those motherfucking kids.' More angry student demonstrations erupted after it became known in April 1970 that the administration had extended the Vietnam War into Cambodia, and Nixon railed against 'these bums, you know, blowin' up the campuses'. During a protest at Kent State University in May, National Guardsmen shot and killed four students. Furious demonstrations erupted in over half of the nation's campuses. Two more students died from police bullets at Jackson State College in Mississippi. Whatever the responsibility of local officers for these tragedies, the rhetoric of the Nixon administration had done nothing to restrain the agents of the law. Polls taken after the Cambodia invasion indicated that about 75 per cent of Americans disapproved of anti-government protests. Nixon's law-and-order stance did him little harm with the working- and middle-class ethnics that he wanted to draw into the Republican camp.

Nixon's inconsistency as a conservative, however, was highlighted by his celebrated 'turnaround' on economic policy, one that he dramatized in a television address. The deteriorating balance of payments combined with inflation had contributed to a critical drain on the country's gold reserves. Foreigners sold dollars on a massive scale and by the summer of 1971 the economy seemed on the verge of collapse. In August the administration 'closed the gold window' by suspending the convertibility of the dollar into gold. It also introduced its New Economic Policy by imposing a temporary surcharge of 10 per cent on imports. 'My basic approach', said the Secretary of the Treasury, 'is that the foreigners are out to screw us. Our job is to screw them first.' Even more striking was a 90-day freeze on prices and wages to control inflation, since such controls were normally anathema to economic conservatives. They revealed the extent of Nixon's alarm over the economy, but there were political reasons for them too. They were designed to keep down prices as the president sought re-election.

By November 1972 there was little doubt that Nixon would be re-elected. His foreign policy coups in Peking and Moscow (discussed in Chapter 18) were followed by the announcement of a breakthrough in the peace talks over Vietnam just before the election. More critically, the tide of domestic politics had turned in his favour, particularly when the Democratic Party nominated George McGovern for president. A powerful critic of American policy in Vietnam, McGovern was the candidate of Democratic insurgents who reviled the legacy of Lyndon Johnson and who had mastered the new party rules requiring more egalitarian procedures. The Democratic platform in 1972, adopted by a convention bereft of the old machine bosses and containing unprecedented numbers of black, female and young delegates, called for an 'equitable distribution of wealth and power', improved welfare rights, school bussing, prisoners' rights and even 'the right to be different'. Even the AFL-CIO repudiated McGovern, the first time in twenty years it had not backed the Democratic nominee. The 'new politics' associated with the Democratic left held little appeal for what Nixon in November 1969 had dubbed 'the silent majority' of the American people. His aide Charles Colson reportedly told him that 'The key voter blocs to go after are Catholics, organized labor and the racists'. After George Wallace had decided against a third-party bid in favour of seeking the Democratic nomination (and was in any case crippled by a gunman in May 1972), Nixon could be sure that his potential voters would not be hijacked.

The electorate was being given the opportunity to repudiate not so much the Democratic Party as the radical political styles that had emerged from the 1960s. The misfortune of the McGovern campaign was its association with the long-haired lifestyle of the counter-culture. Keen to get out of Vietnam and prepared to extend amnesty to draft dodgers, George McGovern's position was inaccurately caricatured as 'acid, amnesty, and abortion'. Richard Nixon may not have been a doctrinaire conservative, but he was at one with the greater part of the electorate in upholding traditional lifestyle values and discountenancing surrender in Vietnam. He secured re-election with 60 per cent of the popular vote. As usual the Democrats retained the control of both houses of Congress, the election again suggesting that presidential politics had become separated from congressional politics.

After the frustrations of his first term, and buoyed by his resounding victory, the re-elected Nixon was ready to move to the right. 'Abroad and at home,' he said in his second inaugural address, 'the time has come to turn away from the condescending politics of paternalism – of "Washington knows best".' He even essayed an awkward counter-echo of Kennedy: 'In our own lives, let each of us ask – not just what will government do for me, but what can I do for myself?' Soon after, his administration announced its intention to slash government spending and end over a hundred Great Society programmes; the OEO itself was finally axed. In 1973 what remained of Lyndon Johnson's Model Cities programme was devolved to the states. Nixon also attempted to further his consolidation of authority in the White House. He asked all non-career employees in the executive branch, including cabinet members, to submit their resignations, and tried to restrict appointments to those personally loyal to him. He hoped that a number of 'Supersecretaries' operating from within the White House would take responsibility for groups of domestic agencies. He was moving towards a model of corporate management, but by the spring of 1973 his administration was in crisis and his bureaucratic reforms could not be sustained.

Whatever plans Richard Nixon may have had for his second term were destroyed by the Watergate débâcle. Employees of the Nixon re-election campaign had broken into Democratic Party headquarters in June 1972 and had been surprised by the police. The break-in had little effect on the 1972 election since the White House was able to profess its innocence, but as journalists and congressional committees probed the affair the presidential office embarked on a series of manoeuvres designed to protect the president. Whether or not he had endorsed the burglary, Nixon's subsequent actions implicated him in the 'cover-up', that is a criminal conspiracy to obstruct the course of justice, or what Daniel Ellsberg characterized as 'a slow coup against the U.S. Constitution'. Nixon was in the habit of secretly recording what was said in the Oval Office, and when these recordings were forced into the public domain the White House's participation in the cover-up and the foul language of the president were exposed, along with circumstantial evidence that he had tampered with the tapes. Among the agents of Nixon's downfall was Judge John J. Sirica (an appointment to the federal bench that Nixon had approved because of his reputation as a 'law and order' judge), whose tough handling of the burglars had forced them to talk, and also the Supreme Court, with its four Nixon nominees, which had insisted that he hand over the tapes. Threatened with impeachment by a hostile Congress, in August 1974 Richard Nixon became the only American president ever to resign his post.

Watergate was a major constitutional crisis, and Nixon became the second president in six years to be forced out of office, a mark of the new insecurity of the presidency. The illegal behaviour of the Nixon White House, and the clandestine and often illegal activities on the part of the CIA and the FBI that came to light, further damaged the reputation of government. Over fifty people were convicted of offences related to Watergate, including several members of the cabinet and the White House staff. The American electorate was already losing its respect for politicians; the various exposures associated with the Nixon presidency reduced public confidence to a new low. A public opinion poll of 1975 found that only 13 per cent expressed 'great confidence' in the executive branch of government.

Late in 1973 Spiro Agnew had resigned from the vice-presidency following the exposure of financial misdeeds earlier in his career, and Nixon had appointed Gerald Ford, the Republican minority leader in the House of

Representatives, in his place. When Nixon in turn resigned, the unelected Ford was precipitated into the White House. For a couple of years Gerald Ford headed a weak caretaker government, still suffering from the fallout of Watergate and the consequent unpopularity of the Republicans. Taking office in a crisis, Ford moved cautiously, appointing moderates, reducing the trappings of the 'imperial presidency', and signalling his willingness to listen to Congress. He tried to heal a wound inflicted by the Vietnam War by offering a conditional amnesty to draft evaders and deserters. More controversial was his fateful decision to issue a pardon to Richard Nixon for any crimes he may have committed. Ford hoped that the pardon would end the media obsession with the fate of the former president, but in the event it proved massively unpopular, Ford's own public standing plummeted and his administration was crippled.

The Watergate affair also encouraged other congressional probes into the behaviour of executive agencies. It was discovered that since the 1950s the FBI had conducted over 200 'black bag jobs' (or illegal break-ins) against domestic targets. The FBI's campaigns against the New Left, Martin Luther King and the Black Panthers were exposed. The CIA too was investigated in 1975; it soon appeared that it had not only implicated the Mafia in plots to assassinate Fidel Castro but had also spied on thousands of American citizens.

The Ford administration also reeled under the early effects of the 'oil shock'. Since late 1973, in the wake of the Yom Kippur War, the Arab countries had stopped supplying oil to the United States, and early in 1974 OPEC quadrupled its prices. An instinctive conservative, Ford's reaction was to curb federal expenditure. High interest rates and price rises dampened the economy and unemployment grew. The development of the worst recession since the 1930s further damaged the standing of the Republican Party, whose candidates fared unusually badly in the mid-term elections of 1974. Thereafter cooperation between White House and Congress grew yet more difficult as Ford faced huge Democratic majorities on Capitol Hill. Like Nixon before him, Ford felt obliged to make frequent use of his veto, resorting to it more often than any other modern president.

Traditionally conservative and personally amiable, Ford was chosen by his party to remain as presidential candidate for 1976, but he was seriously challenged by California's Ronald Reagan, the favourite of the Republican right, who also benefited from the fact that he was untainted by the misdeeds of Washington. Such was the insurgency that Ford was obliged to allow the Reagan wing largely to write the Republican platform. Without Watergate perhaps the conservative currents in the country would have taken the Republicans to another victory in 1976, but damaging too was the economic depression, which prompted a somewhat paler version of the New Deal voter coalition to line up once more behind the Democrats.

Victory went to the Democrats' Jimmy Carter, who also had the advantage of not being identified with Washington. Popular disaffection with the political establishment played into the hands of the former governor of

Georgia, who had never held federal office and who had spent much of his life developing a career outside politics. The rule changes following the Democratic calamity of 1968 had shifted power away from party chieftains and made primaries the principal route to the presidential nomination, opening the process to populist currents. Carter's success in the Democratic primaries owed something to his outsider status, as did his narrow victory in November. He promised to clean up the 'mess' in Washington, a stance that did not endear him to members of Congress. Like Andrew Jackson in 1828, Carter was elected as a kind of public reproof to the Washington establishment.

Jimmy Carter represented no revival of New Deal liberalism. 'I was a southerner, a born-again Christian, a Baptist, a newcomer', remembered Carter later. These rather righteous qualities led him at first to embrace policies that he thought were 'the right thing', but Congress did not prove particularly amenable to such reasoning and, in time, calculated political prudence assumed a larger role. Carter also had a background as an engineer and he valued expertise and administrative competence over political wheeler-dealing. Unlike liberals of the New Deal tradition, he was a fiscal conservative, although he claimed to be liberal on social issues. 'I would consider myself quite liberal on environmental quality, on human rights, civil rights, the race question,' he told a journalist: 'I would consider myself quite conservative on strengthening local government, on balancing the budget, on … businesslike management of government.' If reluctant to spend money, he made constructive use of his powers of appointment, naming many more African-Americans, Hispanics and women as federal judges than had all previous presidents combined.

Disenchantment with the Great Society, the massive rejection of the radical Democratic platform of 1972, and the fashionable nostrums of neoconservatism had had their effect on the Democratic Party. Carter's pollster, Patrick Cadell, dismissed such Democratic notables as Edward Kennedy and George McGovern as 'traditional Democrats … in many ways … as antiquated and anachronistic a group as are conservative Republicans'. Aide Jody Powell later explained that the New Deal coalition 'was no longer a winning coalition in and of itself', and that Carter needed also to reach those who had escaped to the suburbs and elsewhere. During the campaign Carter had promised to cut the number of governmental agencies from 1900 to 200, and as president he at least consolidated some of them. He also looked to community self-help as a means of reducing poverty. 'Government cannot solve our problems …' said Carter in his second annual address to Congress, sounding rather like Richard Nixon: 'It cannot eliminate poverty, or provide a bountiful economy, or reduce inflation, or save the cities, or cure illiteracy, or provide energy.'

Nonetheless Jimmy Carter did try to seize the initiative on energy, a serious political issue through the industrial world since the 1973 Arab oil embargo. In the United States energy prices were artificially low, thanks partly to the federal regulation of domestic oil and natural gas prices, but politicians shrank from the logical solution of sharply raising costs to consumers. Carter called for a 'comprehensive long-range energy policy', warning that the energy problem was the 'moral equivalent of war'. (Unhappily the resulting acronym was MEOW.) Recognizing an obligation to future generations, he wanted to increase conservation and encourage alternative energy development by raising the prices of non-renewable resources like oil. The bill that he presented to Congress in 1977 included taxes on petrol and crude oil and a tax on cars with high fuel consumption. Carter sought to make it palatable not only by emphasizing its conservation clauses but also by distributing costs between producers and consumers and passing some of the revenues generated back to the public via tax credits. But quarrelsome Senate committees delayed the bill and amendments largely removed the proposed taxes so central to its strategy; the National Energy Act of 1978 at least required the phased deregulation of natural gas prices.

Energy-related measures remained difficult to achieve, and following the overthrow of the Shah of Persia in 1978–9 another world oil shortage precipitated steep oil price rises. As long lines formed at filling stations and inflation took another leap, a demoralized president called a series of highly publicized meetings with leading and representative Americans in July 1979; in a televised speech he spoke of the 'malaise' which gripped the nation. He also proposed another energy programme aimed at discouraging the consumption of oil by allowing prices to rise and encouraging the further exploration of energy sources. Some of Carter's proposals, including a windfall profits tax on domestic oil production, were enacted in 1980.

Jimmy Carter also elevated the status of environmental policy, responding not so much to an old New Deal agenda but to new liberal concerns that had emerged in the 1960s, the loose-knit movement aiming at the preservation of the wilderness, the protection of human health and the conservation of natural resources. Carter's ambitious plans, however, again encountered resistance from special interests in Congress, and his growing preoccupation with inflation and the energy crisis diluted his enthusiasm for environmental regulation. But he did not abandon the cause, and some of his major accomplishments came after his electoral defeat in November 1980. In December he signed a bill preserving one-third of Alaska (a huge area) as a wilderness reserve protected from commercial exploitation and another bill creating a 'superfund' to clean up toxic waste sites. While the Carter administration disappointed the more ardent conservationists, it did bequeath a raft of regulatory controls that exasperated the incoming Republicans.

If Carter was willing to extend the regulatory state in protecting the environment, on the faltering economy he aligned himself with those seeking deregulation. Anxious to revitalize business by promoting market competition, he took the initiative in the deregulation of large swathes of industry and commerce, saying in 1980 that his proudest achievement was ending 'government regulations to put free enterprise back into airlines, the trucking and the financial system of our country'. One reason for his relative success in deregulation was that it could often be achieved via executive action. Reform requiring the cooperation of a fractious Congress proved elusive for an administration that had little taste for log-rolling politics.

Above all it was the intractable economic problems that weighed down the Carter administration. When it took office growth was flagging and unemployment high and yet, in defiance of Keynesian assumptions, prices were rising, creating the unprecedented condition of 'stagflation'. Carter found it difficult to steer a clear course in economic policy. After an uncertain start, when he had offered some public works programmes, he concluded that inflation was the most serious problem, and it was indeed accelerating at an unnerving rate. Between 1975 and 1979 the consumer price index shot up from 161 to 217, while the productivity rate actually fell between 1977 and 1980. Carter's more liberal advisers wanted to increase government spending, but that would only intensify the inflationary spiral while exacerbating a deficit that was thought to contribute to price instability. Carter soon dismayed Democratic members of Congress by his insistence on budget restraint. The budget that he proposed in 1978 included a lower increase in government spending than any the prudent Ford had offered. In his 1979 submission Carter called for reduced domestic spending in real terms, but world oil prices shot up again in that year, prompting the president to urge yet further cuts in social services, even as he wanted to increase defence spending. The New Deal wing of the party was appalled by the sight of a Democratic president taking a knife to school lunches and food stamps. 'Long before the Reaganites entered the White House', Bruce J. Schulman has written, 'the Carter administration had already rejected the neo-Keynesian orthodoxy that had governed economic policy making in the United States for a generation and was slouching toward a new one, toward monetarism and supply-side economics.'

The president had failed to devise an effective anti-inflation programme. Rapid inflation intensified grass-roots resentments of taxation and government. In California house price inflation stirred voters in 1978 to approve Proposition 13, requiring a slashing reduction in local property taxes (the state having built up a substantial surplus because of the rising prices). Proposition 13 became a powerful symbol of the anti-tax movement, and the revolt spread to other states over the next two years (and encouraged the major parties, especially the Republican, to weigh the appeal of a tax-cutting agenda). The inflation rate reached 13 per cent in 1980, unemployment rose, and with the Federal Reserve Board adopting a monetarist approach, the prime rate (interest rate) reached 20 per cent. These were disastrous figures with which to go to the electorate, but Carter declined to return to the full employment policies of previous Democratic presidents. Despite voter restiveness over taxes, a tax cut was ruled out while various social programmes were targeted for reductions. As it happened, the election was overshadowed by the hostage crisis in Iran. In November 1979

Islamic students had occupied the US Embassy in Tehran and held fifty-three diplomatic staff hostage. An attempt to rescue them ended in a tragic fiasco, and prolonged diplomatic negotiations eroded public confidence in the administration. The hostages were not released until President Carter's successor was taking the oath of office.

While Jimmy Carter attempted to steer the Democratic Party away from its big spending past, New Deal Democrats had not disappeared. Carter's fiscal caution provoked a revolt among the old guard and Edward Kennedy emerged as a contender for the 1980 Democratic nomination, committed to a Keynesian programme. In the event Kennedy could not amass enough convention votes to displace an incumbent president, but his insurgency underlined the discontent within the party. The president allowed the liberals to write a large part of the 1980 Democratic platform, which included a hefty $12 billion job-creation programme. But the dispiriting aura of failure that surrounded the Carter presidency, the aggravating hostage crisis and the rejuvenated Republican Party rallying around the personable Ronald Reagan doomed Carter to defeat.

Ronald Reagan could be said to personify the changing course of American politics since the New Deal era. As a young man he had voted four times for Franklin Roosevelt. His shoe salesman father, after all, was an Irish Catholic and a Democrat. Graduating from college in 1932, Reagan found a position as a sports announcer for a small Iowa radio station. At ease in the world of sportscasting, he took his communication skills to Hollywood and established himself as a competent actor. During the war, unable to serve because of defective sight, he acted in a number of army morale films, some of the scenes of which were to condition his memory of the 'real' war. He became president of the Screen Actors Guild in 1947, developing considerable experience as a labour leader and a suspicion of Communist machinations in local union politics. Still a Democrat, he made his knowledge of the Hollywood community, with its left-wing activists, available to the FBI. From the mid-1950s he switched his energy to television as host of a prime-time programme, CBS's General Electric Theater. He also toured General Electric's plants in morale-boosting visits and addressed local chambers of commerce. As he honed his communication skills and completed his transition from union to corporate spokesman, he also moved politically to the right. A Democrat for Eisenhower in the 1950s, he registered as a Republican in 1962 and gave a celebrated television address for Goldwater in the 1964 campaign.

In 1966, aided by a group of wealthy businessmen, Ronald Reagan became the Republican candidate for governor of California, pitted against the formidable incumbent, Pat Brown, a Democrat of the old school. But Brown was no match for the telegenic actor. An incalculable Reagan strength was that while his political philosophy was distinctly right wing by the standards of the day, as a person he seemed amiable and humane. Where the rather strident Barry Goldwater had frightened many voters in 1964, Reagan radiated reassurance. In 1966 too he was able to take advantage of the first flickers of discontent with the New Deal style of politics. In the election he swept into the governor's mansion with an impressive fifteen-point lead. This spectacular victory made Reagan a major political figure, and he used the media attention to further his rhetorical campaign against big government, high taxes and sixties-style permissiveness. To Reagan old-fashioned individual endeavour had been the rock on which the country had been built, and he constantly insisted on the superiority of private enterprise over public provision. In his eight years as governor his policies proved more moderate than his rhetoric, partly because of the necessity of compromising with a Democratic legislature, but a coherent conservative vision informed his governance.

'Are you better off than you were four years ago?' Ronald Reagan asked the television audience as he went head to head with Jimmy Carter in the 1980 campaign. Reagan won the election with 51 per cent of the popular vote, ten points ahead of Carter. (A third-party candidate, independent Republican John B. Anderson, took most of the remainder.) The Republicans also fared well in the congressional elections, winning a majority in the Senate for the first time since 1952 and reducing the Democratic majority in the House. The only group to vote as heavily for Carter in 1980 as it had in 1976 were African-Americans. Among the other traditional Democratic constituencies – Catholics, Jews, Hispanics, union members, low-income earners – there were significant defections from the Democratic column, although in some cases Anderson benefited more than Reagan. Reagan's rhetoric identified him primarily with an unreconstructed Republicanism, with its faith in unbridled capitalism, that had seemed to go out of fashion with the New Deal. But the one-time film star was also the beneficiary of the religious right, which approved his pro-family platform. He thus became the first divorced man to be elected president, ironically defeating the impeccable family man and born-again Carter. Reagan could be said to be doubly a beneficiary of the sixties – more permissive values made possible the election of a divorced candidate, even as that candidate benefited from the backlash against permissiveness.

On gaining the presidency in 1968 Richard Nixon had hoped to build a new Republican majority with his blend of economic liberalism and cultural conservatism, a party of the middle class rather than big business. His administration was blown apart by Watergate, which made possible a Democratic comeback in 1976, but the liberal persuasion did suffer in these years. Nixon's crushing re-election in 1972 had left liberals and radicals deeply demoralized, and in a sense the liberal project divided into its component parts, surviving as the discrete movements of feminism, environmentalism, public interest group activity and so on. Many activists preferred to operate in interest groups bringing pressure to bear on government (including the courts) rather than as elements of a party alliance after the fashion of the New Deal coalition. It was left to the right to articulate a broad (if somewhat discordant) vision for the future, aided by the continuing reaction against big government during the economic travails of the 1970s. On the foreign front too the détente policies favoured by moderate Republicans and Democrats were being subjected to increasing criticism by Cold War hardliners in both major parties. This revitalized conservatism, combining a rediscovered faith in free enterprise with a religious rejection of modern permissiveness, placed a confident Ronald Reagan in the White House. Yet its triumph was not quite complete. The Democratic majority in the House of Representatives suggested that voters were not overly eager to forgo the benefits that the New Deal system had afforded them. Conservatives were now setting the agenda but government remained divided.

|18|

The United States and the World
1969–2000

By the end of the 1960s it was becoming evident that the United States could no longer dominate world affairs in the manner that it might have hoped in 1945. The American economy was beginning to lose its miraculous lustre, Vietnam was fatally undermining American self-confidence and the world at large was becoming a more complicated place. The Soviet economy had been relatively buoyant in the 1960s and the Soviet Union was closing the missile gap. China too was a nuclear power. Elsewhere, the growth of the European Economic Community promised greater political independence for Western Europe, Japan had become a major economic power and new nations had emerged in Africa and Asia. John Kennedy himself had begun to question bipolar assumptions and by 1969, as discord over Vietnam legitimized opposition to Cold War strategies, the need to adapt American foreign policy both to the limits of American resources and to multi-polar realities was becoming inescapable.

There was no likelihood of a return to isolationism. For one thing, American presidents, often unable to accomplish much on the stalemated home front, were tempted to try to build reputations instead as world statesmen. One adviser to several of them reckoned that normally they spent about 60 per cent of their time on foreign policy. But Vietnam cast a long shadow and in the final third of the twentieth century Americans were once more wary of foreign entanglements. The United States wanted to exercise power in the world, but not in a way that occasioned serious American casualties. Military interventions did take place, but tended to be either severely circumscribed in scope – as in the Reagan administration's invasion of the tiny island of Grenada – or else characterized by overwhelming force – as in the 1990–1 Persian Gulf War. Further, the consensus over how to conduct the Cold War had vanished, as some Americans urged a measure of accommodation with the Communist bloc and others advocated military strength and vigilant resistance to Soviet wiles. In 1989–91, however, the Soviet empire spectacularly imploded, allowing the United States to claim 'victory' in the Cold War. The United States was left as the only superpower, but in a world that seemed dangerously fragile without the sobering discipline of East–West confrontation.

The awareness of limits that now conditioned American foreign policy was partly rooted in economic constraints. The United States remained an economic giant, but its relative stature was eroding. In 1945 it had produced about half of the world's output; by the early 1990s its share of global production was little more than a fifth. The vulnerability of the American economy had been exposed in the early 1970s, when ferocious speculation against the dollar had obliged Richard Nixon to end its convertibility into gold. The Bretton Woods system, which had structured the post-war international monetary system, was dead. Yet even as its share in the world economy declined, the United States became more deeply entangled in it (not least in its increasing dependence on foreign oil). In 1970 the dollar value of exports (in 1996 dollars) had represented just under 4.5 per cent of GDP; by 1996 the figure had more than doubled to 11.2 per cent, and the overseas activities of American multinationals took the United States yet further into the global economy. In the mid-twentieth century the United States had possessed one of the most self-sufficient economies in the world, but before the century was over it was the largest exporter. The ending of the Cold War raised the prospect of economic considerations no longer being subordinate to military in the international conduct of the United States. Perhaps too there would be more room for humanitarian action.

Richard Nixon took office in 1969 with ambitious thoughts of restructuring foreign policy, and his interest in achieving a new global equilibrium was shared by his National Security Adviser Henry Kissinger. Some kind of easing of relationships with the Communist world would be a major coup for a Republican president. But Nixon had also promised 'peace with honor' in Vietnam, and he desperately needed to disentangle the United States from that imbroglio. He remained a Cold Warrior, but concluded that the way forward was to establish more stable relations with the major powers, which in turn could be expected to control their smaller client states. Cooperation rather than confrontation with the Soviet Union and China would maintain the balance of power and contain aggression. In 1969 the president also announced the Nixon Doctrine, giving notice that in future the United States would help threatened countries with economic and military aid but would not send combat troops. Détente, as the various theories being developed by Nixon and Kissinger became known in the 1970s, might also facilitate withdrawal from Vietnam.

Extricating the country from Vietnam proved frustratingly difficult. 'Peace with honor' seemed to mean that the United States would somehow have to withdraw without being seen to have surrendered, and this in turn meant the survival of the South Vietnam government. Nixon was no more anxious than Lyndon Johnson to be the first president to lose a war, and, in the words of Henry Kissinger, 'we could not simply walk away from an enterprise involving two administrations, five allied countries, and thirty-one thousand dead as if we were switching a television channel'. The strategy settled on was 'Vietnamization'. American soldiers were to be progressively withdrawn and the South Vietnam government forces substantially strengthened, so that Asian boys would once more become the combat troops. But Vietnamization proved disappointingly slow to effect, although the South Vietnamese armed forces were massively enlarged at American expense.

In 1971 Richard Nixon announced that he would visit the People's Republic of China, the very power that was said to be behind the North Vietnamese (although by this date they were growing closer to the Soviet Union). Since 1949 the United States had treated China as a pariah state, denying it diplomatic recognition and trading relations. Nixon's old anti-communist credentials helped to protect him from attacks from the right, while the increasingly acrimonious split between the Soviet Union and China opened an opportunity. In February 1972, as the presidential election campaign was looming, Nixon became the first American president to visit China, an occasion lavishly covered by the media. In his talks with Chinese leaders Nixon agreed to reduce US military forces in Taiwan when possible, and the two sides settled on a series of economic and cultural exchanges. Richard Nixon had won a stunning diplomatic victory, achieving rapprochement with a major enemy.

Withdrawal from Vietnam might also require Soviet help, and three months after winning his accord with China Richard Nixon visited Moscow. His objective was détente and a desire to drive a wedge between the two main components of the Communist bloc. Again the Republican president secured agreements, telling the Soviet premier Leonid Brezhnev that capitalism and communism could 'live together and work together'. The Soviet Union had its own reasons for seeking better relations, not least its fear of a nuclear China. One result was the Strategic Arms Limitation Treaty (SALT), limiting the numbers of offensive intercontinental ballistic missiles maintained by the two powers; their defensive antiballistic missile systems were also to be limited. Where Kennedy and Johnson had sought nuclear superiority over the Soviet Union, Nixon was prepared to settle for 'sufficiency' or parity (or so he said as he continued to add to his stock of nuclear warheads).

But communism was to be contained, not comforted, and it was not to be tolerated just anywhere. When the socialist Salvador Allende sought election as president of Chile in 1970, Nixon, anxious to avert another Cuba, cut off aid to the country. 'I don't see why we have to let a country go Marxist just because its people are irresponsible', Henry Kissinger is reported to have observed. Allende's election was not averted, but the CIA worked for his overthrow and this was effected via a military coup in September 1973. Allende died, reportedly committing suicide.

As it happened the policies of détente proved of little use in disengaging the United States from Vietnam. After two years of 'Vietnamization' US forces in the country had been reduced only by about half. The peace negotiations dragged on dispiritingly too, despite massive bombing campaigns launched by the president to weaken North Vietnamese resolve. Nixon also took the war into Cambodia, through which the North Vietnamese had supplied their forces in the South. Following the secret bombing of Viet Cong sanctuaries there in 1969, in April 1970 he announced an invasion of Cambodia by US and South Vietnamese forces. This extension of the war into another country triggered enormous protests in the United States, particularly on the campuses, and at one, Kent State, four students were killed when the Ohio National Guard opened fire. Congress finally acted to restrain presidential power, prohibiting the return of American forces to Cambodia. And still the peace process dragged on until, in October 1972 (with the presidential election imminent), Kissinger was able to announce that 'peace is at hand'. Finally in January 1973, after another massive bombing campaign against Hanoi, Nixon achieved his 'peace with honor'. American forces were withdrawn and two years later the weak government left in South Vietnam succumbed to the Communists.

The Vietnam War was the only war that the United States palpably lost, and the consequences were to reverberate through the rest of the century. The war deeply divided American society and destroyed the post-war consensus on the American role in the world. While some drew the lesson that the United States' Cold War preconceptions had misled it into seeing a threat to its interests where none existed, others complained that American politicians had been too grudging in providing the military with the weapons needed to win. If some drew the conclusion that foreign interventions were best avoided, others thirsted for a restoration of American pride in the world. The war had also done much to destroy Lyndon Johnson's cherished Great Society, and it intensified the inflation that roared through the economy in the 1970s. It added to the perception that governments enjoyed little power to control either domestic or foreign affairs.

The mortification in Vietnam was one reason for Nixon's search for a new global equilibrium, but almost from the beginning the promise of détente was being undermined by growing instability in other parts of the Third World. Tensions had remained high in the Middle East in the aftermath of the 1967 Six Day War, when Israel had seized extensive land. Refusing to yield Jordan's Left Bank and its other acquisitions, Israel insisted that its security depended on the continued occupation and even settlement of the territories. Also subject to Israeli rule were the Palestinians living in the West Bank and Gaza Strip, whose cause was vociferously upheld by the Palestine Liberation Organization under Yasir Arafat. War broke out again in October 1973 (the 'Yom Kippur War'), when Egypt from the west and Syria from the north launched simultaneous attacks on Israel. After initial losses Israel saw off its assailants, aided by military equipment rushed by the United States. The crisis also jolted the world back to the darkest days of the Cold War. Egypt and Syria had been provided with military supplies by the Soviet Union. American–Soviet relations quickly deteriorated when the Soviet Union threatened to intervene in the war, and the United States ordered its forces across the world on a stage 3 alert, the first nuclear alert since the Cuban missile crisis.

The Arab states retorted to the American favour accorded to Israel by imposing an oil embargo on the United States and the European countries that had supported the Israelis. This was to have momentous consequences. As OPEC (Organization of Petroleum-Exporting Countries) discovered its muscles and cut production in 1973–4, oil prices quadrupled. Powerful inflationary pressures washed across world markets, and the economies of the United States, Western Europe and Japan were shaken. The United States had long ceased to be self-supporting in terms of oil and a major gap in its armour was suddenly exposed. The most powerful nation on earth could be held hostage, it seemed, by a few Arab countries.

But the quadrupling of oil prices did more than draw attention yet again to American economic vulnerability. Since the Second World War there had been relatively steady growth in the global and especially the Western economy, a true 'golden age' as historian Eric Hobsbawm called it, made possible in part by the supply of cheap oil from Saudi Arabia and the Gulf States. The golden age disappeared with the oil crisis. Global economic growth slowed in the last third of the twentieth century, a circumstance that exacerbated political instability in many parts of the world.

By the mid-1970s the policy of détente was also being mocked by the indirect confrontations of the superpowers on the troubled African continent. The Nixon administration had shown more interest in strengthening relations with South Africa, a rich country with a white government, and with the Portuguese and their strategically located colonies of Angola and Mozambique, than with the new governments of black Africa. A revolution in Portugal in 1974 opened the way to the freeing of its African possessions. In Angola, where three main factions vied for supremacy, an array of outside powers, among them the Soviet Union, Cuba, South Africa and the United States, became implicated in these struggles. With the eruption of civil war there in 1975 the CIA directed covert aid to its favoured faction, but American intrigue was frustrated when the People's Movement for the Liberation of Angola established a government with the help of Soviet-financed Cuban troops. Also unwelcome to the White House was the success of the left-wing Frelimo movement in securing internal self-government for Mozambique in 1974 and independence in 1975.

Yet attempts at détente continued under the Ford administration (in which Kissinger remained as Secretary of State). Kissinger reached agreement with the Soviet premier in November 1974 to place limits on the number of strategic weapons possessed by each power, that is on bombers and nuclear missiles. In 1975 the Ford administration and the representatives of thirty-four other nations signed the European Security Treaty in Helsinki, recognizing the post-war boundaries established by the Soviet bloc, and recognizing too the right of peoples to enjoy human freedoms.

But many foreign policy experts were losing confidence in détente. Both major parties were split on foreign policy, with right-wing Republicans coming to loathe détente as personified by Henry Kissinger, and Democrats dividing between liberals scalded by Vietnam and Cold Warriors drawn to anti-communist neo-conservatism. In 1976 fierce attacks were mounted at the Republican presidential convention on the foreign policy of the Ford administration. In the same year the Committee on the Present Danger was formed, in part by officials of earlier Democratic administrations, arguing that the Soviet Union was still aiming at world domination, as evidenced by its expanding military capacity and succour of anti-American movements wherever they emerged. The CPD considered it essential for the United States to build up its own forces and to resist Soviet machinations in unstable Third World countries. In 1980 it would lend its resources to the presidential campaign of Ronald Reagan.

Nonetheless the Carter administration clung wearily to the policy of détente. Like Nixon, Jimmy Carter was wary of the United States assuming too much international responsibility, arguing that the 'time for American intervention in all the problems of the world is over'. In 1977 he claimed that the United States had freed itself of that 'inordinate fear of communism' which had led it to embrace right-wing dictators, seeming to promise a more nuanced approach to foreign problems. The protection of human rights, he insisted, should be 'the soul of our foreign policy'. This seemed to mean encouraging right-wing dictatorships and the Communist regimes to respect the rights of their citizens, and occasioned friction with the Soviet Union when Carter criticized its treatment of its dissidents. But the administration persisted with the SALT II negotiations and reached agreement with the Soviets in June 1979. The subsequent Soviet invasion of Afghanistan, however, turned American opinion strongly against the treaty and doomed it in the Senate.

But Jimmy Carter did correct what some saw as a historic wrong. The US control of the Canal Zone across Panama had always been of questionable propriety. American presidents from Lyndon Johnson onward had recognized that it was but a matter of time before the United States yielded control, but it was Jimmy Carter who courted unpopularity by pushing a revised treaty through the Senate in 1978. Ronald Reagan, wooing the New Right that was revitalizing the Republican Party, damned the move as 'appeasement'. One strand of opinion was illustrated by California Senator H. I. Hayakawa, a conservative Republican, who at first claimed that 'we stole' the canal 'fair and square', but who eventually bowed to reality and voted for ceding it.

Carter also turned his considerable diplomatic energies to the Middle East. In 1977 President Anwar Sadat of Egypt embarked on direct negotiations with Israel, hoping to reach an Egyptian–Israeli accord. But the sticking point was the West Bank territories taken by Israel from Jordan in 1967. In September 1978 the president invited Sadat and Menachem Begin, prime minister of Israel, to Camp David to work out an agreement. Accord could not be reached on all issues, but the Carter initiative eventually led to the signing of the first Arab–Israeli peace treaty in March 1979. Under it, normal diplomatic and trade relations were established between Israel and Egypt, and

Israel was to withdraw from the Sinai Peninsula by 1982. The West Bank issue was not resolved and continued to be a major source of discord in the Middle East.

Jimmy Carter won considerable plaudits for the Camp David Accords, but his administration ended with major foreign crises. Its attempts to improve relations with the Soviet Union received a stunning blow with the Soviet invasion of Afghanistan. A Moslem country, Afghanistan had been ruled by a neutralist government respectful of its Soviet neighbour, but in 1978 a Communist faction seized power in a coup supported by the Soviets. The subsequent unrest threatened to tear the country apart, and in December 1979 the Soviet Union sent troops into Afghanistan and installed a new regime. This military invasion provoked widespread condemnation in the United States and aroused fears of Soviet incursions into the Persian Gulf, with its rich oil resources. Any attempt to gain control of that region, the president warned sombrely, would be 'repelled by any means necessary, including military force'. The Soviet Union was soon at war with Islamic Afghan guerrillas, who received surreptitious aid from the United States.

Carter's reputation suffered even more as a result of events in Iran. The Shah had been a close ally of the United States but also headed an absolutist regime. In deference to Carter's preoccupation with human rights, he tried to lighten his treatment of dissidents in 1977, but the opposition could not be contained. Strikes and riots inspired by fundamentalist Moslem clerics proliferated, and by the autumn of 1978 the country was close to anarchy. The Shah fled, and early in 1979 the Ayatollah Khomeini became the effective leader of a revolutionary regime. The troubles in Iran slashed its oil production, and the renewed shortage doubled the price of oil on world markets and added to the inflationary pressures in the capitalist economies. In October 1979 Carter agreed to admit the Shah to the United States for cancer treatment. There were angry anti-American demonstrations in Iran, and in November the US Embassy in Tehran was invaded by hundreds of Islamic 'students', who proceeded to hold about eighty American occupants hostage (some black and female hostages were subsequently released). The most powerful nation on earth found itself helpless in the face of a bunch of foreign students, who nightly tormented American television audiences by abusing the hostages or burning the US flag.

As the months ticked by and as a presidential election loomed, Carter found himself under intense pressure to attempt some kind of military action. In April 1980 he attempted to free the hostages with a surprise rescue mission using helicopter gunships. But the helicopters never reached their destination. A dust storm disabled some of them and another went up in flames after a collision. News pictures of the burnt corpses publicly underlined the failure of the mission. The hostages remained confined in the embassy and negotiations stuttered on. They were eventually concluded successfully on the last day of Carter's term, by which time he had lost the presidential election.

The failure of the Carter administration to contain what was perceived as Soviet adventurism in Angola, Ethiopia and Central America, and its helplessness in the face of the Soviet invasion of Afghanistan, completed the discrediting of the policy of détente. 'So far, détente's been a one-way street the Soviet Union has used to pursue its own aims', said President Ronald Reagan in signalling a new direction for American policy. A renewed anti-communism was to be accompanied by massive defence spending. Reagan's stance was underlined by his foreign policy appointments. The secretary of state was Alexander Haig, a former NATO commander, whose offer to reduce Cuba to 'a fucking parking lot' apparently disturbed even the president. As ambassador to the UN, Reagan appointed Jeane Kirkpatrick, one of those Democrats who had switched allegiance as their party seemed to lose its empathy with Middle America. She had publicly argued for a distinction between 'authoritarian' (mostly right-wing) regimes, which might evolve in a democratic fashion and which the United States might support, and 'totalitarian' (mostly Communist) regimes, in which there was little hope of nurturing the seeds of freedom. Such theories accorded with Reagan's instincts.

Anti-Soviet rhetoric was a staple of Reagan's early foreign policy. In March 1983 he described the Soviet Union as an 'evil empire', no less than the 'focus of evil in the modern world'. The renewed arms race provoked strong anti-nuclear movements in the United States and Europe. Defence spending increased each year during Reagan's first term, and Reagan capped his vision in 1983 with the announcement of the Strategic Defense Initiative (SDI), otherwise known as Star Wars. This was to be a huge research programme to create a kind of defence shield or umbrella, mounted from space, to ensure that hostile missiles did not reach the United States. This fantastic conception implied a fundamental rethinking of nuclear strategy. Hitherto the superpowers had based their policies on the assumption that a nuclear attack by either would trigger a catastrophic response – 'mutually assured destruction'. Now Reagan promised a space shield which would make nuclear missiles 'impotent and obsolete'. Most scientists seriously doubted whether such a system could work, but the administration pressed ahead with the research.

Soviet–American trade declined as relations between the two superpowers became acrimonious. Their relationship was not helped by events in Poland, where in 1981 the Communist regime was threatened by the Solidarity trade union movement led by Lech Walesa. Under Soviet pressure the Polish government imposed martial law, about which the frustrated Reagan administration discovered that it could do little, although the continued tension in the country allowed Reagan ample opportunity to deploy the provocative rhetoric of freedom.

This rhetoric sat uncomfortably with memories of Vietnam. On the one hand, Reagan wanted to restore American prestige after that experience and after what he saw as the weakness of the détente strategy. But while the Reaganites yearned to see America walk tall again, enough of the Vietnam Syndrome survived to make them wary of committing American military might abroad. Defense Secretary Caspar Weinberger combined tenacious support for a huge escalation in defence spending with a dogged reluctance actually to use military force. Ultimately these contradictions were resolved in what came to be known as the Reagan Doctrine. 'Our mission is to nourish and defend freedom and democracy, and to communicate these ideals everywhere we can ...' said Reagan in 1985, adding that 'Support for freedom fighters is self-defense'. This seemed to mean that while large numbers of troops would not be sent abroad, the United States would support insurgencies against Communist regimes. The CIA, which Carter had made some attempts to rein in, was given its head again under its gung-ho director Bill Casey, who had few reservations about the use of covert action.

One area subject to CIA attention was Latin America, in which the administration espied Soviet meddling. From the late 1970s revolutionary movements in this area, in part the product of deteriorating economies, enjoyed some success. Jeane Kirkpatrick argued that Central America and the Caribbean had become 'the most important place in the world for us', because Soviet interference could disproportionately divert American resources. Under the Reagan Doctrine these countries should not be allowed to become Soviet puppets.

Nicaragua was a particular concern. In 1979 the moribund Somoza dictatorship had collapsed before the revolutionary forces of the Sandinistas, whose new government Jimmy Carter had modestly aided. Within about a year, however, the Sandinista regime under Daniel Ortega established friendly relations with the Soviet Union and admitted Cuban advisers. Ortega was turning Nicaragua into a 'Soviet ally on the American mainland', as Reagan put it, and his overthrow became a priority. The president authorized the CIA to assist Nicaraguan elements who were fighting the government. These Contras, or 'freedom fighters' as Reagan liked to call them, operated in part from Honduras, where they were trained by the CIA. For some years the administration kept its involvement more or less covert, although in 1984 a political storm erupted when it was discovered that the CIA had mined three Nicaraguan harbours, a breach of international law. Even Senator Barry Goldwater, who as chair of the Senate Intelligence Committee had a right to be informed of covert operations, was furious when he discovered the extent of CIA responsibility. 'I've pulled Casey's nuts out of the fire on so many occasions,' he fumed, 'I feel like such a fool.' Congress prohibited further CIA or military aid to the Contras.

Nicaragua was not the only Central American country to warrant attention. Socialist guerrilla activity was continuing in El Salvador, but the supply of CIA and military aid to its government seemed only to provoke a greater rebel offensive. In a confusing situation, in which right-wing military groups used 'death squads' to kill thousands of civilians, the Reagan administration for the most part lent its support to the moderate anti-communist José Duarte. Through the 1980s the United States also provided aid for the military regimes of Guatemala.

The Reagan administration also perceived Soviet influence in Grenada, a small Caribbean island which was part of the British Commonwealth. The reform regime of Maurice Bishop was overthrown in October 1983 by a more militant Marxist faction backed by Cuba. As it happened, the United States was simultaneously humiliated in the Lebanon, powerless as a terrorist explosion killed US marines, but Grenada offered the opportunity to restore American spirits. 'Hey, fuck, let's dump these bastards', advised William Casey. Reagan sent in troops to protect American citizens on the island during the unrest, and to ensure the exclusion of Marxists from a reconstituted regime. Several Latin American governments and NATO allies, including Britain, condemned this outright military invasion, but it secured its objective and the troops were soon withdrawn. Reagan was convinced that he had saved the island from becoming a Soviet base.

In the Middle East Jimmy Carter's Camp David Accords had shifted rather than dispelled tensions. The Lebanon had become a focus of opposing pressures, with its government virtually disintegrating in the face of PLO and Syrian occupations of parts of the country and an Israeli occupation in the South. In 1982 the Israelis tried to vanquish the Palestinian threat with an attack that destroyed the Syrian air force and pushed the PLO out. American marines were despatched to the Lebanon as part of a multinational force to restore order, with little success. Rival militias competed between themselves and with the precarious Lebanese government, and the peacekeeping forces returned after the Christian militia of Lebanon (apparently with Israeli complicity) massacred hundreds of men, women and children at the Palestinian refugee camps of Sabra and Shatila. In April 1983 the US Embassy was bloodily car-bombed. Reagan responded by allowing American ships and planes to use their firepower on behalf of the regime of President Amin Gemayel, thus starkly defining the United States as the enemy of the militia groups. In October a truck careered through the gates of the marine barracks and exploded, taking 241 American lives. Reagan swore that the United States would not 'cut and run', but the marines could not be defended and by April 1984 had been pulled out. The anarchic country became a no-man's-land for Americans and other Westerners, who from time to time were taken hostage by fundamentalist groups.

Like Jimmy Carter before him, Reagan discovered the near helplessness of a superpower when its citizens were taken hostage in hostile territory. The White House made pronouncements about the impossibility of negotiating with terrorists, but secretly it was more pliable – Jimmy Carter after all had lost an election because he had been unable to free hostages. National Security Council officers probed for ways to secure the release of the prisoners, seven Americans being held by Shi'ite groups by 1985. The Shi'ites were closely connected with Iran, an American enemy, but through intermediaries some kind of understanding was reached that a supply of arms to the Iranian regime could secure the release of the hostages. In August 1985 Reagan approved the provision of anti-tank missiles in order to secure the freeing of four hostages, with Israel acting as middleman (Congress having banned arms sales to Iran), but only one American was released. Nonetheless the National Security Office persisted, adding anti-aircraft missiles to the weapons sold to the Iranians. The cornucopia of missiles did little to dislodge the hostages. One was freed in July 1986 but three more were taken prisoner a couple of months later.

By this time the arms-for-hostages initiative had become intertwined with the administration's obsession with Nicaragua. Reagan was still determined to sustain the 'freedom fighters' against what he saw as the Soviet-backed regime of Daniel Ortega. From 1984, when Congress was moving to cut off aid to the Contras, National Security Adviser Robert McFarlane, with his deputy Oliver North and with the president's blessing, had been working to find alternative funds to supply the Contras. McFarlane, his successor John Poindexter, North, and the CIA's Casey, were overseeing both of these covert operations (arms-for-hostages and aiding the Contras), and North realized that surplus funds from the arms sales could be diverted to the Contras. This was done, but in October 1986 a cargo plane carrying arms was shot down over Nicaragua. An American survivor admitted to being part of a CIA-sponsored operation. Somehow, it seemed, the United States was involved in the resupply of the Contras despite the explicit ban by Congress.

The media and Congress demanded an explanation. At the end of November Attorney-General Ed Meese revealed the diversion of Iranian funds to the Contras and a major constitutional crisis erupted. President Reagan flatly denied trading arms for hostages and insisted that he knew nothing of the diversion of funds. His approval rating dropped by over twenty points in a month. North was fired, Poindexter resigned, several investigations were set in train, and something of the secret government within the government was revealed. A joint committee of Congress held televised hearings in the summer of 1987, and while it became clear that administration officials had engaged in illegal actions, destroyed files and lied to Congress, the degree of Reagan's complicity was never fully established, while Oliver North's feisty performance before the committee, playing the part of a wronged patriot, made him something of a folk hero. It seemed that while the American public had no particular wish to see US involvement in Central America, it had some sympathy for efforts to free the hostages in the Lebanon and it more or less trusted the president to do what was right. It could not be conclusively demonstrated that Reagan had wittingly broken the law, and his administration was hurt rather than destroyed by the Iran-Contra affair.

The Reagan administration could have ended in foreign policy disgrace, but in the unlikely event it was the Soviets who rode to the rescue. During his first term, with his anti-Soviet rhetoric and his arms build-up, Reagan's relationship with the Kremlin could hardly have been worse, and he declined to meet a Soviet leader. Yet during his second term Reagan met the Soviet premier on five occasions and the relationship warmed. In part this rapprochement was the product of events in the Soviet Union. In 1985 the premiership was assumed by the relatively young and energetic Mikhail Gorbachev, who was willing to admit the stagnancy of the Soviet economy and the inadequacy of the traditional Soviet method of central planning. The Cold War was haemorrhaging the Soviet economy, and Gorbachev wanted desperately to reduce defence costs and secure greater access to modern technology. His attempts at reform made the Soviet Union more acceptable to Western eyes. By the late 1980s the hardliners of the Reagan administration had mostly left, to be replaced by moderates such as George Shultz as secretary of state and Colin Powell as national security adviser. Less inclined to be deeply suspicious of every Soviet move, the new men around Reagan were reinforced by his wife Nancy, who, assisted by her astrologer, had apparently come to the conclusion that her husband's place in history would be best served by the title of peacemaker.

Thus fortified, Ronald Reagan embarked on a remarkable course of personal diplomacy with the Soviet leadership, convinced that his affability could soften Kremlin attitudes, though Gorbachev proved even more committed to the process. The two met at a series of summits. At Reykjavik in October 1986 the president unnerved his advisers by impetuously agreeing to the abolition of all nuclear weapons, although that summit collapsed because Reagan was not prepared to give up his cherished SDI. It was at the Washington summit in December 1987 that an historic accord was signed. The INF treaty provided for the elimination of both intermediate and short-range ballistic missiles, and the two superpowers agreed to mutual inspections to confirm that the missiles were being dismantled. For the first time ever, by the late 1980s the nuclear arsenals held by the superpowers in Europe were being reduced. The Cold War eased further in 1988 when the Soviet Union began withdrawing its troops from Afghanistan.

By this time the Soviet Union was also indicating to Third World countries that it could no longer afford them aid, a stance that offered the prospect of greater security for US interests in Latin America. In 1989 Nicaragua's Sandinista government accepted a peace plan providing for a ceasefire and open elections. In El Salvador too the erosion of Soviet aid hastened the ending of war and revolutionary activity declined. Hostilities also waned in Guatemala. Fidel Castro remained in command of Cuba, but his revolutionary allies in Latin America were disappearing.

The changing character of the Cold War was illustrated in Latin America when President George Bush launched a major military intervention against a right-wing (rather than a left-wing) dictatorship. Relations between Washington and the increasingly vicious Panamanian regime of General Manuel Noriega had deteriorated during the late 1980s, and by the time Bush took office it was clear that Noriega was profiting hugely from his dealings with Colombian drug lords. A tense atmosphere developed between the Panamanian military and the US forces that remained in Panama to protect the canal. In December 1989 a US marine was killed. George Bush responded by sending in troops and Noriega was overthrown and extradited to Florida, where he was convicted of drugs offences. His removal did nothing to stem the flow of cocaine to American city streets.

In the Middle East too the ending of the Cold War facilitated a military intervention. In August 1990 Iraq's president Saddam Hussein launched an invasion of its oil-rich neighbour Kuwait. Beyond Kuwait lay Saudi Arabia; if Saddam seized that too he would control 40 per cent of the world's known oil reserves. Several other Arab nations condemned the invasion, as, remarkably, did a joint declaration issued by the US secretary of state and the Soviet foreign minister. Within a few days American troops were on their way to Saudi Arabia, and in November the UN Security Council authorized the use of 'all necessary means' to secure the withdrawal of Iraqi forces from Kuwait by 15 January 1991. By that date about 500,000 American troops were in the region and a formidable international coalition embracing twenty-nine countries had been fashioned. By assembling such might Bush hoped for a quick and decisive victory – this was not to become another Vietnam. A massive air campaign was launched against Iraq on 16 January and ground forces followed in February. By the end of the month the Iraqi forces had been overwhelmed, though the Saddam regime survived. The United States had spectacularly mobilized a huge multinational force, secured the acquiescence of the Soviet leadership, and imposed its will. 'By God,' said George Bush, 'we've kicked the Vietnam syndrome once and for all.'

The Gulf War took the course that it did in no small part because the Cold War was sputtering to a halt. If the Russian Revolution of 1917 had been one of the decisive events to shape the twentieth-century world, the collapse of the Soviet Union in the early 1990s was no less momentous. Gorbachev had been pursuing liberalization since the mid-1980s and the Soviet Union was visibly changing. In May 1989 Bush conceded that it was time to move 'beyond containment', though asked for evidence of Soviet good intentions before supporting 'the integration of the Soviet Union into the community of nations'. But events were moving faster than American policy.

Having embarked on arms reduction and withdrawal from Afghanistan, Gorbachev also began reducing Soviet troops in the Eastern European satellites. In Poland, where the Solidarity movement had been flourishing since the early 1980s, the Communist Party unexpectedly failed to win open elections in the summer of 1989 and reluctantly admitted Solidarity to the government. Within months Communist regimes were also crumbling in Hungary, Czechoslovakia and eventually Rumania. The Soviet leadership, preoccupied with its critical domestic reforms and anxious to improve relations with the West, concluded that it could no longer bear the political and financial costs of militarily subduing the resentful populations of its satellites. Each country must be responsible for its own affairs, said Gorbachev; the Soviet Union would not intervene: 'We assume others will not interfere either.'

With the Soviet retreat mass demonstrations swept across East Germany and the hardline Communist government finally collapsed at the end of 1989. The Berlin Wall was pulled down by a new government and celebrating East

Germans. For many its destruction symbolized the end of the Cold War. In March 1990 elections in East Germany returned a government favourable to reunification. This was a highly sensitive matter, it having been a principle of post-war Soviet policy that Soviet security depended on the neutrality or division of Germany, and complex negotiations followed. Eventually Moscow had to bow to the inevitable, and in the course of 1990 Germany was reunified as a member of NATO. Moscow's acquiescence was bought in part by the promise of Western aid for the embattled Soviet economy.

The winding down of the Cold War also provided an opportunity for further arms reductions. In its last years the Reagan administration had sought ambitious cutbacks through the Strategic Arms Reductions Talks (START, replacing SALT) and had reached substantial although not conclusive agreement. With the collapse of the Warsaw Pact – dissolved in April 1991 – the Soviet Union had less to defend and substantial reductions of conventional forces in Europe were agreed. In July 1991 the Soviet Union and the United States signed a START agreement, reducing strategic nuclear arsenals by 30 per cent.

The disintegration of its empire placed immense strains on the Soviet Union. The Soviet Communist Party, through which political power had been wielded, fast lost authority. In the largest of the Soviet Union's fifteen republics, Russia, Boris Yeltsin was elected president in May 1990 and demanded the decentralization of the Soviet Union and the autonomy of each republic, and other Soviet republics soon made similar claims. A failed coup by the old guard directed at Gorbachev in August 1991 spelled the end of the Soviet system. Statues of Stalin were torn down and the Communist Party disintegrated as an instrument of government. In December the Soviet Union was replaced by the Commonwealth of Independent States, a loose confederation joined by most of the old Soviet republics. Its dominant member would be Russia, which took the Soviet seat on the UN Security Council. Finally in October 1992 Congress offered $410 million to further the democratization of the former Soviet republics. This was hardly commensurate with the problem, but Reagan's policies had left the United States heavily in debt.

The United States, it could be said, had 'won' the Cold War, although the Soviet collapse was in no small part a consequence of fundamental weaknesses within the Soviet economic and political systems. Nonetheless the new global configurations raised the prospect of a rethinking of American foreign policy. During the Gulf War George Bush spoke of the likely emergence of a 'new world order', although he failed to articulate a coherent strategy to realize this vision.

However the 'new world order' might evolve, Bush's successor Bill Clinton was determined to put an American imprint on it: 'Today, as an old order passes, the new world is more free but less stable. Communism's collapse has called forth old animosities and new dangers. Clearly, America must continue to lead the world we did so much to make.' The task would be a challenging one, he emphasized, because of the globalization of economic and environmental issues. Yet there were opportunities too for the diffusion of American ideals in this age of instant global communication: 'Our hopes ... are with those on every continent who are building democracy and freedom. Their cause is America's cause.'

If anti-Soviet objectives were no longer to guide American policy, Clinton anticipated that economic issues might loom larger. But that was for the long term. For the moment he groped for a response to the political shockwaves that swept around the world in the wake of the Soviet collapse. His handling was uncertain largely because his overriding passion was for domestic affairs and at first he seemed to regard the outside world as a tiresome distraction. 'What Clinton did not yet understand was that foreign policy never lets an American president go', recalled one adviser.

Arguably the Cold War had imposed a kind of stability on the world, albeit one achieved through a balance of terror. But with the ending of the East–West stand-off there was a tendency for parts of the world to fragment. Nationalism and tribalism erupted as superpower rivalry evaporated. As Clinton observed, 'old animosities' had been called forth. Sometimes the dissolution was peaceful (Czechoslovakia, for example, separated into the Czech Republic and Slovakia). Often it was not. Over a hundred nationalities had lived in the old Soviet Union alone, and some took to arms to secure their self-determination. The Moslem province of Chechnya sought its independence from Russia, which used military force to try to subdue these determined insurgents. Secretary of State Warren Christopher worried in 1993 that 'We'll have 50,000 countries rather than the hundred plus we now have'. But what should the United States do now that its own security was not the paramount consideration? Act only if its own interests were touched, assume the role of humanitarian world leader or work for global order through the United Nations?

Clinton at first responded in an ad hoc way to foreign crises, although in time he was to devote considerable attention to his global role. (By the end of his administration he had visited more countries than any of his predecessors.) He played a part in persuading Russia to withdraw its last troops from the Balkan states, marking, as he put it, 'the real end to World War Two in Europe'. The disintegration of the Soviet empire also left three nuclear powers in Ukraine, Kazakhstan and Belarus at a time when other uncertain regimes – North Korea, Iran, Iraq – seemed also to be developing nuclear capabilities. The Clinton administration had some success in persuading the three republics to scrap their missiles.

The ending of the Cold War meant chaos in the Balkans. In 1991 Yugoslavia split up, as Slovenia and Croatia declared their independence, marking the beginning of years of turmoil. Focused on Bosnia, this was rooted in animosities between the Serbs, who were Eastern Orthodox in religion and generally dominant in Belgrade and the federal government, the Catholic Slovenes and Croats, and the Bosnians, who were Moslem. In the early 1990s the Serbs in Bosnia, supported by the Belgrade government, engaged in 'ethnic cleansing' to drive out the Moslems. Western governments appalled by the slaughter found it difficult to construct a coherent policy. Imposing peace in that mountainous region would require a massive military force, placed there perhaps indefinitely, for which there was little stomach in the West. While Clinton had no intention of committing American forces, the destruction in the Balkans pointed up the superpower's helplessness. An arms embargo and economic sanctions were deployed, UN peacekeepers were used to try to protect Moslem enclaves and ensure a supply of food and medicine, and NATO conducted limited air strikes against the Serbs. But the crisis dragged on. Clinton was nettled in 1995 when the French president remarked that 'the position of leader of the free world is vacant'. Finally prepared to use more force, in the summer of 1995 NATO bombing was intensified, eroding the Serbs' strength and pushing them towards negotiation. Eventually the leaders of the principal factions met under American auspices at Dayton, Ohio and the Dayton Accords were thrashed out. These provided for a ceasefire, the deployment of 60,000 NATO troops (including a US contingent) in 1996 to keep the peace, and the incorporation of elected representatives of the Bosnian Serbs, Croats and Moslems into the Bosnian government.

Peace in the Balkans, however, was not easily preserved. The Serbian leader Slobodan Milosevic turned his attention to Kosovo, a province in the old Yugoslavia settled mainly by Albanian Moslems. By 1997 the Kosovo Liberation Army was fighting for Kosovo's independence from the Bosnian Serb republic and the Serbs were striking back. The Western powers were again reluctant to intervene and by 1998, with the Clinton White House embroiled in 'Monicagate' (the scandal over Clinton's relationship with Monica Lewinsky, discussed in Chapter 19), the violence in Kosovo was intensifying. The NATO powers hoped to contain Milosevic with the threat of bombing, but he remained intransigent. Finally, with Clinton acquitted of impeachment charges in February 1999, he was ready to take action. To placate Congress the president disavowed the intention of using ground troops, but in March, as the Serbians attempted to drive the Albanians from Kosovo, an intensive bombing campaign began. Early in June Milosevic capitulated, unable to withstand high-tech airpower and the defection of his erstwhile Russian ally to the American strategy. Later in the year he fell from power.

Other regions of the world also experienced unrest. Anarchy engulfed parts of Africa. In Somalia, for example, there had been civil war and famine after the ending of the aid provided by the superpowers during their Cold War rivalry, and in December 1992 George Bush sent in marines as part of a UN peacekeeping force. American public support for this humanitarian operation waned, however, after eighteen American soldiers were killed in October 1993, an incident that did nothing to allay widespread American distrust of the United Nations. By April 1994 all US troops had been withdrawn. The United States and other Western countries proved unable or unwilling to end massive massacres in Rwanda, where the number of victims of tribal wars dwarfed the casualties experienced in Bosnia. In a brief three months perhaps a million died in what one author characterized as 'the most efficient killing since the atomic bombing of Hiroshima and Nagasaki'. Huge numbers of refugees fled and conflict in other parts of Central Africa precipitated further migrations, overwhelming the relief agencies. In Zaire the dictator Mobutu Sese Seko had relied on American military aid in the Cold War period, but this was no longer available and he was overthrown in 1997. The implacable tensions in the Middle East also continued to defy the dream of a lasting peace, despite Clinton's energetic efforts late in his presidency. He exerted his influence too on behalf of the troubled peace process in Northern Ireland.

Another symptom of the global instability of the post-Cold War world was the growth of international terrorism. The United States was targeted in attacks on American barracks in Saudi Arabia in June 1996, on US embassies in Kenya and Tanzania in August 1998 (when most of those who died were Africans) and on the USS *Cole* in October 2000. The assault on the two embassies was credited to Osama bin Laden's al Qaida guerrilla organization, and Clinton responded with cruise missiles on a suspected pharmaceutical factory in Sudan and a training camp in Afghanistan. But the action looked more like an attempt to distract attention from the Lewinsky affair than a serious response to the terrorist threat.

There was no easy route to a 'new world order'. No longer needing to subordinate every policy stance to anti-Soviet containment, American leaders remained uncertain about the global role that the United States should adopt. But Clinton did possess a sense of how economics could inform foreign policy. Keenly aware of the various ways in which the United States was enmeshed in the wider world, Clinton looked to trade and commerce to redefine its international role. 'We have put our economic competitiveness at the heart of our foreign policy', he said in 1994. Trade policy linked foreign policy to his vital concern for the economy. Clinton held that American interests and international security would be furthered by working with the forces of globalization and by vigorously promoting free trade. The American share of global production had been declining for decades, but the United States had become the world's largest trader, and it could use this advantage to revitalize its own economy by prising open foreign markets. In a series of remarkable diplomatic initiatives, Clinton pursued free trade agreements with the countries of the Pacific Rim, with the rest of the Americas and with Europe.

The Reagan and Bush administrations had already largely negotiated the North American Free Trade Area, which some warned would mean a drain of jobs to low-wage Mexico, but Clinton was convinced that economic expansion would create more jobs. He defied the protectionist instincts in his own party and pushed the agreement through Congress in November 1993. This was followed in 1994 by the Free Trade Agreement of the Americas signed with the leaders of the other western hemisphere countries – Cuba apart.

In another initiative the heads of the Pacific Rim countries signed an agreement to develop a free trade area over the next fifteen years. Crowning these measures was the endorsement Clinton won from Congress at the end of 1994 for a new GATT pact (the Uruguayan round of the General Agreement on Tariffs and Trade) with its heavy reductions in tariff duties. Also approved was US participation in GATT's strengthened replacement, the World Trade Organization. 'The economic benefits of the tariff reductions we negotiated during the Clinton administration represents the largest tax cut in the history of the world', Treasury Secretary Lawrence Summers would boast.

The military alliances of the Cold War era were being supplanted by free trade pacts. In 1991 a survey had shown that in the opinion of the public the saving of American jobs should be the first foreign policy goal, followed by protecting the interests of Americans working abroad and securing adequate supplies of energy, a lesson pointed up by the Gulf War. Bill Clinton attended the G7 economic summits of the leading industrial countries rather than the geopolitical summits experienced by Franklin Roosevelt and Dwight Eisenhower or the arms summits of Ronald Reagan. Free commerce and instant information, Clinton seemed to be saying, would define the post-Cold War world, and the United States must press home its advantages as the market leader. The businessmen who surrounded the administration of his successor, George W. Bush, were no less interested in the economic benefits that might be wrested from the world, even if their instincts were unilateralist, but after terrorists struck horrendously at the World Trade Center and the Pentagon on 11 September 2001 national security once more became paramount in the shaping of American foreign policy.

|19|

Fin de Siècle: *Reagan, Bush and Clinton* 1981–2000

With the election of Ronald Reagan the American right was finally in the driving seat, or so it believed. The entrepreneurial values of the business élite had triumphed, albeit with the somewhat incongruous assistance of a moralistic right that appealed both to professionals in well-to-do suburbs and to many blue-collar and ethnic voters. 'We talked about the sanctity of free enterprise ... until we were blue in the face', observed Richard Viguerie in 1981, but: 'We never really won until we began stressing issues like bussing, abortion, school prayer and gun control.' What gave the various right-wing constituents a sort of unity was a fear that the United States was being undone at home, by an intrusive federal state and liberal attempts to extend rights. The New Right emphatically disavowed government meddling, whether in the economy or with the patriarchal family. (Rights to abortion, easy divorce and gay sex seemed subversive of traditional family values.) Liberal impulses had struggled for expression during the 1970s, but even the Democrats under Jimmy Carter had signalled their retreat from New Deal and Great Society solutions. With the slowing of economic growth, conservative notions on the limited role of the state gained a new ascendancy, and leading figures in both major parties spoke of reining in government and reducing federal spending. The Reagan White House was passionately committed to these objectives, but even when the Democrats regained office under Bill Clinton in the 1990s the administration talked of the need to 'reinvent government'. There was never any danger in the final straitened decades of the twentieth century of returning to the freewheeling days of Franklin Roosevelt and Lyndon Johnson.

Ronald Reagan brought to the presidency a beguiling simplicity of vision. He was, as Iwan Morgan has observed, 'the most ideological president of modern times', but the very simplicity of his views 'gave his administration a clear sense of direction'. Government 'is not the solution to our problem', Reagan said in his inaugural address. By reversing its growth, he believed, the 'creative energy' of the American people would be liberated.

Reagan's understanding of foreign affairs was informed by a profound anti-communism. The Soviet Union was 'the evil empire', behind most of the world's troubles, and the appropriate response was a massive military build-up. Many of the people around Reagan shared his vision. They believed that the 1980 election had given them a mandate for a 'new beginning'. In their perspective, 1980 was the counterpoint to 1932, heralding a return to a distinctly conservative system of politics, even a 'Reagan Revolution'. But the Reagan people were no more able than their predecessors to overcome the constraints of a divided polity.

Yet 1981 was 'glad morning again' to the Republican right. Determined to undo the mistakes of a generation, the new president surrounded himself with conservatives. Edwin Meese, who had been his chief of staff at Sacramento, became counsellor to the president and worked to ensure that sound conservatives were thickly scattered around the executive departments. James A. Baker, a pragmatic and tough-minded Texan, became chief of staff. Other senior officials included Budget Director David Stockman, a strong believer in free market forces; Secretary of Defense Caspar Weinberger, who believed that American defences had been dangerously neglected; and Secretary of the Treasury Donald Regan, who had enjoyed a successful Wall Street career. While most of these men were clearly conservative they were not ideologues, although James Watt as secretary of the interior was a hero of the New Right, seemingly determined to do away with environmental restraints on the economic exploitation of the public domain.

Reagan made clear his priority in his inaugural address, the greater part of which was devoted to the need to restore a 'dynamic economy'. He equated 'our present troubles' with the 'intervention and intrusion in our lives that result from unnecessary and excessive growth of government', and anticipated a roll-back in federal bureaucracy, reduced taxation and government spending, and a consequentially revitalized economy that would provide employment for all. In February 1981 Reagan unveiled his economic programme, the centrepiece of which was a proposal to cut federal income and business tax rates by a whopping 30 per cent over a three-year period, with high-rate taxpayers benefiting most. In addition there would be reductions in government spending to bring down the deficit and reach a balanced budget by 1985. Since defence expenditure was sacrosanct – the Reaganites wanted it enhanced – the cuts would have to come in domestic spending, that is in various welfare programmes and grants to state and local governments. The programme also promised a tight money supply to control inflation and sweeping deregulation to unleash business. This daring combination of policies was 'Reaganomics'.

The budget proposals represented a clear repudiation of Keynesianism, switching the emphasis from demand to supply-side economics. Two leading Republicans, Representative Jack Kemp and Senator William Roth, had been advocating a large reduction in federal income taxes for some years, influenced by the ideas of economist William Laffer, whose celebrated

Laffer Curve showed that tax revenues disappeared as the tax rate approached either zero or 100 per cent. A 100 per cent tax rate would kill off economic enterprise and no revenues would be collected. High taxes, it was concluded, were a disincentive to work. Reduce the tax rate and people would work harder and save more, business would be reinvigorated and more tax revenues would flow in. Reagan himself had apparently once paid tax at the 90 per cent wartime rate and, in his budget director's words, on hearing of the Laffer Curve he 'knew instantly that it was true and would never doubt it a moment thereafter'. (It also resonated with the grass-roots 'tax revolt'.) Not all of Reagan's advisers possessed the same faith in the Kemp-Roth formula as a miracle cure, but it offered a route to cutting back on welfare and other government expenditures and allowing market forces freer rein. 'Pray God it works', one Republican reportedly grunted: 'If this economic plan doesn't jell, where are we going to get the money for anything?'

Reagan's first year was a remarkably successful one. He scored a major hit for the business right (as noted in Chapter 15) when he defeated a strike by the air traffic controllers, an episode that destroyed their union. Reagan's White House team proved adept at dealing with congressmen, who were also given pause by the president's popularity, and Southern Democrats in particular had some sympathy with his conservative economics. Reagan was reluctantly obliged to reduce his 30 per cent tax cut goal to 25 per cent, but the Emergency Recovery Tax Act of 1981 secured the largest federal income tax cut in American history and also unprecedented reductions in domestic programmes. Unable to repeal the welfare state, the Republicans were now seeking to de-fund it. With a burgeoning fiscal deficit, as Budget Director Stockman later recalled, at some point there would simply have to be 'massive spending reductions':

> The success of the Reagan Revolution depended upon the willingness of the politicians to turn against their own handiwork – the bloated budget of the American welfare state. Why would they do this? Because they had to! In the final analysis, I had made fiscal necessity the mother of political invention.

In the 1990s a Democratic president would be obliged to provide the cuts required to restore the government's financial integrity.

Given the Democratic majority in the lower house the tax cut was an impressive political achievement. Economically it was a more ambiguous victory. The economic programme had always been based on some questionable assumptions, such as an annual 5 per cent growth rate in the economy, and the compromises exacted by Congress further undermined it, so that there was no realistic prospect of eventually delivering the promised balanced budget. Tight monetary restraints were maintained, but the high interest rates insisted on by the Federal Reserve Board pushed the economy into recession before the tax cuts could take effect, and by the autumn of 1982 unemployment had reached over 11 per cent, the highest rate since 1940. As the deficit yawned, in 1982 Reagan secured further cuts in social programmes and even steeled himself to a tax increase, although leaving untouched the celebrated income tax cut and securing the necessary revenue by new excise taxes and other quiet adjustments. Helped by the serious economic recession, in the mid-term elections of 1982 the Democrats increased their majority in the House and thereafter the Reagan White House was never able to regain its influence over Congress.

The increasing federal deficit occurred in part because of another major component of the Reagan agenda. Since 1968 the military budget had declined while the Soviet budget increased, at least until 1978 when the Carter administration began to spend more on defence. To the anti-communist right, the United States was becoming vulnerable to the mighty Soviet nuclear arsenal, and Reagan was one of those who believed that there was no alternative to what he called 'peace through strength'. While his ambitious budget proposals were meant to spark a domestic revolution, there was to be no compromise on military strength. 'Defense is not a budget item', Reagan told his aides, 'you spend what you need.' Between 1980 and 1984 US military spending increased by 40 per cent, the largest peacetime defence build-up in American history.

But other than militarily Reagan wanted to roll back the functions of the federal government. He wished to free industry from regulation (which would also diminish federal bureaucracy), reduce welfare programmes and turn over some functions to the states. The heritage of the New Deal was at last to be addressed. In part the assault was to be administrative. Although the number of federal employees increased in the Reagan years because of the expansion of the defence establishment, agencies responsible for social, economic and health programmes experienced staff cutbacks, in some cases as much as 25 per cent.

Deregulation was a major component of this agenda. The Carter administration had begun to dismantle obstructions to competition in the transportation and communication industries, but the more fervent Reaganites itched to go much further. They also looked askance at controls protecting the environment and even at safety regulations in the workplace. Relying more on administrative than legislative action (which would require the cooperation of Congress), the administration quickly reduced the number of rules to which industry was subject. After the first year in office it was claimed that *The Federal Register*, which provided a regulations checklist, had been reduced in size by a third.

The administration also employed other tactics in its deregulation drive. One was to appoint officials to regulatory agencies who were committed to the Reagan agenda. The most zealous was Interior Secretary James Watt, who assumed office promising that: 'We will mine more, drill more, cut more timber to use our resources.' (Watt divided his fellow citizens into 'Liberals and Americans'.) He was determined on such a wholesale blitz on his department's regulations that no successor 'would ever change them back because he won't have the determination that I do'. He secured the removal of employees whose views he thought unduly environmentalist, rejigged procedures in ways that advantaged corporate interests, allowed mining exploration on public land and stopped the enlargement of national parks. He even talked of turning wilderness areas over to private hands. The EPA head, Anne Gorsuch, possessed a similar outlook (at least until her officials began to persuade her of the value of environmental controls) and the number of hazardous waste prosecutions dropped markedly. Other officials eased the enforcement of anti-trust laws and health and safety regulations, and even the National Labor Relations Board, in adjudicating industrial disputes, increasingly made decisions favouring employers as Reagan appointed more members to it. The regulatory regime was also weakened by squeezed funding. During Reagan's first term the EPA budget was cut by 35 per cent; staff positions in the Consumer Product Safety Commission were reduced by 38 per cent.

Nonetheless the administration's deregulatory assault disappointed its champions. There was resistance in Congress, the courts and among the public, and the pro-business favouritism of some officials led to scandals and often dismissal or worse. In 1983 a toxic waste controversy precipitated Anne Gorsuch's departure from office, and James Watt's indiscretions led to his resignation. Congressional committees probed EPA actions, and by 1984 over twenty of its officials had resigned or been fired. The deregulation of the savings and loan (S&L) banks (which provided services similar to building societies in Britain) was greeted by the president as the 'most important legislation for financial institutions in fifty years'. In fact the removal of controls unleashed a frenzy of speculative ventures, unsafe loans and outright frauds in the S&L business, and before Reagan left office many of these banks were collapsing. The bill had to be picked up by the taxpayer, since the federal government guaranteed deposit accounts, although not until the Bush administration was the size of the problem appreciated. It was then estimated that over thirty years the cost to the American public could amount to a staggering $500 billion.

The attack on environmentalism had provoked powerful resistance from a wide array of lobbies, and environmental organizations actually grew in membership in these years. They took their causes to the courts and into election campaigns. With many environmental aims strongly supported by public opinion, Congress frustrated several administration initiatives and exposed agency circumvention of regulations. Broadly speaking a stand-off was reached by the end of Reagan's first term. None of the principal pan-industrial regulatory laws affecting industry or the environment introduced in the 1960s and 1970s was repealed during the Reagan years. At the same time the environmental movement was unable to secure major new programmes. This was another illustration of the divided governance of the United States in the final third of the twentieth century. And stalemate was not simply the product of a White House at odds with Congress. Business and environmental groups were also facing off against one another and many business interests accepted the need for some constraint. Large corporations often preferred the uniformity of federal rules to a patchwork of state regulations. The courts sometimes called the government to account, while some public agencies succeeded in seeing off the ideologues and remaining committed to their public brief. The regulatory regime was so woven into the fabric of this complex and divided society, and so supported by a miscellany of figures and interests at critical junctures, that it was able to withstand the offensive directed against it.

Much the same obtained of Reagan's attempts to reduce the welfare state. 'The Reagan Revolution', said David Stockman, '... required a frontal assault on the American welfare state.' It did not succeed. The social insurance programmes such as old-age pensions, which enjoyed a large and even middle-class constituency that could not be lightly offended, in fact emerged relatively unscathed. (Social Security contributions were increased to safeguard the fiscal integrity of the fund, negating the benefits of the 1981 tax cut for many low-income earners.) Social Security had originated with the New Deal, and it was the surviving Great Society programmes that were at greater risk. Reagan did succeed in tightening up eligibility to 'welfare' or assistance, and the number of people entitled to such benefits as AFDC cheques, food stamps and student loans was reduced. His 1981 budget act reflected a conservative welfare philosophy in allowing states to require some kind of work from claimants seeking benefits. Over the next few years several states experimented with work-welfare schemes, and a new consensus emerged in favour of this approach, which was to find expression in the Family Support Act of 1988.

Giving states more discretion was part of the Reagan plan to shift governmental functions away from Washington. The aim was to refashion federalism, particularly in handing over programmes relating to community development, education and welfare to the states (which would then have an incentive to keep down costs). The ambitious 1981 budget began this, ending some grant programmes and consolidating others into block grants, allowing the states more discretion on how to spend them. In 1982 Reagan hoped to go much further, proposing that the states assume responsibility for AFDC (the major 'welfare' programme), but he was unable to win much political support for this radical change. Thereafter Congress proved unhelpful in realizing Reagan's vision of a new federalism and the greater part of the responsibilities of the federal government remained with it. Nonetheless the administration squeezed the grants it did distribute. Total federal grants to state and local governments fell by 15 per cent between 1980 and 1987, a substantial reduction at a time when state responsibilities were being extended. Great Society programmes, such as community services and urban renewal, suffered in particular. As a result many states were forced to raise their own taxes or to neglect the public infrastructure, and frequently both. Reagan might be credited with stemming the growth of Washington's authority *vis-à-vis* the states, but his vision of a new federalism was only very imperfectly realized.

After 1983 the Reagan Revolution stalled. By that date the true believers like David Stockman and James Watt had left the administration and

Congress was less susceptible to the president's charms. Yet Reagan's luck remained with him. The economy revived in 1983, in part because of the 'military Keynesianism' of high defence spending, and by the election year of 1984 there was a sense that the good times had returned. Boosted by his foreign policy foray into Grenada, the success of American athletes at the Olympic Games in Los Angeles, and his highly personable television performances, Reagan won by a landslide. Only African-Americans, Hispanics, Jews and the unemployed, the remnants of the New Deal coalition, voted strongly Democrat.

Yet during his second term Reagan's domestic political position weakened, as illustrated by the Democrats' success in regaining control of the Senate in the mid-term elections. Reagan may have been spectacularly successful in improving relations with the Soviet Union, but by late autumn of 1986 the exposure of the Iran-Contra affair (see Chapter 18) was wreaking havoc with the administration. The House and Senate formed committees to investigate, and an independent investigator was appointed to conduct his own inquiry. In fact Reagan's personal popularity held up surprisingly well, but there was little more to be gained in legislative achievement. In the autumn of 1987 the Senate turned down his first choice for a Supreme Court vacancy, the conservative Robert Bork. Reagan's final year in office was also overshadowed by the Stock Market Crash of October 1987. Decisive action by the Federal Reserve Board averted a general economic downturn, but the economy grew at a slower rate.

Nonetheless Reagan, more than Nixon before him, had done something to tip the American polity to the right. He had made right-wing appointments to the Civil Rights Commission and the Equal Employment Opportunity Commission, and after eight years conservatives were generously distributed throughout the executive agencies. By the end of his presidency Reagan had not only named over half of federal judges but a reliable conservative majority had also emerged on the Supreme Court. The president may not have been able to deliver the red meat desired by his avid supporters on the New Right, but tighter appropriations and a range of administrative and court decisions tended to frustrate the demands of the civil rights, feminist and other progressive lobbies.

Yet Reagan's remarkable personal popularity did nothing to build a cohesive Republican ascendancy across the political system. The vaunted Reagan Revolution left the party structure largely untouched. The divisions in the political system were exposed yet again in the 1988 elections. Reagan's vice-president George Bush won the presidency with 54 per cent of the popular vote, his Democratic opponent Governor Michael Dukakis of Massachusetts carrying only ten states. Yet the Democrats narrowly increased their majority in the House and maintained a ten-seat lead in the Senate.

What contributed to Bush's victory was his revival of a version of Nixon's Southern strategy. Early in the campaign the Democratic candidate had enjoyed a substantial lead in the polls, but this slipped away as the Bush camp skilfully depicted Dukakis as the personification of unpatriotic and bleeding-heart liberalism. The most notorious tactic was a melodramatic television commercial focused on Willie Horton, a black convict allowed a weekend's leave by Massachusetts's furlough programme, who had then raped and murdered a white woman, responsibility for which was imputed to the hapless Dukakis. Bush ran particularly strongly in the South, where Dukakis carried no electoral votes (Washington, DC apart). The deployment of negative tactics and the reduction of the campaign to soundbites did little for the public's jaundiced view of politics. Turnout was the lowest since 1924, and two-thirds of those who did bestir themselves to vote admitted that they wished that the choice had been between two different candidates.

George Bush's presidency was dominated by foreign affairs, most notably the disintegration of the Soviet empire and the Persian Gulf War. One aide estimated that Bush spent at least 75 per cent of his time on foreign policy, and he seemed almost indifferent to the course of domestic affairs. During the 1988 campaign he had promised to be the 'education president', but unwilling in the face of the yawning deficit to commit funds his education policy proved to be little more than a series of gestures. Health care had become a major issue, in large part because of its escalating costs and the large number of Americans without health cover, and the issue was exacerbated by the terrifying AIDS crisis. But the president gave health little attention, for which he received widespread criticism. In 1990 *Time* named him 'Men of the Year', picturing two faces, that is, 'a foreign policy profile that was a study in resoluteness and mastery, the other a domestic visage just as strongly marked by wavering and confusion'. Bush noted in 1991 that the 'first rule of economic policy' reminded him of the Hippocratic Oath: 'Do no harm.' A few months later he made the same remark in relation to the government's responsibility for welfare. This attitude seemed to surface in the White House's reaction to the horrendous Los Angeles race riot of 1992, which it attributed to the liberal social programmes of the 1960s, and the president compounded the appearance of aloofness by being slow to visit the area. While the administration hastened to recover by offering aid to the city, which had suffered more deaths than in any other such outbreak in American history, a public opinion poll showed that 49 per cent disapproved of the president's response against 43 per cent approving.

Another issue to attract the wavering attention of the Bush administration was drugs, which the president said would be his number one domestic priority. The use of cocaine was widespread, and even more worrying was the spread of its smokable variety, crack, which was associated with street gangs and inner-city crime. Attempts were made to intercept the supply of drugs from Peru and Colombia and to enforce the anti-drug laws with enhanced policing and jail space. Several critics objected to the emphasis on punishment rather than treatment, and some argued that the programme failed to address the real problem – the growth of an urban 'underclass' that seemed beyond the reach of public policies. The vaunted 'war on drugs' proved no more successful than those previously conducted against poverty, crime and energy waste.

Bush also failed to make much impact on the social issues dear to the heart of the New Right. He did signal his lack of enthusiasm for civil rights when he vetoed what he called a 'quota bill' in 1990, but he retreated in 1991 in signing a modified measure designed to preserve affirmative action. Similarly ambiguous was his record over abortion (which his wife seemed to favour). The White House entered an *amicus curiae* brief in a 1989 case arguing for reversing the *Roe v Wade* decision, but the Court disappointed the religious right in declining to do so, though it did recognize the authority of individual states to place restrictions on abortion in publicly funded hospitals and clinics. The Bush nomination of the conservative African-American Clarence Thomas to the Supreme Court in 1991 also backfired. A major row erupted during the Senate confirmation hearings when a former female assistant, Anita Hill, accused Thomas of sexual harassment, and tensions were raised further when male senators attacked her testimony. Bush stood by Thomas, who was narrowly confirmed, but the affair cost him some female votes in the 1992 election.

George Bush could claim some success on the environment, in which, as a hunter and fisherman, he had an authentic interest. Public consciousness had been raised in 1989 when the oil tanker *Exxon Valdez* ran aground in Alaska, contaminating 6000 square miles of ocean and devastating wildlife. Bush increased funding for the EPA, and in contrast to the Reagan style appointed a professional conservationist to head it. He extended wildlife refuges and wetlands and helped secure the Omnibus Water Bill of 1992 to protect the Grand Canyon. Appropriations for the endangered species programme more than trebled. The White House could claim much credit for the Clean Air Act Amendments of 1990, which tightened controls on the industrial emission of air pollutants, introduced a programme for reducing acid rain, and took the first measures to combat the erosion of the ozone layer.

But it was the economy that presented the Bush administration with its most problematic domestic challenge. The Reagan policies had left the federal government with a huge and widening budget deficit (exacerbated by the S&L débâcle). During the election campaign Bush had promised no new taxes – 'read my lips' – but by 1990 the projected deficit was over $100 billion greater than that permitted by the Gramm-Rudman law of 1985, which had tried to set deficit limits. Moreover, the national debt had almost trebled since 1980. A sustained economic boom might just have generated the revenues needed, but instead the economy slowed. A Democratic Congress reluctant to cut spending and a president committed to no tax increases were soon locked in a protracted deadlock, and divisions within Congress itself rendered agreement even more elusive. Eventually, late in 1990, a compromise was found, and while it involved some spending cuts it also included an increase in the top rate of income tax and higher excise taxes, including on gasoline. Conservative Republicans felt betrayed, not least those in Congress led by the brash Newt Gingrich. The president's approval ratings promptly dropped by twenty-five points.

Perhaps Bush could have sprung back from this humiliating climbdown, particularly as his handling of foreign affairs was widely acclaimed, but the economic slowdown soon deepened into recession. American corporations found it difficult to withstand the impact of growing globalization and were forced to cut back on their workforces. Unemployment rose, not least among white-collar workers, a relatively novel feature, and a disturbing one to politicians aware of the potency of their vote. During Bush's last year in office the annual deficit was up to $290 billion and the national debt reached an unprecedented $3 trillion. Bush may have won the Gulf War, but it had lasted only a few weeks and for most Americans was a television spectacle demanding no commitment on their part; further, the ending of the Cold War implied that other priorities could replace containing communism. To many Americans the economy had become the priority, and it was against this backdrop that the 1992 presidential campaign was fought out.

The Democrats nominated the young Arkansan, Bill Clinton, the possessor of acute antennae that made him a nimble figure in the now volatile world of American politics. A rare intellect combined with drive and charm had catapulted him from a modest background to Georgetown University, Oxford and Yale, and when he turned to politics he had become the youngest governor in the country at the age of 32. Like several other ambitious Democrats of his generation, Clinton could be classified as a neo-liberal, or alternatively as a 'New Democrat', one of those anxious to get away from the 'big spending' image of the New Deal-Great Society tradition. This group tended to be liberal on social issues like civil and women's rights and moderate on economic issues, accepting a need to work with business and to show restraint in budgeting. Some of them, like Clinton himself, were members of the Democratic Leadership Council, a body that had been established in 1985 to explore such ideas. The Democrats could no longer depend on the big city vote, said the DLC's executive director Al From: 'So Democrats need to make inroads into the suburban vote without turning their backs on the cities … Putting new dollars into old programs won't do.' This is not to suggest that the Democrats had lost faith in government. Clinton looked to the state to 'invest' in education, conservation and high-tech research. (Federal spending was being relabelled 'investment'.)

Clinton saw the need in particular to win the support of the middle classes. Low-income groups no longer turned out to vote in great numbers, and it was middle-income voters – referred to by Clinton as 'the forgotten middle class' – who could sway elections. Analyses of the 1984 and 1988 elections seemed to show that the Democratic Party had been hurt by its identification with 'special interest groups', such as organized labour and African-Americans, and Clinton cautiously distanced himself from these progressive constituencies. His middle-class target was not so very different to Richard Nixon's 'silent majority', but Clinton wooed it with skill, emphasizing the positive, such as investment in the infrastructure and education. The negative campaign consisted largely of attacks on the Bush administration for mismanaging the economy. The mantra within the Clinton camp to remind themselves of the central issue of the campaign was, 'The economy, stupid.'

Clinton was not the only candidate to contest the incumbent in 1992. An extraordinary third-party campaign was launched by Texas billionaire Ross Perot, who benefited from the increasing disrespect for professional politicians. He presented himself as a commonsensical businessman who would make Washington work. He would not duck problems but would 'get under the hood and fix them', and he railed in particular at the massive budget deficit. Polls suggested that he drew about equally from the two major parties, although his centres of strength in the South and the West threatened Bush's potential electoral votes the most.

Bill Clinton won the presidential election with a five-point lead in the popular vote over George Bush. Ross Perot took a remarkable 19 per cent though carried no states. The Democrats also retained their majorities in both houses of Congress, and so briefly the same party commanded both the executive and the legislative branches of government. (By this time, however, Reagan and Bush appointments had put conservatives safely in charge of the judiciary.) Nonetheless, Clinton's share of the popular vote was only 43 per cent, the least for a presidential winner since 1912. Most voters had cast their ballots for other candidates.

Clinton advertised his empathy with the people by promising to appoint a cabinet that looked 'more like America than previous administrations'. He recruited four women, four African-Americans and two Hispanics, more in each category than any of his predecessors. But his administration got off to an uncertain start, partly because of campaign promises that he could not easily deliver. The most harmful furore emerged over his promised support for equal treatment of homosexuals in the armed forces. Clinton vacillated and eventually announced a compromise recruitment policy based on the principle 'don't ask, don't tell'. This pleased neither the gays who had supported Clinton nor the military traditionalists and left a harmful impression of pusillanimity. Also leaving an unhappy mark was the administration's handling of a siege at Waco, Texas, where an apocalyptic sect had fortified themselves inside their compound and shot at government agents. After fifty-one days the FBI attacked the compound, which was consumed by a ferocious fire, leaving eighty dead. While public opinion broadly conceded the benefit of the doubt to the administration, paranoid far right groups espied evidence for their conviction that the government was conspiring against individual liberties, and the growing militia movement was further boosted. (On the second anniversary of the Waco tragedy, 19 April 1995, a federal building in Oklahoma City was blown up by militia members Timothy McVeigh and Terry Nichols, killing 168 people.)

But Clinton's first priority was the economy, on which, he said, he wanted to focus 'like a laser'. Further study had persuaded him that even more urgent than measures to boost it was a reduction of the deficit; without that a sustained economic expansion – of a kind which would fund new policies and ensure his re-election – would not be possible. Only low interest rates would provide a productive economy, and these were set by money markets requiring deficit reduction. 'We're Eisenhower Republicans here and we're fighting the Reagan Republicans', Clinton privately complained: 'we stand for lower deficits, free trade, and the bond market. Isn't that great?' Within a month of taking office he laid out an ambitious package designed first to reduce the ballooning deficit, through higher taxes on corporations, the rich and on energy, and through spending cuts. 'Unless we dealt with the deficits first', his wife Hillary later recalled, 'we'd never be able to do any of the other things we wanted to do.' Clinton had not abandoned his campaign pledge to stimulate the economy, although this part of the package was more modest than once anticipated, urging 'investment' in the infrastructure like transport and in 'human capital' like education and skills. The Republicans, convinced that they had lost the election because of Bush's volte-face on taxes, immediately assailed the tax hikes. By dint of compromise, Clinton did manage to squeeze the deficit reduction proposal through Congress, providing for a hefty cut of $500 billion in the deficit over the next five years. 'It sends a clear signal to the markets that interest rates should stay down', said a jubilant president.

Further, while deficit reduction was the centrepiece, Clinton also engineered some liberal measures into the budget. It provided funding for the establishment of AmeriCorps, a national service programme giving participants a year's work in education, health and the environment. And it massively expanded the Earned Income Tax Credit, a programme that had been modestly introduced in 1975 to provide tax relief or refunds to the working poor. Clinton adroitly consummated EITC's conversion into a major social policy, his changes providing an estimated $20 billion in income support to 16 million poor families by 1998. Nonetheless, he had to abandon some of his budget ideas, and the accompanying stimulus programme was torpedoed by a filibustering Republican minority in the Senate. Yet there was more than one way of providing stimulus, and vital to the Clinton economic vision too was free trade (as discussed in Chapter 18). This was not a strategy supported by many congressional Democrats, who feared for the jobs of their constituents if trade barriers were reduced around the world, but Clinton was convinced that aligning the United States with globalist forces would powerfully boost the American economy.

A major initiative was the health care plan to oblige employers to provide health insurance for their employees. When Clinton assumed the presidency the United States had the highest health care costs among industrial nations, yet nearly 40 million Americans were without health insurance. The federal government had spent 9 per cent of its revenue on health care in 1971; by 1991, thanks to the accelerating cost of Medicare and Medicaid, it was up to 21 per cent. The president hoped that a universal programme might enable him to rebuild an alliance of working- and middle-class voters and black, ethnic and white voters. A task force under the First Lady, Hillary Clinton, prepared a plan, which was submitted to Congress in September 1993 to an initially favourable public response. Contributions would be collected from both employers and employees, but the poor and small businesses would be subsidized by the government, and 'sin' taxes (notably on tobacco) would help pay for the programme. The ambitious package, which ran to 1300 bemusing pages, ran foul of a range of conservative lobbies, and some moderate Democrats were unhappy too. Interest groups spent $60 million on a television advertising campaign assailing the proposals and public opinion turned against them. Congressional committees hacked the package about and the administration eventually conceded defeat in the face of Republican obstructionism in the Senate. Having set so much store by health care reform, its defeat was a major setback for the administration.

Repeatedly rebuffed by a Congress in which the Democrats held at least nominal majorities, by the summer of 1994 public opinion polls showed more people disapproving than approving of the Clinton presidency. The confusing health plan suggested that the Democrats had not after all repented their big government ways. The fuss over gays in the military associated Clinton with sixties permissiveness, as did allegations about extramarital affairs, issues that affronted the resurgent Christian right. Exacerbating public disaffection were charges of impropriety over an earlier investment made by the Clintons in the Whitewater resort project in Arkansas (though they had actually lost money in the deal), and suspicions of a subsequent White House cover-up. One press analysis discovered that there had been over 31,000 stories on Whitewater compared to 2400 on the health care proposal since the latter had been introduced. Public discontent was powerfully expressed in the mid-term elections of 1994, when the Republicans astonishingly stormed Congress. Not since 1952, when they had been helped by Eisenhower's coat-tails, had the Republicans won control of both houses, and their routing of the apparently permanent Democratic majority in the lower house suggested that something profound was happening to the electorate.

Many of those elected were Sunbelt and Southern conservatives, viscerally hostile to New Deal policies and liberal permissiveness. As one New Right Republican put it: 'We wanted to politicize everything. Remember the slogan, "The personal is political"? That was feminism, right? Well, that became us, too.' The Republican leader in Congress, Newt Gingrich, had tried to turn the elections into a referendum on the 'Great Society, counterculture, McGovernik' heritage of the 1960s, or what he also called 'the long aberration'. He and other Republican leaders had drawn up a 'Contract with America', which proposed several major initiatives to reverse the thrust of Democratic government. The Contract included an amendment to the Constitution requiring a balanced budget, welfare reform to oblige recipients to work, tax cuts, increased defence spending and deregulation, as well as a series of measures to strengthen family life. While Clinton could claim to be a moderate on the economy and government spending, his earlier admission that as a student he had smoked marijuana (without inhaling), his avoidance of the draft and rumours of his sexual liaisons meant that he could be identified with the permissive culture that so offended the powerful religious right, as could his wife's association with feminist causes. Grass-roots work by the Christian Coalition contributed to Republican success.

Newt Gingrich was elected Speaker of the House of Representatives, in which office he attempted to lead an alternative government, promising to introduce the measures listed in the Contract within a hundred days. But Gingrich found it no easier to govern than did Clinton, and his strident rhetoric tended to alienate rather than attract support, not least that of some senior Republican senators, and he himself became the subject of ethics investigations. Only two minor measures of the Contract were enacted in that session, both enjoining greater responsibility for their actions on members of Congress themselves (although other Contract promises, such as welfare reform, did eventually become law). Clinton also blunted the Republican offensive by moving to the right, recruiting new White House aides of a centrist disposition. His adroit manoeuvres further ensured that the Gingrich Republicans got the blame when the federal government was forced to shut down for short periods in October and December 1995 because the failure to agree a budget deprived it of funds. (There was a similar partial shutdown in 1996.)

The president's sinuous pragmatism was demonstrated in the congressional battle over welfare reform. The Republicans mounted a powerful assault on the 'welfare mess', eager to put an end to the handout culture they believed the New Deal Order had left them. Clinton himself had promised to 'end welfare as we know it', and in 1994 had taken a centrist position, emphasizing the need for welfare recipients to accept job training and suggesting that cash payments be terminated after two years. The Republicans pushed such principles to their political limits. The Personal Responsibility and Work Opportunity Act of 1996 transferred the major welfare programmes to the states, something Reagan had been unable to effect, and provided for a cut-off point at which a person's welfare payments would cease. States were also required to ensure that at least half of their welfare recipients had jobs or were enrolled in job-training programmes. The measure represented a fundamental overhaul of the welfare structure, one in tune with conservative doctrine in its emphasis on 'workfare' and its threat to end payments to substantial categories of people, including single mothers with young children. Liberal Democrats fiercely denounced the bill as regressive, but in 1996, as the presidential election loomed, Bill Clinton signed it into law.

To the AFL-CIO president the act was 'anti-poor, anti-immigrants, anti-women and anti-children – unravelling the safety net Franklin Roosevelt had put in place sixty years before'. But welfare entitlements had been burgeoning since the 1960s and for the most part the Middle Americans that Clinton cultivated had no particular affection for them, suspecting them of being subsidies for the feckless. Over half those polled in 1994 believed that welfare payments should be reduced or terminated. The Democrats had been harried over welfare for decades by conservative Republicans, and Clinton apparently concluded that the old unpopular system had to be abandoned before a new one could be devised. His gamble seemed vindicated by the experience of his second term, when, with assistance from the flourishing economy, welfare rolls dropped by nearly half, the proportion of the poorest women taking jobs rose markedly, and the number of children living with single parents actually declined. (Less happy figures began to emerge when the economy hit harder times after the turn of the century.)

By 1996 the economy was booming and the deficit declining fast. Clinton could claim credit for wise economic management, while the Republicans had been damaged by public perceptions of their congressional leaders' inflexibility over the budget negotiations and responsibility for the government shutdown. The Republican Party chose Bob Dole, a skilful Senate operator, as its candidate, but at seventy-three his age and dour manner counted against him, while the exuberant Clinton excelled in what he did best, schmoozing the electorate. Clinton coasted home with a lead of over 8 million votes, even if he still failed to get 50 per cent of the popular vote; Ross Perot ran again, though his popular vote slipped to 8 per cent. But while the 'Comeback Kid' had demonstrated his peculiar appeal yet again, he had failed to overcome the electorate's dogged preference for divided government, the Republicans retaining control of both houses of Congress. There was no assurance that Clinton's second term would be any more successful than his first.

Clinton's consummate understanding of the budget process did bring him some victories over congressional Republicans in these four years. Reconciling the budget was always a tortuous process with the Republicans in command of Capitol Hill, but year by year the president ensured that progressive programmes received something. Funding for such programmes as Head Start and child-care support was increased, as well as for AmeriCorps. There were new tax credits for higher education, to the relief of millions of middle-class parents, and money for a health insurance scheme for poor children. Decisions taken in these years promoted the use of the Internet, the phenomenal growth of e-commerce as a free trade area, and the boom in mobile phones. Yet these accomplishments received little attention and Clinton barely survived his second term, hopelessly mired as he became in scandal and constitutional crisis.

The charges over Whitewater had refused to go away, but more seriously the president's integrity was ferociously damaged by what became known as Monicagate. Bill Clinton had for years been dogged by rumours relating to extramarital relationships, but early in 1998 a charge emerged that he could not shake off. The partial government shutdowns had meant that the White House had to rely more than usual on young interns rather than the regular messenger service, one of whom the president had befriended. This was Monica Lewinsky, who told a friend of sexual encounters in the Oval Office.

As denials followed the allegations, congressional committees and federal officials unleashed investigations of any improprieties or criminal cover-ups, and the whole sorry episode escalated into an issue that virtually monopolized the headlines and the attention of Congress and the White House. 'I did not have sexual relations with that woman, Miss Lewinsky', the president insisted on television: 'I never told anybody to lie, not a single time. Never.' It turned out that whether he had sex with her depended on the definition of sex, and even on the meaning of 'is'. Clinton had apparently lied under oath and the Republican-led Congress felt that it had little alternative to impeachment proceedings, the second so instituted in the last third of the twentieth century. The humiliated president was tried before the Senate on two counts of perjury and one of obstruction of justice, although he was eventually acquitted because his prosecutors could not secure the two-thirds majority necessary to convict. It seemed that whatever the fury of the religious right, the bulk of the American people had little enthusiasm for destroying a president for his private peccadilloes, and the partisanship of his Republican accusers seemed no more admirable than Clinton's equivocations. (A poll in November 1998 remarkably showed that 54 per cent of Americans trusted Clinton to tell the truth.) Further, the economy was booming – unemployment was at its lowest point in decades – and the world was more or less peaceful. Clinton was generally credited with having done a good job.

'Slick Willy' had escaped yet again, though his political credibility had been so damaged that he was able to achieve little on the domestic front for the remainder of his administration. Clinton continued to be harassed by investigators probing into the various charges that had been levelled at him. Yet he never quite lost the charm with which he had won over a portion of the public, and had he been in a position to stand for a third term in 2000 he could well have been re-elected. As journalist Joe Klein has observed, 'he would leave office with the highest sustained job approval ratings of any President since John F. Kennedy'. But Clinton's capacity to engage with the public could not rub off onto his successor as Democratic presidential candidate. Vice-President Al Gore had the difficult task of distancing himself from the more tawdry aspects of the Clinton presidency while hoping to gain from the booming economy. The Republicans nominated the Texas governor and son of George Bush, George W. Bush, who portrayed himself as a 'caring conservative' (as he also promised a 'humbler America', ironically perhaps in view of the unshackling of American military power in the aftermath of 11 September 2001).

The uninspiring campaign concluded with an election that seemed the natural consummation of a third of a century of divided government. In the final – delayed – count Albert Gore won the popular vote with a lead of over 500,000, but the critical electoral vote was less conclusive. As the various states declared one way or the other, the decisive state proved to be Florida, the governor of which happened to be Bush's brother. Eventually the results declared by Florida officials showed a small lead for Bush, but the whole agonized process had brought to light several irregularities and had incited court challenges. Ultimately, on 12 December, the US Supreme Court itself, most of its members appointed by Republican presidents, had to resolve the impasse, doing so in a complex decision that favoured George W. Bush. The popular vote had gone one way and the electoral vote – so the judges decreed – another. Congress too yet again displayed its split personality. While the Republicans won a modest majority in the lower house, the Senate elections returned fifty Democrats and fifty Republicans. The dispiritingly divided condition of the American polity was reflected in the larger electoral map. For the most part Gore had carried the highly urbanized states, with their mixed racial and ethnic populations, and Bush the more homogeneous smaller states where traditional values remained vibrant. The cultural wars of the late twentieth century were still smouldering.

In September 1901 Theodore Roosevelt had been precipitated into the presidency by the assassination of William McKinley. The assassin, Leon F. Czolgosz, was an anarchist, albeit an American-born one, but he seemed the latest personification of a growing international terrorism that had recently taken the lives of a French president, a Spanish prime minister, an Austrian empress and an Italian king. As it happened, McKinley's murder did not seriously impede the spread of progressive sentiments in early twentieth-century America. By the end of the century another wave of international terrorism was under way, and almost exactly a hundred years after the slaying of President McKinley two planes destroyed the monumental twin towers of the World Trade Center in New York, along with about three thousand people, and another was flown into the Pentagon. These daring strikes on the symbols of American capitalism and military might suddenly exposed the frightening vulnerability of the planet's remaining superpower. The anarchist terrorism of around 1900, conducted with knives, handguns and small bombs, had tended to claim a victim at a time, which may be why McKinley's death did not trigger a general panic and did not deflect the course of American history. The mass destruction of 11 September 2001, however, seemed to be an act of war on the American state, a violent rejection of the role that the United States had come to play in the world in the course of the twentieth century. This awesome assault had the potential to refashion the shape of American politics; perhaps another political order would emerge.

Select Bibliography

Studies of the history of the United States in the twentieth century fill many yards of library shelves and room can be found here only to acknowledge some of the more helpful sources used in this book and to suggest some further reading for interested students.

Books on twentieth-century America began to appear when the century was little more than halfway through. One of the more authoritative is Arthur S. Link, *American Epoch: A History of the United States Since the 1890s* (New York, 1955), although subsequent editions, such as that in which William B. Catton collaborated (3 vols, New York, 1967), took the story to the mid-1960s. Barton J. Bernstein and Allen J. Matusow, eds, *Twentieth-Century America: Recent Interpretations* (New York, 1969) is a useful collection of essays. From a radical perspective is Gabriel Kolko, *Main Currents in Modern American History* (New York, 1976). For a perceptive study of the way in which American politics evolved during the greater part of the century see Robert Harrison, *State and Society in Twentieth-Century America* (London, 1997). An overview of the century focusing on the White House is John Kentleton, *President & Nation: The Making of Modern America* (Basingstoke, 2002). For a different perspective see Douglas Tallack, *Twentieth-Century America: The Intellectual and Cultural Context* (London, 1991). An engaging modern study is David A. Horowitz, Peter N. Carroll and David D. Lee, *On The Edge: A New History of 20th-Century America* (St Paul, MN, 1990), as is Michael Kazin, *The Populist Persuasion: An American History* (New York, 1995).

Economic, Social and Political Background

Useful general studies of the economy are Stuart Bruchey, *Enterprise: The Dynamic Economy of a Free People* (Cambridge, MA, 1990) and Jeremy Atack and Peter Passell, *A New Economic View of American History*

(2nd edn, New York, 1994). More specialized is Robert Sobel, *The Age of Giant Corporations: A Microeconomic History of American Business, 1914–1992* (3rd edn, Praeger, 1993). Valuable for the second half of the twentieth century are Michael French, *US Economic History since 1945* (Manchester, 1997) and William Issel, *Social Change in the United States, 1945–1983* (Basingstoke, 1985). For the same period a vital study is David Calleo, *The Imperious Economy* (New York, 1983). Good on the distribution of wealth through American history is Jeffrey G. Williamson and Peter H. Lindert, *American Inequality: A Macroeconomic History* (New York, 1980), and for the growing inequality of the late twentieth century see Sheldon Danziger and Peter Gottschalk, eds, *Uneven Tides: Rising Inequality In America* (New York, 1993) and Wallace C. Peterson, *Silent Depression: The Fate of the American Dream* (New York, 1994).

On parties and elections in the twentieth century see Walter Dean Burnham, *Critical Elections and the Mainsprings of American Politics* (New York, 1970); A. James Reichley, ed., *Elections American Style* (Washington, 1987); Paul Kleppner, ed., *The Evolution of American Electoral Systems* (Westport, CT, 1981); and Arthur Schlesinger, ed., *The History of U.S. Political Parties* (4 vols, New York, 1980). The growth of government is explored in Robert Higgs, *Crisis and Leviathan: Critical Episodes in the Growth of American Government* (New York, 1987); Jonathan R. T. Hughes, *The Governmental Habit Redux: Economic Controls from Colonial Times to the Present* (Princeton, 1991); and Ballard C. Campbell, *The Growth of American Government: Governance from the Cleveland Era to the Present* (Bloomington, IN, 1995). Other studies relevant to the themes of this book include Joseph J. Broesamle, *Reform and Reaction in Twentieth-Century American Politics* (Westport, CT, 1990) and Samuel P. Hays, *American Political History as Social Analysis* (Knoxville, TN, 1980). Still worth reading are the essays on William Jennings Bryan, Theodore Roosevelt, Woodrow Wilson, Herbert Hoover and Franklin D. Roosevelt in Richard Hofstadter, *The American Political Tradition and the Men Who Made It* (New York, 1948).

For general studies of foreign policy see Walter LaFeber, *The American Age: U.S. Foreign Policy at Home and Abroad* (2nd edn, New York, 1994); Foster Rhea Dulles, *America's Rise to World Power, 1898–1954* (New York, 1955); Thomas G. Paterson and Dennis Merrill, eds, *Major Problems in American Foreign Relations* (2 vols, 4th edn, Lexington, MA, 1995); and Robert H. Ferrell, *American Diplomacy: The Twentieth Century* (New York, 1988).

Indispensable in any serious study of American history is the US Census Bureau's *Historical Statistics of the United States: Colonial Era to 1970* (Washington, 1976), which may be supplemented with the annual *Statistical Abstract of the United States*. Another useful source is Kirk H. Porter and Donald Bruce Johnson, eds, *National Party Platforms, 1840–1964* (Urbana, 1966).

Political History, 1900–33

Good recent introductions to the early twentieth century include Nell Irvin Painter, *Standing at Armageddon: The United States, 1877–1919* (New York, 1987); John M. Cooper Jr., *Pivotal Decades: The United States, 1900–1920* (New York, 1990); Lewis L. Gould, *Reform and Regulation: American Politics from Roosevelt to Wilson* (3rd edn, Prospect Heights, IL, 1996); and Steven J. Diner, *A Very Different Age: Americans of the Progressive Era* (New York, 1998). Two earlier books in the Chicago History of American Civilization remain both essential and eminently readable, notably Samuel P. Hays, *The Response to Industrialism, 1885–1914* (Chicago, 1957) and William E. Leuchtenburg, *The Perils of Prosperity, 1914–1932* (Chicago, 1958).

In the middle of the twentieth century a number of influential studies reinvigorated the historiography of Progressive America, most notably Richard Hofstadter, *The Age of Reform: From Bryan to F. D. R.* (New York, 1955); the Hays volume cited above; Henry F. May, *The End of American Innocence: A Study of the First Years of Our Own Time, 1912–1917* (New York, 1959); Gabriel Kolko, *The Triumph of Conservatism: An Interpretation of the Progressive Movement* (New York, 1963); and Robert H. Wiebe, *The Search for Order, 1877–1920* (New York, 1967). John A. Thompson offered a valuable analysis of the historiography as it then existed in *Progressivism* (British Association for American Studies, 1979). Subsequent revisions have been assisted by such studies as Barry D. Karl, *The Uneasy State: The United States from 1915 to 1940* (Chicago, 1983); Martin Sklar, *The Corporate Reconstruction of American Capitalism: The Market, the Law, and Politics, 1890–1916* (Cambridge, 1988); Richard L. McCormick, *The Party Period and Public Policy: American Politics from the Age of Jackson to the Progressive Era* (New York, 1986); and two by Morton Keller, *Regulating a New Economy: Public Policy and Economic Change in America, 1900–1933* (Cambridge, MA, 1990) and *Regulating a New Society: Public Policy and Social Change in America, 1900–1933* (Cambridge, MA, 1994). Contributing the perspective of a political scientist is Stephen Skowronek, *Building a New American State: The Evolution of National Administrative Capacities, 1877–1920* (Cambridge, 1982).

Other studies of progressive reform include Clarke A. Chambers, *Seedtime of Reform: American Social Service and Social Action, 1918–1933* (Ann Arbor, 1967); Robert Crunden, *Ministers of Reform: The Progressives' Achievement in American Civilization, 1889–1920* (New York, 1982); and Allen F. Davis, *Spearheads for Reform: The Social Settlements and the Progressive Movement, 1890–1914* (New Brunswick, NJ, 1984). For connections with later reform see Otis L. Graham Jr., *An Encore for Reform: The Old Progressives and the New Deal* (New York, 1967).

On Theodore Roosevelt and his times see George E. Mowry, *The Era of Theodore Roosevelt and the Birth of Modern America, 1900–1912* (New York, 1958); William H. Harbaugh, *The Life and Times of Theodore*

Roosevelt (New York, 1975); John M. Blum, *The Republican Roosevelt* (Cambridge, MA, 1954); and Louis L. Gould, *The Presidency of Theodore Roosevelt* (Lawrence, KS, 1991). Paolo E. Coletta, *The Presidency of William Howard Taft* (Lawrence, KS, 1973) treats TR's favoured successor, while Woodrow Wilson has been the subject of extensive study. Most authoritative is Arthur S. Link, *Wilson* (5 vols, Princeton, 1947–1965), although this epic only reaches 1917, but more succinct are the same author's *Woodrow Wilson and the Progressive Era, 1910–1917* (New York, 1954) and *Woodrow Wilson: Revolution, War and Peace* (Arlington Heights, IL, 1979). A perceptive study is John M. Blum, *Woodrow Wilson and the Politics of Morality* (Boston, 1956). Incisive and thoughtful is John A. Thompson, *Woodrow Wilson* (London, 2002); and Wilson is interestingly compared to his great rival in John Milton Cooper Jr., *The Warrior and the Priest: Woodrow Wilson and Theodore Roosevelt* (Cambridge, MA, 1983).

The above titles contain extensive material on foreign policy, but may be supplemented with more specialized studies. Walter LaFeber, *The American Search for Opportunity, 1865–1913* (Cambridge, 1993) examines the United States' entry onto the world stage. Lloyd E. Ambrosius, *Woodrow Wilson and the American Diplomatic Tradition* (Cambridge, 1987) puts the struggle over the League of Nations in context. Christopher Lasch, *The American Liberals and the Russian Revolution* (New York, 1962) and David S. Foglesong, *America's Secret War Against Bolshevism: U.S. Intervention in the Russian Civil War, 1917–1920* (Chapel Hill, 1995) consider the implications for the United States of the Russian Revolution. For a leading isolationist see Richard Coke Lower, *A Bloc of One: The Political Career of Hiram W. Johnson* (Stanford, 1993).

On the First World War see David M. Kennedy's excellent *Over Here: The First World War and American Society* (New York, 1980); also still useful is Edward Robb Ellis, *Echoes of Distant Thunder, 1914–1918* (New York, 1975 and 1996). The political history of the 1920s may be traced in John D. Hicks, *Republican Ascendancy, 1920–1933* (New York, 1960); Ellis W. Hawley, *The Great War and the Search for a Modern Order: A History of the American People and Their Institutions, 1917–1933* (New York, 1979); David Burnham, *The Politics of Provincialism: The Democratic Party in Transition, 1918–1932* (New York, 1968); Robert K. Murray, *The Politics of Normalcy: Governmental Theory and Practice in the Harding-Coolidge Era* (New York, 1973); and Michael E. Parrish, *Anxious Decades: America in Prosperity and Depression, 1920–1941* (New York, 1992). Of the political figures of the era, Herbert Hoover has received the most respectful attention, as in Joan Hoff Wilson, *Herbert Hoover: Forgotten Progressive* (Boston, 1975). Particular episodes and movements have been examined in Robert K. Murray, *Red Scare: A Study in National Hysteria, 1919–1920* (New York, 1955); K. Austin Kerr, *Organizing for Prohibition: A New History of the Anti-Saloon League* (New Haven, CT, 1985); and Kenneth T. Jackson, *The Ku Klux Klan in the City, 1915–1930* (New York, 1967).

John Kenneth Galbraith provides a classic analysis of *The Great Crash, 1929* (3rd edn, London, 1973); and for a brief analysis see Peter Fearon, *The Origins and Nature of the Great Slump, 1929–1932* (London, 1979). Robert S. McElvaine, *The Great Depression, 1929–1941* (New York, 1984) is a vivid account. A wider view is taken in Dietmar Rothermund, *The Global Impact of The Great Crash, 1929–1939* (London, 1996).

Political History, 1933–69

A good collection of essays is Steve Fraser and Gary Gerstle, eds, *The Rise and Fall of the New Deal Order, 1930–1980* (Princeton, 1989). For interesting discussions of the evolution of the liberal tradition through the middle decades of the twentieth century see William E. Leuchtenberg, *In the Shadow of FDR: From Harry Truman to Ronald Reagan* (rev. edn, Ithaca, 1985) and Alonzo L. Hamby, *Liberalism and Its Challengers: F.D.R. to Reagan* (New York, 1985). Political scientists have added their insights in Kenneth Finegold and Theda Skocpol, *State and Party in America's New Deal* (Madison, 1995); David Plotke, *Building a Democratic Political Order: Reshaping American Liberalism in the 1930s and 1940s* (Cambridge, 1996); Sidney M. Milkis, *The President and the Parties: The Transformation of the American Party System since the New Deal* (New York, 1993); and Everett Carll Ladd with Charles D. Hadley, *Transformation of the American Party System: Political Coalitions from the New Deal to the 1970s* (New York, 1978).

William E. Leuchtenburg, *Franklin D. Roosevelt and the New Deal, 1932–1940* (New York, 1963) remains one of the best introductions to the New Deal, and an excellent topical approach is Anthony J. Badger, *The New Deal: The Depression Years, 1933–1940* (Basingstoke, 1989). Much longer is the authoritative David M. Kennedy, *Freedom from Fear: The American People in Depression and War, 1929–1945* (New York, 1999). Peter Fearon, *War, Prosperity & Depression: The U.S. Economy, 1917–1945* (Oxford, 1987) offers the approach of an economic historian. A recent interpretative study of the whole of Roosevelt's presidency is Alan Brinkley, *The End of Reform: New Deal Liberalism in Recession and War* (New York, 1995).

A sympathetic study of the New Deal is Arthur M. Schlesinger Jr.'s trilogy of *The Age of Roosevelt* (Boston): *The Crisis of the Old Order* (1956), *The Coming of the New Deal* (1958) and *The Politics of Upheaval* (1960), though the story is not taken beyond 1936. The doyen of New Deal historians is William E. Leuchtenburg, whose introductory volume is cited above, but see also *The FDR Years: On Roosevelt and His Legacy* (New York, 1995) and *The Supreme Court Reborn: Constitutional Revolution in the Age of Roosevelt* (New York, 1995). Important on the New Deal and the economy is Ellis W. Hawley, *The New Deal and the Problem of Monopoly* (Princeton, 1966). Excellent on the politics is John M. Allswang, *The New Deal and American Politics: A Study in Political Change* (New York, 1978). On Roosevelt's populist opponents see Alan Brinkley, *Voices of*

Protest: Huey Long, Father Coughlin and the Great Depression (New York, 1982). Perhaps the single most influential biographical analysis of Franklin Roosevelt is James MacGregor Burns, *Roosevelt: The Lion and the Fox* (New York, 1956). A recent biography is Patrick Maney, *The Roosevelt Presence: A Biography of Franklin Delano Roosevelt* (New York, 1992).

Authoritative on Roosevelt's foreign policy is Robert Dallek, *Franklin D. Roosevelt and American Foreign Policy, 1932–1945* (New York, 1979); and see also Frederick W. Marks III, *Wind Over Sand: The Diplomacy of Franklin Roosevelt* (Athens, GA, 1987). Particular periods are examined in Wayne C. Cole, *Roosevelt and the Isolationists* (Lincoln, 1983) and Gaddis Smith, *American Diplomacy During the Second World War, 1941–1945* (2nd edn, New York, 1985). Also valuable are Warren F. Kimball, *Franklin D. Roosevelt and the World Crisis, 1937–1945* (Lexington, MA, 1974) and Robert A. Divine, *Roosevelt and World War II* (Baltimore, 1969). A brief general treatment of the United States in the Second World War is Michael C. C. Adams, *The Best War Ever: America and World War II* (Baltimore, 1994); and for a lively general study see William L. O'Neill, *A Democracy at War: America's Fight at Home and Abroad in World War II* (Cambridge, MA, 1993).

On the Allied leadership see Herbert Feis, *Churchill, Roosevelt and Stalin: The War They Waged, The Peace They Sought* (Princeton, 1974) and Christopher Thorne, *Allies of a Kind: The United States, Britain, and the War Against Japan, 1941–1945* (Oxford, 1978). Christopher Thorne, *Border Crossings* (Oxford, 1988) contains suggestive essays on Anglo-American relations. For the resort to the atom bomb see Robert James Maddox, *Weapons for Victory: The Hiroshima Decision Fifty Years Later* (Columbia, MO, 1995). Valuable studies focusing largely on the domestic impact of the war include Richard Polenberg, *War and Society: The United States, 1941–1945* (Philadelphia, 1972) and John Morton Blum, *V Was For Victory: Politics and American Culture in World War II* (New York, 1976).

Good introductions to the post-war period are James Gilbert, *Another Chance: Postwar America, 1945–1968* (New York, 1981); John Diggins, *The Proud Decades: America in War and Peace, 1941–1960* (New York, 1988); and William O'Neill, *American High: The Years of Confidence, 1945–1960* (New York, 1986). Excellent and substantial syntheses are William H. Chafe, *The Unfinished Journey: America Since World War II* (5th edn, New York, 2002) and James T. Patterson, *Grand Expectations: The United States, 1945–1974* (New York, 1996). A recent major interpretation is Lizabeth Cohen, *A Consumers' Republic: The Politics of Mass Consumption in Post-war America* (New York, 2003).

Other helpful studies include Kim McQuaid, *Uneasy Partners: Big Business in American Politics, 1945–1990* (Baltimore, 1994); Elaine Tyler May, *Homeward Bound: American Families in the Cold War Era* (New York, 1988); and Robert Wuthnow, *The Restructuring of American Religion: Society and Faith since World War II* (Princeton, 1988).

Indispensable for tracing the course of public opinion is George Gallup, *The Gallup Poll: Public Opinion, 1935–1971* (New York, 1972).

For the Truman presidency see Alonzo Hamby, *Beyond the New Deal: Harry S. Truman and American Liberalism* (New York, 1973) and Robert Ferrell, *Harry S. Truman and the Modern American Presidency* (Boston, 1983). Barton J. Bernstein, ed., *Politics and Policies of the Truman Administration* (Chicago, 1970) and Michael Lacey, ed., *The Truman Presidency* (Washington, 1989) offer valuable collections of essays. Dwight Eisenhower has attracted many historians, not least Stephen Ambrose, *Eisenhower* (2 vols, London, 1983–1984). For briefer studies see Elmo Richardson, *The Presidency of Dwight D. Eisenhower* (Lawrence, KS, 1979) and Charles C. Alexander, *Holding the Line: The Eisenhower Era, 1952–61* (Bloomington, IN, 1975). An influential revisionist work is Fred I. Greenstein, *The Hidden-Hand Presidency: Eisenhower as Leader* (New York, 1982). Important specialized studies include Gary W. Reichard, *The Reaffirmation of Republicanism: Eisenhower and the Eighty-Third Congress* (Knoxville, 1975) and Iwan W. Morgan, *Eisenhower Versus the Spenders: The Eisenhower Administration, the Democrats and the Budget 1953–1960* (London, 1990).

There are many studies of McCarthyism, among them David Caute, *The Great Fear: The Anti-Communist Purge Under Truman and Eisenhower* (New York, 1978); Robert Griffith, *The Politics of Fear: Joseph R. McCarthy and the Senate* (2nd edn, Amherst, 1987); and M. J. Heale, *American Anticommunism: Combating the Enemy Within, 1830–1970* (Baltimore, 1990) and *McCarthy's Americans: Red Scare Politics in State and Nation, 1935–1965* (London, 1998). A major recent analysis is Ellen Schrecker, *Many Are the Crimes: McCarthyism in America* (Princeton, 1998).

A brief introduction to the 1960s is offered in M. J. Heale, *The Sixties in America: History, Politics and Protest* (Edinburgh, 2001). Good on political history is John M. Blum, *Years of Discord: American Politics and Society 1961–1974* (New York, 1991). David Burner, *Making Peace with the 60s* (Princeton, 1996) emphasizes the destructive effects of the splitting apart of liberalism and radicalism. An excellent recent discussion is Maurice Isserman and Michael Kazin, *America Divided: the Civil War of the 1960s* (New York, 1999). Godfrey Hodgson, *America in Our Time* (New York, 1978), examines the 'liberal consensus' among the governing classes; and emphasizing the changing nature of liberalism is Gareth Davies, *From Opportunity to Entitlement: the Transformation and Decline of Great Society Liberalism* (Lawrence, KS, 1996). Allen J. Matusow takes a critical view in *The Unraveling of America: a History of Liberalism in the 1960s* (New York, 1984).

In national politics the turbulence of the sixties tended to facilitate the revival of conservatism. On this subject see Mary C. Brennan, *Turning Right in the Sixties: The Conservative Capture of the GOP* (Chapel Hill, 1995) and especially Lisa McGirr, *Suburban Warriors: The Origins of the New American Right* (Princeton, 2001) and Rick Perlstein, *Before the*

Storm: Barry Goldwater and the Unmaking of the American Consensus (New York, 2001). Major studies of conservative figures include Robert Alan Goldberg, *Barry Goldwater* (New Haven, 1995) and Dan T. Carter, *The Politics of Rage: George Wallace, the Origins of the New Conservatism, and the Transformation of American Politics* (New York, 1995). Essential reading on the New Left is the participatory history by Todd Gitlin, *The Sixties: Years of Hope, Days of Rage* (New York, 1989). A major study of protest activity is Terry H. Anderson, *The Movement and the Sixties* (New York, 1996).

Good scholarly studies of the Kennedy administration include Herbert S. Parmet, *JFK: the Presidency of John F. Kennedy* (New York, 1983); James N. Giglio, *The Presidency of John F. Kennedy* (Lawrence, KS, 1991); and especially Hugh Brogan, *Kennedy* (London, 1996). Lyndon Johnson was able to provide his own account in *The Vantage Point: Perspectives of the Presidency, 1963–1969* (New York, 1971), though more revealing is Doris Kearns, *Lyndon Johnson and the American Dream* (New York, 1976), written after interviews with the former president. Judicious is Paul Conkin, *Big Daddy from the Pedernales: Lyndon Johnson* (Boston, 1986), while the most authoritative scholarly account is Robert Dallek, *Flawed Giant: Lyndon Johnson and His Times, 1961–1973* (New York, 1998). For the reform programmes see Irwin Unger, *The Best of Intentions: The Triumphs and Failures of the Great Society Under Kennedy, Johnson, and Nixon* (New York, 1996).

A useful introduction to modern American foreign policy is Stephen Ambrose and Douglas G. Brinkley, *Rise to Globalism: American Foreign Policy since 1938* (8th edn, New York, 1997), as are Thomas J. McCormick, *America's Half Century: United States Foreign Policy in the Cold War and After* (2nd edn, Baltimore, 1995) and John Spanier and Steven W. Hook, *American Foreign Policy Since World War II* (14th edn, Washington, 1998). Thomas G. Paterson offers some sharp analyses in *Meeting the Communist Threat: Truman to Reagan* (New York, 1988).

The roots of the Cold War have been located in the Second World War, as briefly discussed in Richard Crockatt, *The United States and the Origins of the Cold War*, 1941–53 (British Association for American Studies, 1990) and more substantially in John Lewis Gaddis, *The United States and the Origins of the Cold War, 1941–1947* (New York, 1972). See also Melvyn Leffler, *A Preponderance of Power: National Security, the Truman Administration, and the Cold War* (Stanford, 1992); Thomas Paterson, *On Every Front: The Making of the Cold War* (New York, 1979); Michael Hogan, *The Marshall Plan: America, Britain, and the Reconstruction of Western Europe, 1947–1952* (New York, 1987); Daniel Yergin, *Shattered Peace: The Origins of the Cold War and the National Security State* (Boston, 1977); Ernest R. May, ed., *American Cold War Strategy: Interpreting NSC-68* (New York, 1993); and Robert Divine, *Eisenhower and the Cold War* (New York, 1981).

A recent brief introduction to Vietnam is Mitchell K. Hall, *The Vietnam War* (Harlow, 2000); see also John Dumbrell, *Vietnam: American*

Involvement at Home and Abroad (British Association for American Studies, 1992); Michael H. Hunt, *Lyndon Johnson's War: America's Cold War Crusade in Vietnam, 1945–1968* (New York, 1996); and Robert J. McMahon, ed., *Major Problems in the History of the Vietnam War* (Lexington, MA, 1995). Substantial, authoritative accounts include George Herring, *America's Longest War: The United States and Vietnam, 1950–1975* (2nd edn, Philadelphia, 1986); Marilyn Young, *The Vietnam Wars: 1945–1990* (New York, 1991); Lloyd Gardner, *Approaching Vietnam: From World War II Through Dienbienphu, 1941–1954* (New York, 1988); and Stanley Karnow, *Vietnam: A History* (New York, 1983). Absorbing on the American war leadership is David Halberstam, *The Best and the Brightest* (London, 1972). Focusing on the Johnson White House is Larry Berman, *Lyndon Johnson's War: The Road to Stalemate in Vietnam* (New York, 1989). For the domestic implications of the war see Thomas Powers, *The War at Home: Vietnam and the American People, 1964–1968* (New York, 1973).

Political History, 1969–2000

The more one approaches the present the more history is supplanted by political science. Textbooks by political scientists are useful for understanding parties and politics, such as Tim Hames and Nicol Rae, *Governing America: History, Culture, Institutions, Organisation, Policy* (Manchester, 1996) and David McKay, *American Politics & Society* (3rd edn, Oxford, 1993). Interesting analyses may be found in Byron E. Shafer et al., *Present Discontents: American Politics in the Very Late Twentieth Century* (Chatham, NJ, 1997). Sniffing the electoral winds at the time of their publication were Kevin P. Phillips, *The Emerging Republican Majority* (New Rochelle, NY, 1969) and Richard M. Scammon and Ben J. Wattenberg, *The Real Majority: An Extraordinary Examination of the American Electorate* (New York, 1970). Fred I. Greenstein, ed., *Leadership in the Modern Presidency* (Cambridge, MA, 1988) is a collection of essays on the presidents from Franklin Roosevelt to Reagan. For valuable essays on modern political trends see Gillian Peele, Christopher J. Bailey, Bruce Cain and B. Guy Peters, eds, *Developments in American Politics 3* (3rd edn, Basingstoke, 1998) and *Developments in American Politics 4* (Basingstoke, 2002); Anthony King, ed., *The New American Political System* (Washington, 1978) and the 'second version' (Washington, 1990); and Richard A. Harris and Sidney M. Milkis, eds, *Remaking American Politics* (Boulder, CO, 1989). E. J. Dionne Jr., *Why Americans Hate Politics* (New York, 1991) is a perceptive account by a political reporter of the period from the 1960s to the 1990s. See also Hedrick K. Smith, *The Power Game: How Washington Works* (Glasgow, 1988) and Theodore H. White, *America in Search of Itself: The Making of the President 1956–1980* (London, 1983).

Thematic studies include Kim McQuaid, *Big Business and Presidential Power: From FDR to Reagan* (New York, 1982); Alexander P. Lamis, *The*

Two-Party South (2nd edn, New York, 1988); Samuel P. Hays, *Beauty, Health, and Permanence: Environmental Politics in the United States, 1955–1985* (New York, 1987); and Kirkpatrick Sale, *The Green Revolution: The Environmental Movement, 1962–1992* (New York, 1993). For aspects of American political culture see Lester Thurow, *The Zero-Growth Society* (New York, 1980); John Kenneth Galbraith, *The Culture of Contentment* (New York, 1992); Arthur M. Schlesinger, Jr., *The Disuniting of America: Reflections on a Multicultural Society* (New York, 1991); and Gertrude Himmelfarb, *One Nation, Two Cultures* (New York, 1999).

The following studies are helpful for significant trends in American politics: Peter Irons, *A People's History of the Supreme Court* (New York, 1999); Mark Silverstein, *Judicious Choices: The New Politics of Supreme Court Confirmations* (New York, 1994); Morris P. Fiorini, *Congress: Keystone of the Washington Establishment* (2nd edn, New Haven, 1989); David K. Nichols, *The Myth of the Modern Presidency* (University Park, PA, 1994); Timothy Conlan, *New Federalism: Intergovernmental Reform from Nixon to Reagan* (Washington, 1988); David M. Ricci, *The Transformation of American Politics: The New Washington and the Rise of Think Tanks* (New Haven, 1993); Larry J. Sabato, *The Rise of Political Consultants* (New York, 1981); Allan J. Cigler and Burdett A. Loomis, eds, *Interest Group Politics* (2nd edn, Washington, 1986); David Vogel, *Fluctuating Fortunes: The Political Power of Business in America* (New York, 1989) and *Kindred Strangers: The Uneasy Relationship between Politics and Business in America* (Princeton, 1996); and Benjamin Ginsberg and Martin Shefter, *Politics by Other Means: Politicians, Prosecutors, and the Press from Watergate to Whitewater* (New York, 1992).

Good studies of long-term political change include Iwan W. Morgan, *Beyond the Liberal Consensus: A Political History of the United States since 1965* (London, 1994). There have been several studies of the rise of the right, including Thomas Byrne Edsall with Mary D. Edsall, *Chain Reaction: the Impact of Race, Rights and Taxes on American Politics* (New York, 1992); Godfrey Hodgson, *The World Turned Right Side Up: A History of the Conservative Ascendancy in America* (Boston, 1996); William C. Berman, *America's Right Turn: From Nixon to Bush* (Baltimore, 1994); Peter Steinfels, *The Neo-Conservatives: The Men Who Are Changing America's Politics* (New York, 1979); and Steve Bruce, *The Rise and Fall of the New Christian Right* (Oxford, 1990).

Richard Nixon was also able to tell his own story in *RN: The Memoirs of Richard Nixon* (London, 1978), and, despite blistering analyses of his role in Watergate, he has received surprisingly sympathetic treatment by at least some biographers, as in Herbert S. Parmet, *Richard Nixon and His America* (Boston, 1990) and Melvin Small, *The Presidency of Richard Nixon* (Lawrence, KS, 1999). An important study is Joan Hoff, *Nixon Reconsidered* (New York, 1994). A recent incisive analysis is Iwan Morgan, *Nixon* (London, 2002). For Nixon's fall see Stanley Kutler, *The*

Wars of Watergate: The Last Crisis of the Nixon Presidency (New York, 1990).

The 1970s are surveyed briefly in Peter Carroll, *It Seemed Like Nothing Happened* (New York, 1982) and enjoyably in Bruce J. Schulman, *The Seventies: The Great Shift in American Culture, Society, and Politics* (New York, 2001); see also Elsebeth Hurup, ed., *The Lost Decade: America in the Seventies* (Aarhus, Denmark, 1996). Gerald R. Ford saw his brief administration as *A Time To Heal* (New York, 1979); and an academic study is John Robert Greene, *The Presidency of Gerald R. Ford* (Lawrence, KS, 1995). Jimmy Carter tells his story in *Keeping Faith: Memoirs of a President* (New York, 1982). For analyses by political scientists and historians see Charles O. Jones, *The Trusteeship Presidency: Jimmy Carter and the United States Congress* (Baton Rouge, 1988); Erwin C. Hargrove, *Jimmy Carter as President* (Baton Rouge, 1988); John Dumbrell, *The Carter Presidency: A Re-evaluation* (Manchester, 1993); Burton I. Kaufman, *The Presidency of James Earl Carter, Jr.* (Lawrence, KS, 1993); and Gary M. Fink and Hugh Davis Graham, eds, *The Carter Presidency: Policy Choices in the Post-New Deal Era* (Lawrence, KS, 1998).

Several of the studies of foreign policy and Vietnam listed in the previous section remain relevant for the evolution of foreign policy after 1969. An interesting recent analysis of the anti-war movement is Rhodri Jeffreys-Jones, *Peace Now: American Society and the Ending of the Vietnam War* (New Haven, 1999). On the anti-war movement's impact see Melvin Small, *Johnson, Nixon, and the Doves* (New Brunswick, NJ, 1988). Revisiting the conflict in which he participated is Robert S. McNamara, *In Retrospect: The Tragedy and Lessons of Vietnam* (New York, 1995). A useful analysis of the post-Vietnam period is John Dumbrell, *American Foreign Policy: Carter to Clinton* (London, 1997). For Jimmy Carter's foreign policy see Gaddis Smith, *Morality, Reason and Power: American Diplomacy in the Carter Years* (New York, 1986). Most helpful on its subject is Robert A. Pastor, *Whirlpool: U.S. Foreign Policy Toward Latin America and the Caribbean* (Princeton, 1992). Several thoughtful scholars have contributed to Michael Hogan, ed., *The End of the Cold War* (Cambridge, 1992). Critical of the Bush administration in the Persian Gulf War is Robert W. Tucker and David C. Hendrickson, *The Imperial Temptation: The New World Order and America's Purpose* (New York, 1992). Other useful studies include George Lenczowski, *American Presidents and the Middle East* (Durham, NC, 1990). A major study of American policy in the 1990s is David Halberstam, *War in a Time of Peace: Bush, Clinton and the Generals* (London, 2002).

The Reagan administration is considered succinctly in David Mervin, *Ronald Reagan and the American Presidency* (London, 1990) and in lively mode in Michael Schaller, *Reckoning with Reagan: America and Its President in the 1980s* (New York, 1992). See also Fred Greenstein, ed., *The Reagan Presidency: An Early Appraisal* (Baltimore, 1983). Haynes Johnson, *Sleepwalking Through History: America in the Reagan Years*

(New York, 1991) is an indictment by a talented journalist; and a friendlier biography is Edmund Morris, *Dutch: A Memoir of Ronald Reagan* (London, 1999). Several members of the administration have published revealing accounts, including David Stockman, *The Triumph of Politics* (London, 1986). On Reagan's successor see David Mervin, *George Bush and the Guardian Presidency* (Basingstoke, 1996) and John Robert Greene, *The Presidency of George Bush* (Lawrence, KS, 2000).

Good on the early Clinton administration is Colin Campbell and Bert A. Rockman, eds, *The Clinton Presidency: First Appraisals* (Chatham, NJ, 1996). Also observing from a halfway point is British journalist Martin Walker, *The President We Deserve: Bill Clinton: His Rise, Falls, and Comebacks* (New York, 1996). American journalist Joe Klein provides some perspective in *The Natural: The Misunderstood Presidency of Bill Clinton* (New York, 2002); and a massive defence of the Clinton presidency by an aide is Sidney Blumenthal, *The Clinton Wars* (New York, 2003).

Labour

Introductory works in labour history include Melvyn Dubofsky and Foster Rhea Dulles, *Labor in America: A History* (6th edn, Wheeling, IL, 1999); Eileen Boris and Nelson Lichtenstein, eds, *Major Problems in the History of American Workers* (Lexington, MA, 1991); David Brody, *Workers in Industrial America: Essays on the Twentieth-Century Struggle* (New York, 1980); Mike Davis, *Prisoners of the American Dream* (New York, 1986); and Robert H. Zieger, *American Workers, American Unions* (2nd edn, Baltimore, 1994). See also John H. M. Laslett and Seymour Martin Lipset, eds, *Failure of a Dream? Essays in the History of American Socialism* (Garden City, NY, 1974). For the period down to the 1970s see Melvyn Dubofsky, *The State and Labor in Modern America* (Chapel Hill, 1994).

Essential for understanding the late nineteenth-century working class is Herbert Gutman, *Work, Culture, and Society in Industrialising America* (New York, 1976). Major studies focusing largely on the late nineteenth century and early twentieth century include Melvyn Dubofsky, *Industrialism and the American Worker, 1865–1920* (2nd edn, Arlington Heights, IL, 1985); William E. Forbath, *Law and the Shaping of the American Labor Movement* (Cambridge, MA, 1991); and David Montgomery, *Workers' Control in America* (Cambridge, 1979) and *The Fall of the House of Labor* (Cambridge, 1987). Valuable too are Dirk Hoerder, ed., *American Labor and Immigration History, 1877–1920s* (Champaign, IL, 1983) and John E. Bodnar, *Workers' World: Kinship, Community and Protest in an Industrial Society, 1900–1940* (Baltimore, 1982).

The years of the New Deal Order were critical for labour history and industrial relations. See particularly Robert H. Zieger, *American Workers, American Unions*, noted above, and Irving Bernstein, *The Lean Years: A History of the American Worker, 1920–1933* (Boston, 1960) and *The*

Turbulent Years: A History of the American Worker, 1933–1941 (Boston, 1969). Influential on the middle years of the century are Lizabeth Cohen, *Making a New Deal: Industrial Workers in Chicago, 1919–1939* (Cambridge, 1990); Nelson Lichtenstein, *Labor's War at Home: The CIO in World War II* (Cambridge, 1982); and, on the 1940s, Howell Harris, *The Right To Manage: Industrial Relations Policies of American Business* (Madison, 1982). Important specialized studies include Steve Fraser, *Labor Will Rule: Sidney Hillman and the Rise of American Labor* (New York, 1991); Gary Gerstle, *Working-Class Americanism: The Politics of Labor in a Textile City, 1914–1960* (Cambridge, 1989); Christopher L. Tomlins, *The State and the Unions: Labor Relations, Law, and the Organized Labor Movement in the United States, 1880–1960* (Cambridge, 1986); and Robert H. Zieger, *The CIO, 1935–1955* (Chapel Hill, 1995).

Vivian Vale, *Labour in American Politics* (London, 1971) is perceptive on labour's political role during the New Deal Order, as is Karen Orren, *Belated Feudalism: Labor, the Law, and Liberal Development in the United States* (Cambridge, 1991). Also helpful are J. David Greenstone, *Labor in American Politics* (New York, 1969) and Graham K. Wilson, *Unions in American National Politics* (London, 1979). George Lipsitz, *Rainbow at Midnight: Labor and Culture in the 1940s* (Urbana, IL, 1994) offers a radical critique and Harvey A. Levenstein, *Communism, Anticommunism, and the C.I.O.* (Westport, CT, 1981) and Barbara S. Griffith, *The Crises of American Labor: Operation Dixie and the Defeat of the CIO* (Philadelphia, 1988) examine particular episodes. Studies of labour decline include Gordon C. Clarke, *Unions and Communities Under Siege: American Communities and the Crisis of Organized Labor* (Cambridge, 1989) and Michael Goldfield, *The Decline of Organized Labor in the United States* (Chicago, 1987).

Welfare history may be approached through Edward D. Berkowitz, *America's Welfare State from Roosevelt to Reagan* (Baltimore, 1991) and through James T. Patterson's studies, *America's Struggle Against Poverty, 1900–1985* (2nd edn, Cambridge, MA, 1986) and *The Welfare State in America, 1930–1980* (British Association for American Studies, 1981). Other major contributions include Margaret Weir, Ann Shola Orloff and Theda Skocpol, eds, *The Politics of Social Policy in the United States* (Princeton, 1988); William R. Brock, *Welfare, Democracy and the New Deal* (Cambridge, 1988); and Linda Gordon, *Pitied But Not Entitled: Single Mothers and the History of Welfare* (New York, 1994).

Women

American women's history has been a flourishing field. A magisterial introduction is Carl Degler, *At Odds: Women and the Family in America from the Revolution to the Present* (New York, 1980). Several leading scholars contribute to Nancy F. Cott, ed., *No Small Courage: A History of Women in the United States* (Oxford, 2000). For an incisive introduction see

S. Jay Kleinberg, *Women in the United States, 1930–1945* (London, 1999); and for more specialized essays, Ellen Carol DuBois and Vicki L. Ruiz, eds, *Unequal Sisters: A Multicultural Reader in U.S. Women's History* (New York, 1990). Students should find useful the collection of essays and documents in Mary Beth Norton and Ruth M. Alexander, eds, *Major Problems in American Women's History* (2nd edn, Lexington, MA, 1996). Focusing more exclusively on the twentieth century are Rosalind Rosenberg, *Divided Lives: American Women in the Twentieth Century* (New York, 1992); Lois W. Banner, *Women in Modern America: A Brief History* (3rd edn, Fort Worth, 1995); and Sheila Rowbotham: *The History of Women in Britain and the United States* (London, 1997). See also Susan Estabrook Kennedy, *If All We Did Was To Weep At Home: A History of White Working-Class Women in America* (Bloomington, 1979). Excellent on economics, employment and income is Claudia Goldin, *Understanding the Gender Gap: An Economic History of American Women* (New York, 1990); see also Alice Kessler-Harris, *Out to Work: A History of Wage-Earning Women in the United States* (New York, 1982).

More specialized studies focusing on the early twentieth century include William L. O'Neill, *The Woman Movement: Feminism in the United States and England* (London, 1969); Aileen S. Kraditor, *The Ideas of the Woman Suffrage Movement, 1890–1920* (New York, 1965, 1981); and Robert Booth Fowler, *Carrie Catt: Feminist Politician* (Boston, 1986). For the evolution from 'first wave' to 'second wave' feminism see Nancy F. Cott, *The Grounding of Modern Feminism* (New Haven, 1987).

For the middle decades of the twentieth century see William H. Chafe, *The American Woman: Her Changing Social, Economic, and Political Roles, 1920–1970* (London, 1972) and *Women and Equality: Changing Patterns in American Culture* (New York, 1977); Susan M. Hartmann, *The Home Front and Beyond: American Woman in the 1940s* (Boston, 1982); Rochelle Gatlin, *American Women since 1945* (London, 1987); Joanne Meyerowitz, ed., *Not June Cleaver: Women and Gender in Postwar America, 1945–1960* (Philadelphia, 1994); and Elaine Tyler May, *Homeward Bound: American Families in the Cold War Era* (New York, 1988).

Betty Friedan, *The Feminine Mystique* (New York, 1963), helped to inspire the feminist revival, and her role is examined in Daniel Horowitz, *Betty Friedan and the Making of* The Feminine Mystique (Amherst, MA, 1998). Important on the origins and character of the modern movement is Sara Evans, *Personal Politics: The Roots of Women's Liberation in the Civil Rights Movement and the New Left* (New York, 1979). See also Leila J. Ruff and Verta Taylor, *Survival in the Doldrums: The American Women's Rights Movement, 1945 to the 1960s* (Columbus, OH, 1990) and Cynthia Harrison, *On Account of Sex: The Politics of Women's Issues 1945–1968* (Berkeley, CA, 1988). There are some important essays in Vicki L. Crawford et al., *Women in the Civil Rights Movement* (New York, 1990).

On the later decades of the twentieth century see particularly Ruth Rosen, *The World Split Open: How the Modern Women's Movement Changed America* (New York, 2001); Flora Davis, *Moving the Mountain: The Women's Movement in America since 1960* (Urbana, 1999); Sylvia Ann Hewlett, *A Lesser Life: The Myth of Women's Liberation* (London, 1987); and Myra Marx Ferree and Beth B. Hess, *Controversy and Coalition: The New Feminist Movement Across Four Decades of Change* (3rd edn, New York, 2000). Also useful are Steven D. McLaughlin et al., *The Changing Lives of American Women* (Chapel Hill, 1988); Arlene Skolnick, *Embattled Paradise: The American Family in an Age of Uncertainty* (New York, 1991); Barbara J. Nelson and Najma Chowdhury, eds, *Women and Politics Worldwide* (New Haven, 1994); Sherri Matteo, ed., *American Women in the Nineties* (Boston, 1993); and R. Darcy, Susan Welch and Janet Clark, *Women, Elections, and Representation* (2nd edn, Lincoln, NE, 1994).

Immigration, Race and Ethnicity

For broad surveys of immigration see Maldwyn Allen Jones, *American Immigration* (2nd edn, Chicago, 1992) and Philip Taylor, *The Distant Magnet: European Emigration to the U.S.A.* (New York, 1971). Focusing on the period since 1965 is David M. Reimers, *Still the Golden Door: The Third World Comes to America* (2nd edn, New York, 1992); see also Reed Ueda, *Post-war Immigrant America: A Social History* (Boston, 1994) and David Heer, *Immigration in America's Future* (Boulder, CO, 1996). Encompassing black and Native Americans as well as immigrants are Ronald Takaki, *A Different Mirror: A History of Multicultural America* (Boston, 1993) and Leonard Dinnerstein, Roger L. Nichols and David M. Reimers, eds, *Natives and Strangers: A Multicultural History of Americans* (3rd edn, New York, 1996). For a suggestive recent study on the themes of immigration, race and national identity see Gary Gerstle, *American Crucible: Race and Nation in the Twentieth Century* (Princeton, 2001).

Both liberation movements and the return of mass immigration in the late twentieth century contributed to a heightened awareness of ethnicity. A broad survey sensitive to this theme is Richard Polenberg, *One Nation Divisible: Class, Race, and Ethnicity in the United States since 1938* (Harmondsworth, 1980). For particular groups see Julian Samora and Patricia Vandel Simon, *A History of the Mexican-American People* (rev. edn, Notre Dame, IN, 1993); Ian F. Haney, *Racism on Trial: The Chicano Fight for Justice* (Cambridge, MA, 2003); and Ronald Takaki, *Strangers from a Different Shore: A History of Asian Americans* (Boston, 1989). For Native Americans see James Wilson, *The Earth Shall Weep: A History of Native America* (London, 1998); James J. Rawls et al., *Chief Red Fox Is Dead: A History of Native Americans since 1945* (Fort Worth, TX, 1996); Robert N. Wells Jr., *Native American Resurgence and Renewal* (Metuchen, NJ, 1994); and Jack Utter, *American Indians* (Lake Ann, MI, 1993).

Michael Novak, *The Rise of the Unmeltable Ethnics: Politics and Culture in the Seventies* (New York, 1971) called for a new ethnic politics; see also Andrew M. Greeley, *Ethnicity in the United States* (New York, 1974). Critical of the prioritizing of cultural ethnicity is Stephen Steinberg, *Ethnic Myth: Race, Ethnicity, and Class in America* (Boston, 1981). The essays in Fred L. Pincus and Howard J. Ehrlich, eds, *Race and Ethnic Conflict* (Boulder, CO, 1994) examine continuing tensions. There has been a thoughtful debate about multiculturalism and its implications. See, for example, Elizabeth Martinez, *De Colores Means All Of Us: Latina Views for a Multi-Colored Century* (Cambridge, MA, 1998) and Michael Lind, *The Next American Nation: The New Nationalism and the Fourth American Revolution* (New York, 1995). An influential scholarly work is David A. Hollinger, *Postethnic America: Beyond Multiculturalism* (New York, 1995).

There are many surveys of the history of African-Americans. The better studies include John Hope Franklin and Alfred A. Moss Jr., *From Slavery to Freedom: A History of African-Americans* (8th edn, Boston, 2000); and for the twentieth century, Thomas C. Holt and Elsa Barkley Brown, eds, *Major Problems in African-American History, Volume II: From Freedom to 'Freedom Now', 1865–1990s* (Boston, 2000). C. Vann Woodward's seminal *The Strange Career of Jim Crow* (3rd edn, New York, 1974) remains a good starting point. Robert Cook, *Sweet Land of Liberty? The African-American Struggle for Civil Rights in the Twentieth Century* (London, 1998) and Adam Fairclough, *Better Day Coming: Blacks and Equality, 1890–2000* (New York, 2001) are excellent recent studies. James T. Patterson, Brown v Board of Education: *A Civil Rights Milestone and Its Troubled Legacy* (Oxford, 2001) examines the issue of school integration through the second half of the twentieth century. Replete with suggestive statistics is Stephan and Abigail Thernstrom, *America in Black and White: One Nation, Indivisible* (New York, 1997). On segregation in the federal government see Desmond King, *Separate and Unequal: Black Americans and the US Federal Government* (Oxford, 1995).

Invaluable for the period of the New Deal Order is Doug McAdam, *Political Process and the Development of Black Insurgency, 1930–1970* (2nd edn, Chicago, 1999). Nancy Weiss has examined the relationship of African-Americans to the New Deal in *Farewell to the Party of Lincoln: Black Politics in the Age of FDR* (Princeton, 1983); on the war period is Neil Wynn, *The Afro-American and the Second World War* (London, 1976).

Space allows mention of only a fraction of the studies of the modern civil rights movement. Valuable syntheses include William M. T. Riches, *The Civil Rights Movement* (Basingstoke, 1997); Manning Marable, *Race, Reform and Rebellion: the Second Reconstruction in Black America, 1945–1982* (London, 1984); Harvard Sitkoff, *The Struggle for Black Equality, 1954–1980* (New York, 1981); and Robert Weisbrot, *Freedom Bound: A History of America's Civil Rights Movement* (New York, 1990). King's role is examined in Adam Fairclough, *To Redeem the Soul of*

America: The Southern Christian Leadership Conference and Martin Luther King Jr. (Athens, GA, 1987); David Garrow, *Bearing the Cross: Martin Luther King Jr. and the Southern Christian Leadership Conference, 1955–1968* (New York, 1986); and the two volumes by Taylor Branch: *Parting the Waters: America in the King Years, 1954–1963* (London, 1988) and *Pillar of Fire: America in the King Years, 1963–1965* (New York, 1998). Important specialized studies include Aldon D. Morris, *The Origins of the Civil Rights Movement: Black Communities Organizing for Change* (New York, 1984); August Meier and Elliott Rudwick, *CORE: A Study of the Civil Rights Movement* (New York, 1973); and Clayborne Carson, *In Struggle: SNCC and the Black Awakening of the 1960s* (Cambridge, MA, 1981). Good on intellectual history is Richard H. King, *Civil Rights and the Idea of Freedom* (Athens, GA, 1996).

There are instructive essays in Hugh Davis Graham, ed., *Civil Rights in the United States* (Philadelphia, 1994). Fascinating on the Great Society's engagement with the race issue is Nicholas Lemann, *The Promised Land: The Great Black Migration and How It Changed America* (London, 1991). For the evolution of race relations in the South see Steven F. Lawson, *Black Ballots: Voting Rights in the South, 1944–1969* (New York, 1976); *In Pursuit of Power: Southern Blacks and Electoral Politics, 1965–1982* (New York, 1985); and David R. Goldfield, *Black, White, and Southern: Race Relations and Southern Culture, 1940 to the Present* (Baton Rouge, 1990). Brian Ward, *Just My Soul Responding: Rhythm and Blues, Black Consciousness and Race Relations* (London, 1998) illuminates the interrelationship between music and African-American politics. On the emergence of Black Power see Stokely Carmichael and Charles V. Hamilton, *Black Power: The Politics of Liberation in America* (New York, 1967); Philip S. Foner, ed., *The Black Panthers Speak* (Philadelphia, 1970); and William L. Van Deburg, *New Day in Babylon: The Black Power Movement and American Culture, 1965–1975* (Chicago, 1992).

The following are helpful on civil rights and related issues in the late twentieth century: Robert C. Smith, *We Have No Leaders: African-Americans in the Post-Civil Rights Era* (Albany, 1996); Steven A. Shull, *A Kinder, Gentler Racism? The Reagan-Bush Civil Rights Legacy* (Armonk, NY, 1993); Paul M. Sniderman and Thomas Piazza, *The Scar of Race* (Cambridge, MA, 1993); Herman Belz, *Equality Transformed: A Quarter Century of Affirmative Action* (New Brunswick, NJ, 1995); and Orlando Patterson, *The Ordeal of Integration: Progress and Resentment in America's 'Racial' Crisis* (Washington, 1997).

Appendix

A

Presidential Elections
1900–2000

Year	Candidates	Party	Popular Vote	Electoral Vote	% Popular Vote
1900	*William McKinley*	Republican	7,218,491	292	51.7
	William J. Bryan	Democratic/ Populist	6,356,734	155	45.5
	John C. Wooley	Prohibition	208,914		1.5
1904	*Theodore Roosevelt*	Republican	7,628,461	336	57.4
	Alton B. Parker	Democratic	5,084,223	140	37.6
	Eugene V. Debs	Socialist	402,283		3.0
	Silas S. Swallow	Prohibition	258,536		1.9
1908	*William H. Taft*	Republican	7,675,320	321	51.6
	William J. Bryan	Democratic	6,412,294	162	43.1
	Eugene V. Debs	Socialist	420,793		2.8
	Eugene W. Chafin	Prohibition	253,840		1.7
1912	*Woodrow Wilson*	Democratic	6,296,547	435	41.9
	Theodore Roosevelt	Progressive	4,118,571	88	27.4
	William H. Taft	Republican	3,486,720	8	23.2
	Eugene V. Debs	Socialist	900,672		6.0
	Eugene W. Chafin	Prohibition	206,275		1.4
1916	*Woodrow Wilson*	Democratic	9,127,695	277	49.4
	Charles E. Hughes	Republican	8,533,507	254	46.2
	A. L. Benson	Socialist	585,113		3.2
	J. Frank Hanly	Prohibition	220,506		1.2
1920	*Warren G. Harding*	Republican	16,143,407	404	60.4
	James N. Cox	Democratic	9,130,328	127	34.2
	Eugene V. Debs	Socialist	919,799		3.4
	P. P. Christensen	Farmer-Labor	265,411		1.0

(*Continued*)

Year	Candidates	Party	Popular Vote	Electoral Vote	% Popular Vote
1924	*Calvin Coolidge*	Republican	15,718,211	382	54.0
	John W. Davis	Democratic	8,385,283	136	28.8
	Robert M. La Follette	Progressive	4,831,289	13	16.6
1928	*Herbert Hoover*	Republican	21,391,993	444	58.2
	Alfred E. Smith	Democratic	15,016,169	87	40.9
	Norman Thomas	Socialist	267,420		1.0
1932	*Franklin D. Roosevelt*	Democratic	22,809,638	472	57.4
	Herbert Hoover	Republican	15,758,901	59	39.7
	Norman Thomas	Socialist	881,951		2.2
1936	*Franklin D. Roosevelt*	Democratic	27,752,869	523	60.8
	Alfred M. Landon	Republican	16,674,665	8	36.5
	William Lemke	Union	882,479		1.9
1940	*Franklin D. Roosevelt*	Democratic	27,307,819	449	54.8
	Wendell L. Willkie	Republican	22,321,018	82	44.8
1944	*Franklin D. Roosevelt*	Democratic	25,606,685	432	53.5
	Thomas E. Dewey	Republican	22,014,745	99	46.0
1948	*Harry S. Truman*	Democratic	24,105,812	303	49.5
	Thomas E. Dewey	Republican	21,970,065	189	45.1
	Strom Thurmond	States' Rights	1,169,063	39	2.4
	Henry A. Wallace	Progressive	1,157,172		2.4
1952	*Dwight D. Eisenhower*	Republican	33,936,234	442	55.1
	Adlai E. Stevenson	Democratic	27,314,992	89	44.4
1956	*Dwight D. Eisenhower*	Republican	35,590,472	457	57.6
	Adlai E. Stevenson	Democratic	26,022,752	73	42.1
1960	*John F. Kennedy*	Democratic	34,227,096	303	49.9
	Richard M. Nixon	Republican	34,108,546	219	49.6
1964	*Lyndon B. Johnson*	Democratic	43,126,506	486	61.1
	Barry M. Goldwater	Republican	27,176,799	52	38.5
1968	*Richard M. Nixon*	Republican	31,085,267	301	43.5
	Hubert H. Humphrey	Democratic	30,760,301	191	42.9
	George C. Wallace	American Independent	9,674,802	46	13.5
1972	*Richard M. Nixon*	Republican	47,169,911	520	61.3
	George McGovern	Democratic	29,170,383	2	37.3
	John G. Schmitz	American	1,099,482		1.4
1976	*Jimmy Carter*	Democratic	40,830,763	297	50.1
	Gerald R. Ford	Republican	39,147,973	240	48.0
	Eugene J. McCarthy	Independent	756,631		1.0

(*Continued*)

Year	Candidates	Party	Popular Vote	Electoral Vote	% Popular Vote
1980	*Ronald Reagan*	Republican	42,951,145	489	51.0
	Jimmy Carter	Democratic	34,663,037	49	41.0
	John B. Anderson	Independent	5,551,551		7.0
1984	*Ronald Reagan*	Republican	54,450,603	525	59.2
	Walter Mondale	Democratic	37,573,671	13	40.8
1988	*George Bush*	Republican	47,917,341	426	54.0
	Michael Dukakis	Democratic	41,013,030	112	46.0
1992	*Bill Clinton*	Democratic	43,728,375	370	43.0
	George Bush	Republican	38,167,416	168	38.0
	Ross Perot	Independent	19,237,247		19.0
1996	*Bill Clinton*	Democratic	47,402,357	379	49.2
	Robert Dole	Republican	39,198,755	159	40.7
	Ross Perot	Reform	8,085,402		8.4
2000	*George W. Bush*	Republican	50,459,624	271	47.9
	Albert Gore Jr.	Democratic	51,003,238	266	48.4
	Ralph Nader	Green	2,882,985		2.7

Candidates with less than 1 per cent of the popular vote are excluded.

Party Composition of Congress
1901–2001

Year	Congress	House			Senate		
		Majority Party	Minority Party	Other	Majority Party	Minority party	Other
1901	57th	R-197	D-151	9	R-55	D-31	4
1903	58th	R-208	D-178		R-57	D-33	
1905	59th	R-250	D-136		R-57	D-33	
1907	60th	R-222	D-164		R-61	D-31	
1909	61st	R-219	D-172		R-61	D-32	
1911	62nd	D-228	R-161	1	R-51	D-41	
1913	63rd	D-291	R-127	17	D-51	R-44	1
1915	64th	D-230	R-196	9	D-56	R-40	
1917	65th	D-216	R-210	6	D-53	R-42	
1919	66th	R-240	D-190	3	R-49	D-47	
1921	67th	R-301	D-131	1	R-59	D-37	
1923	68th	R-225	D-205	5	R-51	D-43	2
1925	69th	R-247	D-183	4	R-56	D-39	1
1927	70th	R-237	D-195	3	R-49	D-46	1
1929	71st	R-267	D-167	1	R-56	D-39	1
1931	72nd	D-220	R-214	1	R-48	D-47	1
1933	73rd	D-310	R-117	5	D-60	R-35	1
1935	74th	D-319	R-103	10	D-69	R-25	2
1937	75th	D-331	R-89	13	D-76	R-16	4
1939	76th	D-261	R-164	4	D-69	R-23	4
1941	77th	D-268	R-162	5	D-66	R-28	2
1943	78th	D-218	R-208	4	D-58	R-37	1

(Continued)

Year	Congress	House			Senate		
		Majority Party	Minority Party	Other	Majority Party	Minority Party	Other
1945	79th	D-242	R-190	2	D-56	R-38	1
1947	80th	R-245	D-188	1	R-51	D-45	
1949	81st	D-263	R-171	1	D-54	R-42	
1951	82nd	D-234	R-199	1	D-49	R-47	
1953	83rd	R-221	D-211	1	R-48	D-47	1
1955	84th	D-232	R-203		D-48	R-47	1
1957	85th	D-233	R-200		D-49	R-47	
1959	86th	D-282	R-154		D-64	R-34	
1961	87th	D-263	R-174		D-65	R-35	
1963	88th	D-258	R-177		D-67	R-33	
1965	89th	D-295	R-140		D-68	R-32	
1967	90th	D-247	R-187		D-64	R-36	
1969	91st	D-243	R-192		D-57	R-43	
1971	92nd	D-254	R-180		D-54	R-44	2
1973	93rd	D-239	R-192	1	D-56	R-42	2
1975	94th	D-291	R-144		D-60	R-37	2
1977	95th	D-292	R-143		D-61	R-38	1
1979	96th	D-276	R-157		D-58	R-41	1
1981	97th	D-243	R-192		R-53	D-46	1
1983	98th	D-269	R-165		R-54	D-46	
1985	99th	D-252	R-182		R-53	D-47	
1987	100th	D-258	R-177		D-55	R-45	
1989	101st	D-259	R-174		D-55	R-45	
1991	102nd	D-267	R-167	1	D-56	R-43	
1993	103rd	D-259	R-175	1	D-57	R-43	
1995	104th	R-235	D-197	1	R-53	D-47	
1997	105th	R-227	D-207	1	R-55	D-45	
1999	106th	R-223	D-211	1	R-55	D-45	
2001	107th	R-221	D-212	2	D-50	R-50*	

D = Democratic, R = Republican

The figures relate to the beginning of the first session of each Congress, reflecting the outcome of the elections in the year immediately preceding.

* Early in the session following the 2000 election one senator elected as a Republican dissociated himself from the party, denying it control of the Senate.

Index